BEYOND EXPERIENCE:
METAPHYSICAL THEORIES AND
PHILOSOPHICAL CONSTRAINTS

Shedding light on a subject that too often seems mysterious and remote, Norman Swartz puts a human face on the study of metaphysics. Far from being the exclusive handiwork of professional philosophers, Swartz argues, metaphysical theories lie just below the surface of every person's own world-view. He uses a number of case studies and an occasional appeal to science-fiction theorizing to make the subject accessible to a general audience.

Two tasks confront metaphysicians. The first is to identify our metaphysical beliefs and their effect on our behaviour and practices. The second is to assess these beliefs once they have been brought to light.

Swartz's own preference is for what he calls 'negative' theories, those that try to solve metaphysical problems without recourse to entities foreign to science. Indeed, one thesis running throughout the book is that metaphysics and science are not separable disciplines but are merely different facets of one and the same discipline.

Among the areas considered in this light are space and time, mental states and brain states, the nature of theories, pain, identity, the concepts of person and property, and the search for extraterrestrial intelligence. To all of them Swartz brings a uniquely refreshing perspective for professional philosopher and lay reader alike. His book is especially well suited to courses as a lively introduction to key problems in contemporary metaphysics.

NORMAN SWARTZ is Professor of Philosophy at Simon Fraser University. He is the author of *The Concept of Physical Law* and co-author, with Raymond D. Bradley, of *Possible Worlds: An Introduction to Logic and Its Philosophy*.

For Sylvia, Diane, Efrem, Eva, Harry, Paul, and Lorna (Theresa).

And in loving memory of my father, Martin.

NORMAN SWARTZ

BEYOND EXPERIENCE
Metaphysical Theories and Philosophical Constraints

UNIVERSITY OF TORONTO PRESS

Toronto Buffalo London

© University of Toronto Press 1991
Toronto Buffalo London
Printed in Canada

ISBN 0-8020-2783-0 (cloth)
ISBN 0-8020-6832-4 (paper)

Printed on acid-free paper

Canadian Cataloguing in Publication Data

Swartz, Norman, 1939–
  Beyond experience

  Includes bibliographical references and index.
  ISBN 0-8020-2783-0 (bound)
  ISBN 0-8020-6832-4 (pbk.)

  1. Metaphysics.   I. Title.

  BD111.S89 1991   110   C91-093664-1

         72820

This book has been published with assistance
from the Canada Council and the Ontario Arts
Council under their block grant programs.

Contents

Foreword

Grappling with issues that are both inherently interesting and unavoidably controversial is the lifeblood of philosophy. A good introduction to the subject must convey the sense of excitement that characterizes lively controversies. Doing this well – avoiding the mock combat of straw men and artificial opponents – is far from easy, which is why relatively few good introductions are the work of one single writer. The present book is an exception to this rule. For Norman Swartz has managed to combine a good sense of the complexities that always lurk behind the surface of philosophical issues with an easy, nontechnical mode of exposition accessible to the interested nonspecialist. His book is at once readable, informative, and stimulating.

One can learn *about* philosophy by reading, but one can learn to *philosophize* only by thinking about the issues. But philosophical thinking requires recourse to problems, concepts, and methods, and these are obtained most efficiently and effectively via the printed page. What a book can do is to extend a congenial invitation to learning. The difficulty is finding books with the right combination of accessibility-with-profundity and of breadth-with-depth. In this regard, the interests of the beginner – student or interested reader alike – are well served by *Beyond Experience* which, I have found, provides constantly stimulating discussion of a wide range of challenging questions.

The very nature of philosophy is such that it is easier to pose problems than to enforce conclusions. Even the plausible data of the field – the deliverances of 'plain logic', of ordinary common sense, and of science – are not of so fixed a character that they always resist the corrosive impact of critical scrutiny. Moreover the 'data' of philosophy (whatever they are) underdetermine the conclusions: there are always alternatives that must be weighed by standards that we bring to our philosophizing rather than extract from it. To present philosophy in a dogmatic way is accordingly to betray the enterprise by impoverishing it – by putting out of sight concepts, issues, and problems that deserve and need to have their place in philosophy's complex terrain. In this connection, what is particularly appealing about this book is its undogmatic approach. Its author is more concerned that readers should appreciate the many-sidedness and complexity of the issues than that they take away a predilection for one particular answer. This insistence on readers thinking for themselves rather than pressing for the endorsement of one particular view is certainly one of the book's most attractive features.

Those who give *Beyond Experience* an attentive reading are in for a treat. They will come away not only with a better sense of what philosophy is all about, but will also experience the enjoyable stimulus of thinking philosophically.

Nicholas Rescher
University Professor of Philosophy
University of Pittsburgh

Acknowledgments

Four colleagues, three of whom I have never met, have played essential roles in making it possible for me to bring this book into being.

William Saywell, the president of Simon Fraser University, took it upon himself to recommend to the board of governors a sabbatical leave for me under special terms for the academic year 1988-89. Without his confidence in the project, his enthusiasm, and his arranging supplementary financial support, I would not have been able to undertake writing this book.

If William Saywell provided the opportunity, Nicholas Rescher provided the sustenance. In the fall of 1988, when I had written about the first third of the manuscript, I read Rescher's editorial in the *American Philosophical Quarterly*:

> A substantial divide apparently separates the issues that intrigue philosophers themselves from those which non-philosophers think that philosophers ought to discuss. For, like other professionals, we philosophers favor shoptalk over popularization and prefer addressing our colleagues and 'the public' at large. We incline to salve our consciences with the comforting reassurance that our field has become too technical for that sort of thing.
>
> But has it? Perhaps we have simply become too impatient to deal with the complexities of simple exposition and self-indulgently prefer technicalities laden with presuppositions and laborsaving complexities to the clear and patient discussion of fundamentals.
>
> A considerable host of philosophers from Hume to Russell and beyond show that it is possible to do both technical philosophy and popular communication – occasionally even in one and the same book. ... If philosophy loses out on its educative

mission towards the reading public at large, the fault lies not in our stars – or in the very subject – but in ourselves. ([172], 347)[1]

Once you have read chapter 1 in this book, you will understand why I was startled and delighted to find Rescher writing this. On opposite sides of the continent, we were simultaneously writing identical thoughts about the practice of philosophy. I sent him immediately what I had already written, and he wrote back, encouraging me in my effort and graciously accepting my invitation to write the Foreword to this volume. But his kindness did not end there. Throughout the year that followed, when I often became exhausted and discouraged, Rescher kept pushing me on with reassurances and suggestions. There is no way I can repay him. But neither – I am sure – does he expect repayment. All I can hope is that someday I might, in turn, be privileged to pass such generosity on to some other writer.

If Saywell was the impetus and Rescher the sustainer, then Ron Schoeffel, senior house editor, and Bill Harnum, marketing manager, at the University of Toronto Press, were the patrons. I had earlier discussed this project with some other editors, but they had warned that the general public would not read philosophy. Schoeffel and Harnum reacted differently. They were not willing to 'write off' the general public, believing that not just university students and their teachers, but nonacademics as well, have both an appetite and an ability to read serious philosophy.

But it must be clear that a book of this size cannot have called upon the assistance of just four other persons. Many others, as well, contributed substantially to this volume.

The British Columbia provincial government, under its Work/Study Program, and Robert Brown, the dean of arts at Simon Fraser University, provided funding for my two stalwart research assistants, Hyne-Ju Cho and Armin Meyerholz.

Moira Gutteridge, a friend and colleague (Fraser Valley College and Capilano College), drew the splendid illustrations for chapters 8 and 11. Lorraine Ourom, executive editor at the Press, was in charge

---

1. Abbreviated citations are used throughout this book. Bracketed numbers in parentheses are cross-references to the References section, pp. 415-26. Numbers following the brackets are page citations. Thus "([172], 347)" refers to page 347 in the item cited as no. 172 in the References section.

of the production editing. Throughout the months of preparing the manuscript for publication, she good-naturedly accommodated an inordinate number of fussy requests from this author. John St James copy-edited this book. Unfortunately, a good copy-editor's contribution to a book, unlike a good illustrator's, is by its very nature invisible. But those who have seen my original manuscript and have seen John's expert, extensive, and indispensable repair of it know what a considerable improvement he has wrought. Probably unwisely, I have sometimes refused his advice. What stylistic idiosyncrasies occur, I assure you are my own.

Two readers who were engaged by the University of Toronto Press, and who remain anonymous, painstakingly read the penultimate draft of the manuscript. They provided a number of astute suggestions which I have been pleased to adopt, and they caught some errors which I have corrected. But I am sure that they have not spotted every error or challenged me on every unclarity. In due course, readers may tell me what these are. But whatever these errors may turn out to be, I, who wrote them, am alone responsible for them.

Dennis Bevington and Professors John Len Berggren, Raymond D. Bradley, Roger C. Buck, Warren Goldfarb, Raymond E. Jennings, Hugh Johnston, E.L. Pattullo, Mark Skinner, Kenneth B. Storey, Don Todd, and Robert Todd provided invaluable assistance in tracking down some of the bibliographical materials I needed.

Professors Harvey Gerber, Leigh Palmer, and Lawrence Dill obligingly lent a hand with certain details in mathematics, astronomy, and ichthyology, respectively.

And the editors of *Analysis*, *The Canadian Journal of Philosophy*, and *Ratio* kindly gave permission for me to reprint, as sections of chapters in this book, revised versions of certain of my earlier papers. The particulars of original publication are to be found herein as footnotes at the outset of each of the relevant sections. The curator of the Joseph Regenstein Library, University of Chicago, gave me permission to quote from the unpublished papers of Clarence Darrow.

Last to be mentioned, but foremost in importance, is Sylvia, my wife and helpmate. Throughout the thousands of hours I spent working on this book, by her quiet encouragement and unfailing love, she provided the needed perspective and balance. For she is the secure reminder that I am first a husband and a father, a son and a brother, and then – but only then – a philosopher.

N.S., Simon Fraser University, Burnaby, BC

BEYOND EXPERIENCE:
METAPHYSICAL THEORIES AND
PHILOSOPHICAL CONSTRAINTS

CHAPTER ONE

Presenting philosophy

"For whom is this book written?" The question has two answers, one short, the other rather long.

The short answer is that I have written this book for my children. At various times during their growing-up years, they asked me, "Dad, what is philosophy?" I explained to them that the question "What is philosophy?" has no easy answer; that they would need to take a course or read a book to find the answer. And thus it was, in part, a desire to answer their question that prompted my undertaking to write this book. But in the meantime, the older of my two children, Diane, has gone on to university, has taken several philosophy courses, and so now has a good idea what philosophy is. For her, this book will not be so much an introduction to philosophy per se as it will be an entree to her Dad's own thoughts about philosophy. For both her and her younger brother Efrem, this book will be, then, a testament of their father's interests and reflections.

But this book was scarcely undertaken solely for my children. I have a much wider audience in mind. And it is to you of this wider audience I now turn to make a few remarks explaining what I try to do herein.

In a way, the question "For whom is this book written?" is a remarkably *contemporary* question, very much the sort of question which arises naturally in the late twentieth century, but would not have been nearly so apt in previous times. Nowadays it is the fashion when writing 'learned books' to address them either to specialists (cognoscenti) in one's own specialized discipline, or to nonspecialists, often students, and in the latter case to present the material in the familiar form of a textbook.

If we look into historical practices, however, we see few instances of this kind of division of labor. Books were not written to be read only by specialists or only by tyros, but were addressed broadly to the educated and would-be-educated public alike. Plato, Aristotle, Aquinas, Locke, Berkeley, Hume, Kant, Frege, Russell, Sartre, Camus, Austin, etc., never – not one of them – ever wrote a *textbook*. They – all of them – wrote philosophy books, books which they intended to be read by persons interested in philosophy, never mind whether those readers were professional philosophers or lay readers. The philosophy textbook is pretty much a product of the twentieth century. It has, however, become so entrenched in the current teaching of philosophy that we often forget that it is an upstart and that it is possible – if one makes the effort and has the interest – to write philosophy both for one's professional colleagues and for the interested lay reader. At least I hope it is still possible. Of course I may be wrong. Philosophy may have become so specialized, so technical, in recent decades that it is no longer possible to address the same book both to one's professional colleagues and to the interested, educated adult reader. I hope this is not so.

The style of the bulk of the writings of Karl Popper gives one cause for some optimism. Many of his numerous articles and the greater part of his several books are read and enjoyed both by his professional peers and by interested readers who are far from being professional philosophers. His popularity is no accident. He is, after all, a fine and important philosopher. But there is a significant additional element as well, a craftsmanship about which I heard him speak often.

When I was a graduate student, I was fortunate to take a course from him. Time after time, Popper exhorted his students to try to write so clearly that virtually anyone could understand the material. He warned that if your presentation was so dense that it could be read (I would say "deciphered") only by a learned colleague, then you should go back and rewrite it again and again until it was pellucidly clear. His own work, for the greatest part, really does exhibit the very virtue he urged on the rest of us. I have found his advice compelling and have tried to follow it and commend it to others. I will try here to write a book in the old-fashioned style. It is intended as an antidote to the modern textbook. I will try to make the material accessible and comprehensible to a wide audience. However, I will not condescend to simplify. Quite the contrary, some sections of this book have earlier been published as journal articles for professional colleagues.

Much – far too much, I would hazard – of recent philosophical writing apes the lamentable style of contemporary articles in physics and chemistry journals. Historically, scientists did not write in the compressed, antiseptic, manner currently favored in the scientific journals. In centuries past, much of the humanity of scientists, their disappointments, their triumphs, and their frailties, was obvious in their writings. Thus, for example, we find Count Rumford (Benjamin Thompson) positively delighting in the effect of his experiment (c. 1790) of heating water by friction (emphases are Rumford's own):

> At 2 hours 20 minutes it was 200° [Fahrenheit]; and at 2 hours 30 minutes it ACTUALLY BOILED!
> It would be difficult to describe the surprise and astonishment expressed in the countenances of the bystanders, on seeing so large a quantity of cold water heated, and actually made to boil, without any fire.
> Though there was, in fact, nothing that could justly be considered as surprising in this event, yet I acknowledge fairly that it afforded me a degree of childish pleasure, which, were I ambitious of the reputation of a *grave philosopher*, I ought most certainly rather to hide than to discover. ([176], 15; gloss added[1])

(We will return in chapter 4, to examine Rumford's experiment in closer detail.)

Today, perhaps because of the sheer volume of scientific writings, most articles have been reduced to a kind of formula prose which simply tells what was done and the results of the experiment. Only those scientific magazines which are expressly written for the lay public (e.g. *Scientific American* and *Discover*) preserve any modicum of literary worth. But as regrettable as the situation has become in science, it is worse in philosophy. For in philosophy there are no magazines targeted for the public. And thus nonspecialists find themselves, year by year, further removed from the researches and writings of philosophers. This unhappy state of affairs can only be to the detriment of both the public and philosophers themselves.

Why do persons become philosophers? No one ever gets hired as a philosopher without years of preparatory training. No more so than do doctors or lawyers. Persons become philosophers because they are intensely interested in philosophical problems. And yet so little of this genuinely, deeply felt interest comes across in their professional writ-

---

1. Hereinafter, when I interpolate a gloss within a quotation I will not call explicit attention to the insertion. The square brackets alone will indicate my editorial elaboration. Also, see footnote 1, p. xiv.

ings. All sense of adventure, of personality, of struggle, and, yes, on occasion, of fun, is sucked out of most that is written in philosophy nowadays. Journal articles and books often are tortuously dry reading and are almost entirely in the third person, as if they had been written, not by living, breathing, feeling, human beings, but by disembodied oracles. Far too many authors, in trying to affect a modish kind of objectivity, end by writing a prose which is so painfully impersonal that it reads like a technical manual for the disassembly of a carburetor. One can read entire philosophy books and never once find therein the word "I" or "you", as if these two comfortable English words were somehow vile subjective dissonances.

This book will be different. In the third sentence of this introductory chapter, I have already used the word "I", as I will many, many times subsequently. And from time to time, I will use the word "you" too, remembering that I am writing this book to be read by interested persons, and not just to be soaked up by the silicon chips of the microcomputer on which I happened to have typed these words.

R.G. Collingwood's aphorism "every new generation must rewrite history in its own way" ([51], 248) might equally well be said for philosophy. Not only do we each have a uniquely personal perspective from which we regard our world; there is also something of a cultural perspective, and certainly, too, something of a parochial perspective, especially if – as I do – one belongs to a certain school of thought. In my case, I am a product of an undergraduate degree in physics and a graduate degree in Anglo-American (so-called Analytic) philosophy. I make no apology for this mind-set: it is impossible to do philosophy without a mind-set. One cannot transcend all mind-sets and aspire to The Truth. That kind of Presuppositionless Objectivity is quite beyond the capabilities of human beings. All that we can do is to be honest about our own approach and to try to get as clear as we can about just what it is that we are doing.

Philosophy, like so many other twentieth-century studies, has broadened its compass enormously. I am no polymath; I can only offer my own opinions, grounded in my own particular training and perspective. This book, like every other book in philosophy, however much some writers try to pretend otherwise, is a *personal* statement by its author. There are no authorities in philosophy. There are only gradations of plausibility.

These views explain why, then, I will try to do *two* things in this book. To be sure, I will devote much of what follows to exploring some traditional problems in metaphysics; I will review a variety of theories that other philosophers have offered as solutions; and I will on occasion criticize these theories; and I will, too, sometimes offer my own ideas as to what solutions might be. But I will try to do something else as well, and this 'something else' accounts for the "Philosophical Constraints" which figures as the second part of the subtitle of this book.

I want to try to explain why philosophers disagree, why the seeming consensus which exists in something like, let us say, physics seems so often unattainable in philosophy. Many newcomers – particularly those used to the textbooks of public high schools, where all controversy and intellectual struggle have, deliberately and systematically, been expunged – are dismayed at the indecisiveness of so much of philosophy. "All those questions; never any answers" I have often heard some of my students complain. There is no disguising the fact: there is much disagreement in philosophy. But, as we shall see, there is much – or at least there is room for as much – disagreement in physics, chemistry, and biology, too. In chapter 4, I will argue that philosophy is not really any worse off in this regard than the so-called hard sciences. The difference is that the very existence of controversy itself is one of the central concerns of the philosophical enterprise, and thus tends to become spotlighted. But controversy is the fuel of any and every intellectual discipline. As this book progresses, I will try to explain the *nature* of philosophical controversy, or to be more exact, the aspects and parts of philosophical controversy familiar to me. Indeed, the very nature of controversy itself turns out to be a controversial topic within philosophy. Different philosophers have different accounts of the origins of, and the possibilities for resolving, controversy. And thus, to be perfectly frank, when I subsequently offer my views as to the nature of controversy – why it exists and what role it plays in the intellectual enterprise – I will not simply be presenting a settled matter of fact, but will, by that very attempt, be engaging in a piece of philosophizing which, like all philosophy, is itself a proper object for debate and analysis.

But before we begin our studies, allow me a cautionary note. Professional philosophers are constitutionally incapable of succumbing to the danger I am about to alert you to. But if you are new to philosophy, be careful. Philosophy ought not to be something that one acquires like a piece of purchased material goods. Philosophy ought to be acquired by struggling *yourself* with its problems and exploring a variety of proposed solutions looking for the 'best answer'. For only in the crucible of the clash of ideas can we hope to construct good theories.

If you find yourself interested in the questions I am about to pursue and find yourself attracted to the tentative answers I am about to offer to some of those questions, do not accept my own answers by default. The answers I proffer in this book (at least at the time of my writing this book) seem right to me. But if you, like me, find that these questions are fascinating, then you owe it to yourself not to accept any one person's answers – neither mine nor anyone else's – until you have savored and reflected on a variety of answers, even a variety of approaches. Then you can make up your own mind. In short, if it turns out that I have been privileged to introduce you to metaphysics and to philosophy, and if you find that you resonate – as some do – to these kinds of ideas, then I urge that you let this be only the first of many books you read on these subjects. For philosophy is, in the end, an attitude or a process of thought; it ought not to be regarded as a finished product.

CHAPTER TWO

The metaphysical impulse

A while ago, in my introductory philosophy course, we had reached
the section dealing with metaphysics. I tried to explain to my students
what metaphysics is by mentioning a variety of problems which traditionally have been regarded as falling within that area. Among these
problems is the nature of space and time, and I began to recount the
fascination, and in some instances the bewilderment, a variety of persons have felt through the centuries in contemplating the concepts of
space and time. I recounted to my students how Lucretius (Titus
Lucretius Carus, 95-52 BC)[1] wondered what would happen if a person
were at the 'end of space' and hurled a spear. Where would it go? If
there really were an edge to space, then there would have to be more
space beyond; but if there were no edge, space would have to go on
'forever'. Either way – Lucretius reasoned – one could never actually
be at the edge of space, and so Lucretius argued to the conclusion that
space, as he put it, "goes on and has no bounds".[2]

> ... there can be no end to anything
> without something beyond to mark that end
> and show where nature and sense[3] can go no further.
> ... if we should theorize that the whole
> of space were limited, then if a man ran out
> to the last limits and hurled a spear,
> would you prefer that, whirled by might and muscle,
> the spear flew on and on, as it was thrown,
> or do you think something would stop and block it?

1. The dates of most persons mentioned in this book are listed in the Names
Index, pp. 427-32.

2. Later, in footnote 3, p. 151, I will say a bit more about his argument.

3. I.e. sensory perception

One or the other you must assume and grant.
But either cuts off escape and forces you
to grant that the All goes on and has no bounds.
For whether your spear is checked and stopped by something
from tracing its path and landing at its goal,
or flies free, where it started was not the end.
So it will go: no matter where you spot
the end, I'll ask, "What happens to my spear?"
([127], 23-4)

I recounted, too, to my students how the teenaged Martin Buber (1878-1965), twenty centuries later, in adopting the same sort of vivid imagery as Lucretius's, was driven to despair and to the brink of insanity.

> ... what stirs and terrifies ... [man] ... is not the ... infinity of space ... It is the fact that, by the impression of infinity, any concept of space, a finite no less than an infinite, becomes uncanny to him, for really to try and imagine finite space is just as hazardous a venture as really to try and imagine infinite space, and makes man just as emphatically conscious that he is not a match for the world. When I was about fourteen years of age I myself experienced this in a way which has deeply influenced my whole life. A necessity I could not understand swept over me: I had to try again and again to imagine the edge of space, or its edgelessness, time with a beginning and an end or a time without beginning or end, and both were equally impossible, equally hopeless – yet there seemed to be only the choice between the one or the other absurdity. Under an irresistible compulsion I reeled from one to the other, at times so closely threatened with the danger of madness that I seriously thought of avoiding it by suicide. ([37], 135-6)

And I told the students, too, how I myself as a youngster, knowing nothing of Lucretius or Buber, would often wonder – like countless others before me and doubtless countless more in the future – about these same problems. Even as a child, I resolved to write a book about these problems. Today, I remember only the resolve; I have totally forgotten what I thought I might write. That forgetfulness is probably all for the best. For I am sure that if I could remember my childhood ruminations on these problems, they would embarrass me by their naivety and youthful exuberance. In any event, I recounted all this to my students, and then found myself asking how many of them, too, had harbored similar wonderment and perplexity.

About half the class raised their hands and we got to talking. It turned out, as I suspected, that many of them had wondered about such matters. But a surprise lay with the other half of the class. As we talked, some of the latter group confided that they had never, ever thought about the matter. They told us that as they looked up at the stars on cloudless nights (and that they all did, from time to time), they never found themselves wondering how big the universe was – whether finite or infinite – or whether space 'went on forever' or 'stopped somewhere out there'. I am afraid that my response, after hearing several of them profess such uninterest, was "How can you *not* think about such things!?"

Two days later, in one of the tutorial groups in that same course, one of my students objected to my remark. She wrote me a note which reads, in part: "One of the reasons why I have failed to worry about such problems as where space ends or when did time begin is because I prefer to concern myself with dilemmas that have relevance to life right now. There are many current crises that require immediate attention ... This ... point of view may make me appear ignorant of intellectual thought but I don't feel comfortable worrying ... [whether] the universe expanded last night because whether it did or not, I can still function the same as I did yesterday." It was clear that this woman had been put on the defensive by my unfortunate manner of expression "How can you *not* think about such things!?" I say "unfortunate" because it had certainly not been my intention to berate those who do not share my concern with such problems. I was not suggesting – as this student thought I was – that everybody *ought* to be fascinated by such puzzles. Instead I was merely expressing my own surprise at, not my objection to, other persons' not being seduced by these problems. Once again, this time to explain the thrust of my remark, I found myself recounting to my students still another piece of personal history.

When I was in my early twenties, I dated a woman who, on our third date, happened to mention that she did not like chocolate. My response on that earlier occasion had been identical, save for the last phrase. For I had said to her: "How can you *not* like chocolate!?" I certainly was not finding fault with her. There is no fault in someone's not liking chocolate. Nor is it that I thought that she should like it or that if she would just give herself a chance, she would learn to like it.

Nothing of the sort. I was simply amazed that her reactions could be so dissimilar to my own. So, too, it is with metaphysics.

All of us, whether trained in philosophy or not, subscribe to a great variety of metaphysical theories. Some of us, however, are predisposed to examine these theories, to probe their strong and weak points, to hold them up for comparison with alternative theories, and sometimes to abandon one in favor of another. Some persons – like myself and many, but not all, of my students – find themselves pondering metaphysical questions without being provoked or goaded to do so. We just do it naturally. Others come to find such problems interesting when they find their friends and teachers talking about them. And still others find no particular interest or reward in examining the merits of the metaphysical views they hold, and grow impatient with the exercise of intellectual self-examination. You may already know into which category you yourself fall. But for some of you, philosophy will come as a new challenge, and you may find the uncovering and the analyzing of your own world-view a fascinating route to self-discovery.

What do I mean when I say that each of us, whether professional philosopher or not, holds a great variety of metaphysical theories? I will try to illustrate with a few examples. The exercise will serve to begin to illuminate what a metaphysical theory is.[4]

Metaphysical theories inform world-views, and by this I mean not just that they shape what we say about the world, or what we might believe about the world, but that they affect our actions, our reactions, and our emotions. To this extent, they resemble religious views, but unlike religious views, there need not be any supernatural component to them, and unlike religious views, they invite critical scrutiny and revision.

It is surprising that metaphysical theories which may resist being judged true or false by empirical, or experiential methods, i.e. which

---

4. Traditionally philosophy has been regarded as having four main divisions: Metaphysics; Epistemology (Theory of Knowledge); Logic; and Value Theory (incorporating both Aesthetics and Ethics). But these historical partitions within philosophy are not immutable; they are mere conveniences. Many problems and methods, particularly in the twentieth century, crisscross several of these areas. Although my concern in this book is principally with metaphysics, occasionally the discussion will touch upon areas customarily regarded as lying outside of metaphysics.

have no *testable* consequences, may, nonetheless, have profound *practical* consequences. Buber, as we have already seen, contemplated suicide because he could not see his way through a metaphysical puzzle. Indeed, he probably did not even realize that he had unwittingly subscribed to a bad (conceptually bad, not of course morally bad) metaphysical *theory*. His mistake, I will argue later in this book, was very basic: he conceived of space as if it were similar to familiar physical objects, i.e. as if it were similar to the sorts of things which have a surface and which are located at a place. He saw his way out of the puzzle, finally, only by casting off the one metaphysical theory in favor of another. It is interesting to note that he was rescued by discovering a book of metaphysics, and thereby coming to realize that his was, after all, a metaphysical conundrum. Picking up the passage I quoted just above and now continuing, we find:

> Under an irresistible compulsion I reeled from one to the other, at times so closely threatened with the danger of madness that I seriously thought of avoiding it by suicide. Salvation came to the fifteen year old boy in a book, Kant's *Prolegomena to all Future Metaphysics*, which I dared to read although its first sentence told me that it was not intended for the use of pupils but for future teachers. This book showed me that space and time are only the forms in which my human view of what is, necessarily works itself out; that is, they were not attached to the inner nature of the world, but to the nature of my senses. ([37], 136)

Fortunately Buber believed he had solved the puzzle and was able to cease agonizing over it. Kant's theory at least had the virtue of convincing Buber that space itself is not to be likened to objects in space. But as it turns out, Kant's was not the only alternative theory then available, at the end of the nineteenth century, which could have solved Buber's problem. There was, in fact, another theory also available, one which I regard as vastly superior to Kant's, but Buber either did not know of that theory or found it less convincing. In any event, later in this book I will offer a solution to Buber's problem modeled after the theory, not of Kant (1724-1804), but of Leibniz, who had flourished (1646-1716) in the century before Kant.

For a second example let us turn from concerns about the end of space to one about the end of life. One of the most troubling problems confronting modern society has been the realization of the scope of, and the devastation to families that is wrought by, Alzheimer's disease. Many an unfortunate older woman, herself suffering failing heath and often having meager financial means, is faced with the terrible burden of caring for a husband dying of Alzheimer's disease. There can be few greater human tragedies. For as the disease progresses the patient is able less and less to respond *in a human fashion* to the ministrations, the care, and the love of his own suffering wife. In the last, most horrible days of the disease, the patient is unable even to thank his benefactors, or even to recognize them, and finally unable even to talk to them. The patient falls into what is sometimes brutally, but aptly, called "a vegetative state".

How the wife and the family react to this unfolding tragedy is to a great extent determined by which metaphysical theory of personhood they subscribe to. More often than not, families are unaware that their actions in such circumstances are informed by anything as grand-sounding as 'a metaphysical theory', but their actions and attitudes really are.

What, after all, is it to *be* a person? Is the dying, semiconscious patient 'really' a person? Beliefs*[5] differ. Some families go through their grieving process midway through the course of the illness. At some point, even months perhaps before the patient is pronounced clinically dead, the family might say something of the sort, "Father is gone; all that is left is the shell of his body." When clinical death follows months later, the members of such a family experience relief, not grief. But other families react in a totally different way. Up until the moment of clinical death they regard the patient as 'husband' and as 'father', and will permit themselves to grieve only after the clinical death. It is not just the time of grieving which differs in the two cases. There may well be resentment and anger in the latter case where the family has for years felt themselves obliged to cater to the bodily needs of the ailing patient, often at a terrible sacrifice in their own lives. The wife may be consumed with enormous guilt. After all, she pledged, and she takes her pledge seriously, to "cleave to her husband unto death". But when, exactly, does a person die? Is it *just* a figure of speech to say – as some families do – at some point, long before the

---

5. Terms having distinctive meanings within philosophy and technical terms which may be unfamiliar to the nonspecialist reader have been flagged on their first appearance with an asterisk and are explained in the Glossary, pp. 397-407.

clinical death of the body, that an Alzheimer's patient is dead?

Which account of personhood one subscribes to can have profound effects on one's own attitudes, on one's sense of obligation, and on one's own measure of self-worth when one finds oneself entrusted to care for an Alzheimer's patient. "I pledged myself to care for my husband 'unto death'. Is this wracked body which used to be that of my husband still my husband? Or has my husband already died, and am I the victim of a cruel joke of Nature, left to care for this vegetative body as if he were still alive? Am I a wife or a widow? Is this my husband or merely his breathing body? I married and swore my love and care to a person, but is this a person? How far does my obligation to care and love go? If his body were not breathing, he would be dead. But this body is merely breathing; there is no recognition, there is no human response, there is nothing reciprocated. Is my husband dead?" Few of us, mercifully, are in positions where these questions are forced on us. And thus few of us actually go through such exercises of mulling over the alternative answers.

Sometimes persons who find themselves caring for vegetative patients are unaware (as was Buber, albeit in a very different sort of case) that they do subscribe to a particular metaphysical theory. They simply unthinkingly, unreflectingly either believe that the patient has died or believe that the patient has not died. They take their belief from their own parents, or their church, or their friends. They fail to realize that the matter is not so clear-cut, that it can be argued what the proper attitudes should be, that it cannot either be simply assumed that the person has died or be simply assumed that the person has not died. In short, what answers one gives to such questions, and what attitudes one takes in getting through one's day if one is forced to care for an Alzheimer's victim, depend on what particular metaphysical theory of personhood one subscribes to. And it is remarkably easy to subscribe to one theory or another without even an inkling that one *is* subscribing to a metaphysical theory, one which, almost certainly, many other persons, just as matter-of-factly, reject. But we need not be in the dark about these remarkably different beliefs and attendant attitudes. It is possible to become aware that our own views about what a person is constitute a *theory*, not a settled 'fact', and are thus open to examination, to critical probing, and to revision if not outright replacement.[6]

---

6. Even persons who are not clinically ill can change so much as to make identity problematic. "When [television newscaster Jessica] Savitch's end

These two problems, the one concerning the end of space, the other the end of life, seem at the outset to have virtually nothing in common. Even the appearance of the word "end" in the statement of the two problems is more of an accident than a genuine commonality, for the term is equivocal. In the first case "end" means something like "boundary" or "edge", while in the latter it means "cessation" or "extinction". And yet, there is a remarkable connection between these two problems.

For both problems, as we will see later, intimately concern the concept of a physical (material) body. Does space exist independently of the objects (material bodies), e.g. the stars, planets, and comets, which are said to 'occupy space'? Are persons anything other than certain kinds of physical objects, viz. living human bodies? Are persons, that is, to be *identified* with their bodies, or are persons conceptually distinct from their bodies? The two problems, one about the nature of space, the other about the nature of personhood, come together in requiring that one attend to the concept of what it is to be a physical object (material body). But while there is this common feature in both these problems, certainly not all metaphysical problems share this particular commonality.

Still another instance where a metaphysical theory informs our world-view occurs in the case of our judging the proper response to a person's wrongdoing. Some determinists believe that punishment is never warranted. Such persons believe that whatever a person does is determined by that person's genetic makeup and environment, where "environment" is understood broadly to include *all* the stimuli which impinge on that person. But if these are *all* the 'determiners' of a person's behavior, and if neither your genetic makeup nor the stimuli which assail you are of your choosing, then there can be no sense in which you are responsible for your own actions. And thus someone who subscribes to this particular theory will argue that punishment, to the extent that it is retributive and not rehabilitative, is never morally justified.[7]

---

finally came in a freak car accident in 1983, one close friend had already finished mourning: the Jessica she had once known had died years before" ([220], 63).

7. I have argued in [201], chapters 10-11, that this particular version of determinism assumes a certain account of the nature of physical laws, and that if that account is abandoned, then the conclusion that we are never responsible

Can one really believe such a theory? It certainly appears that the famed trial lawyer Clarence Darrow (1857-1938) did.

> Every one knows that the heavenly bodies move in certain paths in relation to each other with seeming consistency and regularity which we call [physical] law. ... No one attributes freewill or motive to the material world. Is the conduct of man or the other animals any more subject to whim or choice than the action of the planets? ... We know that man's every act is induced by motives that led or urged him here or there; that the sequence of cause and effect runs through the whole universe, and is nowhere more compelling than with man. ([53], 76-7)

> The principal thing to remember is that we are all the products of heredity and environment; that we have little or no control, as individuals, over ourselves, and that criminals are like the rest of us in that regard. ([52], 15; quoted by permission)

Darrow often used such arguments in the murder cases he defended. In the mouth of such a skillful and theatrical orator, these metaphysical arguments seem to have been highly persuasive, for never once in his long career did he lose a client to the death penalty.

The impact of metaphysical theories is not reserved exclusively for such momentous issues as the extent of the universe, the nature of personhood, and the existence of free will. Metaphysical theories inform our behavior, as well, in what might be regarded as the mundane.

A person who believes in souls and who believes that pain is of moral consequence only in a creature with a soul, and who believes that animals lack souls, may believe that it is morally permissible to kill animals without trying to lessen their pain. Nowadays many of us are repelled by the idea of causing an animal needless pain. But such attitudes have not been the historical norm. Even nowadays many persons who would be appalled at someone's inflicting injury on a dog may not give a moment's heed to catching a trout by means of a barbed hook in the creature's mouth. The familiar justification for the difference in attitude is often summed up in the formula: "Fish are cold-blooded creatures and cold-blooded creatures do not feel pain."

---

for our actions does not follow. I will not, however, explore these issues further in this book.

In part, but only in part, is the verdict on whether or not fish feel pain a scientific one. Science can tell us how highly developed is a fish's central nervous system. What science cannot possibly tell us is to what extent any creature feels pain.[8]

What, if anything, makes this diverse sample of puzzles metaphysical? It is important to recognize that there need be no answer to this question other than tradition. There may, that is, be many metaphysical problems which bear little more in common than that they are *regarded* as metaphysical puzzles. To this extent, "metaphysical" may be like "interesting" or "popular" or "taboo", i.e. the term may describe something extrinsic, a way of our regarding the thing described, rather than any intrinsic feature of the thing itself. It may well be that there is no way other than by giving examples to explain what is to be regarded as a metaphysical puzzle.

If this is true, there should be no cause for alarm. For if this is true, metaphysics is no worse off in this regard than is, for example, mathematics. There is no single determinate feature, other than tradition, which makes some puzzle or some technique a mathematical one. When certain persons at the end of the sixteenth century set their minds to developing what has come to be known as algebra, many mathematicians did not know what to make of the newly developing techniques and body of knowledge ([112], 122-6). Was algebra, or was it not, mathematics? Or, again, at the turn of this century, as set theory was being developed at the hands of a few mathematicians, it was being roundly condemned by others ([112], 203-4). Was set theory a genuine part of mathematics or not? Mathematicians, without of course ever taking a vote on the question, but rather just by their accepting and using algebra and set theory, collectively decided (not discovered!) that these new techniques and their attendant concepts were to be regarded as mathematical. Similarly today there is a debate among physical anthropologists whether 'forensic archaeology' is a bona fide discipline alongside forensic anthropology.[9] There is no court of appeal to address one's questions to, to settle such discipli-

---

8. For a taste of just *some* of the many problems involved in trying to understand the consciousness of nonhuman creatures, see Thomas Nagel's "What Is It Like to Be a Bat?" ([140]).

9. One anthropologist, revealing his hostility, has characterized forensic archaeologists as "'fringe' elements who analyze ceramics from vandalized sites" (reported in [98], 2).

nary disputes. Nowhere is it authoritatively written what is, and what is not, to count as being mathematical; nowhere is it written what is, and what is not, to count as falling within the sphere of forensic anthropology. And – to make the point I am driving at – nowhere is it, nor could it be, authoritatively written what is, and what is not, to count as being a metaphysical problem.

This is not to say, however, that anything and everything is eligible for being regarded as being a metaphysical problem. No more so than is everything eligible for being regarded as being a mathematical or an anthropological problem.

To what extent, then, can we say what a metaphysical problem is, or put another way, what metaphysics itself is? There is no simple answer. The scope of metaphysics changes somewhat from generation to generation (remember the quotation [p. 6] from Collingwood, speaking of history); it may even change from philosopher to philosopher. I think it would be foolhardy to attempt to give anything like a definition or some formula whose application would give a verdict: "Yes, this is a metaphysical problem"; or, "No, this is not a metaphysical problem". To learn what metaphysics is, or better, what sorts of problems philosophers regard as being metaphysical problems, one should look into a variety of philosophical books. And in doing that, one will quickly discover that a great many, remarkably diverse, problems are regarded as being metaphysical ones.

This essential vagueness must be terribly unsatisfactory for the newcomer. There is always the expectation that one should be told at the outset what the nature and scope is of the studies to be pursued. Actually, I have tried to anticipate this presumption with the preceding examples. But doubtless some of you would like something more by way of characterization. So, bearing in mind the warnings I have just given about the hazards and indeed the futility of the attempt, let me say just a little bit more about what metaphysics might be regarded to be. But understand that whatever anyone could say at this point could be nothing more than a kind of signpost.

Human beings come equipped with several sensory modes. Aristotle (384-322 BC) thought we had exactly five: seeing, hearing, touching, tasting, and smelling.[10] So venerated was his philosophy that this

---

10. See [10], book III, 424b20-3. Aristotle not only thought that there were exactly five senses, he thought that it was provable that there could not be any more than five (see 424b24-425a14).

wildly wrong opinion was, and still is, accepted by many persons as indubitable truth. But the simple fact is that human beings have more than five senses, and I am not talking about esoteric senses whose very existence is highly debatable, such as precognition, clairvoyance, or telekinesis. I mean perfectly ordinary, common, garden-variety senses: of temperature, of balance, of pain, etc.

Our senses serve up to us a rich variety of information about the world external to our skins and internal to our skins. But our curiosity runs beyond our ability to probe the universe with the sensory tools we are born with. We extend, and indeed supplement, our human senses with artfully crafted scientific instruments. Our scientific instruments extend the range of our senses, to the infrared, to the ultra-violet, and beyond; to the subaudible, to the cryogenic, to the microscopic, etc. Our instruments, too, can make discriminations much finer than we ourselves are personally capable of: the nanosecond, the micron, the milligram, etc. And our instruments can even reveal features of Nature to which our senses seem to be blind, such as the polarization of the sky, the magnetic field of the Earth, or the direction of an electrical current. Such knowledge, as provided by our senses and by the extension of those senses through the use of scientific instruments, is considered to be *experiential* knowledge.

Only a little of experiential knowledge is passive. The greatest part is the result of our (individually and collectively) actively examining and manipulating the environment with an eye to gaining knowledge. Our creative talents are pressed to the limits in this enterprise and reach their greatest fruition in our creating science. Few of the workings of Nature are written on the surface, as it were. To understand how the world operates we need to guess about its workings, to test those guesses, and then to guess again and again when those guesses turn out to be incorrect. Popper has called the method of science "conjectures and refutations". Just as aptly it could be called "a creative guessing game".

The growth in experiential knowledge has been prodigious in extent and remarkable in its variety. Science has revealed to us many of the nearly infinitesimal components of the atom and much of the structures of galactic clusters; many of the secrets of inorganic matter and those of living tissues; a considerable number of the operations of the insensate, and some of the infinitely more subtle operations of the consciousnesses of human beings.

What is there about hydrogen and oxygen that allows them to form a molecule? What is there about these same elements which prevents each of them from forming molecules with seven of their own kind, i.e. why are there no molecules consisting solely of eight atoms of hydrogen, and none consisting solely of eight atoms of oxygen? What is the normal evolution of stars? How are genes replicated? How do muscles contract? These are the sorts of questions which science can answer.

Nonetheless, experiential knowledge, whether the product of passive, unaided human sensory perception or the result of the most highly imaginative and sophisticated scientific hypothesizing combined with controlled experimenting with technically refined instruments, still can take us only so far. Our desire for explanations forever transcends what experience, even when pushed to its limits in science, can possibly offer us. Experience cannot answer a question such as "What must a world be like in order that there should be able to exist within it such things as physical molecules?" Experience cannot tell us, for example, whether a human being, in the final stages of Alzheimer's disease, who has lost all ability to recognize and interact with other human beings, is still a person. Experience cannot tell us, for example, whether a (future) computer which perfectly imitates the behavior of a human being is conscious. Experience cannot tell us, for example, whether human beings have free will. And experience cannot tell us whether human beings have immortal, immaterial souls.

These questions, which go beyond the ability of experience, beyond the ability of science, to answer, are metaphysical questions. This, at the very least, is the one common thread in all metaphysical questions. Etymology is not always a good indicator of meaning, but in this instance "meta", meaning "beyond", is apt.[11] Metaphysical questions are questions whose answers lie "beyond" physics, i.e. beyond science, beyond experience.

---

11. We want to be careful, however, not to carry the etymology back *too* far. For although the etymology does provide a useful insight, it turns out to be more fortuitous than it might at first appear. There were neither quotation marks nor italics in ancient Greek. Andronicus of Rhodes (c. 70 BC) introduced the term "metaphysics" in editing Aristotle's writings. At its first appearance, "metaphysics" meant, not "beyond physics", but "after *Physics*"; that is, Andronicus used the expression to refer to Aristotle's sequel to the treatise *Physics*. It was only subsequently that the term "metaphysics" came to be understood, not as indicating the position of certain of Aristotle's writings within his corpus, but rather as the kind of material treated in those writings. (See [54], 1.)

It does not follow, of course, that the converse is true, that every question which lies beyond the abilities of experience to answer is to be regarded as a metaphysical one. Quite the contrary, many such questions are traditionally thought not to be metaphysical ones at all. Questions of ethics and of aesthetics, for example, if their answers really do lie outside of experience, are not usually thought of as being part of metaphysics.

So what we find is that the best we can do is to characterize metaphysical problems as being *among* those problems whose answers take us beyond experience. But what makes one problem in this latter class a metaphysical problem and another a non-metaphysical problem is probably something that, ultimately, can be decided only by examining the history of philosophy to find the verdict of tradition.

Metaphysics can be pursued on a grand scale or it can be narrowly focused on one or a few specific problems. When Bruce Wilshire, for example, begins his book on metaphysics by writing "Metaphysics seeks a comprehensive view of the world" ([215], 13), he clearly is talking of metaphysics conceived in the former manner. And what he tries to do is to explore the rise and fall of a number of historical attempts at creating large-scale metaphysical theories. Metaphysics need not be pursued in that fashion, however. One need not try to solve every metaphysical problem simultaneously by the proposing of a comprehensive theory. One can choose to work piecemeal, by solving, or at least elucidating, specific metaphysical problems. Thus, for example, in this century we have seen a number of books, by a great variety of philosophers, devoted to single problems within metaphysics, e.g. on the nature of mind, on the analysis of causality, on the analysis of free will, on the relations between particulars and universals, and on the nature of space and time. Philosophers who choose to pursue metaphysics in this latter fashion may have no overarching scheme which informs their researches. A philosopher choosing to analyze, for example, the possibility of the existence of free will may, but certainly need not, have a philosophical theory about the nature of space and time.

This book is of the latter design. I examine in subsequent pages only a select number of metaphysical problems. My criterion for choosing is very straightforward: these are the problems which have interested me most in recent years. Utterly no value judgment is intended about the relative merits of the greater part of metaphysics which is not pursued in this book. I am temperamentally disinclined to the kind of grand system building which has attracted some philosophers. I am also somewhat pessimistic about the prospects for success if one endeavors to create a comprehensive system. The probability of error increases with the magnitude of the task. Grand system building is vastly more risky than focusing on specific problems. Indeed, the latter is quite difficult enough for me.

In contrast to Wilshire's opening sentence, which foreshadows an examination of large-scale metaphysical schemes, the opening sentence of P.F. Strawson's book lays the groundwork for his pursuing metaphysics in a more modest fashion: "Metaphysics has been often revisionary, and less often descriptive" ([200], 9). Strawson explains the difference this way:

> Descriptive metaphysics is content to describe the actual structure of our thought about the world, revisionary metaphysics is concerned to produce a better structure. ... Perhaps no actual metaphysician has ever been, both in intention and effect, wholly the one thing or the other. ... This book is, in part, and in a modest way, an essay in descriptive metaphysics. Only in a modest way – for though some of the themes discussed are sufficiently general, the discussion is undertaken from a certain limited viewpoint and is by no means comprehensive. ([200], 9, 11)

It should be clear, from what I have already said, that this book, like Strawson's, is one intended by its author to be "undertaken from a certain limited viewpoint and is by no means comprehensive." My aim is to try to lay bare the 'inner logic' (if I may be permitted such a phrase) of some of our most fundamental concepts. But – as Strawson explains – descriptive metaphysics is virtually always accompanied by revisionary metaphysics. And thus I usually will not be content simply to say, "This is the way such-and-such a concept is standardly used." Frequently, I will venture to say something bolder, to wit, something tantamount to "This is the way such-and-such a concept *ought* to be understood." When I do that, I will not merely be reporting how the concept is used; I will be suggesting how we might profitably revise or refine our concept for further use.

CHAPTER THREE

Theories:
What they are and
what they are not

In chapter 2, I invoked the concept of *theory* several times. In chapters 4 and 5, I will discuss what differences there are between metaphysical theories and scientific theories and what the problems are in generating and testing theories. But we will pause here to examine the concept of *theory* itself.

A theory is, in the broadest sense, one or more hypotheses about some particular subject matter, such as mechanics, optics, international trade, disease transmission, learning, pest control, ethics, infinite numbers, or sexual maturation. A theory is, in brief, an attempt to come to grips with, to make sense of, to explain, and in some instances to control and predict, something of particular interest to us, often some feature of the world (children's growth, climatic changes, audio reproduction, etc.), but sometimes something as 'abstract' as provability or existence in mathematics.

On this account, we all construct theories constantly. Some of them may be relatively long-lived; for example, you might theorize that investing one-tenth of your net income in government bonds is the best manner to save for your retirement and might subscribe to this theory and put it into practice (follow its precepts) for all of your working lifetime. Other theories might be rejected almost immediately; for instance, the theory that the noise in a distant part of your friend's apartment was caused by someone's knocking on a window. It may happen that no sooner does this theory cross your mind than it might immediately be discarded, particularly if you happen to recall that you are visiting in an apartment on the forty-second floor.

It might strike you as rather overstated, even a bit pretentious, to call a momentarily entertained belief that someone is knocking on the window a "theory". You may find that you want to reserve the term "theory" for something somewhat more elaborate, more specialized –

for example, a theory about chemical reactions, or immunization, or electromagnetic radiation. You might, that is, be inclined to reserve the term "theory" exclusively for recognizably scientific contexts.

But there is no particular need to be diffident about conceiving of commonplace, even momentary, beliefs – e.g. about the cause of a noise in an apartment – as theories. Scientists have no more proprietary claim to "theory" than they have to terms like "experiment", or economists have to terms like "profit". To be sure, there is, for example, a *specialized* sense of "profit" which economists adopt in their economic writings, but that sense is certainly not the only viable sense. We can, and do, for example, talk about the *profit*, not monetary or capital gain certainly, in reading a good book, or taking a vacation, or quitting smoking. There unquestionably is this more general notion of "profit" having to do with gaining a good of any sort. So too is there a notion of "experiment" which includes, but is not restricted to, the kinds of deliberately crafted laboratory experiments conducted by scientists. The four-year-old child, in rubbing one crayon over a mark made by another crayon, is *experimenting* with colors and textures; a chef substituting one spice for another specified in a recipe is *experimenting* with flavors; and so on. And so it is with the term "theory". Theorizing is not something confined to the scientific context, nor is it the sole preserve of the trained scientist. All of us theorize. We theorize about the cause of the delay in the mail, the best way to handle the grievance from the shop steward, whether there is an afterlife, how to avoid having to buy a new vacuum cleaner, whether it would be profitable to search the house for our missing notes for the report we are writing or whether to assume that they are forever lost and it would be best to try to reconstruct them, etc.

(You may recall, a moment ago, at the very end of chapter 2, I wrote: "Frequently, I will venture to say something bolder, to wit, something tantamount to, 'This is the way such-and-such a concept *ought* to be understood.' When I do that, I will not merely be reporting how the concept is used; I will be suggesting how we might profitably revise or refine our concept for further use." Notice that this is precisely what I have just been doing, in discussing how the concept of *theory* is to be understood, and I will continue to do so throughout the rest of this current chapter. I am not merely saying that such-and-such is the way the concept *theory* is used; I have been arguing, and will continue to argue, that to adopt a certain usage is useful and profitable. In short, I am not just engaging in a piece of descriptive lexicography,*[1] but I am here *doing* philosophy, in this particular case, recommending how we might best, or at least usefully, regard the concept of *theory*. I have, that is, started upon a philosophical theory about, interestingly enough, the very concept of *theory* itself. Hereinafter, however, as I continue this sort of exercise for a variety of other concepts, I will not again explicitly direct your attention to the fact that I am not only reporting how a concept is ordinarily used, but also, and more importantly for my purposes, making a proposal how I think it might better be used. Concepts, after all, are intellectual tools. We are not duty-bound to leave them as we find them. We are entitled to tamper with them, to experiment with them, in an effort to try to improve them. And having wrought modifications in a concept, we are entitled to offer those changes to others, along with our reasons for the revisions and with samples of their uses, so that others may have grounds for accepting, rejecting, criticizing, or modifying our handiwork in turn.)

Some authors like to make a distinction between hypotheses on the one hand and theories on the other. The distinction is akin to that between sentences and paragraphs: a paragraph may consist of a single sentence, but it may also consist of a great many sentences grouped together by a common subject matter. Similarly, a theory may consist of a single hypothesis, but it may also consist of a great many hypotheses grouped together by a common subject matter. Because theories are, in the end, collections of one or more hypotheses, I will not usually distinguish between the two. I am as happy to talk about hypotheses as I am about theories.

A theory, on this account, is a guess, sometimes a remarkably insightful guess, sometimes one containing several propositions*, but a guess, hypothesis, or conjecture nonetheless. I use all these terms, "guess", "conjecture", and "hypothesis", almost interchangeably. The only difference is that while all hypotheses are guesses, not all guesses are hypotheses. A child may hide a jelly bean in one of her fists and ask her brother, "Which one?" If the brother tries, using his knowledge of his sister's typical behavior, to figure out in which hand she is likely to have concealed the candy, then he is constructing a hypothesis. But if he chooses at random, makes a stab in the dark as we say, he is merely guessing, not hypothesizing. The difference is that a hypothesis is something more, but often little more, than *just* a guess.

---

1. See "descriptive definition" in Glossary.

It is an attempt to make sense of, or to predict the truth of some feature of the world by calling upon one's prior knowledge of the world
and some rational grounds for expecting it to be of one sort rather than
another. But with this said, I will not trouble myself further with
trying to offer a decisive account of the difference. Guesses and
hypotheses are similar enough to one another that – for present purposes – a precise account of their subtle differences is not required.

Some theories – e.g. that someone is knocking on the window –
may be regarded to be among those things which may be judged true
or false. But other theories do not lend themselves to being judged
true or false – e.g. the theory (next chapter) that we should prefer explanations of natural events in terms of causes rather than in terms of
purposes. These latter sorts of theories must be judged on other
criteria; for instance, Is the adopting of the theory useful? Does it
allow us to get on better than do alternative theories? Is it simpler than
alternative theories? We will return to the matter of appraising such
theories later, in chapter 6, where we will examine metaphysical theories in greater detail.

Theories of the sort which allow for being judged true or false do
not cease to be theories when their truth or falsity becomes known. A
theory – just like a guess – may be true; equally well a theory may be
false. This is not to say of course that any one theory may be both true
and false. I mean simply that something's being a theory does not
preclude its being true: it may be, or then again, it may not be. And
thus a theory does not cease to be a theory when its truth comes to be
regarded as a virtual certainty. Geometrical optics is sometimes held
up as a example of a body of knowledge whose truth is a practical certainty and whose details have been agreed upon, virtually without
change, for about a hundred years. But despite its durability, it is still
appropriate, within the meaning of the term, to call geometrical optics
a "theory". So, too, is it appropriate to talk of the *theory* that poliomyelitis is caused by a virus. This latter claim is, so far as I know, universally assented to within the medical profession. But it is still perfectly
appropriate to call the claim a theory.

I emphasize the point that a theory may be *true*, that this is no contradiction in terms, because there is a bogus, quasi-political, argument
to the contrary which we would do well to scotch.

Some creationists have argued that Creation Science deserves to be
taught in the public schools alongside evolutionary theory, because
both are conjectures and neither can be regarded as established fact.
The flawed argument runs like this: "The very name 'evolutionary

theory' signifies that the claims being made are not proven. Whatever is proven is called a 'fact', not a 'theory'. Evolutionary *theory* is not proven. It is conjecture; it is a set of beliefs. But insofar as evolutionary theory is just that, a theory, i.e. unproven, then so too does creation theory, admittedly also not proven, deserve to be taught alongside as an alternative viewpoint." The creationist has in this argument made heavy weather of the word "theory", stating explicitly that the term implies "not proven". This is simply incorrect. It is perfectly proper to regard a body of propositions which have a certain explanatory power, and which are generally regarded as true, as a "theory". Witness: the special theory of relativity, today so well established that it is not much challenged; the theory of conic sections, believed by most, if not all, mathematicians to be absolutely correct and not profitably to be challenged; and the theory of logarithms. All of these are theories, and all of them – just like the previously mentioned theories of poliomyelitis and geometrical optics – are reasonably to be regarded as true.[2] If espousers of Creation Science, then, want to make a case for the teaching of Creation Science in the public schools, they must do so on grounds other than the claim that evolution and creation are both theories. For, from the fact that something is a theory, nothing whatsoever follows about its worthiness, or unworthiness, to be taught in the public schools. Whether Creation Science deserves to be taught depends, rather, on what *kind* of theory it is: for example, whether it is religious or scientific, whether it is amenable or immune to revision, and whether it is strongly or weakly confirmed* by the evidence offered in its support.

Theories which are true or false are called "truth-valued theories". (Being "truth-valued" simply means being "either true or false".) Among truth-valued theories, just as some may, with virtual certainty (conviction), be regarded as being true, others may, with equal certainty, be regarded as being false; e.g. the theory that flies spontaneously generate from putrefying meat; the theory that human beings are the only tool-making animals on this planet; and the theory that it is possible to construct a perpetual-motion machine. But most truth-valued theories fall somewhere between the two extremes, some close to one end or the other, while other theories fall closer to the middle.

---

2. The list goes on indefinitely: e.g. the theory that light travels at a fixed, finite velocity; the theory that blood circulates within the human body; or the theory that genetic information is coded in the DNA molecule.

This is not, of course, to say that truth-valued theories fall along a continuum from true to false. There is nothing 'between' truth and falsity. Any truth-valued theory is either true or it is false; there is no other alternative. There is, however, a continuum between our attitude of resolute conviction on the one extreme and our attitude of total disbelief on the other. We may well be strongly inclined to view some particular theory as true, another theory as false, and still another as one whose truth or falsity we are unsure about. Thus it is possible, although relatively rare, to be badly mistaken about a theory's truth. We might, for example, take a false theory to be indubitable, even though – in this case – we happen to have made a mistake, and the theory is, in fact, false. As human beings, wanting to get on in the world, we must make reasoned judgments about the truth or falsity, or the utility as the case may be, of many of our theories. We may, even, feel ourselves justified in adopting an attitude of certainty about particular ones among our truth-valued theories. On occasion, however, the world fools us; on occasion, the world surprises us. What we are convinced is true sometimes turns out – for all that – to be false; and what we are convinced is false sometimes turns out – for all that – to be true.

In the previous chapter I mentioned that many persons hold to a variety of theories without even being aware that they do so. I think, in fact, that we each hold not to just a few such theories, but to a great many. These theories typically are not especially well-articulated. Indeed, I am sure that most of the theories each of us subscribes to are held rather inchoately, below the level of conscious examination. Not only are we often not aware that we hold them, we would have some difficulty in articulating them were we to try. The case is analogous to a person's knowing the meaning of a word, but without being able to give a definition of that word. This is especially true of children. Children know, that is, are able to use correctly, a great many words. But they are not able to define those words or tell you what those words mean. Being able to use a word and being self-consciously aware of the meaning of the word are two quite different skills. The latter comes only later in one's intellectual development, if it comes at all. Similarly for theories. Each of us subscribes to an enormous number of theories but we may be totally unaware that we do, and may be unable to articulate many of the theories we in fact believe and act upon.

Theorizing begins at a very early age. Even as the young infant lies in her crib, she begins exploring her environment and theorizing about it. Laboratory data suggest that it takes some weeks before the infant 'catches on' to the fact that when objects pass out of view (e.g. Mother or Father leaving the room) or one object passes behind another object, the obscured object does not 'go out of existence' ([115], 451-3). But what exactly do we mean when we say that the infant 'catches on' to the fact that most material objects persist (continue to exist) even though obscured from view by some other physical object? The most natural way to explicate this notion of 'catching on' is to say of the infant that she has posited* the hypothesis (constructed the theory) that obscured physical objects continue to exist, and that, by experimenting, has come to accept this hypothesis. Note, of course, that we are not saying that the infant has a concept of *hypothesis* or of *theory*. One may create a theory without having the concept of a theory, just as one may walk or talk without having the concept *walking* or the concept *talking*. And it bears remarking, too, that some theorizing at least – for example, this very case of the young infant hypothesizing the persistence of obscured physical objects – can proceed without a language. Indeed animals which lack languages can also be regarded as engaging in theorizing, although at a much less sophisticated level than human beings. Just as animals, e.g. cats and dogs, can be regarded as having certain kinds of unsophisticated beliefs, they can as well be regarded as engaging in a kind of low-level, unsophisticated, theorizing.[3]

Two hundred years ago Kant hypothesized (recall the second quotation from Buber in chapter 2, p. 13) that the human mind is so constituted as to interpret the data of our senses in such a way that the external world would present itself to our consciousness so as to be perfectly describable by Euclidean geometry. If someone were to try to salvage this theory, and render it in a more modern idiom, it would probably emerge as the theory that our brains are hard-wired (preprogrammed) to apply a Euclidean computation to the data provided by

---

3. These sorts of claims – about beliefs and theories held by animals – are programmatic. At the current level of theory within psycholinguistics, we are unable to state very precisely just what it is for an animal to have a belief. As a matter of fact, we are unable to state with much clarity and conviction what it is for a human being to have a belief. In a way, the claims that animals can have beliefs and can engage in theorizing are pre-theoretical. They constitute, not the results of well-confirmed theories in psycholinguistics, but rather some of the intuitively grasped *data* which we would like to see such theories, in due course of their development, accommodate.

our sensory organs. Modern engineers use the technical term "filter" to describe any 'black-box device' which alters, in a determinate manner, signals or information passing through that device ([102], 352). Thus polarizers placed on a camera lens are filters, but so too are bass and treble controls on a stereo amplifier, and so too are many computer programs, e.g. ones which chop text files into readable chunks of twenty-five lines, or which justify lines of text so that they are all of uniform width on a page. In modern terminology, then, Kant's theory was that the mind acts as a filter on the raw data of sense to transform them in such a way as to conform to the calculus of Euclidean geometry, or to put it still another way, the mind is itself a Euclidean filter. Now this particular claim, both in its original form and in its modern transformation, is probably false. We probably are not preprogrammed to view the world with the kind of specificity inherent in Euclidean geometry. We may not, that is, be preprogrammed to interpret the world so that, for example, doubling the lengths of the sides of a triangle would leave all the angles unchanged. (This latter is a theorem of Euclidean geometry, but not of some other geometries.) But we *may* be preprogrammed to interpret the world in more general ways, e.g. to conceive of it as having movable, enduring, physical objects; or to conceive of it as having objects at varying distances from our personal loci of perception. In this century, some experimental psychologists and linguists have turned to examine these sorts of questions empirically: What sorts of beliefs, if any, do we seem predisposed to adopt? What sorts of concepts, if any, do we seem naturally to use?

Some of the pioneering work in this field, in particular Piaget's investigations into children's understanding of the concept of *causality*, remains among the most interesting and philosophically illuminating ([152]). His experimental data showed that children take several years to develop anything like an adult's understanding, and use, of the concept of *causality*.[4] Perhaps this very fact that it takes children so long to master the concept of *causality* may help to explain why philosophers have had such a difficult time in trying to explicate it. The concept of *causality* may take so long to acquire because it is so com-

---

4. Some more recent research (see [96], 2-3) would tend to lower, somewhat, the ages Piaget found for the various stages of mastery of the concept of *causality*. Nonetheless, his original finding that it takes children several years to acquire the adult's understanding of the concept remains intact.

plicated and multifaceted, and indeed probably is not one single concept, but rather a family of concepts.

It should be clear, from the examples I have been giving, that theories need not be (sets of) mathematical formulas. Certain philosophers, however, in trying to explicate the concept of a theory, have focused their attention on the sorts of theories one finds in physics and chemistry. For example, Ernest Nagel, taking his inspiration from Norman Campbell (1880-1949), writes:

> For the purposes of analysis, it will be useful to distinguish three components in a theory: (1) an abstract calculus that is the logical skeleton of the explanatory system, and that "implicitly defines" the basic notions of the system; (2) a set of rules that in effect assign an empirical content to the abstract calculus by relating it to the concrete materials of observation and experiment; and (3) an interpretation or model for the abstract calculus, which supplies some flesh[5] for the skeletal structure in terms of more or less familiar conceptual or visualizable materials. ... However [these distinctions] ... are rarely given explicit formulation in actual scientific practice, nor do they correspond to actual stages in the construction of theoretical explanations. ([139], 90)

By an "abstract calculus", Nagel means a mathematical equation or a statement expressed using the symbolism of modern mathematics or logic, e.g.

(3.1) $F = ma$

(3.2) $I = E/R$

(3.3) $Z = \sqrt{[R^2 + (X_L - X_C)^2]}$

Such symbolic expressions are, in the first instance, to be conceived only as formulas which may be manipulated by the rules of some system. The "F", the "m", the "a", etc. are to be regarded merely as variables, in much the same way that a high-school teacher may

---

5. The metaphor, "skeleton" and "flesh", which Nagel adopts here is not just his own: it is a familiar one which dozens of other philosophers of science have appropriated as well.

instruct students to manipulate expressions in algebra, such as "$x^2 + 11 = 29.49$", without specifying whether the variables are to stand for dollars, acres of farmland, milliliters of sulfuric acid, or scores on tests of eye blink frequencies. Only at the second stage is meaning to be assigned to the symbols, e.g. "F" may be said to stand for "force", "m" for "mass", and "a" for acceleration, so that a formula such as (3.1) above might then be read as expressing Newton's second law of motion. Similarly, under the proper interpretation of "I", "E", and "R", (3.2) above may be read as expressing Ohm's law, and under a proper definition for "Z", "R", "X_L", and "X_C", (3.3) above may be read as expressing the formula for calculating the impedance of a resistor-capacitance-inductor circuit.

To be fair, Nagel explicitly denies that this philosophical reconstruction which he is offering is meant to portray precisely what you might expect to find in physics texts and journals, nor is it meant to capture the "actual stages in the construction of theoretical explanations". Nagel's explication, which is promoted by a great number of other philosophers of science as well, is intended to reveal no more and no less than the 'logical structure' of scientific theories.

Philosophical 'reconstruction' is a peculiar business. Even among philosophers who nominally belong to the same school of philosophy, there are remarkably different opinions as to what, properly, ought to go into a philosophical reconstruction. Nagel,[6] in this passage, has allied himself with the so-called formalist branch of Analytic philosophy. The formalist approach may be contrasted with the contextualist (or ordinary-language[7]) approach. The differences between these two approaches were more clear-cut and topical in the 1950s than they are in the latter quarter of this century, but something of the attitudes each wing took toward philosophy still characterizes many contemporary

---

6. Incidentally, there are a few well-known, widely read, twentieth-century philosophers all bearing the name "Nagel". I am here writing of Ernest Nagel.

7. Neither "contextualist" nor "ordinary-language" are particularly good descriptions of the analytic philosophers who are not formalists. A more apt, but even less explanatory, description would be simply "non-formalist". Very crudely, the non-formalists put more stock into trying to incorporate into their analyses of concepts something of the context-dependency of their uses and the intentions of their users, i.e. what are often called the 'pragmatics' of their use.

philosophers. Although not pledging unreserved allegiance to either wing, many contemporary philosophers tend to identify more strongly with one approach than with the other.

On the matter of explicating the concept of *theory*, I depart widely from the formalists. To focus exclusively, or even primarily, on the mathematical and logical features of certain refined theories in physics, chemistry, and economics strikes me as drawing too restricted a sample and ignoring too many other critical features. Of course some theories are highly mathematical (quantum theory, special and general relativity, string theory [in cosmology], etc.), but this must not cause us to overlook that the greatest number of our theories are *not* mathematical ones. We will fail to understand what role theories – both scientific and metaphysical ones – play in our lives if we blinker our analysis by conceiving of *theory* overly narrowly. Theorizing permeates our human approach to the world. It is not something reserved exclusively for the accomplished, trained scientist. All of us theorize constantly, on political matters, human relationships, humankind's place in the world, children, earning a living, friendship, loyalty, death, etc.

Philosophers differ, too, as to whether, and how much, a philosophical analysis ought to try to capture the route or means by which a concept is acquired. Formalists will usually dismiss the matter of concept- and theory-generating as 'psychologizing', arguing that it has no proper place in the concerns of philosophy. Again others, I among them, take the opposite point of view.

Pick up any textbook which attempts to teach a person physics or chemistry. The actual mathematical formulas typically will comprise no more than 5% of the total text, in some books vastly less, perhaps no more than 1%. Attend some introductory classes in *any* science, whether physics, chemistry, economics, sociology, or anthropology. There you will hear the lecturer speaking almost entirely in English or some other natural language. Usually the lecturer will write down the mathematical parts of the lecture on the blackboard, and students will copy that math into their notebooks. An outsider, looking at those class notes, might easily mistakenly infer that the lecture was almost entirely in mathematics. But this is clearly not so. To teach a theory, to explain it to other persons, to get those other persons to understand the theory – so that they in turn can use it, can apply it to the world in an attempt to understand, manage, and predict what is going on in the world – one must communicate in a *natural language*. We never *learn* theories by first being taught an uninterpreted calculus, and then, having mastered the manipulation of the symbols, by being informed, at a second stage of initiation as it were, what those symbols refer to. No, teachers first try to explain to their students what the concepts of (for instance) *mass*, *profit*, *capital*, *velocity*, and *neurosis* are, and then and only then do they proceed to introduce symbols for those concepts.

To understand why the formalists find the sort of analysis offered by Nagel both alluring and plausible, one must understand that this sort of analysis has had some very striking historical successes. It is, to my mind, still the best account available to explain how it is possible that there can be alternative geometries. For two thousand years, from the time of Euclid to the mid-nineteenth century, there had been but one geometry: Euclid's. The prevailing view as to why there was exactly one geometry was to the effect that, in some sense, either because geometry was a logical necessity or because geometry was imposed by the mind on the data of sense (Kant), there *could not be* any more than one. When, finally, several geometries were discovered (invented) which competed with Euclidean geometry, an explanation had to be found. The sort of analysis offered by Nagel and other formalists serves that purpose admirably. By conceiving of each and every geometry as, in the first instance, consisting of just a set of uninterpreted formulas, the way was found to place them all on an equal footing. All geometries are simply abstract, uninterpreted calculi saying nothing whatsoever about the real world, and thus none of them is either true or false. Only when an uninterpreted system is 'fleshed out' with an interpretation, for example, linking the uninterpreted term "*L*" with something in the actual world that is to count as a line, can the interpreted geometry thereby created then be tested for truth or falsity.

Thus the model Nagel presents is powerfully historically motivated. It has had some stunning success. And indeed I continue to use it regularly to explain to my own students how it is possible that there are bona fide alternative, non-Euclidean, geometries. But the question remains as to how far this particular formal analysis of *theory* may be extended. And it is in answering this question that some of the most fundamental differences in philosophical attitude become vocally contested among analytic philosophers.

Plato is reputed to have had inscribed in the lintel of the entrance to his Academy the motto "Let no one who is not a geometer enter." The slogan had a point. Plato looked upon geometry as the 'ideal' of knowledge. It was the 'most perfect' form of knowledge. Non-geometrical propositions were regarded as approximating to knowledge to the degree that they exhibited the rigor and style of geometry.

To be sure, there is something quite remarkable, audacious, even aesthetically pleasing, that is to say, beautiful, in geometry. It is a marvel of the powers of human reason. But to what extent any given masterpiece, whether a geometry, a musical composition, or an act of bravery, ought to set the standards by which others of that genre are to be judged remains an issue over which all of us, philosophers and non-philosophers alike, will perennially argue.

Nagel and other formalists tend to offer specific, *idealized*, reconstructions of many of our most fundamental concepts – e.g. of *theory*, of *cause*, of *explanation*, indeed even of *space* and of *time*[8] – growing out of analyses of some especially favored particular cases. Carl Hempel, for example, in explicating the concepts of *theory*, *cause*, and *explanation* ([90]), invoked the case of a car's radiator cracking when the temperature fell below freezing – a case lending itself to prediction by citing antecedent conditions (drop in temperature, lack of antifreeze, etc.) and known scientific laws (concerning the expansion of water when frozen, the tensile strength of metals, etc.).

Non-formalists are temperamentally disposed to cast their nets far wider, to collect a much greater diversity of cases from which to begin and then to try to accommodate as much as possible of this diversity in their analyses. Critics of the formalist approach will argue, for example, against the appropriateness of Hempel's favored example, objecting that it is an artificially simple case, unrepresentative of cases such as explaining someone's purchasing theater tickets in anticipation of surprising arriving guests. In the latter case, of human behavior, there is little expectation of our being able to predict the purchase nor can we deduce the description of the event from antecedent conditions and known scientific laws. Wittgenstein (1889-1951), although himself having once been a formalist, denigrated the formalists' approach when he wrote in his posthumous *Philosophical Investigations*:

---

8. It is a fascinating, and eye-opening, investigation to compare the writings of a formalist on the topic of time (see e.g. Grünbaum [84]) with those of sociologists, anthropologists, and psychologists (see e.g. Gurvitch [85]). Sometimes it is difficult to discern in just what sense these persons are writing about the 'same' thing.

... in many cases where the question arises "Is this an appropriate description or not?" The answer is: "Yes, it is appropriate, but only for this narrowly circumscribed region, not for the whole of what you are claiming to describe." ([216], §3)

A main cause of philosophical disease – a one-sided diet: one nourishes one's thinking with only one kind of example. (§593)

It would be tempting to ask, "Well, who is right, the formalists or their critics? Which is the correct way to go about doing a philosophical analysis?"

If only such questions had straightforward answers. But they do not. I can see no way at all to offer an answer without begging* the very question being posed. Formalists will answer in one fashion, non-formalists in another. But who, or where, is the neutral, objective referee who can adjudicate the debate? So far as I can tell, at this point, when we have begun to ask questions about how philosophy is to be done, there can be no definitive or authoritative answers. As I said earlier, each of you must sample philosophical approaches to find one suitable for yourself. At some point argumentation comes to an end and it becomes time simply to choose.

When I was much younger, I did not at all have this attitude toward philosophy. I was convinced that there must be good arguments for the resolution of any philosophical question. My teachers seemed so *sure* of their own philosophical bearings. They never seemed to experience, let alone confide in us students, any qualms or misgivings concerning what they so confidently professed. And for a while I, too, shared something of what I took to be their attitude: that one can achieve knowledge and certainty in philosophy, that with effort and conscientiousness one could aspire to truth in philosophy just as one could in science. I believed that there were objective standards in philosophy just as in science and that we philosophers could, if we were willing to do the work, achieve consensus in our philosophy.

Twenty-five years later that youthful optimism has completely evaporated. I have unburdened myself of that comfortable delusion. Indeed, I have gone one step further. Unlike my own teachers, I often and emphatically explain my own views about philosophy to my students, telling them quite explicitly that although I am prepared to present my views with as much verve as I can, I do not want them to mistake my enthusiasm for a conviction of certainty. I am *certain* of almost nothing I teach my students. (And likewise for the bulk of this book.)

My lack of certainty, however, has not dulled my interest. Certainty has given way to what I regard as a more mature understanding of human theorizing. We do the best we can, but in the end we can *prove* almost nothing of what we believe, say, or write.[9] Why, exactly, this is so, or, more precisely, why exactly I believe this, I will try to explain in the following two chapters. There I will argue that our theorizing is *underdetermined* by the evidence we offer in support of our theories. And I will argue that this indeterminacy is not just a feature of our philosophizing, but permeates our attempts to do science as well. But this is to anticipate.

Some contemporary anthropologists and psychologists have taken to describing *Homo sapiens* as the storytelling species, and by this they mean that we human beings are constantly constructing stories (hypotheses/theories) in order to make sense of both the usual and the unusual. These stories range from the myths of primitive societies to the highly sophisticated theories of quantum mechanics and astrophysics, from the commonplace ("there are parallel black marks on the pavement; probably a car skidded") to the highly speculative ("there is intelligent life elsewhere in this galaxy") and to the outrightly metaphysical ("there is in each of us an immortal soul"). But whether this metaphysical view – that there exists within us a deep motivation to try to construct ever more and ever better explanations – ever achieves wide acceptance, there is one thing that must be said of it: it has an endearing kind of self-illustration, for it would itself appear to spring from the very source it purports to describe.

---

9. "... the cause of philosophical disagreement ultimately lies in conflicting 'cognitive values' that relate to such matters as importance, centrality, and priority. ... Despite the inevitable strife of systems, scepticism regarding traditional philosophy is not warranted. Because values – cognitive values included – are important to us as individuals, philosophy remains an important and worthwhile enterprise, notwithstanding its inability to achieve a rationally constrained consensus on the fundamental issues. Indeed, given the nature of the enterprise, consensus is simply not a sensible goal, and failure to achieve it is not a defect" (Rescher [171], xi).

CHAPTER FOUR

Underdeterminism (I)

To understand how it is even possible to pursue metaphysics, it is necessary to begin by understanding the limits of what experience can tell us of the world,* and to understand how experiential (scientific) knowledge and metaphysics enjoy a symbiotic relationship.

4.1 The interconnectedness of science and metaphysics

Earlier in this century, there was a philosophical movement (c. 1920-45) which was openly hostile to metaphysics. The disaffection of the Logical Positivists (also known as Logical Empiricists) sprang principally from their antipathy to the highly speculative metaphysics of a number of nineteenth- and early-twentieth-century philosophers. Carnap mentions by name Fichte, Schelling, Hegel, Bergson, and Heidegger ([44], 80). He illustrates (1932), with a quotation from Heidegger, the sort of metaphysics which he is intent to eliminate.

> What is to be investigated is being only and – *nothing* else; being alone and further – *nothing;* solely being, and beyond being – *nothing. What about this Nothing? ... Does the Nothing exist only because the Not, i.e. the Negation, exists? Or is it the* other way around? *Does Negation and the Not exist only because the Nothing exists? ... We assert: the Nothing is prior to the Not and the Negation. ...* Where do we seek the Nothing? How do we find the Nothing. ... We know the Nothing. ... *Anxiety reveals the Nothing. ...* That for which and because of which we were anxious, was 'really' – nothing. Indeed: the Nothing itself – as such – was present. ... *What about this Nothing? – The Nothing itself nothings.* ([44], 69; italics in the original; translation by Arthur Pap[1])

---

1. The translating of Heidegger's writings into English has always been

A.J. Ayer continued the attack (1936) and used for his own example of unacceptable metaphysics ([16], 36) a slightly edited version of the last sentence of this passage from F.H. Bradley:

> ... pure spirit is not realized except in the Absolute. It can never appear as such and with its full character in the scale of existence. Perfection and individuality belong only to that Whole in which all degrees alike are at once present and absorbed. This one Reality of existence can, as such, nowhere exist among phenomena. And it enters into, but is itself incapable of, evolution and progress. ([33], 442)

Modern scholarship is not nearly so unsympathetic to these initially obscure-sounding pronouncements. Many modern writers claim to find in them intelligibility and significance not at all apparent to Carnap, to Ayer, or to their fellow Logical Positivists. Be that as it may, there is an undeniable difference between the style, the vocabulary, and the accessibility, on the one hand, of the metaphysics of Heidegger and Bradley, and on the other, of that of Strawson, for example, of whom we spoke briefly at the end of chapter 2. Suppose we compare the selection from Heidegger with one drawn from the first chapter of Strawson's *Individuals*. Both Heidegger and Strawson, we note, are endeavoring to explain what metaphysics is.

> We think of the world as containing particular things some of which are independent of ourselves; we think of the world's history as made up of particular episodes in which we may or may not have a part; and we think of these particular things and events as included in the topics of our common discourse, as things about which we can talk to each other. (Strawson [200], 15)

Metaphysics – at least as written by some philosophers – we see *can be* perfectly straightforward and readily comprehended.

With examples drawn from the most speculative extremes of meta-

---

problematic. What Pap translates as "being", Hull and Crick translate as "what-is" ([88], 358); and where Pap coins the verb "nothings" and translates Heidegger as saying "The Nothing itself nothings", Hull and Crick say "Nothing 'nihilates' of itself" ([88], 369).

physics, the Logical Positivists embarked on a program to try to devise linguistic and logical tests by which they could separate 'scientifically meaningful' statements from what they called "pseudo-statements". Some of them were so incautious, even, as to call all of metaphysics, not just that which gave rise in the first instance to their disapprobation, "literal nonsense".

Nowadays metaphysics again needs no apology. The Logical Positivists' attack on metaphysics was relatively short-lived. For a variety of technical reasons, their program to create what they called "a criterion of empirical significance" was to prove impossible to carry through. In due course, the Positivists came to realize the futility of their enterprise and abandoned it. Several philosophers (see e.g. Hempel [91]), including some of the Positivists themselves, carefully chronicled the successive attempts Positivists made along the way. Many explanations have been offered as to why the program was destined, ultimately, to fail.

The most common explanation for the failure is that there is no particular identifying feature of metaphysical statements. If a scientific theory happens to contain 'metaphysical' statements, then those statements cannot be distinguished from the other 'non-metaphysical' components of that theory. The source of the problem (from the Positivists' point of view) is that scientific theories are collections of diverse statements, and that sets of statements can only be tested *altogether*, i.e. one cannot, as a matter of logic, draw from a scientific theory testable implications whose truth or falsity redounds to the truth or falsity of individual members of the set (see, for example, Hempel [91], 129). In short, according to this explanation, there seems to be no way, either logically or linguistically, to isolate the 'metaphysical' components of a scientific theory from its 'non-metaphysical' components.

Such an explanation is, I think, incomplete. The problem lies deeper. The Positivists' program was doomed, not just because it is impossible to isolate the metaphysical components of a scientific theory, but rather, and more importantly, because metaphysical components are *essential* to any reasonable scientific theory. Scientific and metaphysical theorizing go hand in hand; it is impossible to do either one without the other. Science is impossible without *some* metaphysical presuppositions; metaphysics is impossible, or at the very least sterile in the extreme, unless informed by science (experience). Science and metaphysics are one of a kind; the difference is merely one of degree. The most fundamental presuppositions of science, those furthest removed from 'observational' data, tend to be regarded as 'metaphysi-cal'. It is these which change most slowly, which are so much a part of working scientists' conception of the world that scientists scarcely attend to them in day-to-day work, spending most of their energies instead on that part of science which lends itself most easily to con-firmation, disconfirmation, or revision in light of observation and experiment.

There is no question of logical or temporal priority in the interplay between our scientific and our metaphysical beliefs. Together they form a world-view. This world-view is in constant flux. As science progresses, our metaphysical views gradually change; and as meta-physical views change, adjustments are made within our science.

4.2   Case study: Francis Bacon's account of induction

"What is heat?" The question is deceptively simple. One is tempted to think that its answer ought to be a relatively trivial matter to settle. After all, heat is not an unfamiliar, rare commodity. We encounter it, in varying degrees, throughout all our waking hours: in stoves, hot-water taps, light bulbs, automobile engines, noxious cigarettes, active muscles, etc. Surely all a scientist has to do, we might be tempted to believe, is to examine instances of many such cases and it will be quickly obvious what heat *is*. Francis Bacon (1561-1626), for one, explicitly said exactly this in *The New Organon* of 1620:

> ... a nature [phenomenon] being given, we must first of all have a muster or presentation ... of all known instances which agree in the same nature, though in substances most unlike. And such collection must be ... without premature speculation ... For example, let the investigation be into ... heat. ...
>
> 1. The rays of the sun, especially in summer and at noon.
>   ...
> 3. Fiery meteors.
> 4. Burning thunderbolts.
> 5. Eruptions of flames from the cavities of mountains.
> 6. All flames.
>   ...
> 9. Liquids boiling or heated.
>   ...
> 16. All bodies rubbed violently, as stone, wood, cloth, etc.

insomuch that poles and axles of wheels sometimes catch
fire ...

...

25. Aromatic and hot herbs ... although not warm to the hand
..., yet to the tongue and palate, being a little masticated,
they feel hot and burning.

...

28. Other instances. ([20], 130-2)

Bacon thinks, however, that humankind lacks the requisite intelligence
to infer the nature of heat from a table consisting solely of positive instances. The difficulty stems from the fact that, presented with any
collection of items however much seemingly initially unlike one
another, we can – with a little ingenuity – find not just one but several
common features. A rug, a chair, and a tea bag – to invent just one
example – may share any number of features in common: they may all
be the same color; they may all be imported; they may all, to some
degree, be manufactured; they may all be purchased goods; they may
all be flammable; and so on. Drawing a single, correct, inference from
a list of positive instances, Bacon thus believes, would be possible
only by God and the angels, and perhaps by other higher intelligences
(p. 151). Humankind, lacking the special faculties of divine intelligence, can reduce the number of detected commonalities only by
supplementing the list of positive instances with lists of negative instances. Thus, for example, where the rays of the sun had been the
first item in his own list of positive instances, he contrasts this with
"the rays of the moon and stars and comets [which] are not found hot
to the touch" (133), and similarly, for each of the other twenty-one
specific items in his original list. And finally, he produces yet a third
list, this time of some forty-one items, discussing a variety of instances in which heat comes in various degrees. For example, the
twenty-fifth item in this third list reads: "Some ignited bodies are
found to be much hotter than some flames. Ignited iron, for instance,
is much hotter and more consuming than flame of spirit of wine
[alcohol]" (147).

These methods of Bacon were to have a profound influence on phi-
losophy. Two centuries later, we find them little changed, repeated in
J.S. Mill's *Logic* (1843) as the Method of Agreement, the Method of
Difference, and the Method of Concomitant Variations.

Having gathered his data, and having rejected a great number of hypotheses, e.g. the texture of materials, light or brightness, and rarity (pp. 154-5), Bacon states his conclusion:

> From a survey of the instances, all and each, of which the nature of heat is a particular case, [heat] appears to be motion. (156)

In spite of its modern sound, it is clear that Bacon's notion of the nature of heat is very unlike that of modern science. His subsequent comments reveal that he has not made the modern distinction between heat and temperature. Modern science tells us, for example, that two equal masses of water and iron at the same temperature contain different amounts of heat. It takes 8.4 times as much heat, for example, to raise 1 kg of water from 40°C to 41°C than it does to raise 1 kg of iron from 40°C to 41°C.[2] Nor does he conceive of heat as a quantity of fixed amount, i.e. he has no inkling of the law of the conservation of energy.

> ... when heat is produced by the approach of a hot body, this ... depends ... on the nature of assimilation or self-multiplication. (157)

> ... assimilation multiplies and transforms bodies and substances. ... Heat does not diffuse itself, in heating a body, by communication of the original heat but simply by exciting the parts of the body to that motion which is the form of heat. (242)

My purpose is not, however, to fault Bacon's conclusions. My concern lies with his discussion of how he supposedly arrived at those conclusions.

At the most crucial point in all of this, at the juncture between having completed his review of his data and drawing his conclusions, Bacon offers no account whatsoever of how he proceeded to move from the former to the latter. Instead of an explanation, we find simply a label: Bacon calls the process of moving from data to conclusion an "induction" (130). Earlier, he had spent several pages (18-23) explaining that this was to be regarded as a new kind of induction, a 'legitimate' sort of induction.

---

2. This is to say, the *specific heat* of water is 8.4 times that of iron.

> ... what the sciences stand in need of is a form of induction which shall analyze experience and take it to pieces, and by a due process of exclusion and rejection lead to an inevitable conclusion. ... The testimony and information of the sense [i.e. of sensory perception] has reference always to man, not the universe; and it is a great error to assert that the sense is a measure of things. ... The mind, when it receives impressions of objects through the sense, cannot be trusted to report them truly, but in forming its notions mixes up its own nature with the nature of things. ... The intellect is not qualified to judge except by means of induction, and induction in its legitimate form. (20-3)

For Bacon, human senses can, and often do, deceive. The human intellect, either alone or in concert with the senses, is inadequate to the task of finding the route to Nature's "first principles ... [which] lie at the heart and marrow of things" (20). The only way, according to Bacon, to proceed is by induction. And he thought, too, not only that his induction could generate new 'notions' but that it provided the only means to do so: "induction must be used ... in the formation of notions" (99).

But while Bacon is expansive in his praise of induction, he is strangely silent in explaining precisely what it is supposed to be or how it works. He is completely silent about *how* induction might get us from observational data to explanatory hypothesis, or how one might learn the technique or teach it to someone else. There are no rules stated; there are not even any hints given. This seemingly minor oversight is of the utmost importance for our understanding how science is underdetermined,* and for identical reasons, how metaphysics is underdetermined.

Bacon did not explain how he was able to generate his conclusions from his data, not, as some might suppose, because he simply neglected to make the details of the step explicit. Rather the explanation for the omission is that no such account (of the step which generates conclusions from data) is even possible, and this for the reason that it is overwhelmingly likely that there is in fact no such step at all. Bacon never did, his claims to the contrary, generate his conclusion about the nature of heat from the survey he had conducted.

The statistics branch of mathematics has, since the late eighteenth century, provided us with a certain, steadily increasing, collection of inductive techniques. For example, modern polling techniques attempt to predict the behavior or choices of a wider population on the basis of sampling a subset*[3] of that population. In this instance, the inference is from the few to the many. Sometimes a statistical inference may go the other way, as, for example, from the knowledge that 81% of the children in a school system are black, one might infer that more than 60% of the children in some one school in the system are black. In these instances, what we find is that features of certain aggregates are posited to hold of other aggregates (often a subset or superset*[3] of the original aggregates). What it is essential to note in these and in many other sorts of inductive inferences sanctioned within statistics is that it is typically the *scope* of a feature which is being extrapolated, not the introduction or discerning of new features. Bacon's 'induction' is remarkably different. Indeed Bacon takes some pains to contrast his own kind of induction with statistical forms which he calls "simple enumeration" (98). Bacon claims that by using his considerably more powerful induction, he can glean from his data, taken collectively, certain features of each individual item, features which are anything but apparent in those individual items themselves. The inference thus is very unlike the inference that "Sally Jones has green eyes; her brother has green eyes; therefore all the other Jones's children as well have green eyes." In this latter instance, the data explicitly contains the information about each child examined that he/she has green eyes. Bacon's data is not at all like this.

Many, if not most, of his data items contain no *explicit* mention of motion. Consider item 17: "Green and moist vegetables confined and bruised together, as roses in baskets; insomuch that hay, if damp, when stacked, often catches fire"; or item 13: "All villous [long-haired] substances, as wool, skins of animals, and down of birds, have heat" (131). One looks in vain for any explicit or implicit mention here of "motion". Indeed, on the basis of 'data' such as this, if, that is, we were to consider wool as 'having heat', most of us would be positively insistent that whatever it is we are trying to explain, call it heat or whatever, is surely not a form of motion. What, after all, is more inert, i.e. motionless, than a clump of wool? It is clear that one cannot 'read off' of data such as this the conclusion that heat is motion. The trouble is that Bacon has adduced a conclusion intended to explain all of his data but in which there occurs a descriptive term "motion" which does not occur in all or, for that matter, in even very many of

---

3. For definition in Glossary, see under "set".

his premises. Indeed, Bacon's conclusion was not to prove convincing either to his contemporaries or to several subsequent generations of scientists. When a majority of scientists finally did begin to adopt the theory that heat is motion, in the mid-nineteenth century, it was for reasons remarkably different from the sorts of reasons (and reasoning) advanced by Bacon.

In twentieth-century philosophy it is common practice to distinguish two, fundamentally different, senses of "induction". On the one hand we recognize the historical use of "induction" in the sense we have just seen promoted by Bacon. In this first sense, "induction" is said to describe the inferential step from data to a hypothesis explaining that data. On the other hand, "induction" is also used to describe the logic which endeavors to explain, and indeed in some cases to assign numerical values to, the amount of weight a certain body of evidence lends to the support or credibility of a hypothesis. In this latter case, there is no suggestion of one's being able to *generate* the hypothesis from the data; both hypothesis and data (evidence) are taken as 'given' (however each might have been arrived at), and the only matter to be examined by induction is the extent to which the evidence supports the hypothesis. Briefly, the distinction between the two senses of "induction" is reflected in the two phrases "logic of discovery" and "logic of justification".

Bacon clearly thought his inductive methods constituted a logic of discovery, that by the careful, systematic, unbiased collecting of data one could 'by induction' simply 'read off' from that data its explanation.

Throughout much of this century a number of philosophers – including, especially, K. Popper, H. Reichenbach, R. Carnap, and C. Hempel – have scorned this Baconian concept of induction. The contrary thesis, that there is a logic of discovery, had – until very recently – been defended by only a tiny handful of philosophers, principally J.S. Mill (1806-73), C.S. Peirce (1839-1914), and N.R. Hanson (1924-67).[4]

---

4. In 1962, the historian Thomas Kuhn published *The Structure of Scientific Revolutions* in which he clearly sides with the opinion that there is no logic of discovery. But he argues further that there is no logic of justification either, that the process of accepting or rejecting a scientific theory does not lend itself to appraisal or prediction by logical rules, that ultimately a great number of nonlogical factors influence scientists' decisions to abandon an old theory

Those philosophers who have argued against the very possibility of there being a Baconian logic of discovery have been able to use a so-called bottom-line argument, in effect saying: "If there really is a logic of discovery, show it to us, state its rules and principles so that we and anyone else can apply it to do useful work of scientific discovery."

Unexpectedly, the challenge was taken up. Researchers in Cognitive Science have, for the last twenty years, been actively engaged in precisely this pursuit.[5] They have been trying to discover the ways human beings actually go about making scientific discoveries and have been trying to emulate those methods in computer programs.

As each new science has developed it has revealed an underlying order where none had been previously noted. If we lacked scientific knowledge, most of what happens in the world would appear to us as capricious, random, or the presumed handiwork of a hidden supernatural intelligence. But science frequently reveals an underlying order: in the ways elements form compounds; in the ways living bodies fight diseases; in the ways characteristics are passed from parent to child; in the ways earthquakes come about; in the ways objects fall; etc. Even something as seemingly haphazard as the meandering of streams is found to be explainable (Einstein [65]). So, too, with the subject matter of Cognitive Science. What, prior to recent research in Cognitive Science, appeared to be one of the most capricious, undetermined, of all activities, viz. problem solving, has been revealed, under careful study, to have an unsuspected underlying

---

and to accept a new one. (We will see for ourselves below, when we come to the next case study, how scientists can resist abandoning one theory even when experimental data are produced which are found to be compelling refutation in the minds of some other scientists.) Arguments similar to those of Kuhn are found, too, in the writings of Paul Feyerabend (see e.g. [71]). To a limited extent, this modern historiographical repudiation of a logic of justification had been foreshadowed by Pierre Duhem and by Max Planck. Planck had written: "An important scientific innovation rarely makes its way by gradually winning over and converting its opponents. ... What does happen is that its opponents gradually die out and the growing generation is familiarized with the idea from the beginning" ([154], 97; see also [155], 33-4). The views of Duhem, Planck, Kuhn, and Feyerabend have not, however, won unanimous endorsement from other philosophers and remain controversial.

5. Much of this research – theoretical and experimental – was both undertaken and inspired by Herbert A. Simon. See, e.g., [111].

order. Although they are not at all obvious to casual observation, the study under controlled conditions of problem solving is revealing sets of strategies and ploys used by virtually everyone. Problem solving turns out not to be a wild flailing about in a search for anything at all that 'works'. Problem solving is often methodical and systematic.

Those cognitive scientists who have lately revived the claim that there is a logic of discovery base their assertion on their equating scientific discovery with nothing but (a specialized kind of) problem solving: "A hypothesis that will be central to our inquiry is that the mechanisms of scientific discovery are not peculiar to that activity but can be subsumed as special cases of the general mechanisms of problem solving" (Langley et al. [119], 5).[6] But how legitimate is such an identification? Can scientific discovery realistically be equated with problem solving, or is there something more to scientific discovery than merely solving a problem?

Of course scientific discovery is some kind of problem solving. It would be pointless to deny that. Bacon had a problem: "What is heat?" And his eventual answer, "Heat is motion", might, in some sense, be regarded as a 'solution' to that problem. But was his 'route' to his 'solution' via a *logic*, as he claimed; or was it something else, as a great many other philosophers subsequently insisted?

The way Bacon conceived of inductive logic, and the model criticized by many of his successors, was as a logic of discovery understood to be something akin to a calculation. The idea was that one should be able to gather data, subject it to a calculation in accord with some specifiable formula or recipe, and generate therefrom a solution. Metaphorically we can conceive of a logic of discovery as being a kind of 'logic engine': one feeds in the data as input, one turns the crank, and the engine outputs the solution. Such a model suggests a possible realization, not in some visionary apparatus, but in something as mundane as a modern, large-scale digital computer. Indeed cognitive scientists[7] regard the test of their theories to reside just in

---

6. This book, *Scientific Discovery: Computational Explorations of the Creative Process*, contains an extensive bibliography of important work in this field.

7. In the remainder of this chapter I will use the expression "cognitive scientists" for those researchers in cognitive psychology, artificial intelligence (AI), etc. who advance the theory that scientific discovery is a kind of problem solving replicable (in principle) in a program for a digital computer. In

their (eventually) programming computers to act as engines of discovery.

Can such an engine of discovery be built? Equivalently, can computer programs be devised which will generate explanatory hypotheses from observational data? The cognitive scientists say, "Yes ... in principle." Their opponents say, "No."

Critics of the claim that a logic of discovery is nothing but a kind of problem solving point to two major differences between what cognitive scientists offer as cases of problem solving and what often have been applauded as cases of scientific discovery. As in any new science, there is a great deal of optimism, a slighting of difficulties, and a tendency to exaggerate the significance of initial findings.[8] And, in this particular case, there has also been a marked penchant for the disputants to argue past one another, often because of subtle shifts in the meanings of central terms in the debate.

A substantial part of the writings of cognitive scientists lays out the experimental findings which reveal how persons will systematically search through what these scientists call "the hypothesis space" (more on this later, footnote 25, p. 187). Their intent is to show that persons do not search among alternative hypotheses aimlessly but do so using what have come to be called *heuristics*: rules of thumb, earlier successful techniques, etc.

But to argue, as some cognitive scientists frequently do, that these findings are good evidence in support of there being a logic of discovery is to overstate the case. For the philosophers who have argued against the logic of discovery do not contend that there is no rational way to select among alternative hypotheses for testing. Their claim, rather, has been that there is no rational means for generating the hypotheses in the first instance. Their objection is that these cognitive

---

using this term in this fashion I am of course distorting the ordinary meaning of the expression. It is just that there is no agreed-upon alternative expression, and I am loath to coin a neologism. I hope that no confusion will result.

8. In the 1950s and 1960s, for example, researchers in machine translation of natural languages and in machine (visual-)pattern recognition believed that within a few years they would be able to program computers to emulate human abilities. Subsequent developments, however, revealed that the problems they were tackling were very much more difficult than supposed at the outset. Initial progress was rapid, but soon gave way to steadily diminishing gains as the remaining problems grew harder and harder.

scientists are helping themselves to too much, are starting, as it were, too late in the day. Given a wealth of hypotheses, one might well argue that there is some strategy for moving among them to select candidates for testing. But that is to misrepresent the problem. The *real* problem lies earlier: in the formulating of the hypotheses initially.

But perhaps the point on which the cognitive scientist and the philosopher-critic will differ most is on the second, viz. the prospects of adducing a set of heuristics capable of yielding those special scientific discoveries which we regard as standing in an exalted, privileged niche: the scientific breakthroughs, the new scientific *theories*.

Much of what cognitive scientists regard with pride as being cases of scientific (re)discovery their critics will dismiss as cases of mere curve fitting.[9] These critics argue that what is needed to generate a genuinely new scientific theory – a theory which goes beyond being a single law and is instead a comprehensive way of looking at a large body of varied data – is precisely the abandonment of heuristics. What is needed are not rules of thumb, or familiar strategies for solving problems, but an act of creative imagination. As long ago as 1949, Herbert Butterfield laid the groundwork for an objection to regarding scientific discoveries, particularly those discoveries we call 'breakthroughs' or 'revolutionary', as being cases of (ordinary) problem solving:

> ... of all forms of mental activity, the most difficult to induce
> ... is the art of handling the same bundle of data as before, but
> placing them in a new system of relations with one another by
> giving them a different framework, all of which virtually means
> putting on a different kind of thinking-cap for the moment. ...
> The supreme paradox of the scientific revolution is the fact that
> things which we find it easy to instill into boys at school ... –
> things which would strike us as the ordinary natural way of
> looking at the universe, the obvious way of regarding the be-
> haviour of falling bodies, for example – defeated the greatest
> intellects for centuries, defeated Leonardo da Vinci and at the

---

9. Trying to find computer programs to generate formulas to fit graphed data (curve fitting) is a task which engineers have been pursuing in industry since at least the 1950s. Forty years ago, no one regarded such programs as modeling scientific discovery. It is only more recently that cognitive scientists have come to regard them in that way.

marginal point even Galileo, when their minds were wrestling on the very frontiers of human thought with these very problems. ([40], 1-2)

No existing computer program (least of all the ones ironically named "BACON.1" to "BACON.6" [119]), nor any likely to be developed along lines currently being pursued by cognitive scientists, could possibly emulate or replicate Bacon's own thought processes (whatever they were) which led him to hypothesize that heat is motion. No realistically foreseeable computer program can bridge the gap between data which list a variety of hot things and the creation of the hypothesis "Heat is motion."

Or consider, as another example, Newton's second law of motion published in the *Principia* in 1687 (here reworded): "An object will experience an acceleration directly proportional to, and parallel to, the resultant of the total forces acting on it, and indirectly proportional to its mass." No amount of observing the world could ever provide data from which to generate such a law. For eons, presumably for all of time, prior to Newton's appearance on the scene, there had been massy objects, i.e. objects having mass. But mass, unlike weight, is a feature of the world which is *not* directly observable by any human sense. Newton did not observe the property mass, he posited it, i.e. he hypothesized it as part of a solution to a puzzle. He did that by inventing the *concept* of mass, or, if you find the notion of inventing a concept problematic, you could say that Newton *introduced* the concept of mass to science.[10] His posit was insightful and profitable beyond

---

10. There is an important distinction to be made between our having a concept (e.g. our having a concept of a unicorn, our having a concept of the superego) and there being anything in the world which exemplifies that concept (e.g. there actually being a unicorn, there actually being a superego). I personally happen to have a fairly 'realistic' attitude concerning the status of the referents of useful concepts in science. That is, if a concept in science seems to do the job, if it allows us to state useful and approximately true hypotheses, then I am inclined to regard that concept as referring to some actually existent thing or property in the world. However, a concept may prove useful, even necessary, to a scientific theory without there being anything in the world which it describes (refers to). For example, Newton also posited 'punctiform' masses, i.e. objects having mass but occupying only a mathematical point in space, that is, having zero depth, length, and

his ability to foresee. (It was also, we might note with some interest, eventually to be significantly emended by Einstein more than two centuries later, in 1905.) Newton's invention (introduction) of the concept of mass was a product of his fecund creative imagination, not of any superior powers of observation, not of his possessing a logic of discovery, and not of his utilizing some 'heuristic'.[11] It was as novel, and as free of being governed by a logic or set of recipes, as was, for

---

height. Few physicists, if any, believe that there actually are any punctiform masses in Nature, however useful the concept *punctiform mass* may be in their theories. Realism need not, then, be an unqualified belief in the actual existence of things or properties corresponding to every theoretical term of science. Scientific realism usually is something less than a one-to-one mapping of theoretical terms onto unique features of the world.

Although I have just incidentally admitted that I am a realist about mass, it is important to mention that there is considerable dispute about the wisdom of adopting such a realist position about the relations between the concepts of science and features of the world. One may, instead, adopt an instrumentalist attitude, arguing that scientific concepts may be justified by their successful role within a scientific theory and that one need not take the further step of believing that these concepts refer to bona fide features of the world. The dispute between scientific realists and instrumentalists runs very deep. I will return to a discussion of the concept of *property* in chapter 9; however, I will not pursue in this book the dispute between scientific realists and instrumentalists. Although it is an important dispute within metaphysics, it is not on the agenda for this particular book.

11. Langley et al. cite Clark Glymour's reconstruction ([78]) of the route by which Newton likely arrived at his second law of motion, $F = ma$, and assert that these steps are capable of being programmed so as to permit a computer to output the same formula given Newton's data as input ([119], 54-6). But Newton's accomplishment was not simply the stating of a mathematical relationship between certain variables, "F", "m", and "a". In Newton's hands, these were *interpreted* symbols, standing for, respectively, force, mass, and acceleration. What Newton could do, and computer programs of the sort described by Langley et al. cannot do, is to utilize the *concept of mass* in a comprehensive view, i.e. *theory*, of the world. To output the string of symbols "$F = ma$", as a computer might do, even as a solution to a particular problem we set for the computer using Newton's data, is not to have a theory or to have invented the *concept of mass*. The symbol "m" is not a concept. To describe a computer's outputting of "$F = ma$" as a 'rediscovery' of Newton's second law of motion is to caricature, indeed to misrepresent egregiously, Newton's accomplishment.

example, Beethoven's composing the *Waldstein* Sonata. Just as there are no known rules by which to write sublime music, there are no known rules by which to invent new scientific concepts or to generate scientific hypotheses in which these new concepts occur.[12]

The insistence, by many philosophers, that there are no such generative rules, either known or unknown, strikes many persons who are approaching philosophy for the first time as mistaken. These persons recall having been taught in high school something called 'the scientific method'. "Surely," they want to retort, "there is a method for generating scientific hypotheses."

If there were, then the history of science ought to have been very different from what it in fact has been. If there really were a logic of discovery, some logical procedure, some set of rules, by which one could get from observation to explanatory hypothesis, we should expect that the history of science would simply be a history of successive successes without any controversy or false starts. But the history of science is not at all of this latter sort. It is, instead, a history of a succession of guesses, of controversy, of disputes, of competing theories, of occasional successes, and of far more failures.

The world furnishes up to us its secrets extremely begrudgingly. Nature's 'deep secrets' are not written on the surface, as it were. No amount of careful *observation* can ever reveal the greater part of what we want to know. Observation of the world, no matter how carefully done, is an inadequate tool by itself for understanding the world. To understand the world, we need essentially to proceed by guessing, or if you like, by hypothesizing, and by testing those guesses (hypotheses).[13]

----

12. A third objection to the cognitive scientists' claim that there is logic of discovery, an objection which argues that heuristics are not effective algorithms, will be examined in the following section. Unlike the two objections just leveled, this third objection will be rejected, the counterargument being that although heuristics are not effective, to demand effective algorithms for a logic of discovery is to set an impossibly high requirement.

13. Later (in section 10.7, pp. 311ff.) we will examine a contemporary problem, "What is mind?", that is remarkably similar to Bacon's problem, "What is heat?", in that it, too, defies answer by recourse to simple observation or by an analysis which would construe it as a problem to be solved via heuristics. We will see how the answer to this contemporary puzzle can come about only through bold imaginative theory-construction.

4.3   Metaphysical strands in *The New Organon*

How, we might ask, did Bacon manage to make such a grievous error about scientific methodology*? How might we explain how he came to believe that one could 'read off' of Nature its secrets? I think it worthwhile, particularly given the wider purposes of this book, to dwell a bit longer on this remarkable episode in history.

It is easy, but nonetheless mistaken, to conceive of Bacon, in advancing his methods, as engaging solely in a piece of philosophizing. One may think of his *implementing* his methods, or his *illustrating* those methods, by his actually constructing the various tables we have sampled above, as his *doing science*. Used, as we have become, to insisting on a distinction between doing philosophy and doing science, we may be tempted to try to partition the material of *The New Organon* into nonoverlapping categories: the *description* of the methods is philosophy; the *practice* of those methods is science. Even if Bacon himself did not mark out his work in that way, we, in hindsight, working with more refined concepts, can.

I think that were we to do this, we would commit an error. For I think the best way to make sense of what Bacon was doing is to try to reconstruct what world-view he might have held which would lead him to advance the methods he did. Once we have done that, the result, I suggest, will defy categorization as either philosophy alone or as science alone. In short, if we try to imagine Bacon's world-view, we will discover that his methods were neither philosophy nor science alone, but an inseparable amalgam of the two.

One might think that it is possible to know *a priori** that Bacon's methods could not work. After all, the inductive leap from observational data to an explanatory hypothesis is universally acknowledged to be risky, i.e. not one guaranteed to reveal the truth. Even cognitive scientists who have argued that scientific discovery is a kind of problem solving, all of which proceeds via heuristics, have been careful to insist that heuristics are not effective algorithms*, that heuristics carry no guarantee of even a single solution, and hence no guarantee of a unique solution, still less any guarantee of providing 'the correct' solution. Without an ironclad guarantee, however, it might be supposed, strictly as a matter of logic, that any and every attempt to create a logic of discovery is doomed to failure. It might be thought, that is, that it is *logically* impossible that there should be a logic of discovery.

This pessimistic conclusion is too strong. If one makes it a matter of the very definition of the term "logic" that its results must always be certain, i.e. that logic is truth-preserving in the sense that applying its rules to a set of true premises can produce only true conclusions, then – just as a matter of definition – there can be no logic of discovery. But if we allow a weaker sense of "logic", by which we mean a set of stated, although not foolproof, rules (heuristics) by which to proceed, as when, for example, we talk of the 'logic' of making a medical diagnosis, it remains an entirely open question whether even a crude 'logic' of discovery is possible for the generating of explanatory hypotheses from observational data. It is this weaker sense of "logic" which philosophers such as Peirce and Hanson and present-day cognitive scientists have clearly had in mind when they have tried to defend the thesis that there is some 'logic' governing the activities of scientists in their search for laws.

It may well be that we never do succeed in devising a useful set of rules by which we can generate powerful explanatory hypotheses from observational data. But we will not know whether or not the goal is possible without our actively trying. Whether or not anything like a logic of discovery is possible depends on two critical factors: one, on the way the world is; and two, on our cleverness in making explicit canons (heuristics) for discovery. Although I am strongly of the opinion that a logic of discovery which goes beyond curve fitting and finding generalizations in data to being able to generate powerful explanatory theories is not realizable, my pessimism is not grounded in a priori or metaphysical principles. It stems, rather, from a conviction arising from my own experiential assessment of how complex the world is and how ingenious and multifaceted our explanations of the world have had to be in order to make sense of, and be able to explain, that complexity. Like cognitive scientists, I, too, believe that the question whether there is a logic of discovery is strictly an empirical* one (i.e. one to be decided solely by experience, not by a priori reason). But unlike many cognitive scientists I am convinced that scientific discovery is like ordinary problem solving only up to a point, that beyond that – when one comes to making scientific breakthroughs, doing what is sometimes called "revolutionary" science – what is called for is not the application of familiar heuristics, but the creating of unforeseen and radically new ways of explaining the old and familiar.

We cannot know what sort of world this is without actively exploring it. It might have been a terribly simple world, one in which Nature really does reveal (pretty much) all that is to be known simply by our observing it. It just may be that there is some possible world (here I anticipate chapter 6) in which the sorts of rudimentary methods Bacon advanced would prove very much more successful than they have proven in this world. The point is, however, that neither Bacon nor anyone else could know precisely which sort of world this one happens to be without actually trying out their methods to see whether, and if so to what extent, they worked. It turns out that this world is vastly more complicated than Bacon supposed. The subsequent course of science has found it more and more necessary to hypothesize all sorts of features hidden from direct observation (e.g. subatomic particles, electromagnetic fields, gravitational fields, free markets, capital, information content, and placebo effects) in order to explain those features which are observable. One could not know a priori that extraordinarily imaginative and creative hypothesizing along with the positing of arcane features would be needed for significant advancements in science. Such knowledge is attainable only by the verdict of experience, by actually trying simple methods to see whether they could be made to yield successful theories and by finding that they cannot.

To try to sort out in Bacon's methods what in particular was prompted by 'metaphysical' considerations and what by purely 'scientific' considerations is a hopeless task. Is the belief that Nature is relatively simple a scientific or a metaphysical belief? Our first, natural, response is to regard this question as a metaphysical one. But if one has – as Bacon had – a relatively simple science, and if that science, confining its observations pretty much to what unaided perception can furnish, produces results which are generally accepted and found useful, and if its explanations are regarded as satisfactory, then is the belief that Nature is simple not a belief warranted, not by metaphysics, but by science itself? Such a question strikes me as having no determinate answer. There is no determinate answer, I suggest, because doing science and doing metaphysics blend into one another to such a degree as to make any attempt at dissociation futile.

Bacon's views about the possibility of a logic of discovery were a product of a scientific outlook informed by late-sixteenth-century science. Sixteenth-century scientists and philosophers had no idea, nor could they have had an inkling, how *complex* the world is and how much the future course of scientific development would come to rely on positing a staggering complexity 'behind the appearances'. They could not have known, until they actually tried, and found wanting, methods which relied more heavily on observation than on creative imagination. To find excessive error in Bacon's manner of doing science is to believe that the criteria for judgment are ahistorical. If they are, then our own methods may come to be regarded as being as 'mistaken' as Bacon's. But if Bacon's 'methods' were a product of the late-sixteenth- and early-seventeenth-century world-views, his own views about the nature of explanation itself were rather more fore-sighted.

There is no authoritative account of the nature of explanation. What sorts of accounts are considered to be 'explanatory' change from time to time and place to place. Today many persons find it peculiar that throughout much of history so many persons were content with what we now, somewhat pejoratively, call 'teleological' explanations. For our ancestors, very often to explain why an event occurred was to state what purpose it served in the 'grand scheme of things'. Why was a person born? An answer might have been "to seek the good" or "to glorify God". Today an answer more likely will be in terms of antecedent events: two sexually mature adults had sexual intercourse; a sperm fertilized an egg; or some such account. We have, in modern times, switched our expectations about the very nature of explanation itself. We rarely offer or expect explanations, particularly within the 'non-life' sciences (such as physics, chemistry, astronomy, geology, and meteorology), to be in terms of purpose; rather we expect explanations in those sciences to cite causal factors. Only within the 'life' sciences, biology and medicine, does one still find teleological explanations – e.g. "the purpose of the kidneys is to filter impurities from the blood" – and even there a preponderance of explanations are causal, not teleological.[14] Bacon, himself, was one of the principal critics of the traditional teleological mode of explanation. He argued strenuously for the adoption within physics of the causal model instead:

> ... the treating of final causes [i.e. the search for purpose] in physics has driven out the inquiry of physical ones, and made men rest in specious and shadowy causes, without ever searching in earnest after such as are real and truly physical. ... "The leaves of trees are to defend the fruit from the sun and wind. The clouds are designed for watering the earth," etc. All ... [such examples] ... in physics are impertinent and ... hinder the

14. In contemporary social science, many explanations which may at first appear to be teleological are often disguised causal explanations. To say of a person that she did something "with the goal (or purpose) of ..." is to offer that person's having the goal as a cause of her behavior.

sciences from holding on their course of improvement, and introduce a neglect of searching after physical causes. ([19], chap. VI, p. 97)

Bacon's views about the roles of teleological and causal explanations were, in due course, to prevail; they were, it turns out, farsighted, almost prescient. But we must be careful not to think that Bacon (and we) now have 'got it right', that earlier in history when persons were as likely as not to offer and accept explanations in terms of purpose, they had 'got it wrong'. We must be careful not to think that causal explanation is 'right' and teleological explanation is 'mistaken'.

Is it possible to know a priori whether there is purpose in Nature, or is this an empirical question? If empirical, what would show it to be true? to be false? If a priori, how could we know it to be true? to be false? My own inclination is to regard the question whether or not there is purpose in Nature as a metaphysical one, one which 'goes beyond' the possibility of experience to answer. But in saying that it is a metaphysical question, I do not mean that it can be settled a priori; quite the contrary, whether we choose to favor teleological or causal explanations depends to a very great extent on the manner in which we practice science and on whether that way is successful. We *adopt* the causal model (or 'paradigm' in Kuhn's terminology), not because there are persuasive a priori arguments in its favor, and not because there is compelling empirical data to warrant that belief. We favor causal explanations because, given our data, given the way science has developed, the causal paradigm suits our purposes, and guides our research, better.

The causal paradigm has gradually, over several centuries, nearly entirely displaced the teleological paradigm, but there were no crucial, definitive, empirical data uncovered, and there were few strong philosophical arguments offered, to have warranted the changeover. It is rather that, as science progressed, as more and more causal explanations were found, and were found useful, persons gradually came to abandon the one model of explanation for the other.

4.4   Case study: Rumford and the Calorists

Questions such as "What is heat?", "What is mind?", and "What is a person?" cannot be answered by *observing* Nature, neither casually nor in the most conscientious, scrupulously diligent manner possible. If one really could settle such a profound question as "What is heat?"

by *observing* Nature, then Bacon – with his elaborate lists – would have settled the matter. But the subsequent three and a half centuries of scientific speculation, that is, right up to and including present-day research, about the nature of heat provide compelling evidence of the insufficiency of Bacon's optimistic methods. Bacon's methods, although possibly suited for some world or other, an imagined world very much simpler than this one, were woefully inadequate to guide the developing course of science in the actual world.

Bacon published *The New Organon* in 1620, some twenty-eight years after Galileo had invented the first (crude) thermometer. These earliest thermometers lacked scales and, because they were open to the surrounding atmosphere, were significantly affected by changes in barometric pressure. It was not until 1641 that the first sealed thermometer was invented and not until the 1660s that standards emerged for calibrating the scales of thermometers ([174], 120-25). But once scientists had in hand serviceable instruments to measure temperature, the investigation of heat permanently switched from the sort of natural history practiced by Bacon to quantitative research. In the one hundred years after Bacon's death, scientists discovered that various materials had remarkably different specific heats (see footnote 2, p. 44) and discovered the phenomenon of latent heat (the heat of fusion, i.e. the heat needed to melt a substance, and the heat of vaporization, i.e. the heat needed to vaporize a substance). Where Bacon had merely produced lists of items 'having heat', his successors turned their efforts to measuring the amounts of heat needed to effect changes in substances.

While the developing quantitative and experimental methods seemed well suited to answering such questions as "How much heat is absorbed by one pound of ice in melting?", these same quantitative methods seemed unable to answer Bacon's initial, and 'deeper', question "What is heat itself?" Bacon's own answer had been, we have seen, that heat is motion. This theory is sometimes called the "dynamic" view, and later, toward the end of the nineteenth century, came to bear its modern name, the "kinetic" theory of heat. The dynamic theory was, in effect, that the heat of objects and of gases is due to the vibration of their constituent particles ("atoms" or "molecules" in modern terminology). These postulated vibrations were also sometimes referred to as "intestine [internal] tremors". But the trouble with Bacon's conclusions about the nature of heat was that those conclusions could not be seen by his successors, in spite of his claim that those conclusions were reached by an induction, to be in any way dictated by or generable from his data. Nor, for that matter, was his theory the sort which was much favored in the eighteenth century. For at that time, the scientific climate favored a static theory.

Gases, it was readily observed, were 'elastic': they resisted compression and would expand to fill their container. How was one to explain this phenomenon? According to Newton, all material objects (the particles of gases included) *attract* one another. Why then should a gas expand to fill its container, rather than collapse into a liquid or a solid? Obviously – so reasoned many scientists – there must be a repulsive force as well, a force opposing the gravitational attraction of the particles. Where did such a repulsive force originate? An 'internal tremor' seemed not especially promising as a source of repulsive forces. (To cite a modern analogy: the vibrating strings of a guitar do not seem to repel one another.) Instead, theorists turned to adapt what they could of Newtonian theory, the most successful physical theory that humankind had yet produced. Just as material particles attract one another under gravitational forces, there 'must be' – they reasoned – another kind of substance whose particles repel one another and which lie between the particles of matter.

The route to the theory is fairly obvious: if forces are pushes or pulls (the only sorts of forces recognized in Newtonian mechanics) and if material particles attract one another, and if gases expand rather than collapse, there 'must' then be other sorts of particles, nonmaterial ones, whose nature it is to repel one another, rather than to attract. It was understandable, then, that theorists should postulate another, nonmaterial, kind of stuff, a stuff which permeated gases and physical objects, and which tended to drive apart the material particles. This posited stuff came to be regarded as a kind of fluid and was called "caloric". Inasmuch as most materials and gases expand when heated, it was an easy and obvious step to identify this caloric with heat itself. Why do material objects expand when heated? Simply because more caloric had been added to them and the additional caloric exercised a stronger repulsive force causing the expansion. There was no need in this theory for attributing any motion, vibrational or random, to the particles of caloric. Their sheer number, not their activity, was what accounted for expansion, sensations of elevated temperature, melting, etc. And thus the caloric theory was regarded as the 'static' theory of heat. On this theory, heat was a kind of stuff; it was not a vibration or tremor or motion of material particles.

There was at least one other major factor favoring the caloric theory. In areas of physics outside of heat – in light, in magnetism, and in electricity – all the best theories of the time were theories of special kinds of fluids, i.e. light, magnetism, and electricity were all thought to be accountable for in terms of special, subtle, weightless fluids. It would be an understatement, indeed something of a distortion, to say that positing the existence of caloric was done *on analogy* with the theories of light, electricity, and magnetism. Quite the contrary, the positing was done in accord with the overriding model of what the world was like. To posit a fluid to account for the nature of heat was as natural and as acceptable in the eighteenth century as it is in our own day to posit a virus as the cause of some particular disease. If today we were to describe a scientist who posited a virus as the cause of, let us say, multiple sclerosis, as proceeding by constructing an analogy with the explanation of the cause of poliomyelitis, we would, I think, feel that we had seriously underdescribed (if I may be permitted to coin such a word) the situation. Positing viruses nowadays as the causes of specific diseases is not so much constructing an analogy as it is simply following the normal, accepted, and expected practices of biological theorizing. Put another way, our positing a virus in this instance is in keeping with our world-view, call it "physical", call it "metaphysical"; it makes no difference. So too (and this statement *is* an analogy) was positing caloric in the eighteenth century. That was not a bold, analogical conjecture. It was, by that time, simply the obvious theory to promote. Such a hypothesis enjoyed, at that time, the fullest measure of scientific approbation and naturalness. It was, that is to say, fully in keeping with the then-current physical/ metaphysical world-view.

Thus we find Joseph Black (1728-99), for one, arguing explicitly against Bacon's 'dynamic' theory, first on the grounds that it was counterintuitive,[15] and second, on the grounds that it was contrary to experimental findings:

> I cannot form to myself a conception of this internal tremor, that has any tendency to explain, even the more simple effects of heat, or those phenomena which indicate its presence in a body; and I think that Lord Verulam [Bacon] and his followers have been contented with very slight resemblances indeed, between those most simple effects of heat, and the legitimate

---

15. I will have more to say in chapter 6 (p. 105) about the role of so-called intuitions in informing our world-views.

consequences of a tremulous motion. I also see many cases, in which intense heat is produced in this way, but where I am certain that the internal tremor is incomparably less than in other cases of percussion, similar in all other respects. Thus the blows, which make a piece of soft iron intensely hot, produce no [appreciable] heat in a similar piece of very elastic steel. ([30], 32-3)

Black has here raised what he regards as a crucial objection to Bacon's theory: if heat were motion, then in hammering equally two different pieces of iron, one soft and one elastic, the two pieces of iron should heat up equally. But they do not. Therefore, Black suggests, the theory that heat is motion is refuted.

In hindsight, living in an age where the dynamic (kinetic) theory has supplanted the caloric theory, and where the dynamic theory (in conjunction with quantum mechanics) can and does explain why some hammered materials heat up more than others, we may be inclined to regard Black's 'refutation' of the dynamic theory as disingenuous. But any such criticism would be anachronistic, in effect faulting Black for not having foreseen the subsequent development of science.

Black, like most eighteenth-century physicists, strongly preferred the caloric theory to – what he regarded as – Bacon's insupportable, vibrational theory. But one year before Black's death, Count Rumford read a paper (25 January 1798) before the Royal Society of London, describing a series of experiments which, some fifty years later, came to be regarded as strong evidence of the correctness of the vibrational theory and of the inadequacy of the caloric theory. But at the time, at the end of the eighteenth century and through much of the first half of the nineteenth, Rumford's experiments were either dismissed or their results believed to be accountable for within the prevailing caloric theory.

Rumford's name at birth had been "Benjamin Thompson". He was born in 1753 in Massachusetts, which was then still a colony of England. When the revolutionary war came, Thompson remained a loyalist, and when the British army evacuated Boston in 1776, he sailed for Europe. Although he was to maintain a correspondence with persons in America, and was to donate generous sums for scientific research there, he never returned. On the Continent, Thompson entered the service of the Elector of Bavaria, and in due course became the minister of war, gaining the title "Count Rumford" in 1791. In his capacity as minister of war, he became the superintendent of the military arsenal in Munich. And it was there that he undertook his most famous experiments on heat.

> Being engaged lately in superintending the boring of cannon ..., I was struck with the very considerable degree of Heat which a brass gun acquires in a short time in being bored, and with the still more intense Heat (much greater than that of boiling water, as I found by experiment) of the metallic chips separated from it by the borer.
>
> ... *whence comes* the Heat actually produced in the mechanical operation above mentioned?
>
> Is it furnished by the metallic chips which are separated by the borer from the solid mass of metal?
>
> If this were the case, then, according to the modern doctrines of latent Heat, and of caloric, the *capacity for Heat* of the parts of the metal, so reduced to chips, ought not only to be changed, but the change undergone by them should be sufficiently great to account for *all* the Heat produced.
>
> But no such change had taken place. ([176], 4-5)

Rumford begins by examining one possible hypothesis the calorists might have offered for the rise in temperature: the heat is being generated by pulverizing the metal. The idea here is that the total amount of heat in a large block of metal is greater than that in its smaller parts, and that in reducing the original to chips and shavings, the 'surplus' heat of the whole is released. But Rumford then reports on an experiment in which he compares the amount of heat furnished to a given mass of shavings and an equal mass of metal strips (taken from the same original block of brass), by submerging them first into boiling water and then into cold water to see how much heat each absorbs from the hot water and how much each in turn releases to the cold water. He finds no appreciable difference between the shavings and the larger strips.

These initial results, even if they hardly constitute definitive disproof of the caloric theory, are interpreted by Rumford as evidence that there is something seriously amiss in that theory. He begins to believe that the heat being generated is not anything 'latent' in the cannon itself, but is coming about through the conversion of the mechanical energy needed to turn the machinery. In short, Rumford now strongly suspects that heat is not a kind of fluid, but is, in his words, 'excited by friction'. But how can he *prove* any of this?

Rumford then undertakes a series of four further experiments: (1) to measure quantitatively the amount of heat produced by friction (taking the precaution of insulating his apparatus); (2) to determine what the effect of excluding air would be (he finds none); (3) to see what effect there would be if the apparatus were surrounded with a water jacket (the water rises in temperature and eventually boils [see p. 5 above]); and (4) to test whether filling the bore with water will change the results (he finds that it does not). With these further experiments in hand, his conclusions are uncompromising:

> What is Heat? ... Is there anything that can with propriety be called *caloric?*
>
> We have seen that a very considerable quantity of Heat may be excited in the friction of two metallic surfaces, and given off in a constant stream or flux *in all directions* without interruption or intermission, and without any sign of diminution or exhaustion.
>
> From whence came the Heat which was continually given off in this manner in the foregoing experiments? Was it furnished by the small particles of metal, detached from the larger solid masses, on their being rubbed together? This, as we have already seen, could not possibly have been the case.
>
> Was it furnished by the air? This could not have been the case; for, in three of the experiments, the machinery being kept immersed in water, the access of the air of the atmosphere was completely prevented.
>
> Was it furnished by the water which surrounded the machinery? That this could not have been the case is evident: *first*, because this water was continually *receiving Heat* from the machinery, and could not at the same time be *giving to*, and *receiving Heat from*, the same body; and, *secondly*, because there was no chemical decomposition of any part of this water.
> ...
> Is it possible that the Heat could have been supplied by means of the iron bar to the end of which the blunt steel borer was fixed? or by the small neck of the gun-metal by which the hollow cylinder was united to the cannon? These suppositions appear more improbable even than either of those before mentioned; for Heat was continually going off, or *out of the machin-*

ery, by both these passages, during the whole time the experiment lasted.

And, in reasoning on this subject, we must not forget to consider that most remarkable circumstance, that the source of the Heat generated by friction, in these experiments, appeared evidently to be *inexhaustible*.

It is hardly necessary to add, that anything which any *insulated* body, or system of bodies, can continue to furnish *without limitation*, cannot possibly be *a material substance;* and it appears to me to be extremely difficult, if not quite impossible, to form any distinct idea of anything capable of being excited and communicated in the manner Heat was excited and communicated in these experiments, except it be MOTION. ([176], 20-2)

It is interesting to compare the similarity of phrases, but the diametrically opposed views of Black and of Rumford, concerning the very possibility of entertaining the other's point of view. Black: "I cannot form to myself a conception of this internal tremor, that has any tendency to explain, even the more simple effects of heat." And Rumford: "it appears to me to be extremely difficult, if not quite impossible, to form any distinct idea of anything capable of being excited and communicated in the manner Heat was excited and communicated in these experiments, except it be motion." Two eminent scientists, writing at virtually the same time, are incapable – each confesses – of being able to subscribe to the opposing theory.

For the half-century following the publication of his experiments, Rumford's conclusion – that heat is a form of motion – was not only not accepted, it was positively and actively rebutted by calorists. His opponents were not crank scientists, but were among the best of their day.

On 5 June 1801 William Henry read a paper (actually written two years earlier, almost immediately after Rumford first made his experiments public) to the Manchester Literary and Philosophical Society, in which he raised serious objection to Rumford's theory: "... the Count has observed that water could not, at the same instant, be in the act of giving out and receiving heat. ... But I cannot admit that the argument is demonstrative, in proving the evolved caloric not to be derived from external substances; for no absurdity is implied in supposing, that a body may be receiving caloric in one state, and giving it out in another" ([92], 606-7).

Even as late as 1856, some fifty-eight years after Rumford had read his first paper to the Royal Society, we can still find strenuous defenses of the caloric theory. Thomas Traill, the editor of the eighth edition of the *Encyclopaedia Britannica*, undertook himself to write the article on Heat in which he explicitly argued against the vibratory theory.

> The other opinion, which has been maintained by Bacon, Boyle, and several other philosophers,[16] considers heat as a mere quality of matter, and ascribes it to a vibratory movement among the intimate particles of bodies; an idea which was adopted by Rumford to explain his curious experiments on the excitation and communication of heat by friction. This opinion, however, seems vague and unsatisfactory. If we say that heat is motion amongst the particles of matter, still we have no explanation of the manner in which this motion is produced; for we cannot conceive any movement without an impulse, nor an impulse without material agent. ... [If heat were to] consist in vibrations or motions of the particles of other matter, it should pervade elastic bodies with the greatest celerity; which we know not to be the fact. ... If we mingle together equal quantities of water at different temperatures, the resulting temperature will be an exact mean between the extremes. But if heat consisted in such vibrations, there ought to have been a loss of heat, as in all other communicated motions. ... Still more difficult is it to conceive how a permanent temperature could subsist among a great system of bodies, as the planets, if heat were nothing more than a vibration of the particles of bodies; for the original impulse ought to diminish with each communication. ([205], 260)

Among a variety of other objections, we can see here that Traill musters some strong counterevidence to Rumford's theory. Heat is supposed, on Rumford's theory, to be an internal mechanical vibration of a physical object. It presumably, then, ought to be conducted through physical objects with the same speed that mechanical im-

---

16. It is surprising to learn that the very term "scientist" is of very recent origin, having been coined by William Whewell (1794-1866) in 1840 (see Medawar [134], 9). As we can see, it had not achieved universal adoption by 1856.

pulses are transmitted through those objects. In steel, for example, mechanical impulses are transmitted at the speed of 4975 m/sec. Were you, then, to rap one end of a meter-long steel rod sharply, you would feel the impulse at the other end 0.0002 sec (two ten-thousandths of a second) later, i.e. virtually instantaneously. But were you, grasping one end of that same rod, to plunge the other into a fire, it would take some appreciable time, several minutes perhaps, before the end in your hand would grow noticeably warm.

Rumford's theory, we can see, met with opposition for a variety of reasons, not least because it did not offer a *quantitative* account of the nature of heat. Moreover, his theory seemed to contradict, without explanation, certain fundamentals of mechanics, the most basic and respected scientific theory of the day. But even that was not the end of it. For as Henry points out, it rested on certain quite unproven presuppositions, e.g. that a body could not be simultaneously gaining and losing caloric. Such assumptions, while they might have commended themselves with virtual a priori certainty to Rumford, were not in fact demonstrated by experiment or grounded in any theory accepted at that time, and were not nearly so 'self-evident' to Henry or other calorists.

The remarkable French philosopher-scientist-historian Pierre Duhem, early in this century, offered this perspective on such disputes.

> Now it may be good sense that permits us to decide between two physicists. It may be that we do not approve of the haste with which the second one upsets the principles of a vast and harmoniously constructed theory whereas a modification of detail, a slight correction, would have sufficed to put these theories in accord with the facts. On the other hand, it may be that we may find it childish and unreasonable for the first physicist to maintain obstinately at any cost, at the price of continual repairs and many tangled-up stays, the worm-eaten columns of a building tottering in every part, when by razing those columns it would be possible to construct a simple, elegant, and solid system.
>
> But these reasons of good sense do not impose themselves with the same implacable rigor that the prescriptions of logic do. There is something vague and uncertain about them; they do not reveal themselves at the same time with the same degree of clarity to all minds. Hence, the possibility of lengthy quarrels between the adherents of an old system and the partisans of a

new doctrine, each camp claiming to have good sense on its side, each party finding the reasons of the adversary inadequate. ([60], 217)

4.5   The ineliminability of unproved presuppositions

The ensuing debate between the two schools of scientists – the kineticists (as they were eventually to be called) and the calorists – is not atypical. Quite the contrary: the sort of dispute we have seen in this instance has occurred, and will continue to occur, frequently in science. Controversies about scientific theories and the degree to which any given theory is confirmed or disconfirmed by experiment and observation are inevitable; they are, in fact, virtually mandated by certain logical principles.

The testing of scientific theories is not at all the straightforward, unambiguous, procedure it has often, historically, been portrayed to be. An experiment, and its overarching theory, which may be utterly convincing to one scientist, may be just as unconvincing to another. Such differences are not usually to be accounted for in terms of stubbornness, intellectual blindness, dishonesty, conservatism, or the like. Disputes between scientists usually arise, not because of psychological differences between personalities, but because of important principles at play in the *logic* of subjecting scientific theories to empirical testing.

It can be proven – relatively easily as a matter of fact – that for any set of data about the world (i.e. for any set of contingent* data), there must exist logically independent alternative sets of explanations for that data, indeed there are an infinite number of such alternative sets. Intuitively, in less technical vocabulary, this means that the 'fit' between theories and experimental and observational data is remarkably 'loose', and that for any proposed theory or explanation of a phenomenon, there must, theoretically, exist alternative theories or explanations which are compatible with the data. This is not to say, of course, that all such alternative explanations are equally probable or that they are equally attractive to us. The point is that experiment and observation are never themselves sufficient to eliminate all possible contenders among alternative explanations.

Rumford's conclusions were not convincing to his critics. The calorists had no difficulty whatsoever in homing in on all sorts of unproven presuppositions in his arguments. Clearly, Rumford's conclusions survived or floundered upon the correctness or incorrectness of these many, many presuppositions. But he was not in a position to test these presuppositions. Had he attempted that, his experimenting could have gone on forever.

The presuppositions we must bring to any of our experiments are virtually without limit, and there is no practical way of markedly reducing their number. Even as simple an 'experiment' as measuring a room for a carpet is encumbered, we find, by vast numbers of untested presuppositions. What sorts of presuppositions must be true for our measurements of the floor area to be correct? Our tape measures must be accurate; the walls of the room must meet at right angles, or, if not, we must have some means for measuring those angles; our tape measures must not change length as we move about in space; the area of the room must be calculable by some known formula; measurements of length must be independent of the time of day; the visual appearance of the room must have certain known relationships to its physical layout; etc. Were we to put some of these presuppositions themselves to the test, those very tests would themselves, in their turn, carry a number of untested presuppositions. For example, were we to test the angles of the walls, we should then have to ask whether our measuring instruments were accurate. How shall we test *them*? By using still other instruments. But what about the latter? We are faced with the potential of an infinite regress of presuppositions which it is impossible to complete.

Throughout the greater part of the twentieth century, and to a greater degree than any of his contemporaries, Karl Popper has emphasized the role, the ineliminability, and the potential inexhaustibility of untested presuppositions in our doing of science. At first, the very existence of such untested and ineliminable presuppositions may be thought to give the lie to, indeed to make utterly impossible, the claim that science is 'objective'. But Popper argues that this pessimistic conclusion is not forced upon us. In his view, objectivity does not – and more importantly, *could not* – consist in our being able to prove a theory to be true. The number of presuppositions in each of our theories seems to be without limit. They range from highly specific presuppositions of particular theories, e.g. that no physical object can take in and give off caloric at one and the same time, to the most general (often labeled "metaphysical") presuppositions which ground virtually all our theories, e.g. that we will not wake up in an hour and discover that what we have taken to be reality was in fact nothing but a dream. If objectivity consisted in being able to prove a theory *true*, and if proving a theory true involved proving that every presupposition of that theory is true, then simply because the latter – proving the presuppositions true – would be an infinite task, nothing could be deemed to be objective. Popper's reply to this – one which I think is fundamentally sound – is to argue that this latter conception of objectivity is useless. It is useless because it never could apply to anything. Instead Popper urges that we conceive of objectivity, not as an *accomplishment*, but rather as an *attitude*: a critical frame of mind. A scientist is objective, not if he attends open-mindedly to his data and lets it 'dictate' the theory, but rather if he admits to his presuppositions and recognizes that his conclusions rest on those presuppositions and does not try to prejudge a priori or dogmatically what further tests of those presuppositions might reveal.

The logic of testing *scientific* theories is important, for illustrative purposes, because it is, as well, the logic of testing *any* theories, not just scientific, but the most mundane through to the most 'metaphysical'. There is no logic special or unique to the sciences. The logic of theory testing is the same for the child in her crib theorizing about the persistence of unperceived objects as it is for an adult theorizing about the efficacy of using a tape measure to fit a room for a carpet, as it is for the scientist theorizing about the nature of heat, and as it is for the metaphysician theorizing about the nature of space and time. What may differ is the degree to which the theorizing lends itself to empirical testing. But the logic is the same throughout, and the possibility of conclusive proof is not to be realized: there are only degrees of probability (about which – incidentally – there are enormous differences of opinion among researchers in the philosophy of logic).

To be sure, we do not actively *entertain* all, or even many, of the infinite number of potentially confounding factors when we proceed to do something as commonplace as measuring a room. But it is equally clear that these factors must *be* as we just described, if we are to have success. Only if, for example, tape measures do not change length as we move about the room, can our measuring the room work. As we go about our lives, doing what we commonly do, searching for misplaced scissors, measuring rooms, cooking meals, driving cars, turning on radios, etc., we do so in a context of making untold numbers of unproven assumptions. You may seem to recall having had a glass of milk last night. But how good is your memory? Is it perfect? Couldn't somebody have substituted soybean extract which you mistook for milk? Etc.

The point is the same when it comes to doing science, only the degree of uncertainty of the presuppositions is greater. You may reasonably be sure (but ought you to be utterly convinced?) that the walls of your room are square; but what, if anything, entitled Rumford to his – unproven – belief that an object could not simultaneously gain and lose caloric? What warranted his unproven belief that caloric could not be communicated to his apparatus by means other that those he had examined? Simply: he was not justified in these beliefs. He held them because – taken with his theory – they seemed to him to provide a better explanation of what was going on than did the competing caloric theory. But these very presuppositions did not seem compelling, indeed seemed false, to other equally rational scientists, the calorists.

Identical claims may be made for the practice of metaphysical theorizing. In metaphysics – just like commonplace theorizing, and just like scientific theorizing – theories are underdetermined by empirical data. We cannot *prove* that the world did not spring into existence ten minutes ago complete with fossil records, libraries, adult human beings with (apparent) memories, etc. But we theorize that such did not happen, and we do so because an alternative theory seems to work better. But there is nothing that can be regarded as a conclusive test of the truth of either theory.

Some philosophers and a somewhat greater number of cognitive scientists, however, have tried to take the sting out of underdeterminism by arguing that although there are potentially, from a *logical* point of view, an infinite number of different explanations of any given phenomenon, there are generally only a very few alternative explanations *psychologically* available. They will often cite in these arguments the fact that until Einstein's physics appeared, there was no good or reasonable alternative to Newtonian mechanics; that even now there are not many, if any, contenders against Einstein's special theory of relativity; and that there are few, if any, challengers to quantum mechanics. But the trouble with this defense and its complacent attitude about the possibility of underdeterminism is familiar: it focuses on too few examples taken from but one highly specialized area of human knowledge. What is, as we have seen, at best only a half-truth* about physics is surely not true of other areas of human interest. When we look outside of physics, we often do not find dominant, relatively unchallenged theories. Often we will find many, sometimes a bewildering variety of, alternative theories offered as answers to some of our most interesting and pressing concerns.

What is the concept of *causality*?

What are rights and obligations? How are we to recognize and/ or agree to them?

What is a person?

How is knowledge possible?

What is a mind?

What is a soul?

Is there purpose in the universe?

Does God exist?

What are beliefs?

How does language work?

Can the language of science be translated into the language of logic?

To what extent is the atmosphere able to absorb industrial pollutants? Of what kinds?

How shall "gross national product" be defined?

Is punishment morally justified?

Does free will exist?

What makes a particular piece of art worthy or good?

Is *intelligence* a meaningful concept and, if so, can intelligence be measured in a society-independent manner?

Is a value-free science possible?

Are there historical forces?

How best should a society protect minority rights?

What moral justification is there for limiting immigration?

Do animals have rights?

Do males and females differ in their ability to do mathematics?

Etc.

Directing attention to just the first of this list, to the question regarding the analysis of *causality*, we find not just one, or even just a few, but a very great number of theories. One recent author ([94], 14-21) lists ten contemporary theories. And even at that, his list is incomplete.

Having a plethora of alternative theories, far from being 'psychologically unlikely', is in fact the norm. Underdeterminism is not just a logical possibility. It is in fact one of the most pervasive features of our attempts to make sense of the world. All of our theorizing, without exception, whether in science, philosophy, jurisprudence, etc., is underdetermined by the empirical data. We can never hope to 'read the truth off the world' as it were. All we can ever hope to do is to propose theories to try to make sense of the flood of data and to work at trying to improve these theories and to replace theories with better ones. If we do not recognize the underdeterminism in our theories, then we will unwittingly become dogmatists thinking all the while that we 'have seen the truth'.

Truth there well may be. But human beings, unfortunately, have no privileged access to truth when we try to construct scientific and philosophical theories about the world. In generating and adopting such theories there is for us no other method than the dialectical one of trial, error, trial, error, ...[17]

---

17. Learning that a hypothesis is false rarely ends our trials. Our interest lies with highly specific hypotheses, ones which have what is called a high 'information content'. On a scale of 0.00 to 1.00, we desire hypotheses with information content close to 1.00 (see e.g. [34], 370-81). Learning that a hypothesis which has high informational content (e.g. 0.998) is in error is to learn the truth of a proposition whose informational content is very low (e.g. 0.002). For example, you may guess (hypothesize) that my telephone number is 555-9993. You put this hypothesis to a test (trial) and learn that it is false. You now have learned something true alright, but its informational content, and its practical value to you, is virtually nil. Inasmuch as there are – in principle – 10 million different 7-digit telephone numbers, learning (the truth) that 555-9993 is *not* my telephone number puts you only one ten-millionth closer to finding out what my telephone number actually is. Discovering that a hypothesis is false may be useful as a goad to further hypothesizing; but it is, in general, no substitute for learning that a hypothesis has withstood falsifying and may, therefore, be true.

CHAPTER FIVE

Underdeterminism (II)

In the previous chapter I have discussed how Nature does not offer up its secrets willingly, how it requires creativity and imagination to find hypotheses which are useful for explaining and predicting the way the world is, and how it is possible for rational persons to disagree about the merits of a hypothesis. In this chapter I want to explore an extension of those issues, but here my reflections are considerably more speculative than those preceding. What follows below is not so much an argument whose soundness seems clear to me, but a series of worries and concerns, in a way, an expression of disquiet I have about some of the metaphysical assumptions underlying certain contemporary scientific research. These sanguine, common assumptions may be *methodologically* justified. However, it is far from clear that empirical evidence supports them in any strong way, and at the very least they deserve closer scrutiny than they usually have elicited.

5.1   Human history

When I was a high-school student studying algebra and geometry, I found those subjects so straightforward, so intuitive (if you will permit me to describe them that way), in short, so easy, that I fantasized that had they not already been created, I myself could have invented them with some hard work. The self-delusion continued. In university, I believed that I, too, could have found for myself many of the tricks mathematicians had discovered at the turn of the century for solving differential equations. But with additional learning, particularly in studying the history of mathematics and science, I came, in due course, to realize what an extraordinary hubris I had been suffering.

I am sure that the cause of my exaggerated belief in my own abilities had a good deal to do with the kind of education I had been given in high school, a kind of education which, so far as I can tell, in looking at contemporary textbooks and in talking with my students and with my children, is still the norm. The trouble, as I said earlier, is that modern textbooks typically avoid controversy. They ignore the route by which thinkers struggle to reach their hypotheses. Worst of all, textbooks usually are silent about, or simply dismiss as having been 'proven wrong', the successions of abandoned theories strewn on the wayside along the road to current theories. If history teaches us anything, it is that many current theories will themselves in due course be superseded. Too little is made of this point in ordinary classroom teaching.

So much of mathematics and science is presented to students as 'fact', as *fait accompli*, as natural and as certain, that it takes on an almost irresistible appearance of inevitableness. "Yes, of course; clearly it can be seen that that is the way the world is", students may all too easily be beguiled into thinking as they are presented with a seemingly finished science. Students are led to believe that virtually all the work has been done, only the mopping-up details remain.

I remember myself what a shock it was, and what at the same time an illuminating lesson it was, to learn of the history of the invention of what I – from my twentieth-century perspective – regarded as so 'obvious' that at first I could hardly believe that there was ever a time when humankind lacked the concept: a symbol for the number zero. But history tells us that not only was the symbol late in coming, so too was the very concept of zero's being a number. Using a symbol for zero was a monumental breakthrough in the history of mathematics. But it took generations of mathematicians laboring away at arithmetic before a symbol for zero came to be widely adopted; so too for representing numbers themselves with digits whose *place* indicated powers of a so-called base. Notice that in antique Roman numerals, the symbol, for example, for the number eight "VIII" is twice as long as that for nine "IX" and four times as long as that for one hundred "C". In modern (Hindu-Arabic) notation, no number has a longer symbolic representation than a larger number, but this 'obvious', and exceedingly useful (for computational purposes), device took *thousands* of years to emerge. Having been reared on it, we take it to be 'natural'. But it is not 'natural', it was not there in Nature to be 'read off'; it was an invention of genius. And we flatter ourselves in the extreme if we think that any ordinary one of us could have or would have invented it had we not already found it in the world into which we were born.

It took more than three billion years[1] for life on this planet to evolve from the bacterial form to a primate. That it did run this course seems

---

1. 1 billion = 1,000,000,000 = 10^9.

to border on the miraculous, for it is easy to imagine any number of 'accidents' which could have prevented it. Recall, the dinosaurs died out. But conditions suitable for the emergence of a primate are only part of the story.

That human beings, intelligent, rational, language-using, symbol-using creatures who have invented mathematics, physics, chemistry, have tamed the Earth and the seas and the air, should exist at all is – just on the basis of probability – tantamount to a miracle: a miracle of blind Nature or a miracle ordained by God, but a miracle in either case. But once there walks on the face of the planet an intelligent, language-using creature, what happens next? From the evidence, the answer seems to be: not much. The greatest part of human history, save for the last few thousand years, seems pretty much of a piece. Only comparatively recently did human beings plant and irrigate fields, create cities, track the stars, count and multiply, refine ores, and teach themselves to read and write.

As anthropologists have spread out across the globe they have discovered 'primitive' or 'stone age' tribes living here and there, in pockets isolated from civilization, subsisting as did our common ancestors of tens of thousands of years ago. These primitive tribes had not enjoyed (if that is the right description) the progress of most of European and Asian societies. Some of these tribes, at the time of their discovery, had not yet reached the invention of the wheel. Most had no written language. Many had not learned to craft metals. Some knew little or nothing of agriculture or animal husbandry and survived by hunting and gathering.

The point is that human progress should not be regarded as a historical inevitability. It takes the right ecological conditions, of course. But it also requires something more: it requires an act of creativity, either technological (making a wheel, hammering metal, melting sand, etc.) or intellectual (placing a symbol – on a cave wall, or clay tablet, or on some such thing – of not just a scene but an *idea* or a *fact*, inventing words for abstract concepts [*one, two*], etc.). There is nothing inevitable about the occurrence of such breakthroughs. They may, but they need not, occur. The primitive tribes which have survived into the twentieth century are evidence that these breakthroughs need not occur. Had these tribes not been discovered by explorers from civilization, one might speculate, not unreasonably, that they might have persisted in their static state indefinitely, perhaps for tens of thousands of years more, perhaps, even, forever.

Science, mathematics, philosophy, music, technology, medicine, commerce, etc. are all products of the creative genius of countless persons whose names have been forever lost to us. We shall never know the name of the man or woman who first attached a sharpened rock to a wooden shaft, or created a bow and arrow, or tried to write a sentence, or carried a bunch of counting stones to reckon numbers with, or deliberately lit a fire, etc.

There is no inevitableness in our having an arithmetic, in our having a geometry (many of them in fact), in our having calculus, in our having physics, chemistry, or biology. There is no inevitableness, either, in our formulating theories of personhood, in our codifying logics, in our exploring the bases of morality, or in our wondering about the validity of our senses. Science and philosophy both – like music – are the products of creative imagination. There was no more inevitability in humankind's enjoying Newtonian physics than there was in its being the beneficiary of Beethoven's creative genius.

Persons who study political history see certain kinds of events, such as wars, movements of populations, and political alliances, constantly repeated. Focusing on *these* sorts of phenomena one might well come to believe that there is a certain inevitability in history. Certain kinds of events are 'destined' to occur, not just once but time and time again.

But focusing on intellectual history, an entirely different sort of picture emerges. Here there is not repetition but novelty. Here there is not inevitability, but uniqueness, creativity, imagination, and genius. It was not inevitable that a number system would evolve; it was not inevitable that grammarians would appear; it was not inevitable that humankind would figure out the relationship between the sides of triangles in a Euclidean space; it was not inevitable that humankind would figure out the relationship between the sides of triangles in non-Euclidean spaces; it was not inevitable that Locke (chapter 6) would concern himself about the personality of a prince being transferred into the body of a cobbler; it was not inevitable that Bach would write the Chaconne; it was not inevitable that Newton would invent the concept of *mass*.

Far too much has been made of a few cases where one piece of goods, either a material invention or an intellectual invention, was simultaneously created by two or more persons. Cases often cited are Newton's and Leibniz's independent invention of the calculus; Edison's and Cros's invention of the phonograph; Benz's and Daimler's invention of the gasoline engine; Gauss's and Lobachevsky's invention of non-Euclidean geometries. One must not lose perspective, however.

Non-Euclidean geometries arose out of a critical examination of Euclid's geometry created some two thousand years earlier. It took, that is, two thousand years before Euclid's geometry was understood well enough so that variants became possible. But if it took that long just to *understand* Euclid's geometry, is it reasonable to suppose that someone or other, other than Euclid, would have invented his geometry had he not done so? The very fact that it took so long to create a non-Euclidean geometry attests, I would like to suggest, not so much to the inevitability of someone's creating that geometry, but instead to the extraordinary intellectual novelty it was. If the creating of geometries were anything like being 'obvious', non-Euclidean geometries should have occurred not in the nineteenth century AD, but in the first century BC. Then, too, although Leibniz may be regarded as the co-inventor of the calculus, there is nothing in history to suggest that he, or any contemporary, was simultaneously co-inventing mechanics along with Newton. Leibniz had not conceived of *mass*; Leibniz had not conceived of the planet Earth accelerating toward a falling body; Leibniz had not conceived of universal* gravitation; and Leibniz had not conceived that for every action there was an equal and opposite reaction.

There are also a few cases cited within biology itself, not just within recent human intellectual development, which have been used to argue for a certain goal-directedness operative in Nature. The phenomenon of so-called 'convergent' evolution (along very different phylogenetic paths) of, for example, the eye of the mammal and the eye of the octopus has sometimes been offered as evidence of goal-directedness in evolution. (See, for example, [80], 198.) And from the supposition of this directedness, it has been further argued that evolution would probably (or inevitably) produce a creature whose mathematics and physics would resemble ours. But forbidding problems are found in this argument when it is dissected. First is the fact that convergent evolution is a relatively rare phenomenon, providing only weak evidence – at best – of a goal-directedness in evolution itself. Second is the fact that even if one were to posit a goal-directedness in evolution as an explanation of convergent evolution, that goal-directedness would be toward the development of similar physiological structures. It is only on an *analogy* that one moves beyond a goal-directedness of physiological structure to a goal-directedness of rational thought. Formally, i.e. its particular content aside, the argument thus begins with citing a fact about a relatively rare phenomenon and then proceeds in a series of steps each of which is itself of significantly low probability.

The cumulative effect is to make the probability which the factual premise confers on its speculative conclusion no more than very small. It is one thing to argue that something *could* be so (i.e. has a nonzero probability) and quite another to provide solid grounds for believing it *is* so (i.e. has a high probability [greater than 50%]). In short, the argument – which moves from the detected similarities in physiology between the octopus eye and the mammalian eye to the conclusion of the inevitableness of someone or other producing the geometry and physics of Euclid and Newton – is far too weak to justify its conclusion.[2]

Neither occasional instances of co-invention nor irregular occurrences of convergent evolution provide a strong base on which to posit a goal-directedness or historical determinism in Nature pointing toward the probable (still less the inevitable) unfolding of our own particular intellectual history.

5.2   Listening and probing for extraterrestrial intelligence

Once humankind had reconciled itself to the fact that the Earth is not the center of the universe, that not even the Sun is the center of the universe, that there are billions of galaxies in the vastness of the universe, and each galaxy in its turn contains billions of planets, the question naturally arises: Is there intelligent life elsewhere in the universe? In the last twenty years, centuries of speculation have at last turned into active empirical research. The United States government has from time to time funded the program SETI (Search for Extra-Terrestrial Intelligence) (albeit sometimes unwittingly[3]) and has even lofted (1972) into the heavens, on a flight beyond the solar system, a gold-anodized aluminum plate bearing an engraving of a man and a woman along with a (crude) star map of Earth's position among the planets orbiting the Sun. The hope motivating this project has been that somewhere, some time, this disk might be intercepted by alien intelligences and something of our own appearance and accomplishments would then

---

2. For more on convergent evolution and the emergence of intelligence, see Mayr [133], 28, and Raup [166], 35-7.

3. In 1978 Congress terminated funding for SETI. NASA, however, continued SETI without publicity under its exobiology* program, spending $1.5 million on SETI in 1980-1. But in 1981, Congress discovered the subterfuge and explicitly forbade any further expenditures by NASA on SETI ([190]).

be made known beyond our own tiny speck of a planet. Radio telescopes – although not funded by NASA – daily scan the skies searching
among the countless sources of radio waves for some telltale traces of
an origin, not in some natural process, but in a deliberate, contrived,
intelligent broadcast ([59], 70).

But how reasonable is this hope that there is intelligent extraterrestrial life with whom we might communicate? The arguments motivating the modern empirical search for such intelligent life conceal a
host of metaphysical assumptions worthy of close philosophical scrutiny.

It is notoriously difficult to assign a probability to the existence of
intelligent extraterrestrial life. And I must confess to being mildly
bemused by the attempts other persons have made to actually calculate
the probability of there being intelligent life elsewhere in the universe.[4] The assumptions on which these calculations are based seem to
me to be so tenuous and so numerous as to undermine any reasonable-
ness whatever of the conclusions reached. I, for one, find it premature,
at the current level of scientific knowledge, to try to assign a numerical value to the probability of intelligent life arising in a waterless or
carbonless world. What conditions are necessary for life? Certainly
those on Earth have proved ideal. But how far can conditions depart
before life of any form is physically impossible?[5] Is water needed? Is
carbon needed? Is starlight (sunlight) needed or might the radiating
heat of a planet's molten core do as a substitute? What temperature
range? What atmosphere, etc.?

It is altogether improbable that evolution on other planets will have
produced a human being. Intelligent life elsewhere in the universe,

---

4. The standard approach to this problem is currently via the Drake equation
(see e.g. [80], 345-51), devised by the astronomer Frank Drake. Carl Sagan
gives a slightly variant version ([183], 12-24). Typically, the probability of
there being civilizations in our own galaxy with whom we can now communicate is figured as the product of several independent factors, usually seven in
all, including such things as the fraction of planets per planetary system
having conditions ecologically suitable for the evolution of life, the fraction
of planets where life actually develops, and the fraction where life progresses
to the stage of technology.

5. For a detailed examination and criticism of the assumptions made by ex-
obiologists and cosmologists in trying to determine the numerical values of
the terms in the Drake equation, see [129], esp. 80-6.

almost certainly, will be nonhuman. These nonhumans may lack eyes or have light-sensitive organs very different from our own; they may lack ears or have auditory organs quite unlike ours; they may have senses we lack; they may lack senses we have; their emotional responses may be very dissimilar to our own, perhaps even incomprehensible to us; etc.[6] What – given all these myriads of possible differences in our biologies – can we expect to share in common? What subject matter should we choose when we try to establish communication? How shall we communicate with an alien life-form?

Steven Spielberg gave one answer, of a sort, in his film *Close Encounters of the Third Kind* (1977). Many newspaper and magazine reviews of the movie were extravagant in their praise of Spielberg's using music as the medium for communication between aliens and ourselves. But as one thinks about it critically, surely the praise for that particular aspect of the film is undeserved. Music is hardly a universal medium for communication. It is certainly not a language: while it may evoke emotions, it cannot be used to state facts. But even more important, for our purposes, is the fact that music must, to a far greater extent than a language, be tailored to fit the peculiar biology of a species.

If we ever do succeed in making contact with the members of an alien civilization, we certainly would not expect to find pianos in their homes. Pianos are designed in their keyboards and pedals to fit the anatomy of a human being: ten fingers, two feet, and upright posture. And the piano's equal tempering, i.e. being tuned in a certain fashion, indeed its even producing fundamental tones in the audible range of 33 Hz to 4000 Hz, is tailored to the atmosphere of the Earth and the

---

6. For a minority, dissenting, opinion, see Bieri [29]. The guiding assumption of Bieri's argument is that the actual route which evolution has followed on Earth is the route which would be followed on virtually any planet. Given such a premise, his conclusions are not improbable. But that initial assumption needs powerful independent justification, and Bieri does not offer it. In its finer details, his argument is of this sort: "Strong arguments can be advanced for the presence of only two eyes for binocular vision and two ears for binaural hearing" ([29], 456). Unfortunately, Bieri leaves it at that; he offers not even a hint as to what these "strong arguments" might be. And he gets more specific still, being convinced, for example, that humanoids on other planets will not have green skin (457). But again, he offers no argument whatsoever for his assertion.

auditory mechanism of human beings. We can expect few, if any, of these necessary* conditions for our having created a piano to be replicated on other planets.

But even putting aside the purely physical means of producing music, ought we to expect the music itself of alien civilizations to resemble our own? I think there is no good reason to suppose that it would. Given the inordinate number of factors which fuel the evolution of a species, it strikes me as highly improbable that the nervous systems of extraterrestrials would develop in a manner parallel to that of human beings on Earth. It is far more likely that the aesthetic experiences of extraterrestrials, if indeed they have aesthetic experiences at all, would be totally inaccessible to ourselves. Aliens may not, for example, be capable of sorting out the separate lines in a piece of polyphonic music, may be insensitive to color or to geometrical perspective, etc. Their own aesthetics, in turn, may be as incomprehensible and as unmoving to us as our own best accomplishments, e.g. Michelangelo's Sistine Chapel or Schubert's String Quintet, apparently are to cats and dogs.

But if our aesthetic goods are not to be exchanged with alien intelligences, might intellectual goods? Leaving Hollywood behind, and turning to the scientific and philosophical literature, we find that many writers do believe that there are at least some intellectual goods we would share in common with any technologically advanced life-forms: mathematics and science. The idea is that mathematics and science are 'objective', that mathematics will be the same throughout the universe, and that science will be as well, provided, of course, in this latter instance, that the laws of physics are the same throughout the universe.

> What, then, can we hope to communicate with any 'technological' species? It appears that purely symbolic constructs which can be reduced to a postulational system, for example, mathematics (which might include much of physics as well as even basic rules of social organization), can be communicated. Surely a preliminary phase of communicating simple axioms to educate the alien intelligence and let them educate us in basic concepts is first required. However, it seems unlikely that we could share ideas which involve affect and emotions; for example we would be unable to communicate the feel rather than the abstract description of perceiving something. (Arbib [9], 76)

Our main hope for interstellar communication is based on the belief that a technological civilization must have numbers. It is hard to conceive of a psychology which could do technology without being able to count, and add, and multiply. To do the geometry necessary to describe the motion of planets it must have some theory like conic sections or calculus. Thus one might expect such things to be in the repertoire of a scientist in any technological culture. ... One might expect (though Drake's ideas on neutron stars may suggest a counterexample) that Newton's laws hold anywhere as a reasonable first approximation, so that any scientist would eventually begin to recognize that you are talking about Newton's laws. After a while, you have a language in which you can describe the motion of particles, no matter what the senses of the creature are, or whether he perceives these motions by vision, x-ray, touch, or another method. (Arbib [9], 77)

Arbib's optimism is based on a very great number of unarticulated presuppositions. Many of these I regard as highly dubious. I am not at all confident about the possibility of an alien life-form, indeed another human being for that matter, understanding the symbolism of our physics without our already sharing a common natural language. That is, Arbib and many others who have promoted the search for extraterrestrial intelligence believe that two creatures who do not share a common natural language can recognize, just by the passing back and forth of symbols, not only that the symbols are being used to express science and mathematics, but more specifically that the science is Newtonian physics and the mathematics is ordinary arithmetic. It strikes me that altogether too much credit is being given to the power of the message itself, and far too little to the need of a prior commonality of the languages and thought-structures of the would-be communicators.

Suppose the tables were turned. Suppose it were we who were the recipients, rather than the senders, of such a message. The message contains a series of marks which we take to be written in an attempt to establish communication by the senders instructing us in the rudiments of arithmetic and physics. The trouble is that there is no single way, or even just a few ways, to axiomatize either arithmetic or Newtonian physics. Any number of different ways exist to axiomatize arithmetic, some doubtless containing concepts we have never even imagined, perhaps even concepts which we are incapable of having.[7] Similarly for Newtonian physics. Must one have a concept of mass, for example, to do Newtonian mechanics? We might at first think so, since that is the way it was taught to most of us. We have been taught that there were, at its outset, three 'fundamental' concepts of Newtonian mechanics: mass, length, and time. (A fourth, electric charge, was added in the nineteenth century.) But it is far from clear that there is anything sacrosanct, privileged, necessary, or inevitable about this particular starting point. Some physicists in the nineteenth century 'revised' the conceptual basis of Newtonian mechanics and 'defined' mass itself in terms of length alone (the French system), and others in terms of length together with time (the astronomical system).[8] The more important point is that it is by no means obvious that we would recognize an alien's version of 'Newtonian mechanics'. It is entirely conceivable that aliens should have hit upon a radically different manner of calculating the acceleration of falling bodies, of calculating the path of projectiles, of calculating the orbits of planets, etc., without using our concepts of mass, length, and time, indeed without using any, or very many, concepts we ourselves use.

Their mathematics, too, may be unrecognizable. In the 1920s, two versions of quantum mechanics appeared: Schrödinger's wave mechanics and Heisenberg's matrix mechanics. These theories were each possible only because mathematicians had in previous generations invented algebras for dealing with wave equations and with matrices. But it is entirely possible that advanced civilizations on different planets might not invent both algebras: one might invent only an

---

7. Again, see Thomas Nagel [140].

8. James Maxwell (1831-79) introduces the topic by writing: "We shall call the unit of length $[L]$. ... We shall call the concrete unit of time $[T]$. ... We shall denote the concrete unit of mass by the symbol $[M]$ in treating of the dimensions of other units. The unit of mass will be taken as one of the three fundamental units" ([132], 3-4). But then he immediately proceeds to explain that it is not necessary to take mass as fundamental: "When, as in the French system, a particular substance, water, is taken as a standard of density, then the unit of mass is no longer independent, but varies as the unit of volume, or as $[L^3]$. If, as in the astronomical system, the unit of mass is defined with respect to its attractive power, the dimensions of $[M]$ are $[L^3T^{-2}]$" ([132], 4). See also Lord Kelvin (William Thomson 1824-1907) [109].

algebra for wave equations, the other only a matrix algebra. Were they to try to communicate their respective physics, one to the other, they would meet with incomprehension: the receiving civilization would not understand the mathematics, or even for that matter understand that it was mathematics which was being transmitted. (Remember, the plan in SETI is to send mathematical and physical information before the communicating parties attempt to establish conversation through natural language.) Among our own intellectual accomplishments, we happen to find an actual example of two different algebras. Their very existence, however, points up the possibility of radically different ways of doing mathematics, and suggests (although does not of course prove) that there may be other ways, even countless other ways, of doing mathematics, ways which we have not even begun to imagine, which are at least as different as are wave mechanics and matrix mechanics.

My point is not so much to worry about the possibility of our actually ever communicating with extraterrestrial intelligences, but to expose the metaphysical presuppositions of the kinds of scientific, epistemological,* and metaphysical views which inform much of the current discussion. So very much of this contemporary discussion strikes me as being premised on a naive view that mathematics and science can be of only one sort and that any 'successful' mathematics or science must be recognizable as such and translatable into our own. These views, in their turn, seem to me, ultimately, to be traceable back to the naive Baconian idea that Truth can be 'read off' of Nature, that ultimately there can be only one science, because – once the hypothesizing and the testing are done – Truth will be manifest. I cannot prove that these modern views are incorrect. But I am sure – and this is the important point – that they cannot be proven to be true.

As a species, we are faced with something of a methodological dilemma. If we do not assume that communication is possible, if we do not assume that mathematics and physics will be the same and will be recognizable for other technologically advanced civilizations, then we shall never succeed in finding intelligent life elsewhere in the universe by listening to radio signals. That is, these particular, unprovable metaphysical assumptions are a necessary condition for our finding what we seek. But they are not sufficient* conditions. They may be wildly wrong. There may be intelligent life in the universe which has devised mathematics and science, and has managed admirably to cope with its environment, in ways totally unimagined, indeed unimaginable, to us. If so, we will not find them with our technology. Making the assumption that mathematics, science, and technology will inevitably and universally be recognizably similar to our own is our only route to success, just as our hoping that there is to be found (invented) a cure for cancer is our only hope of ever finding (inventing) such a cure. But the hope is no guarantee of success; it is merely a psychologically and politically necessary condition for getting on with the job.

I see no good reason to believe that if we ever manage to detect life on other planets (e.g. by manned or unmanned probes), then we will find that the life-forms there will have succeeded in replicating our own history to the point where they too will have had a Newtonian revolution. Quite the contrary, it strikes me that the probability of other 'intelligent' life-forms throwing up a Newton is of the same order as their throwing up a Beethoven. I no more expect alien life-forms to have duplicated our physics and mathematics than I expect some one of them to have duplicated the *Waldstein* Sonata. And I see no inevitability, either, in any other course of evolution ever producing a Plato or an Aristotle or a Hume or a Kant.

Galileo, Brahe, and Kepler paved the way for Newton. But it was Newton alone who made the breakthrough of conceiving not of the Earth attracting the falling object, but of both the Earth and the falling object attracting one another. No one before Newton ever imagined that an object's falling and accelerating toward the Earth was reciprocated by the Earth's accelerating (but so minutely as to be imperceptible) toward the falling object. This was no minor change in a long-standing theory. Newton's rethinking the situation was breathtaking in its audacity. It was not even remotely to be conceived as being 'read off' of Nature. And it is by no means clear that *anyone* else ever would have replicated Newton's conjecture had Newton himself not authored it. Newton had been born prematurely; as an infant his head had to be supported by a cervical collar; he was a sickly youth ([49]). Had he not lived to adulthood, the modern scientific/industrial era may not have come into being.

Of course I cannot prove that no one but Newton could have figured out what we now call "Newtonian mechanics". All I can do is to reveal the differing metaphysical views we bring to such speculations. I, for one, am especially struck by the fact that so many other persons, working away at the same problems, from ancient times right up to Newton, did *not* conceive of the world the way he did. I am struck by the singularity of his accomplishment. Others, in looking at precisely the same historical data, will interpret it differently. These others will see in that data a steady intellectual evolution and will come to regard Newton's accomplishments as something of a historical necessity. They see the emergence of Newtonian mechanics as something which was bound to happen, if not exactly at the hands of Newton, then at least by somebody or other. We have already seen something of this attitude implicit, I believe, in the paragraphs above from Michael Arbib. To date, the debate between those, including myself, who believe that mathematics, science, philosophy, art, etc. are more of an accident than an inevitability and those who take the contrary view remains speculative. We each will cite the same historical data but will draw glaringly different conclusions.

That the same body of data can be, and often is, interpreted in radically different ways, indeed often in ways inconsistent with one another, is a pervasive fact virtually guaranteeing differences in our worldviews. We find another example, rather akin to the current one about the inevitability of something like Newtonian mechanics emerging eventually in the intellectual history of an intelligent race of creatures, in the debate over the existence in evolution of a goal or purpose. Religious-minded persons, not necessarily creationists or persons opposed to the evolutionary account, looking at the same history as evolutionists and seeing in it how any number of 'accidents' would have derailed its arriving at its present stage, find in that history clear evidence of the hand of a guiding God. The empirical data of evolution may be agreed upon by both atheist and theist. Yet where one sees merely life adapting to a changing environment, the other notices the contingency of all of this so much so that he or she cannot conceive of its having happened at all except as having been guided by something or someone supernatural.

If SETI is successful, if our radio telescopes succeed in finding within the radio noise of the universe signals which bear the unmistakable mark of intelligent origin, those who take the contrary view from me, those who believe that other civilizations can and will progress to radio communication, will have won the day. If diligent search, however, does not lead to success, my view will not have been proven correct; the debate will remain inconclusive.

What is the upshot? It is simply this: I see the development of mathematics, of science, of philosophy, of art, etc. all fairly much of a piece, i.e. as the product of creative genius. But if we are to discover intelligent life elsewhere in the universe we shall have to assume the contrary, namely that extraterrestrial mathematics and science will have evolved along lines pretty similar to our own and that at some point are, or were, at the stage we now find ourselves. I find these assumptions not particularly well-founded, and they seem to me to issue from some very dubious assumptions about the manner in which intelligent beings are able to make sense of, and control, their environments. Be that as it may, I also recognize that unless we make these – to my mind, dubious – metaphysical assumptions, then our hopes of finding extraterrestrial intelligent life are pretty much doomed. The only counsel I would be prepared to make is this: let us proceed with SETI, but let us also take care that it not absorb too many resources, resources which could be better spent on more immediate and pressing needs of humankind.

CHAPTER SIX

Putting concepts under stress (I)

6.1   The limits on science

Aristotle was a physicist and a biologist; Francis Bacon, a physicist; Descartes, Newton, and Leibniz also were physicists; so was Immanuel Kant; Charles S. Peirce was a physicist, astronomer, and geodesist; William James was a psychologist; Ludwig Wittgenstein, an aeronautical engineer; Pierre Teilhard de Chardin, a paleontologist; and Noam Chomsky, a linguist. The list of philosophers who were also scientists goes on and on. Indeed, until the nineteenth century there was little distinction between philosophy per se and science. Both were concerned with plumbing the secrets of nature. Departments of physics in universities were usually called "natural philosophy". Scientific journals often incorporated the word "philosophy" in their titles. One modern physics journal retains its title of 1798: *Philosophical Magazine*.[1] The oldest (1744) scientific society in the United States, the American Philosophical Society, still bears the name given it by its founder, Benjamin Franklin ([23], 5-9). Only in the nineteenth century, particularly with the growing emphasis on the distinction between a priori knowledge and empirical knowledge, did the partnership of two thousand years between philosophy and science begin to become undone. Within the universities, physics departments and psychology departments split off from philosophy departments in order to practice 'empirical' science, leaving philosophy – it was

---

1. *Philosophical Magazine* is published each month, in three volumes, "A", "B", and "Letters". The journal is devoted to topics "in the experimental, theoretical and applied physics of condensed matter. Part A deals with Defects and Mechanical Properties; Part B with Structural, Electronic, Optical and Magnetic Properties." (See "Notes for Contributors", vol. 58A, no. 6 [Dec. 1988].)

imagined – to pursue knowledge in the a priori manner of mathematics and logic.[2]

The split was a historical aberration. It came about through the naive belief that natural science could be pursued free of philosophical ideologies or metaphysical world-views. But there never has been a time when science was essentially and solely empirical and there never has been a time when philosophy was essentially and solely a priori. The difference between the practice of science and of philosophy is, and always has been, one of a matter of the degree to which researchers conduct empirical research. No science is ever totally free of philosophical components, and little, if any, philosophy ever springs out of the resources of pure reason uninformed by any empirical data whatsoever. Even if few philosophers themselves conduct laboratory experiments, they must nonetheless take cognizance of the results of experimental research in their own philosophical pursuits.

Because it was prompted by mistaken views about the very nature of science and of philosophy, the artificial parting of philosophy and science in the nineteenth century never could be very thorough. Too many problems in the sciences – the record is virtually endless – have since cropped up which positively demand philosophical examination: the advent of non-Euclidean geometries; the demise of the absolute theories of space and time; the attack on the Newtonian world-view; the rise of evolutionary theory; the unleashing of nuclear destruction; the appearance of artificial intelligence; the discovery of split-brain phenomena; the challenge of the possibility of paranormal experiences; the technological ability to extend bodily functions past brain death; etc. Bare empirical science is inadequate to provide a human context, a sophisticated understanding, of the implications and relevance of such a flood and diversity of information. The techniques of empirical research do not provide the scientist with the conceptual tools needed to synthesize a satisfactory, comprehensive world-view out of these disparate pieces.

---

2. Some philosophy departments were to experience successive, if not exactly systematic, fragmentation. At Harvard, for example, the Department of Political Economy broke away from the Philosophy Department in 1879; the Department of Social Ethics, in 1906; and the Division of Education, also in 1906 ([38]). The Psychology Department, however, unlike those at most other American Universities where the split had come earlier, remained as a division within Philosophy until 1934 ([24], 24, and [118], 459-63).

If science cannot cope without philosophy, the latter, in its turn, withers without the stimulus of science. Ethics could never be quite the same once travelers brought back news of the incredible diversity of moral norms in different, far-off societies. Newton's theory of absolute space (the 'sensorium of God') had to give way once Einstein had published his special theory of relativity. The simple dualism of a unified mind and a single brain has had to be rethought in light of discoveries about the differing functions of the right and left cerebral hemispheres. The concept of an object's being at a determinate place at a particular time is challenged by the indeterminacy inherent in quantum mechanics. And the very categories themselves in terms of which we analyze language have had to be re-examined in light of the discoveries of cybernetics and the quantification of information. The discoveries and theories of science provide much of the driving force of modern philosophy. Indeed, it strikes me as a certainty that the greater part of modern philosophy simply would never have been conceived except as a response to the information explosion in the sciences. Dozens of philosophers have spent years writing volumes on the relativity of space and time, on multidimensional spaces, etc. only because of the stimulus of twentieth-century physics. Countless philosophers today pursue issues in, for example, medical ethics, sociobiology, linguistics, and artificial intelligence only because of the *need* within the many sciences for help with conceptual puzzles.

In the late twentieth century, science and philosophy have begun to forge new alliances. The historical parting of the ways is being reversed. The discipline of cognitive science, for example, is as much philosophy as it is psychology and linguistics. Researchers in artificial intelligence do not fit comfortably into the strict categories of engineer or philosopher, but often are a bit of both. Economists, too, particularly those doing research in welfare economics, straddle the historical boundaries between empirical research and ethics.[3]

One of the most pervasive, but mistaken, notions of our modern era, a notion which is a clear holdover from nineteenth-century views about knowledge, is that each of our beliefs may be assigned to one of

---

3. In the last fifteen years, many new interdisciplinary philosophy journals have been launched, including *The Journal of Medicine and Philosophy* (1976), *Linguistics and Philosophy* (1977) [successor to *Foundations of Language*], *Law and Philosophy* (1982), *Economics and Philosophy* (1985), and *Biology and Philosophy* (1986).

three categories: either a belief is, or can be, judged true or false by scientific investigation, e.g. that aluminum has a lower melting point than tungsten; or a belief is a matter of ethics to be decided either by convention or the pronouncements of some religion or other, e.g. that it is wrong to institute affirmative-action policies in admitting students to universities; or, finally, a belief is essentially just a matter of opinion, e.g. that some particular work of art or piece of music or sculpture is better than some other one. The first of these categories is, often honorifically, called "objective"; the third, often pejoratively, called "subjective"; and the second, something neither quite the one nor the other, viz. "conventional" or "God-given".

Neither the exclusiveness nor the exhaustiveness of these three categories is given much credence by philosophers any longer. The lines of demarcation between these categories are not nearly as clear-cut as formerly imagined. More important, these categories certainly do not include all the ways we human beings have found to explore truth and to ground beliefs.

It is not my purpose here to explore matters of ethics or of aesthetics. It will suffice, for my purposes, simply to warn that pursuing the answers to ethical questions and to aesthetic questions is never *just* a matter of convention or opinion. Like science and metaphysics, these areas of perennial concern must be informed by empirical data and by human reason.

What is of particular concern to me is to challenge the mistaken idea that so many persons have of the potency of science to answer questions lying outside of ethics, religion, and aesthetics. Science can take us only so far. Whatever results issue from a scientific experiment will always fall short of answering all the questions we contrive for ourselves. Consider, for example, Descartes's theory of the relationship between minds and brains.

In the seventeenth century, René Descartes (1596-1650) gave expression to one of the most enduring theories of mind and brain. He argued that minds and brains are distinct – i.e. different kinds of – substances, in particular that brains are *physical* things, all of which take up (occupy) physical space, while minds are *mental* things and do *not* take up physical space. Each of us, when alive, is a curious amalgam, then, of two different *kinds* of things, or substances: a physical thing, i.e. a human body including its brain, and a nonphysical mind or psyche. The problem, then, became to try to offer a theory explaining the relationship between these two substances. How is it possible for these two, essentially different, kinds of things to interact in a causal manner? How, exactly, does a cut in your finger cause (bring it about that you feel) pain? Wounds, on this theory, are *physical* events, while pains, on this theory, are supposed to be *mental* events. How does something which occurs in space (an incision in your finger) cause something which is not in space (the pain you feel)? Or, taking another example, this time going the other way, how is it possible that your desire for a drink of water, your desire being – on this theory – something that exists in your mind and is thus not physical, causes your body, a physical entity, to rise up out of a chair, cross the room, turn on the kitchen tap, and lift a drinking glass to the stream of water issuing from the faucet? Descartes's successors, to this very day, struggle with these problems.

Other philosophers have offered quite different theories. Some have argued that Descartes's fundamental distinction, that is, between minds and brains, is misconceived. Some of these critics have argued, for example, that minds are not distinct from brains, that mental states and events are nothing other than states and events in the central nervous system. And needless to say, there are a variety of other theories, as well, which are variations on these two principal themes. In the latter half of the twentieth century we enjoy (or suffer, depending on your attitude about these sorts of things) several different theories about the relationship between minds and brains.

The point of bringing up this embarrassment of riches is to focus on a certain naive attitude some persons bring to these debates. Every teacher who has ever introduced students to the problem of the relationship of mind and brain has learned to expect that some students will regard the question as one to be settled by empirical research in the laboratory. To these students, the question initially appears analogous to questions such as "What is the relationship between fever and infection?" and insofar as this latter question permits of empirical resolution, so, too, does it seem to them that the former, about the relationship between mind and brain, ought to permit of empirical resolution. These students express confident belief that – just given enough time, money, and resources – scientists will be able to decide such issues by their usual methods.

Nothing that emerges from the experimenters' laboratories can ever, or indeed could ever, settle the issue between dualists, persons who hold, like Descartes, that mind and brains are fundamentally different kinds of substances, and monists, persons who hold that there are not these two kinds of substances.

It has often been alleged that the reason science cannot provide a definitive answer to Descartes's puzzle is because science is essentially directed to exploring material, or physical, features of the world, that science is incapable of exploring nonphysical entities. But the explanation of the source of the difficulty is, I think, really much more profound. For it is simply false that science is essentially incapable of examining nonphysical things. Suppose, just for the sake of argument, that minds, or more exactly mental states and mental events, *are* nonphysical. Suppose, just for the sake of argument, that mental states and events are – let us say – weightless, have no exact position within our bodies, lack color, have no scents, etc., i.e. lack most, if not all, of the properties we usually find in physical entities. Nevertheless, even if all this were true, science could still explore and learn a very great deal about mental states and events. Science might learn, for example, whether it were possible for persons to 'think themselves out of' pain, whether bright patches of red in our visual fields are succeeded by green patches, whether certain odors might evoke certain memories, whether musical acuity correlates with mathematical ability, etc. As a matter of fact, these sorts of experimental researches are precisely the kinds psychologists regularly do pursue, and indeed do so without having settled the issue whether mental states and events are, or are not, brain states and events. In short, the inability of science to answer the question whether mental states are brain states does not arise because science is essentially incapable of examining nonphysical entities. For all we know mental states may be nonphysical entities. If they are, then science is, even now, examining nonphysical entities.

The real source of the difficulty in trying to decide the relationship between mind and brain is that in exploring the mind of a subject, psychologists have no non-question-begging test to tell them whether they are looking at some physical feature of that subject's central nervous system or at some other, nonphysical, feature of that subject which, although possibly correlated with some physical feature, may – for all that – be distinct from it.

Suppose a dualist and a monist were having an argument. Suppose the dualist were to offer the theory that pains *accompany* or *are caused by* certain kinds of nerve firings but are not literally those firings themselves, while her colleague, the monist, were to argue that the pains were not something *accompanying* the nerve firings but were, literally, the nerve firings themselves. They may perfectly well agree about the experimental data: that increasing the rate of firings increases the reported magnitude and duration of pain; that anesthetizing certain nerves blocks the pain; that bombarding the subject with intense so-called pink noise also blocks the pain; etc. What would any of this show about the correct answer to the question whether pains are physical events? It should be clear that none of this would settle the matter. The question, and its resolution, goes well beyond the experimental data.

This is not, of course, to deny that empirical data have a bearing on the issue. They do. But only up to a point. If there were no detectable *correlation* between pains and physical states, if pains seemed to occur randomly without any physical cause whatever, then we probably would be positively disinclined even to consider that they might be physical states. But we already know enough about the world to know that pains, more often than not, do occur when certain sorts of physical events occur. What experimental research tells us, then, is that there is not just a bare possibility of dualism's being false, but that there is empirical evidence which is consistent with another theory, viz. monism.

The empirical data which we have about minds and brains are consistent with (at least) two *different* theories of the relationship between minds and brains. And from an examination of the sorts of data which empirical research is capable of yielding, it is clear that no forthcoming or future data could ever settle the dispute. It is at this point that the problem, having originated within science, must go beyond science, to metaphysics.

How, if not by empirical research, is metaphysics to be pursued? We have already seen, in chapter 4, that Logical Positivists had been convinced that metaphysics is an impossibility and that any pretensions it might have to furnishing us knowledge are illusory. That particular opposition has pretty well, in time, damped down. But the challenge remains. We really must address the problem how, if not by empirical research, one can hope to answer the sorts of questions science must leave unanswered. To what might one take recourse?

I hope that the answer should already be beginning to become clear in light of what I have been saying in the previous three chapters about theories and underdeterminism. We pursue metaphysics by trying to construct the best theories we can to explain, i.e. to make sense of, the puzzling aspects of our world which science is incapable by itself of explaining. As we venture further from the empirical base, our theorizing becomes more difficult and less determined, or if you will permit me an ugly (but informative) phrase, our theorizing becomes *more underdetermined.*

Metaphysical theories about, for example, the ultimate relationship between minds and brains, theories which presuppose and try to accommodate all the empirical data of the experimental laboratory, but which also try to go beyond that data, are probably destined never to convince all rational persons. Being even more underdetermined than the scientific theories on which they ride piggyback, they probably always will be the object of dispute and of criticism. But this is simply our human condition. No matter how much empirical data we gather, however diligently and conscientiously, that data always will be insufficient to establish our scientific theories as true and always will be insufficient, to an even greater degree, to establish our metaphysical theories as true. Yet we human beings seem insatiably curious. Our knowledge has no natural stopping point. Most of us rebel at the very thought that our knowledge may be at an end. Even if the methods and tools of psychologists and physiologists cannot, in principle, tell us, for example, finally whether minds are, or are not, brains, we still persevere in wanting to know such a thing. And if science cannot tell us, then we will go beyond science, to metaphysics.

6.2 Vagueness

Metaphysical theories are proffered solutions to *conceptual* puzzles. What is the concept of *mind*? What is the concept of *person*? What is the concept of *identity*? What is the concept of *material object*? What are the concepts of *space* and of *time*? Etc.

It is not essential that we try to get very clear what a concept is. That exercise may be left for books on the philosophy of language and of mind. Let me say only this: persons have a concept of – let us take as an example – redness, if they are able, for the most part, to use correctly the word "redness" or some other word, in some other language, which means pretty much what "redness" does in English. To be sure, there are a fair number of things about which one could seek clarification in this brief exposition. But let me add only that, on this particular explication, concepts are not words themselves, but are expressible by words. Speakers of different languages, then, e.g. English and French, may have the same concepts although they will use different words to express them, e.g. "redness" and "rougeur".[4]

----

4. I have stated a quasi-sufficient condition for having a concept, but not a necessary one. Animals, e.g. dogs and cats, probably have certain concepts, but dogs and cats lack languages. Thus, having certain linguistic abilities

Bertrand Russell (1872-1970), in a famous paper, once wrote that "all language is vague" ([180], 84). He also wrote that "all knowledge is vague" (90), that words are vague (85), and "that every proposition that can be framed in practice has a certain degree of vagueness" (88). What all this comes down to is that the concepts which figure in the propositions we frame, i.e. in our beliefs, theories, musings, doubts, certainties, etc., are themselves vague. Vagueness in beliefs, in theories, etc. is traceable to vagueness in our concepts.

In what I am sure was intended as a facetious remark, Russell added, "whatever vagueness is to be found in my words must be attributed to our ancestors for not having been predominantly interested in logic" (84). Had he reflected upon this remark, I am sure Russell would have had to admit that history could not have been otherwise. For general terms, such as "red", "warm", "bald", and "tasty", to be useful, indeed to be learnable by persons not born already knowing a language, those terms *must* be somewhat vague. Concepts could not be taught, and could not be learned, except if they were vague.

A term, or a concept, is vague if there are particular cases (instances, things, etc.) which do not fall clearly inside or outside the range of applicability of the term. At what point exactly does an object cease being red? How much hair exactly must a man lose to be judged bald? In what manner and to what degree must a person hold theological beliefs and practice the dictates of some religion to be regarded as religious? Such questions admit of no precise answers and the concepts *redness*, *baldness*, and *religious* must be regarded as vague.

If most of our workaday concepts were not somewhat vague, we probably could never have learned them, and we certainly would have grave difficulty in applying them. Indeed we can easily see how utterly counterproductive it would be to attempt to reduce the vagueness inherent in the concept *bald*. Suppose we were to stipulate that anyone who had fewer than 2089 hairs on his scalp was to be regarded as bald. (This of course presupposes that we have already similarly stipulated where one's scalp leaves off and one's face begins. The difficulty thus begins to mushroom. What begins as a problem in making the concept *bald* more precise quickly also becomes a problem in revising the concepts of *face*, *scalp*, *hair*, etc. But we will not trouble

---

suffices in the case of human beings to show that those human beings have certain concepts, but those linguistic abilities should not be taken as the very same thing as having those concepts.

ourselves over this appreciable further difficulty, since we have problems enough with the very first level of reform.) On this new, refined,
concept, some persons would clearly be seen to be bald, others clearly
not so. But there will be cases for which we would have to count hair
shafts to be sure. Now, given the sorts of taboos in this society, and
given our sorts of interests, we are not much inclined to go about con-
ducting an inventory of the precise number of hairs on an acquaintance's scalp. If we were to impose the imagined precision on the concept *bald*, we would, almost certainly, immediately supplement that
precise, and now fairly useless, concept with a vaguer, more practical
one, one which for all intents and purposes would simply duplicate
our present concept of *baldness*. In short, any suggestion that we have
vague words in our language, vague concepts in our conceptual
scheme, only because our ancestors did not make the effort to be more
precise would be wildly wrong. We have vagueness in our concepts
because of the way we learn language and because some vagueness is
positively required.

For a conceptual scheme to be workable it is essential not only that
some concepts be relatively vague but that there also be mechanisms
for reducing vagueness as the need arises. No legislator could possibly
envisage all the ways there might be to create a public disturbance or
to threaten the public health. At the turn of this century only a clair-
voyant could have imagined the nuisance potential of portable stereo
radios and the threat to health posed by the careless use of DDT or by
the promiscuous behavior of an AIDS sufferer. Key terms in legislation
– "public good", "intellectual property", "privacy", etc. – must always
remain somewhat vague and thus open to later refinement in light of
changed circumstances.

What is true of legalese is true as well of English at any stage of its
gradual evolution. Our concepts are adjusted to allow us to cope with
the world pretty much as we find it now. As our knowledge expands,
as new technology appears, as our sense of right and wrong gradually
changes over time, our concepts must be revised to allow us to operate
with these changes. The *word* "justice" has not changed for a few
hundred years, neither has the *word* "art", nor the *word* "death". But
our *concepts* of justice, of art, and of death surely have changed in that
period. It was not too long ago, for example, that a person whose heart
had stopped beating was considered dead. Not any more. Nowadays a
person whose heart has stopped beating may be considered, like persons who have temporarily stopped breathing, not dead but in a life-
threatening situation which may warrant heroic resuscitative meas-

ures. In short, we have, in the last fifty or so years, in response to a changed medical technology, revised, not the word "death", but the *concept* of death.[5]

6.3   Conceptual analysis

To solve a metaphysical puzzle is, ultimately, to make a suggestion, i.e. to offer a theory, about how we *do* in fact use a concept or – more often – how we *ought* to use (i.e. revise) a particular concept. When Hume, for example, began his examination of the endurance through time of material objects, he took care to insist that as we ordinarily conceive of a thing's enduring we allow for the thing to change somewhat.[6] He asks us to imagine how we would respond to the situation of something's changing counterfactually* (i.e. contrary to the way the world actually is) by the acquisition or loss over time of some small part. He anticipates that we would not, ordinarily, count that as destroying the thing's identity, and takes that expected response as evidence of how we actually do use the concept. (We will return to this sort of technique, construing its counterfactual aspect as the describing of a possible world, in section 6.4. There we will examine Locke's attempt to elicit our ordinary concept of *person*.)

This first kind of conceptual analysis, I will call "narrow analysis". Some authors prefer the expression "pure analysis". "Narrow analysis" simply means an assay of the standard or typical conditions for the applicability of a concept. Thus Hume's preliminary remarks about endurance through time can be regarded as narrow analysis. And so, too, can the example Bradley and I offered in our book *Possible Worlds*, when we argued, in effect, that the concept of *knowledge* is a complex concept ([34], 183) and that it has the concept of *belief* as one of its constituents (23). Put another way, we argued that it is part of the *analysis* of the concept of *knowledge* that any case of *knowledge* is also a case of *belief*, e.g. to know that it is raining entails (among other things) believing that it is raining. The example we

---

5. Certain English words have changed enough over a period as brief as two hundred years so as to make reading some eighteenth-century philosophy problematic. One must recognize, for example, in reading Locke and Hume, that words such as "idea", "impression", "power", and "necessity" simply do not mean to modern readers what thèy did to eighteenth-century readers.

6. The passage from Hume ([101], 255-6) is quoted below, p. 331.

chose is perhaps more controversial than one would like for illustrative purposes. Nowadays I think I would be more inclined to choose as an example the concept of *triangle*, and would argue that it is part of the *analysis* of the concept of *triangle* that all triangles have three sides.[7] Such knowledge as this is standardly called "analytic knowledge", and on the account preferred by some philosophers at least, Bradley and I certainly among them, would be deemed to be a priori knowledge.[8]

But there is a second kind of analysis, one which may be called "broad analysis", which goes far beyond the limited descriptive nature of narrow, or pure, analysis. In this latter kind of analysis there is a significant component of revision. (Recall the quotation from Strawson in chapter 2, p. 23.)

When we read Hume's discussion of the concept of *causality*, and more especially Kant's response to that discussion, we detect a far greater degree of revision than appeared in the discussion of endurance. Kant, in trying to figure out how and why we make causal attributions, given Hume's claim (which Kant accepted) that causal con-

---

7. There are, of course, additional concepts involved as well, viz. that triangles have straight sides, and that the figure is closed. The concept *three-sided* is, then, but one constituent of the concept *triangularity*.

8. Let me quote from my explication of a priori knowledge which appears in the Glossary at the back of this book: "When philosophers say that a statement can be known without experience, they mean that no particular experience of the world, *save perhaps learning a language*, is necessary to be able to figure out the truth or falsity of the proposition." The italicized qualification is essential. Learning a language can only be through experience. We are not born knowing any language. But learning a language, learning under what conditions it is appropriate to apply words such as "red", "bald", "triangle", "knowledge", etc., is not to have empirical knowledge of this world. Learning English is not, for example, sufficient to inform us whether all triangles are red, or whether all squares are fragile, etc. I might learn, for example, to speak Swahili, and might learn the Swahili words for certain foods I never have laid eyes upon. But merely learning to use these words would certainly not put me in a position to know whether these various foods are ever served at the same meal together, or whether there might be religious strictures barring their appearing on the same table together. To come to know the latter, one would have to go beyond mere knowledge of the meaning of (Swahili) words, to *empirical* knowledge of the mores of the Swahili people.

nections can never literally be perceived – i.e. that all that is perceivable is *sequences* of events – proposed a new concept of *causality*: one which, like his analysis of space and time, theorized that *causality* is imposed on the data of sense 'by the mind'.[9]

When one undertakes to revise a concept, as Kant has done in the case of *causality*, the task is considerably more challenging, and likely to draw fire, than when one tries merely to report how we typically use a concept. Contributing to the difficulty is the fact that there is no one way to go about inventing and arguing for changes in our conceptual scheme. Nor are there probably just a few ways. There are many different ways, some of which are historically and currently stylish, others – no doubt – not yet even imagined, i.e. others are surely to be invented, developed, polished, and pursued by our descendants long after all of us are dead.

There is as much, or as little, method in the practice of metaphysics as there is in science. The commonly broadcast claim that there is something called 'the scientific method' is for the most part – as I have tried to show earlier – more fable than fact. Whatever scientific method exists is not something to be captured in a set of recipes, either by Bacon or by Mill or by a modern successor. What method there is to the practicing of science is something learned by apprenticeship, by imitation, by trial and error, by imagination, and by exposing one's scientific work to the scrutiny and criticism of fellow scientists. The practice of metaphysics proceeds in a parallel fashion.

The practice of metaphysics must be learned by apprenticeship, by reading the writings of metaphysicians, by attending to criticisms of those writings, and by daring to construct theories on one's own, theories which – just on the basis of probabilities – like most new theories, will prove to be, in one way or another, defective. Metaphysics, like science, is not for the fainthearted, and if it is to be done well, is certainly not for the dogmatic.

But if there is no particular method to be followed in metaphysics in our attempts to *generate* revisions to our concepts, there are, nonetheless, certain desiderata to be looked for in *judging* whether a proffered revision of a concept is to be accepted or rejected. Rudolf Carnap (1891-1970) has provided us with one of the best, most insightful discussions of the features by which to judge the worthiness of a philosophical reconstruction ([45], 3-8). Carnap uses the term "explication"

---

9. See the quotation on p. 13 and the discussion on p. 30.

to describe the process of revising a concept, what has here been called "broad analysis". The concept to be revised, he calls the "explicandum"; and the new concept, the one which *replaces* the original, he calls the "explicatum". The latter, the new concept, the explicatum, is supposed to be less vague than the original concept, the explicandum. But there is no question of the explicatum's being perfectly precise. The explicatum is devised to be an improvement; it is not to be thought of as a finished product suitable for use in all subsequent circumstances.

Other authors use different technical vocabulary. Where Carnap uses the term "explicandum", other authors sometimes use another Latinate term, viz. "analysandum", while still others prefer the technical English phrase "pre-analytic concept". And where Carnap speaks of the "explicatum", other authors speak of the "explicans", the "analysans", the "reconstruction", the "explication", and the "analysis", in the last two instances using the terms "explication" and "analysis" both for the process of philosophical reconstruction and for the product of that reconstruction.

Since the 1950s, the terms "analysis" and "analytic philosophy" have achieved a remarkable philosophical vogue. But that fashionableness has been accompanied by an unfortunate ambiguity. Occasionally "analysis", without any accompanying adjective, is used as I have used the expression "narrow analysis"; very often, however, it is used as I have used the expression "broad analysis", or "revisionary analysis", or as Carnap has used the term "explication". On balance, when other philosophers use the term "analysis" *tout court*, they probably mean the latter sort of analysis, viz. "explication". Although the truncated expression "analysis" is not entirely apt, and perhaps even a little misleading, it is so well established within the philosophical lexicon that it would be futile to try to avoid it. So hereinafter, "analysis" will be understood to mean "explication".

Carnap argues that in judging a philosophical analysis (i.e. an explication or reconstruction), there are four factors to be considered, viz., that the explicatum (the revised concept) is to be

1. *similar* to the explicandum (the pre-analytic concept)
2. as *exact* as possible
3. *fruitful*
4. as *simple* as possible.

There can be little question that in assessing and criticizing philosophical analyses (reconstructions), these four factors do play a pivotal role. Critics will praise or fault an analysis according to the degree they judge the analysis to satisfy these requirements. But there is no mechanical or precise way to go about quantifying these requirements, and disputes among philosophers can be fierce as to the relative merits of an analysis. Thus, for example, as we saw earlier, the formalists admire and promote a particular theory of explanation, the so-called covering-law model, which reconstructs explanations as arguments, in which universal or statistical laws, along with statements of antecedent conditions, figure as premises, and the statement describing the event to be explained figures as conclusion (e.g. recall Hempel's example [p. 36] of a car radiator cracking).[10] This analysis is prized by the formalists for its exactness (Carnap's second requirement) and its relative simplicity (Carnap's fourth requirement). But other philosophers are adamantly opposed to the covering-law model, arguing that it does violence to our pre-analytic notion of explanation which is heavily context-dependent and turns on the background knowledge of the person seeking the explanation and on whether that person succeeds in understanding the explanation. In short, critics of the covering-law model protest that the explicatum departs too far from the explicandum, i.e. that the model fails on the first of Carnap's requirements.

Philosophical disputes, such as that between the covering-law theorists and their opponents, are inevitable. The trouble is that the various desiderata in a philosophical explication are usually in conflict with one another. Exactness and simplicity are often purchased at the price of severely constricting our pre-analytic concept. Such clashes are, in the main, inescapable. Our pre-analytic concepts often get into trouble as they are extended to handle cases beyond the 'typical' ones, i.e. they are not suitably clear or precise enough to comprehend new, problematic cases. But there never is, nor could there be, any one way to modify a concept, and there is bound to be disagreement about the benefit of suggested changes.

---

10. Beware not to confuse *explanation* with *explication*. We explain, for example, historical events, biological processes, the means to start a car, and – on occasion – we explain the uses of a term (as I am doing right here, now). But we never explicate historical events, biological processes, etc. In reconstructing a concept, in offering a theory as to how it might be revised, we explicate that concept, we do not explain it. Thus, it is possible, as we see here, to explicate the *concept* of explanation. To do so is not to explain explanation.

All of this presupposes that concepts are not the sorts of things which are 'out there' in some sort of absolute realm not of human making. Concepts are not the sorts of things which we human beings discover and either, as it were, comprehend 'correctly' or – because we make a mistake, through carelessness, inattention, confusion, etc. – comprehend 'incorrectly'. That sort of theory of concepts has been so thoroughly dismissed in modern philosophy that it no longer bears refutation. The concepts human beings use are not fixed entities to be mined in an intellectual realm, but are human inventions, although of course – as mentioned earlier – there may be physical constraints placed on what sorts of concepts we are capable of inventing. (As I said before, it is possible that human beings are so physically constructed, 'hard-wired' in our central nervous systems, as to be capable of forming and entertaining only certain sorts of concepts. Animals – e.g. Thomas Nagel's example of bats – may be incapable of forming the concepts we human beings use; and we, in turn, may be quite incapable of forming the concepts animals use.) In *inventing* and *revising* concepts, there can be no question of our 'getting it right' in the sense of our reconstruction being *true*. Philosophical analyses, although having elements which may be judged true or false, are not, overall, to be regarded as the sorts of things which are true or false. Whether an explicatum is similar to an explicandum can, to a certain degree, be considered something admitting of a judgment which is true or false; similarly the judgment whether an explicatum is fruitful or simple or exact may, too, be regarded as something having aspects of truth and falsity. But to judge an explication as fruitful, or simple, or exact, does not address the questions whether the concept is fruitful *enough*, whether it is *simpler* than rivals, and whether its exactness is *purchased* at the price of its simplicity and similarity to the pre-analytic concept. For these latter sorts of judgments, one cannot argue simply on the basis of 'fact' or pretend that one's claim is somehow manifestly true or that a competing explication is manifestly false. In making these latter judgments which are inherently part of judging the worth of a philosophical analysis, many factors *other* than truth and falsity come into play.

(It bears remarking that there is one particular term which is often also invoked in these contexts, but which may prove a pitfall for the unwary, viz. "intuition". Unless one is aware that philosophers use this term in a specialized, technical sense, confusion is bound to result. When philosophers speak of "pre-analytic intuitions" and "prephilosophical intuitions", and say of an analysis that it is, or is not [as the case may be], "counterintuitive", they are *not* using the term "intuition" as it is ordinarily used, to mean something like "knowledge prior to, or independent of, experience", as for example, when biologists might say that a bird's ability to build a nest without having been taught to do so is intuitive [or instinctual]. In the context of philosophical analysis, or reconstruction, when philosophers talk of intuitions, they refer to our judgments about the pre-analytic concept, the *analysandum*. And when they say such things as "the analysis is counterintuitive", they mean that the proffered reconstruction strongly departs from the original concept. Thus, for example, were a philosopher to complain that some particular analysis of mind was counterintuitive, she would not be objecting that the analysis contradicted some in-built, or a priori, knowledge, but would – rather – be making the more reasonable claim that the analysis was very unlike the original, pre-analytic, concept.[11])

Philosophical analyses of concepts are nothing like dictionary definitions. Dictionary definitions are esteemed for their brevity. Philosophical analyses are anything but brief. Carnap's discussion of the requirements for a philosophical explication occurs in his book *Logical Foundations of Probability* (1950) in which he explicitly says he is trying to explicate one particular concept of probability. The ensuing explication of what he calls "logical probability" consumes well over 500 pages. Or, again, when Gilbert Ryle endeavored to offer his analysis of mind in *The Concept of Mind* (1949) his explication ran to more than 300 pages. And John Rawls's analysis of justice, *Theory of Justice* (1971), spans 607 pages. To revise a concept is no easy or trivial matter. One must try to get clear how the concept has been used, how it runs into trouble for certain cases, and how altering it in a cer-

---

11. The strongest case I know of a philosopher arguing for the importance of intuitions in judging a philosophical analysis occurs in Saul Kripke's *Naming and Necessity*: "... some philosophers think that something's having intuitive content is very inconclusive evidence in favor of it. I think it is very heavy evidence in favor of anything, myself. I really don't know, in a way, what more conclusive evidence one can have about anything, ultimately speaking" ([116], 42). But even with this said, Kripke proceeds to argue that intuitions are not inviolable. For he immediately states that persons who find a particular philosophical thesis – that there are accidental* properties – unintuitive have their intuitions "reversed". Clearly, Kripke thinks both that some intuitions are to be preferred to others and that some intuitions can be successfully challenged by cogent argument.

tain fashion might be thought to provide a way out of the difficulties.

If philosophical analyses are not like dictionary definitions, they are not like proofs in mathematics either. Unlike what I have called "narrow analyses", philosophical analyses (explications) are not the sorts of things whose correctness (validity) may be demonstrated a priori. There is far more empirical content in philosophical analyses than is usually recognized. Because the two different kinds of analysis have not always been clearly distinguished and because few philosophers ever conduct original scientific research, e.g. because few philosophers ever themselves mix chemicals, construct electronic equipment, peer through microscopes or telescopes, dissect animals, unearth ancient pottery, or drill boreholes, it has been easy to form the mistaken idea that philosophy is an a priori science. And probably more than a few philosophers themselves have believed just this. Some persons, in noting that philosophers typically conduct no empirical research, have come to believe that philosophy is just simply the product of deep thought, that philosophy – at its best – springs from pure, unaided reason and that the less contaminated it is by crass facts, the more it aspires to independence of 'the facts', the better it is. The truth is, however, that any such philosophy would be grievously impoverished. If philosophers themselves do not conduct empirical research it is only because they depend, secondhand, on the empirical research of others to infuse their own theories. We have here something of a separation of labors, but nothing like an exclusivity of objectives or interests.

Metaphysical analyses of personal identity, for example, depend heavily and crucially upon certain *empirical* facts about material objects (e.g. their impenetrability, their endurance through time) and upon certain empirical facts about memories (e.g. that memories are causally related to witnessed events in one's own lifetime). Similarly, philosophical analyses of *art*, of *labor*, of *agency*, of *free will*, of *miracle*, and of *justice*, etc., all presuppose an enormous background of *empirical* facts. One cannot get far in discussions of justice, for example, without a host of empirical presuppositions, both psychological and sociological: e.g. that there is a scarcity of material goods; that human abilities, desires, and opportunities are not distributed equally; that certain desires conflict with those of other persons; that disease and physical handicaps afflict some, but not all, persons; that individual lifetimes differ greatly; that knowledge and information are commodities which are not universally accessible; and that decisions are often taken in ignorance of what other persons are doing. Thus, in trying to devise a philosophical explication of justice, no philosopher ever could hope to fashion such a theory a priori or hope to fashion a theory which would be applicable in every conceivable set of circumstances. Quite the contrary, what is involved in fashioning a philosophical theory is the desire that that theory should be applicable to this particular world. Metaphysical theories must have substantial empirical content; they must, that is, be tailored to this world, not to any and every possible world.[12]

And yet, paradoxically, one of the most powerful tools philosophers sometimes use in creating and testing their theories is to put the concepts at play under stress by asking what we would want to say if the circumstances were markedly different from the circumstances that ordinarily prevail. This technique is so surprising, and yet so useful and widely practiced, that it demands particular scrutiny.

6.4   Possible worlds

The aim in developing a philosophical theory is to clarify and possibly revise some of our concepts. How might we do this? One way, particularly favored among metaphysicians, is to place the concept under stress, to subject it to a kind of test wherein we ask whether or not we would want to persevere in applying the concept to *counterfactual* cases, cases which are sometimes far from ordinary; indeed, in many instances, which are physically impossible.

Thus, for example, in one of the most famous passages in philosophical literature, John Locke (1632-1704), in trying to analyze the concepts of *person* and *personal identity* writes:

> ... should the soul of a prince, carrying with it the consciousness of the prince's past life, enter and inform the body of a cobbler as soon as deserted by his own soul, everyone sees he would be the same person with the prince, accountable only for

---

12. "... many concepts of philosophically central interest are collage-like: they are internally diversified *combinations* of logically separable elements that are held together by the glue of a theoretical view of the empirical facts. Such concepts rest in an essential way on an empirically-based, fact-laden vision of how things work in the world. ... Our concepts are not framed to suit *every possible* world but in significant measure adjusted to *this* one" (Rescher [169], 120).

the prince's actions; but who would say it was the same man? The body too goes to the making the man and would, I guess, to everybody, determine the man in this case, wherein the soul, with all its princely thoughts about it, would not make another man: but he would be [taken to be] the same cobbler to everyone besides [i.e. except] himself. ([124], book II, chap. XXVII, §15)

Unfortunately, Locke's prose can be maddeningly obscure at times. This paraphrase of the passage may help to make it clear what (I think) Locke is trying to say:

Suppose the consciousness of a deceased prince were to enter and infuse the body of a cobbler immediately upon the cobbler's own consciousness leaving his body. Anyone who knew of this transference would immediately regard the living person not as the cobbler, but as the prince. But were someone ignorant of the transference, then, in judging from the evidence of the physical body, he would take the person to be the cobbler.

All of this is more than a bit strange. So far as we know, consciousnesses, souls, psyches (call them what you will) do not flit from body to body. Indeed, so far as we know, not only do such things not happen, the transference of consciousnesses is physically impossible. Why, then, should Locke, in trying to understand the concepts of *person* and *personal identity*, even consider such an outlandish counterfactual scenario? The explanation is immediately forthcoming:

I know that in the ordinary way of speaking, the same person and the same man stand for one and the same thing. ... But yet when we will inquire what makes the same *spirit*, *man*, or *person*, we must fix the *ideas* of *spirit*, *man*, or *person* in our minds; and having resolved with ourselves what we mean by them, it will not be hard to determine in either of them or the like when it is the *same* and when not. ([124], book II, chap. XXVII, §15)

Locke is here using the term "man" much as we would today use the term "human being", i.e. as designating a certain kind of physical creature, a member of the species *Homo sapiens*. Locke notes that the expression "same man" (or "same human being") and the expression "same person" generally – or as he puts it, "in the ordinary way of speaking" – stand for one and the same thing. Of course he is right: whenever you judge some man (human being) to be the same man as, for example, when you judge the clerk in the drugstore to be the same *man* as the man who used to work in the bakery, you could equally well say that this *person* is the same person who used to work in the bakery. In the ordinary way of speaking, "same human being" and "same person" may, stylistic considerations aside, be considered *interchangeable*. You could even say that this *man* who is now working in the drugstore is the same *person* who used to work in the bakery. But in spite of this – and this is the crux of Locke's point and of his strange example – the two concepts are not after all the same. The concept *human being* – Locke tries to show through his counterfactual supposition – is different from the concept of *person*. Although all human beings may, as a matter of fact, be persons and all persons may, as a matter of fact, be human beings, nonetheless the concepts of *human being* and *person* are different.

Suppose, just for the sake of an example, that every creature which has kidneys also has a heart and, conversely, that every creature with a heart has kidneys (this example is Quine's [162], 21). Suppose, further, that you wanted to argue that the concept of *having kidneys* is not the same concept as *having a heart*. One thing you could not do would be to display some creature which has the one kind of organ but which lacks the other, for, by hypothesis, there are no such creatures. To demonstrate the conceptual difference between *having kidneys* and *having a heart*, you might take recourse to imaginary (counterfactual) cases. You could say something of the sort: "Imagine an animal which has blood and an organ to pump that blood, but in which there is no specific organ which filters waste products from the blood. Instead, waste products pass directly through the walls of the blood vessels, through the surrounding flesh, and are evaporated on the surface of the skin." The described animal is, of course, a creation of science fiction, i.e. does not exist so far as we know. But whether it exists or not, it serves your purposes admirably. The mere *logical possibility* of its existence suffices to show us that the concept *having kidneys* and the concept *having a heart* are not the same concept.

Now, of course, it must be admitted that we knew this all along. None of us for a moment was tempted to confuse, or conflate, the two concepts of *having kidneys* and *having a heart*. We knew these concepts were distinct before, and indeed without, your telling the science-fiction tale we just related.

But how, exactly, did we know this? We knew it because, even without perhaps ever having encountered a creature which had the one kind of organ and not the other, we were easily able to imagine such a creature. We could imagine, that is, that one of the two concepts might be applicable to some one creature and not the other one as well. That trivial piece of imagining suffices to demonstrate that the two concepts are distinct.

Now we can see what Locke was up to. Perhaps every human being we have ever encountered has been a person; perhaps every person we have ever encountered has been a human being. But are the concepts *human being* and *person* the same concept or not? (The fact that they are expressed by different English words is irrelevant to making the decision. The two words "asteroid" and "planetoid" are certainly different: the former has eight letters, the latter nine; etc. Even so, differences of expression aside, the concept of *asteroid* is the very same concept as *planetoid*.) Locke tries to show that there are certain describable counterfactual cases which, if they were to obtain, would be ones to which one of the two concepts, *human being* and *person*, would apply and the other one not.

If the mind of the prince were to enter the body of the cobbler, we would have such a case. For if this were to happen, and we were to know that it happened, we would – Locke confidently predicts – know that although this is now the body of the cobbler, i.e. this *human being* is the human being who used to be the cobbler, this *person* is the person who used to be the prince. (You may find yourself disputing Locke's prediction about how you would interpret such a case. You may, for example, be disinclined to conceive of minds – or personalities – in such a way that they could even be the sorts of things which might migrate from one body to another. We will return to your misgiving later. For the moment, let us confine ourselves to trying to understand what is thought to be shown by such counterfactual examples.)

Twentieth-century philosophers have borrowed a piece of terminology which was popularized in the seventeenth century by Leibniz, but which he, in turn, had adopted from Scholastic (medieval) philosophy.[13] The scenes and situations depicted in these short counterfactual

---

13. Leibniz's phraseology is familiar, even in popular culture: "Why did God create this world? Because this is the best of all possible worlds". His actual words were: "There were an infinity of possible ways of creating the

(or science-fiction) tales, which are used to place selected concepts under stress, have come to be called by many contemporary writers "possible worlds".[14] When Locke considered the *possibility* of the prince's personality migrating from the prince's body to that of the cobbler's, he was not describing this world (i.e. the actual universe) but an imaginary world, a possible world different from the actual one.

In the twentieth century, the technique of probing concepts by subjecting them to stress within a (described) possible world is commonplace. Contemporary philosophical literature abounds with such examples. Friedrich Waismann, in an attempt to show that the concept of *physical object* does not entail the concept of *physical impenetrability*, asks us to consider a possible world in which two chairs occupy the same place at the same time ([209], 201-2). John King-Farlow, in an attempt to show (among other things) that speaking a language does not require the speaker to have a concept of *self*, asks us to consider a possible world in which trees describe the scenery by rustling their leaves ([110]). Sydney Shoemaker, in an attempt to show that time can pass with nothing whatsoever happening, asks us to consider a possible world in which specific regions are periodically subject to total freezing (i.e. subject to total so-called suspended animation) ([191]). Anthony Quinton, in an attempt to show that not all physical objects need stand in spatial relations to one another, asks us to consider a possible world in which any number of persons, upon falling asleep in England, share a dream of being on a tropical island ([164]). And Peter Strawson, in an attempt to show that certain non-tangible objects can be re-identified over time, even though not being continuously observed, asks us to consider a possible world consisting solely of sounds ([200], chap. 2). (We shall return to some of these examples in subsequent chapters.)

---

world, according to the different designs which God might form, and each possible world depends upon certain principle designs or ends of God proper to itself" ([120], 36). And, "It follows from the supreme perfection of God, that in creating the universe he has chosen the best possible plan ... The actual world ... must be the most perfect possible" ([121], 325).

14. Some authors use other vocabulary. For example, Swinburne ([202], 167), uses the term "myth" instead; King-Farlow talks of "parables"; and still others talk of "fables". But many, of course, persist with "counterfactual situations".

6.5 Methodological concerns

Like every other currently practiced philosophical method, that of examining concepts by subjecting them to stress within a possible-worlds story is an object of controversy. There are two main concerns.

The first has to do with the *limits* of the method. The technique of putting a concept under stress in a possible-worlds setting may be used modestly – as a tool for discovering how we actually use that concept – or aggressively – as a means to promote a particular revision of that concept. Nicholas Rescher is relatively sanguine about using the method in the first way, i.e. as a tool of narrow analysis, but has severe misgivings about using it in the latter revisionist manner.

> ... the analyst must take care not to press his would-be clarification beyond the cohesive force of the factual considerations that hold together the concept as such. And this has definite implications regarding the usability of the science-fiction type of thinking [i.e. a possible-worlds story]. ... A science-fiction hypothesis can effectively bring to light the significant fact *that* certain of our concepts are indeed multi-criterial [depend on several logically independent factors] and rest on empirical presuppositions. But what this method cannot do is to serve as a basis for precisifying [i.e. making more precise] our *existing* concepts, because the supposedly more precise account that results in these circumstances will not and in the nature of the case cannot any longer qualify as a version of the concept with which we began. ([169], 113-14, 115)

Where Carnap, we saw earlier, was enthusiastic about making a concept more precise, Rescher, in contrast, is considerably more hesitant, particularly when that revision comes about through the telling of a possible-worlds tale. Rescher worries that the kind of revision that often results in this latter instance is especially prone to sever just those essential empirical roots which give our actual concepts their usefulness. His uneasiness is well-founded. But his critique does not end in a wholesale rejection of the method. He cautions: "The point of these observations is not to advocate an unbudging conservatism in the conceptual area. No doubt there might conceivably be substantial advantages to giving up some of our concepts in favor of others" ([169], 115-16).

Whether the result of some proposed philosophical reconstruction departs unacceptably far from our original concept is something that can be known only on a case-by-case basis; it can never be determined in advance, and certainly not solely on the basis of the method used to generate that proposed revision. Examining and revising our concepts by telling possible-worlds stories has its risks, and those risks unquestionably increase as one passes from merely assaying a concept to replacing it. But carrying a risk does not render a philosophical technique useless. It merely entails that its results must be judged individually and never accepted or rejected in a blanket fashion.

The second concern over the use of possible-worlds stories in the practice of philosophy stems from a heightened examination, and more than just a little criticism, of the concept of *possible world* itself. There have been in recent years a great many books (see e.g. [126], [122], and [72]), and a much greater number of journal articles, devoted to such questions as: "Just what *is* a possible world?" "What are the contents of a possible world?" "In what sense might a possible world be thought to exist?" "Are possible worlds logically prior to propositions, or are propositions logically prior to possible worlds?"

We need not, however, have settled views about such esoteric subtleties in order to utilize the technique of telling possible-worlds tales. One need not settle all philosophical issues, or even for that matter express an opinion about some, to proceed with others. This is true even when the concepts invoked are fundamental and at the core of one's method.[15]

Otto Neurath (1882-1945), in the midst of (what I regard as) a misguided argument against metaphysics, did offer an insightful, now famous analogy:

> What is first given us is our ordinary language with a multitude of imprecise, unanalysed terms. ... We are like sailors who have to rebuild their ship on the open sea, without ever being able to dismantle it in dry-dock and reconstruct it from the best components. ... Imprecise 'verbal clusters' are somehow always part of the ship. If imprecision is diminished at one place, it may well reappear at another place to a stronger degree. ([143], 91-2)

---

15. Recall that one does not need a rigorous concept of, e.g., *number* in order to be able to do quite sophisticated work in arithmetic and other branches of mathematics.

The sailors cannot begin with an unsheathed keel (at the foundation as it were) and build anew. All they can do is gingerly replace parts from time to time, taking care not to sink the ship as they proceed.

In doing philosophy, we must start with a great many assumptions, techniques, and with a history. Of course any and every bit of this is eligible for examination and eventual revision, or even rejection or replacement. But what we cannot do is to begin with nothing and build 'from the bottom up'.

It must be conceded that the concept of *possible world* needs elucidation (explication), that there are many, as yet, unsolved puzzles about the concept. No one could read current journal articles and be in the slightest doubt about this. But none of this shows that the concept cannot be used with great success in the explicating of selected *other* concepts. One does not have to have a sophisticated theory of possible worlds to invoke the concept of *possible world* and to get much mileage out of that concept in attempts, for example, to probe the concepts of *time*, of *physical object*, of *cause*, etc. Indeed, legions of philosophers have not felt themselves in the slightest deterred by certain unclarities in the concept of *possible world* from using it in just these sorts of pursuits. Although some considerably more refined concept of *possible world* may be necessary for technical advances in such fields as logic and the philosophy of language, an *intuitive* or ready-at-hand concept of *possible world* has been and remains adequate for use as a tool in explicating many metaphysical problems.

For example, the concept of *possible world* needs no apology when it is used in explicating the concept of *person*. A great number of philosophers, beginning with Locke and continuing through the present day, have implicitly or explicitly invoked the concept of *possible world* for this very purpose. But their doing so then raises the question why anyone should want, or for that matter should even be tempted, to refine the concept of *person* along the lines we have seen emerging in Locke's discussion. Why, if – as earlier claimed – the two concepts *human being* and *person* may always, or nearly always, be interchanged, might we want to try to distinguish them?

To this last question, there is no one answer, nor are any of several possible answers absolutely straightforward. Again, we find ourselves examining the very reasons some of us are attracted to metaphysics and others not.

The concepts, the beliefs, the theories and the myths each of us operates with are to a large extent inherited from generations of ancestors and from the culture in which we live. There is no compelling *necessity* that any of us ever should distinguish between *human beings* and *persons*. It is easy to conceive of a society (note here how natural it is to fall into yet another, brief possible-worlds tale) in which there were no such distinction and, moreover, in which it never occurred to anyone to make such a distinction or even to ask whether it might be useful to make any such distinction. We can imagine a society in which all human beings were regarded as persons, all persons were regarded as human beings, and that was the end of it. But the simple fact is, that is not this society. (The truth of the matter is that *this* world is not such a world, i.e. this world is not the *possible* world just described.) For in this society, there is a long history of philosophers, lawyers, scientists, novelists, etc. who have asked, and will continue to ask, "What is a person?" and who have not assumed that the answer is a foregone conclusion: "a human being". Our philosophical, histori-cal, mythological, and literary writings are filled with such examples: in Plato's *Phaedo* where – in trying to solve the problem of knowl-edge – he hypothesized that persons exist prior to birth; in some religious writings, where persons are claimed to be able to survive bodily death; and in our myths, e.g. where Merlin was supposed to have been able to inhabit the bodies of animals. In his philosophical novel *You Shall Know Them*, Vercors has his protagonist, Douglas Templeton, intentionally kill his own nonhuman offspring, the product of his mating with an apelike creature. The question posed by such a (possible-worlds) fable is: "Has Templeton killed a person?" If he has, then he is guilty of murder; if not, then he has merely killed an animal.

Anyone who can be engaged by the play of concepts in Vercors's novel has implicitly already made the distinction between being a *human being* on the one hand and a *person* on the other; has recog-nized that it is conceptually possible for these two concepts not to apply to the same creature; and has allowed himself to be receptive to a discussion of what, exactly, we are to understand by the concept *person*. The eventual answer is not to be found by a kind of philo-sophical excavating, i.e. the answer is not 'out there' for the discover-ing. The answer, if it is to be forthcoming at all, will be the product of suggesting ways we might want to extend our intuitive (or pre-analytic) concept. We may even want to try to imagine how we might react if placed in Vercors's imaginary, possible, world. Confronted with the offspring of a human being and an apelike creature, would we be inclined to regard that offspring as being more like a person or more like an animal? What sorts of factors would enter our decision? Perhaps appearance: how much does it look like a human being?; perhaps intelligence: how clever is this creature?; perhaps linguistic abilities: can it learn a language?; etc. But this is hardly the end of it. Other authors have taken more extreme cases and press the concept of *person* even further. In Arthur C. Clarke's *2001*, Hal (*He*uristically programmed *AL*gorithmic computer) seems to have 'a mind of its own', so much so that it turns rogue, subverts commands, mutinies, and murders human beings, and when its crimes are uncovered, pleads not to be disassembled and despairs at the prospect of its impending loss of consciousness:

> "Dave," said Hal, "I don't understand why you're doing this to me. . . .I have the greatest enthusiasm for the mission. . . .You are destroying my mind. . . .Don't you understand? . . .I will become childish. . . .I will become nothing. . . ." ([48], 156)

Hal is made of the typical stuff of computers: wires, transistors, etc. Hal, clearly, is not a *human being*. But might Hal be a *person*? One of the principal goals of contemporary research in artificial intelligence is to come to learn the operations of human cognitive processes well enough so that they can be replicated in a machine. If that comes to pass, what is now regarded as just a possible world – a computer threatening and pleading with us – we might discover is really a future period of this, the actual world.

CHAPTER SEVEN

Putting concepts under stress (II) – Pains

Sleep and pain tend to inspire poets and philosophers; micturition [urination] and defaecation do not. With psychoanalysts, it is the other way round. – Peter Nathan, *The Nervous System* ([142], 104)

7.1   Case study: Shared out-of-body pains

The constructing of possible-worlds tales to place concepts under stress in an attempt to refine or revise those concepts is no talisman guaranteed to produce success. It is just one method, among several, used by philosophers in their work. And its results, far from being consensual, sometimes provoke disputes as intense as those which prompted the use of the method in the first instance.

To see how the technique might be used, and to see the sorts of objections it might elicit, let us discuss the possibility of public, objective, out-of-body pains. At the outset, it is necessary to say that the question we will be examining – viz. "Might there be public, objective (i.e. shareable), out-of-body pains?" – is not to be regarded, in the first instance at any rate, as an *empirical* question. Only at a second stage of inquiry, can such a question be regarded as amenable to investigation by empirical means. For it is essential, first, to determine whether such a question is even meaningful (intelligible), and only if the answer to this preliminary question is affirmative, can we then proceed to the second. The preliminary question, then, might be stated this way: "Could the concept of *pain* apply to something public, out-of-body, or is its use reserved exclusively for sensations located within a living body and perceivable only to the person whose body it is?" The challenge posed by such a question is to determine how one might go about trying to answer it.

Newcomers to philosophy often immediately turn to the resource they have standardly used to determine the extent or range of application of concepts, namely, their dictionaries. But it quickly becomes clear that dictionaries are not about to help with this particular question. There will always be vagueness in our concepts. Although we may from time to time reduce the vagueness of some of our concepts, we will never eliminate it entirely. Dictionaries cannot adjudicate the proper decisions to make when one operates within the penumbra of the meaning of a term; they are incapable of settling boundary disputes. When we ask ourselves whether we should apply a concept to some phenomenon which falls within the penumbral region of a term, dictionaries, which are designed to report standard usages, must fail us. We must take recourse to other means.

What the task comes down to is looking to see whether we can describe a situation in which it would be reasonable to say that something has occurred which is enough like ordinary 'in-body' pain to be regarded as pain, and yet, is outside of one's body and is perceivable by more than one person. We will begin by reviewing current theories of pain and its causes.

In the case of seeing, hearing, and touching, the perceived 'object' (for lack of a better name) is almost invariably on or, more likely, external to (i.e. at some distance from) our skin. To be sure, we occasionally do hear the rumblings of our own stomachs and do use our hands to touch and feel various parts of our bodies, but for the most part, what we see, hear, and touch are physical objects external to our bodies. We see houses, buildings, human beings, trees, motor vehicles, dogs, etc.; we hear screeching tires, the voices of human beings, the music of a piano, the high-frequency whistle of the flyback transformer of a television set, etc.; we feel the knife and fork in our hands, the slipperiness of a bar of soap, the grip on the handle of a golf club; etc. In short, most often the 'objects' of seeing, hearing, and touching are external physical objects.

The 'object' of pain – or, to put it somewhat more perspicuously, what we feel when we feel a pain – is not a physical object. I may accidentally prick my finger with a pin, or cut my thumb with a blade, but the ensuing pain is not my feeling *of the pin* or *of the blade*. The pain begins, to be sure, with the pin's pricking my finger, but it lasts for some time after the pin is removed. The actual pricking may take only a minute fraction of a second, but the resulting pain may last several minutes, long after the pin is removed from the site of the injury. In feeling pain, I am not feeling the pin, but the *injury* caused by that pin.

Physical injury may occur anywhere within one's body. But while no part of our body is immune to injury, only certain parts contain nerves which give rise to pains. Most persons are surprised to learn that their intestines, for example, are insensitive to incision, and that bowel biopsies may be performed painlessly with no anesthetic whatever. Similarly, the human brain lacks pain-generating nerve endings. But many sites throughout the body are sensitive to pain.

How do we know where a pain is? How do you know, for example, that there is a pain in, let us say, the thumb of your left hand? Young children, even those who have acquired a certain facility with language, are often notoriously bad at localizing their pains. Many children, obviously in pain and obviously having a serious ear infection, frequently are unable to pinpoint their pain; they may not even be able to localize the region of their body where it hurts (i.e. are unable to localize the pain as being above their necks). It might seem, then, that we *learn* over a period of time, by trial and error, to locate pains within our bodies. Perhaps at some early stage of our lives, we may, for example, have experienced a pain and, in looking about our bodies, spotted an injury on our hand.[1] In touching the wound, we may have discovered that the pain increased (or decreased) and thus came to believe that the pain was occurring at the site of the injury. Later, we were able to identify pains which originated from that location directly, i.e. without our having to look with our eyes, or probe with our fingers, for an injury. But in spite of its initial plausibility, this conclusion – that we *learn* through trial and error to identify the sites of our pains – may be too strong. For there is some contrary experimental data which suggest that newborns are able to 'home in' on the site of (at least some) pains directly, without a learning process: "… a newborn can remove an irritant from his nose with his hand or get rid of an irritant on one leg with his other foot" ([32], 19). What confuses the issue is the fact that it is conceivable that this ability of newborns to localize (some) pains is only temporary, like their ability to reach for visual objects. Perhaps, just as in the case of the latter visual-motor ability ([32], 45), the newborn may lose the innate ability to localize pain directly, and may have to 'regain' it in the ensuing

---

1. This picture is somewhat oversimplified. Some, but by no means all, injuries cause an energetic reflex movement, a flexion withdrawal of the limb, a fraction of a second before the pain impresses itself on one's consciousness. Given this muscular reflex, one's subsequent attention is naturally drawn to that limb itself.

months by a learning process. In short, it is unclear how much of our ability to locate pains directly is innate and how much is a learned response. In any event, well before we reach adulthood our ability – whatever its origin – to locate pains directly is firmly in place.

(Some researchers have suggested that we locate pains directly by utilizing an 'internal map' [either learned or innate] of our own bodies, on which we place, more or less correctly, the incoming signals from the many nerve pathways according to their points of origin. How much stock is to be put in such a theory? Does postulating an 'internal representation' of our bodies help to explain this ability to locate pains directly, or is this merely a metaphorical manner of redescribing the very phenomenon itself? We can well understand why researchers differ in their attitudes toward such models. Some researchers regard this model – of an internal, representational map – as the best, if not the only, way to account for the ability to locate pains and to know directly the disposition of our limbs. Other researchers regard the explanatory content of such a hypothesis as nil. They regard the postulating of such a map as unempirical and, indeed, as an entirely dispensable piece of baggage. The debate is but one instance of a century-old controversy about the utility of models in scientific explanations. The dispute can be expected to continue indefinitely.)

Our ability to locate pains directly, good though it often is, is far from perfect as being an ability to locate the injuries which are the physical causes of those pains. For there are a number of instances in which persons will locate pains in their bodies far from the sites of the injuries causing those pains. The best known of these is the pain caused by a rupture (popularly misnamed a "slip") of the fifth lumbar disk. The ruptured disk presses on the sciatic nerve within the spinal column. But the ensuing pain is nearly always felt some centimeters, or even nearly a meter, removed from the site of the trauma. The pain is often felt in the hip, or down the back of the leg, or even in the toes. Such so-called referred pains sometimes mislead diagnosticians. Doctors will sometimes misdiagnose spinal injuries as pulled back ligaments or as hip injuries. It is essential, then, to distinguish carefully the site of a pain (i.e. where the pain is felt) from the site of the injury which causes that pain. Usually they coincide; occasionally, they do not.

The most dramatic case of referred pain is the phenomenon, well-documented in medical literature, of the so-called phantom limb. A person who has had a limb amputated may complain of pains which feel as they would had that limb not been amputated. For instance, a person who has had his left leg amputated may complain of pains of just the sort he would have had if that limb were still attached to his body, i.e. it *feels to him as if he still has a left leg and that there is a pain in that leg*.

From a physiological point of view we can explain the phenomenon in this way. The nerve endings of the niociceptor class of 'Ad' (fast) and 'C' (slow) fibers at the site of the amputation (i.e. on the remaining stump of the limb) are firing and sending impulses along these fibers to the spinal cord, where they interact with a variety of other impulses (e.g. indicating touch or pressure) along with descending signals from the brain. If these impulses are not masked or blocked in the spinal cord, then signals proceed to the thalamus and eventually to the cerebral cortex (see, e.g., [219], 103). These latter signals are so like those which used to originate within his leg that they are 'mistaken' for signals which originate, not on the stump, but from within the (nonexistent) leg itself.

Now while this, or something very like this, physiological explanation is probably true, it does not by any means imply that the pain is not exactly where the person says it is. The crucial thing to recognize is that the location of pain, and the location of the injury causing that pain, need not – and occasionally do not – coincide. The person complaining of pain in his hip, who in fact has no injury whatever to his hip but has, rather, a ruptured fifth lumbar disk, has made no mistake about the location of his *pain. The pain really is in his hip.* He and his doctor make a mistake only if they infer from the pain's being in a particular place that the injury causing that pain must also be in that same place.

So too with the case of the phantom limb. The pain, as distinct from the cause of that pain, is just where it is felt, e.g. 20 cm or so below the stump.

It is just at this point, where we say that a sufferer's pain may be 20 cm beyond the surface of his skin, that many persons will, perhaps unwittingly, suddenly switch theories about the criteria for locating pain. In cases where the pains are *within* a sufferer's body, most persons are perfectly content to use the patient's own report as to the location of the pain as being definitive. The orthopedic specialist who asks her patient to place his fingers on his pain, sees the sufferer place his fingers on his hip. The doctor does not correct her patient, saying, "No, you are wrong. The pain is really where your ruptured disk is pressing on your sciatic nerve, just about here" (placing her own fingers close to the injury) "in the spinal column." Instead she might say, "That sort of pain in your hip is caused by an injury which is actually several centimeters away from the site of the pain, here in your spinal column." None of us has any trouble understanding this distinction.

But let the location of the pain be out of one's body, let it, for example, be felt as being 20 cm below the stump of an amputation, and immediately many persons will abandon the clear knowledge that pains and their causes may be remote from one another and will revert to a radically different account of pain, one which totally blurs the distinction between pains occurring where they are felt to be and pains occurring where the injuries giving rise to them are located. Faced with the report of a patient who says that it feels to him as if he still has a leg and that there is a pain in that leg, these revisionists will argue that the person's pain simply is not where it is reported to be, but must instead be located at the site of the injury, i.e. on the stump of the amputation.

A person who, under the circumstances described, takes recourse to this latter theory has, I would strongly suggest, taken a retrograde step. To argue in the case of a phantom-limb amputee that he is mistaken as to the location of his pain challenges not just the amputee's ability to locate pain, but everyone's, amputee and non-amputee alike. If the amputee's report of the location of his pain is not to be given credence – if, that is, the actual location of his injury is to be given primacy over his report – then there is no reason not to apply the same criterion for every other report of pain as well, in the case of toothaches, spinal injuries, etc.

The revisionists' theory – that pains occur, not where they are felt to be, but rather where the injuries giving rise to them occur – thus departs flagrantly from our ordinary concept of pain. It is a proposal which sacrifices much of what we ordinarily say and think about pain for the expediency of not having to attribute pains to locations outside of bodies in the case of phantom limbs. But the price is too high. It is far preferable to allow that pains can and do occasionally occur outside of one's body (as in the case of phantom limbs) than to subscribe to the theory that in every case of referred pain we have made a mistake as to the location of the pain itself.

An orthopedic specialist still would need to know, as an aid to making her diagnosis, that it *feels* to the patient *as if* there is a pain in his hip. That crucial medical symptom does not disappear in adopting the revisionist's proposal: it simply makes its description awkward. If we were to adopt the revisionist's proposal, then where we had earlier spoken simply and directly of the 'location of the pain', we would now have to talk clumsily of 'the impression as to the location of the pain', or 'the place where the patient *reports* or *believes* the pain to be'. Far preferable, it seems to me, is to argue that the revisionist has confused two quite different things: the pain and its cause. Pains are exactly where they are felt to be: often at the site of an injury, but sometimes at another place.

If we resist the revisionist's illicit conflating of the location of pains with the location of their causes, then the phantom-limb phenomenon must count as a genuine case of an out-of-body pain. The only reasonable conclusion, it seems to me, is to insist that not only are out-of-body pains possible, they are in fact actual, i.e. they exist, in the case of phantom limbs.

But having argued that there are in fact out-of-body pains is not yet to have proved what I initially set out to establish, namely, the possibility of the existence of *public, objective* out-of-body pains. While the phantom-limb experience is, I want to urge, best regarded as being a genuine out-of-body experience, it still falls short of demonstrating the possibility of there being publicly objective, i.e. shareable, out-of-body experiences. To have proceeded this far is still only to have taken the first step along the way to the intended goal. To proceed past this point, we must now take recourse to a possible-worlds tale.

> So prodigious was his talent, so obvious was his promise, that even as a young teenager, having not yet graduated from high school, Michael Robins had been wooed by all the best music schools of the country. But there really was no choice. He had, since childhood, set his heart on studying the cello with Janos Starker, and so was quick to accept the offer from Indiana University when it came.[2] To persons unfamiliar with the school at

----

2. Just as certain novels and romances, e.g. E.L. Doctorow's *Ragtime* ([57]), are fictionalized histories through which ostensibly real persons parade, many possible-worlds tales incorporate characters and places patterned after those in the actual world. These fictive entities, e.g. Indiana University and Maestro Janos Starker in the present case, are said to be "counterparts" of the similarly named entities in the actual world. They are, however, still creatures of fiction.

Bloomington, the Midwest had seemed an odd choice. But that was only because they did not know of the visionary presidents and deans who in a labor of love, in a small town surrounded by corn fields and limestone quarries, had conceived and created one of the world's finest and largest music schools.

Michael flourished under Starker's instruction, and when he graduated, he landed the position, which had just fallen vacant, of first cellist in the recently resurrected NBC Symphony Orchestra.

His career seemed to be virtually assured, except that he had begun to experience, at first slight and then increasingly severe, pains in his right knee. X-rays and a biopsy confirmed the worst: a malignant tumor. Surgery was performed within hours, but his right leg, from mid-thigh, had to be amputated. Being a cellist, there was no question that he would be fitted, as soon as possible after the surgery, with a prosthetic leg so that he could resume playing.

For nearly two weeks after the surgery, Michael was given heavy doses of morphine to kill the pain. But as the drug was gradually withdrawn he began to experience classical phantom-limb pains. Mercifully, this new pain was not at all as debilitating as that prior to the surgery, but it was there, naggingly, nonetheless. It felt to Michael again as if there were a pain in his right knee. Of course he had no right knee, he could *see* that he had no right knee. But the pain 'knew nothing of that'. The pain *felt* as if it were in his right knee. The doctors tried to assure him that in most cases such phantom pains gradually subside, but they did warn him that he could not be absolutely assured that his pain would. In some few cases, phantom pains had been known to continue for the rest of a person's life.

A few weeks later, Michael was fitted with his first prosthesis, a mechanical affair, with a spring and hydraulic knee and a similarly contrived mechanical ankle. There was no electronic circuitry in the prosthesis and no connections whatever to either the muscles or nerves in the stump of his leg. The apparatus simply strapped onto the healing stump.

The phantom pain continued. But as he grew used to the prosthesis and would occasionally forget that he was wearing the mechanical device, he would absentmindedly lean over to rub the location of his pain in an attempt to assuage it a bit. Each time, as his fingers felt the cold plastic of the artificial leg, his hand recoiled as he discovered his 'foolish' mistake and he felt chagrined (much as does a university lecturer who, in the agonies of nicotine withdrawal, has been known to 'take a puff' from the piece of chalk in his hand).

After having worn the prosthesis for two years, Michael became quite used to the novel phenomenon of moving about the world with a pain that was 'not quite in his body'. The pain moved along with his body; but instead of being – like most persons' pains – *inside* the body of its sufferer, Michael's pain was outside his body, not terribly far removed to be sure, only 20 cm or so, but definitely outside.

There would be nothing particularly remarkable about this case were it not for what happened on the day of Michael's third annual checkup. His surgeon wanted him to try a new prosthesis. Where the original device had used stainless-steel strengtheners, this new one used carbon fiber. The new leg was attached and seemed to work perfectly. The doctor then asked Michael where the phantom pain was. Without looking, Michael reached down and tapped the knee joint and said "right here". The doctor grinned. "Mike", he said, "look what you've done. You've pointed to your old appliance, not the one you're wearing." Michael looked down, dumbfounded. He moved both mechanical legs about, first the one attached to his stump by contracting (what remained of) his thigh muscles, and then the discarded original prosthetic leg by taking it in his hands and waving it about. "I don't understand", he said. "The pain moves about as I shake the old unattached leg, not as I swing the attached leg. What's going on? The pain seems to be *in* the knee joint of the unattached prosthesis, not 20 cm below the stump of my right leg as it has been for the last three years." Panic was mounting in Michael's voice and the doctor was quick to recognize the symptoms. "Perfectly natural", he lied with all the credibility he could muster. "Here, let me give you a sedative. It will calm you down a bit." Michael did not protest.

The next few days made medical history. Michael's initial report of the incredible transference of the pain to his first artificial leg turned out to be irrefutable. In one test, Michael was blindfolded and the old prosthesis was moved silently about the room. Michael could unfailingly point to the pain and correctly judge how far it was from him.

But still stranger developments were in store. One of the

researchers working with Michael's surgeon wondered what would happen if another person were to wear Michael's first prosthesis, the one in which Michael's pain seemed now to be housed. Another amputee, who had never experienced a phantom pain, was fitted with the leg. Within eight hours, he too was complaining of a phantom pain: a pain, that is, several centimeters below his stump, as if he had a leg and there was a pain in it. The prosthesis was immediately removed, but it was too late. The pain did not subside, it simply moved farther away, as the prosthesis itself was moved about. Now there were two patients feeling the identical out-of-body pain! (The hospital administrators began to have visions of a malpractice suit.)

Obviously, research would have to proceed cautiously. Since the pain was not terribly severe, it was agreed to use paid, informed volunteers, explaining carefully to them that they might be left with a permanent out-of-body pain. Most interviewees were repulsed by the prospect, but a few were so intrigued that, in spite of the dangers, they actually begged to participate in this historical experiment. They gladly signed the necessary waivers absolving the researchers and the hospital of any legal liability. One even made a sizable donation to the hospital.

The experiment lasted for years. Every precaution imaginable was taken. Elaborate measures were instituted to prevent cheating or fraud. In due course, it was discovered that one did not have to be an amputee to experience the effect. Merely strapping the artificial leg to one's own good leg for twelve or more hours would induce the remarkable phenomenon. The subjects in the experiment were thereafter able to sense the pain even when the leg was removed out of sight to other rooms; indeed, the pain could be felt at distances of up to 150 km, well beyond the visual horizon. Ultrasophisticated electrograms revealed that there was spinal-cord and brain activity associated with this pain sensation but there were no particular afferent signals originating in the peripheral nervous system, i.e. the nervous activity giving rise to the sensing of 'distant pain' (as it had come to be called) appeared to originate directly within the spinal column itself. All the standard analgesics – morphine, acupuncture, etc. – remained as effective in alleviating distant pain as they were for ordinary in-body pain.

Many skeptics believed that the phenomenon of distant pain

was a case of mind-reading, mass hysteria, or some such thing; but a few of them volunteered for the experiment and, without exception, every one reported that he felt the pain in the artificial limb and that so far as he could tell he was not reading anybody else's mind. Eventually, some 237 different persons could all together feel the same pain, in the same place.

In fact, it was because of the great number of persons all sharing the same pain that the experiment was eventually stopped. Several of these subjects had increasingly, over the years, grown annoyed at feeling a distant pain which moved about from time to time. As long as the mechanical leg was left in one spot, the pain was so constant as to hardly intrude upon their consciousnesses. But when the leg was moved about, in being fitted to a new subject, etc., the movement proved distracting to many of the previous subjects. Eventually several of them who lived within the critical 150-km radius of the research center protested the continued activity so vigorously that the matter was put to a mail vote. Over two-thirds of the affected subjects responded, and of them, more than 80% requested that the leg be retired. Michael's surgeon then donated the leg to his alma mater, the Harvard Medical School, where it may now be viewed in a sealed display case. No one, it is reassuring to mention, has ever experienced an out-of-body pain from merely looking at the leg.

Controversy over how to explain the phenomenon swirled for a generation. But the account which gradually seemed to win favor was that somehow (no one offered an explanation of this particular part of the phenomenon) Michael Robins had, quite unintentionally, managed to 'project' (or 'displace' [there really never was a very good word to describe such an unparalleled occurrence]) his pain into his first prosthesis. The pain was really 'there' *in the prosthesis*: it could be felt – and indeed would continue to be felt – by anyone who was keen (or fool) enough to strap it tightly onto, or alongside, his own leg for a half-day or more.

As the extraordinary discovery became widely known (*New England Journal of Medicine*, *Lancet*, etc.), was discussed in medical and psychology textbooks, and was the subject of several science programs on television ("Nova", "National Geographic", "The Nature of Things", etc.), a gradual broadening took place in popular thinking about pain. No one ceased to regard pains as sensations; but what did change was that people now began to talk easily and matter-of-factly about the possibility of pain sensations occurring not only within one's own body, but also in external objects where they might even be experienced (shared) by two or more persons. And when they came across early-twentieth-century philosophy texts which denied the logical possibility of pains being shared or being external to one's body, many of them thought it odd that any writer should have had such a blinkered conception. But, of course, persons who adopted this uncharitable view of their predecessors had not placed the earlier views in their historical context. Would they, themselves, have had a view much different from the earlier one if they had not witnessed for themselves the extraordinary events in Michael Robins's life?

There is, so far as I can tell, nothing logically incoherent in this possible-worlds story. It is, granted, wildly implausible. Indeed, I am certain that nothing like this is likely to occur in this world. But foretelling the future was not the point of the tale. The point of telling the tale was to see whether one could, without logical self-contradiction, describe a case of a public, objective, out-of-body pain. I submit that I have done this. If so, then we may conclude that it is no part of the *concept* of pain that pains *must* be private, internal sensations.

Certain philosophers will sometimes object to exercises such as the one just gone through here, by protesting that the results are 'linguistically deviant'. They might put their objection by saying, "You cannot say such things." By this they mean, not to deny that one can utter certain sentences, but that if one does, then one speaks nonsense. "No meaning has been given in ordinary English", they might say, "to an expression such as 'a publicly sensed pain in a nonliving physical object'." My reply is: The possible-worlds tale, once told, explains how the notion might apply, and thus succeeds – if there had not been an intelligible sense previously – in giving us that sense. If the notion was 'linguistically deviant', then it is no longer; if "public, objective pain" has heretofore lacked a sense, then it has one now. A concept need not apply to anything actual to be intelligible. There may never have been any unicorns, but the concept of *unicorn* is intelligible; there may never be any public, objective pains, but the concept of a *public, objective pain* is perfectly intelligible.

7.2   Case study: Unfelt pains

The sensing of pains (e.g. headaches) is usually regarded as quite unlike the sensing of 'external' objects (e.g. tables and chairs). External objects, we usually think, are not dependent upon our experiencing them for their existence: they can – and usually do – exist without our experiencing them. But pains are usually thought to be different sorts of things. Pains are thought to exist only insofar as they are experienced. A pain must be someone or other's pain; there are no such things as 'free floating', unexperienced pains, in the way, for example, a chair may exist without being experienced. To account for this alleged difference, some philosophers adopt different theories of perception for external physical objects (e.g. tables and chairs), on the one hand, and internal 'feelings' (e.g. headaches, ennui, anxiety, euphoria, fear), on the other. For the first kind of experience, they will adopt what is called an "act/object" or "relational" theory of experience. The experiencer is regarded as being in a perceptual relationship with a certain kind of 'object'.[3] For the second kind of experience, they will adopt what is called an "adverbial" theory of experience. On this latter account, the experiencer is not aware of an 'object', but is having a certain kind of sensation. Pain, for example, on this account is regarded not as the object of an act of sensing, but is regarded as sensing *in a certain way*.

These two theories are not so much competing theories as they are complementary. They are designed to account for different *kinds* of experience. And it is thus possible for a person to subscribe to both of these theories without inconsistency.

But how viable is the alleged distinction which prompts the creating of the relational and the adverbial theories of experience? Is there something about the 'felt aspect' (the phenomenology*) of sensing colors, for example, which is different from the 'felt aspect' of having a pain, a difference which warrants our creating, and subscribing to, two different theories of experience? If the difference is not to be accounted for by anything inherent in the nature of the sensations themselves, then might it be something we learn, through science, about the nature of this world?

---

3. We will here ignore the various versions of this first theory. We will ignore, for example, whether the 'objects' of perception are physical objects or what some philosophers have called "sense-data" or "sensa".

Two thousand years ago, Plato created one of the most enduring possible-worlds tales, his famous "Allegory of the Cave" ([156], book VII). He asked us to imagine persons growing up, chained in a dark cave so that they could see only straight ahead. On the wall in front of them were the shadows of moving objects which themselves were out of sight. (A modern version would be a person in a movie theater who is restrained so as to be able to see only the images on the screen and nothing more.) In particular, the chained person is unable to move about, to touch any of the things he sees. He can talk to other persons who are similarly chained, but none of them can see or touch one another. Plato's purpose in telling this particular possible-worlds tale (what he called an "allegory" or a "parable") was to argue that ordinary perception stands to reality as shadows do to the objects which cast them. I want to make quite another use of his story.

There are, to be sure, profound problems with the story as originally told. Putting aside questions of the unethicalness of chaining innocent persons in such abominable conditions, it is very unlikely that persons who are raised from childhood prevented from moving about and examining physical things ever could learn a language. Persons raised in Plato's cave would be worse off than feral children, i.e. children raised not by human beings but by animals. Such children do not acquire language ([77], 246-8). But we will ignore these complications and pretend that the chained prisoners can see, talk, and hear, and that they occasionally feel pain, anxiety, hunger, and the like. What would they make of such sensations? In particular, would they have any reason to think that visual sensations and auditory sensations, for example, were any more like one another than either was like the sensations of pain and hunger?[4] In not being able to explore

---

4. Jean-Paul Sartre (1905-80) writes: "... if I hear voices, what proof is there that they come from heaven and not from hell, or from the subconscious, or a pathological condition? What proves that they are addressed to me? ... If a voice addresses me, it is always for me to decide that this is the angel's voice" ([185], 19-20). Sartre's pre-eminent concern is our ability, indeed our being condemned, to make choices. That overweening interest sometimes makes Sartre overlook some very obvious distinctions. Under certain circumstances it might be *rational* to attribute a voice to another person, or to an angel, or to the effects of a drug, etc. Perhaps for dramatic purpose in this passage Sartre has suppressed these distinctions; but surely they matter. How *do* we go about sorting out the origins of the voices we hear? Only by being able to interact physically with other persons and with material objects. When

the world, they would have no warrant whatever for associating their visual sensations with images on a distant wall or their auditory sensations with vibrations in the larynxes of other human beings. Would they have any reason, then, to believe that these visual and auditory sensations were of external objects, while pain and hunger were not?

Under the circumstances described, there would seem to be no grounds whatsoever to prompt the distinction between 'internal' and 'external': sensations would simply exist and that would be the end of it. Why should they attribute to other persons the 'voices' which answer their questions? These 'voices' just appear in their auditory spaces, just as hunger pangs occur from time to time in their gustatory spaces, and colors in their visual spaces.[5] Without being able to move about the world, they would regard all sensations on an equal footing in that their sensations would flit in and out of consciousness. Colors would be different from sounds, both would differ from smells, and all would differ from pains. But other than the fact that colors, smells, sounds, and pains would all form distinct categories, there would be no grounds on which to regard any of them as 'internal' or any as 'external'.

If a conclusion can be drawn from our use of Plato's myth, it would be that there is nothing inherent or intrinsic in the having of a sensation which marks it as 'external' or 'internal', as being better explained by a relational theory of experience than by an adverbial theory. Why we treat colors and sounds as 'objects' and pains as 'manners of sensation' has to do, not with the phenomenology of these sensations, but with certain empirical facts we discover about this world. We discover empirically – experimentally and not introspectively – that other persons share our visual sensations but do not share our pain sensations.

A.J. Ayer put the point this way, in his own possible-worlds tale:

   Suppose, for example, that people's feelings were very much

---

the latter opportunities are denied to us, then – and only then – might our decision as to the cause of the voice come down to a matter of 'choice'. For ordinary circumstances, Sartre has considerably overstated the role of choice. But for Plato's cave, where the denizens are physically restrained and unable to probe their environment, something like Sartre's (arbitrary) choice is their only recourse.

5. We will have more to say of this use of "space" in the next chapter.

more uniform than they actually are, so that whenever anyone felt bored, or happy or angry, or depressed, his neighbours nearly always felt the same. In that case, we might very well find use for saying that there was not a multiplicity of feelings, one to each person, but a single feeling, one and the same for all, which different people experienced in different ways. Certain people might fail to experience it at all, just as certain people fail to perceive physical objects which are in their neighbourhood. There might be illusions of feeling, corresponding to illusions of perception. But the feeling would still be there, just as the physical object is there whatever illusion someone may be having. To make the analogy with physical objects closer still, one might make it possible [by telling a possible-worlds tale] for feelings to exist when no one was actually feeling them. This might be said in cases where the normal conditions in which the feeling habitually occurred were present, but some special factor, such as the drugging or hypnotizing of the person in question, intervened. ...

The point of this fantasy is to show how *the distinction between what is public and what is private depends upon a contingent matter of fact*. We do not find it useful to publicize [i.e. regard as being public] feelings, or sensations, or thoughts, or images, because they vary so much from person to person: we do find it useful to publicize physical objects because of the extent to which the perceptions of different people agree. But it is not difficult to imagine that the two should be on a level, or even that the position should be reversed. ([18], 201-2; italics added)

For Ayer, what makes for the 'internality' of pains and the 'externality' of tables and chairs is something we discover, not by examining our own pain sensations, our own visual sensations, our own tactile sensations, etc., but by examining the world and the reports of other persons.

For Ayer, it is a contingent fact about this world, nothing inherent in the nature of pain sensation itself, that pains are not public objects like tables and chairs, and that pains do not exist unperceived. Ayer is quite prepared to allow (as I have argued in section 7.1) that pains could be public, shareable sensations. And Ayer goes one step further. He suggests that, were the world a certain way, we would want to acknowledge the existence of unperceived pains. If a pain can be experienced by several persons (again, see section 7.1), then were one of those persons to be shielded from the pain, by medication, hypnosis, etc., the situation would be perfectly analogous to a person's being shielded from perceiving a physical object by, e.g., blindfolding him or erecting a wall across his field of view. Just as the obscured physical object would still be regarded as existing, although not perceived, so too would it be reasonable to regard the pain as still existing although it, too, was not being perceived.

In short, unfelt pains are no logical impossibility. That they do not exist is an empirical discovery we have made about this particular world. There is nothing inherent in the concept of pain, or in the sensation of pain, to preclude public, shareable pains, pains which can exist without being felt by anyone. The alleged differences which have prompted the creating of two side-by-side theories of experience, the relational and the adverbial theories, are differences which are not inherent in the nature of sensation itself but only in empirical facts we have discovered about other persons.

7.3   Case study: Pains in the absence of nervous systems

In this last century, we have learned enough about neurophysiology to be able to say confidently that our pains are, with virtual certainty, attributable to chemical and electrical activity (i.e. certain specific physical 'goings-on') in specific substructures of our central nervous systems. Even in cases of so-called psychosomatic pains, we have good reason to believe that often, if not always, such pains are, again, attributable to physical goings-on, although, unlike the cases of physical injuries and trauma, not originating in lesions, bruises, infections, etc. In short, we are much inclined – being knowledgeable of some of the data of modern medical research – to attribute the sensing of pains to physical activity in our bodies.

The possible-worlds tale of section 7.1 – which told of the sensing of an out-of-body pain (the strange affair of Michael Robins and others) – still capitalized upon, indeed invoked, the very account being reviewed here. Although the 'initiating cause' of the distant pain was not the firing of the sensitive ending of a peripheral nerve, the pain sensed did come about because of certain activity in the spinal cord and the brain. To that degree, that tale did not depart from contemporary scientific accounts.

Nevertheless, in spite of this familiar scientific background, I want to insist upon a *conceptual* distinction between pains or, better, 'the felt aspect of pains' and their physical origins. This particular distinction, between pains (or the felt aspect of pains) and their specific physical origins in the central nervous system, is one of the most troublesome for some persons to grasp, and takes us right to the heart of one of the most difficult and controversial distinctions in philosophy, one which some writers insist upon and which others reject.

Suppose, as I am perfectly willing to concede as being highly probable, that all pains without exception are attributable to certain kinds of physical goings-on in a living creature, and suppose, further, that whenever there is an occasion (episode) of such physical goings-on there is a felt pain. At least two theories, as we have earlier seen, have been proposed to explain such correlations: either the pain literally *is* the physical goings-on themselves (this is part of the so-called identity theory of mind and brain) or the pain is *caused by* the physical goings-on (the so-called causal theory). But whichever of these theories we might want eventually to settle upon, I would still want to insist upon the *conceptual* difference between one's pains and physical goings-on in one's body.

Now this latter claim – that pains are conceptually distinct from the states of the central nervous system which 'account for' the presence of those pains – is bound to strike some persons as particularly strange. For how can I, on the one hand, allow that pains might literally *be* physical goings-on and yet, on the other hand, insist on the *conceptual* difference between pains and physical events or states? It all depends, of course, on what exactly is meant by 'a conceptual distinction'.

In the analysis I have been proposing, two concepts are distinct if, for each of them, it is *logically possible* for there to be a situation (thing, event, state, etc.) to which that concept applies and not the other one. According to this analysis, then, one can say that there is a conceptual distinction between having a pain and having the brain-state which 'gives rise to' (or even 'is' that very pain), if it is *logically possible* to apply the one concept to an organism and not the other.

But as so often happens in philosophy, we have answered one question only in turn to have prompted another. For now the question arises, "How shall we tell when attributing one concept to a thing while withholding another is logically possible?" We can of course *say* such a thing as "He is in pain, but nothing is happening to him physically to account for that pain", but we also know that it is possible to say things which (if taken literally) describe logically impossible situations, e.g. "He traveled across town in an empty taxi" or

"Her elder brother is an only child." Being able to *say* something does not make what is said logically possible. The test for logical possibility must be something else.

Again, we invoke the technique of constructing a possible-worlds tale. To show that there is a conceptual difference between the two concepts, we might attempt not just to utter a single sentence or two, but to fill in details, to tell a more robust tale, in which it is appropriate to apply one of the two concepts to the situation and explicitly withhold the other. If this can be done *without contradiction*, then this may be taken as evidence that the two concepts are – after all – distinct.

Thus, in the case of pain, if we want to argue for the *conceptual* difference between pains and physical goings-on in a central nervous system, we might try to construct a possible-worlds tale in which creatures experienced pain but in which those same creatures did not have the physical goings-on that are usual when you and I feel pain. Here is such a tale.

> Once upon a time there was a universe in which there was a planet, Htraenon, very like Earth in certain respects but very unlike it in others. Outwardly its creatures resembled those of Earth remarkably, but internally they were surprisingly different. The 'human beings' of that planet looked pretty much as human beings do on Earth: each had a head, two eyes, two ears, a nose, a mouth, two arms, a torso, two legs, ten fingers, and ten toes. By our own standards, we would consider all of them extremely good-looking. Their social life was much like ours as well: they laughed, told jokes, complimented one another, prayed, sang songs, elected officials, instituted moral codes, educated their children, exchanged goods and services for money, and occasionally indulged in metaphysical speculations. They were also subject to many of the same sorts of ailments and frailties that befall the likes of you and me. They had illnesses, they suffered occasional pains, they sought medical treatment, they grew old, and each of them eventually died. But in one respect they were very different from us.
>
> Up until about the time they began to use microscopes and electronic devices in medicine, their history and science were unfolding in a parallel fashion to our own. But once they began to examine the internal functionings of their own bodies, using devices much more sensitive than their own eyes and ears,

they discovered a physiology which is remarkably different from yours and mine. For one thing, they had no central nervous system. It is not that they failed to find such a thing. It went beyond that: they really had no central nervous system at all. Now failing to find a central nervous system did not surprise them in the slightest. After all, they had had no reason to hypothesize, and even less reason to believe, that such a thing existed. They had no beliefs attributing their pains to specific goings-on in a central nervous system, no more so than they had beliefs at the beginning of their modern period of chemistry about glands in their bodies releasing hormones to regulate, for example, the level of glucose in their bloodstreams.

In time, as their science grew in sophistication and they continued to perform physiological, chemical, and microscopic examinations of their own bodies, they discovered within themselves a hormonal system, came to understand its regulatory functions, and even managed to synthesize all of these hormones in their pharmaceutical laboratories. But they never made comparable discoveries about a central nervous system, and this for the aforementioned reason that they did not have a central nervous system. Thus, it was inevitable that these people simply persisted with their timeworn theory that pains, thoughts, musings, etc. were somehow features or characteristics of themselves, but did not think it necessary, or warranted, to attribute them to any particular physical goings-on in their bodies.

When, in due course, several centuries later, scientists from a distant galaxy arrived on Htraenon for the first time and discovered that the Htraenonites had no central nervous systems, they were initially dumbfounded. But soon, the incredulity of the visiting scientists crumbled. After only a few weeks adjusting to such an unexpected jolt to their beliefs about the physiology of sensations, most of these latter scientists found themselves working handily with the idea that some creatures (themselves, for example) feel pain as a result of certain goings-on in their central nervous systems, but that other creatures (e.g. the Htraenonites) feel pain without, so far as could be ascertained, anything in particular happening within their bodies, besides the injuries themselves, which could be correlated with those sensations.

Although the world just described is merely a possible world, i.e. is not this, the actual world, it is meant to mirror the history of the actual world up to the point in our own history when we began to discover the existence of, and the secrets of the functioning of, the central nervous system. Until that point in our own history, we (actual) human beings did not associate pains with goings-on in a central nervous system. So ignorant were our forebears of the existence and operations of the central nervous system that we find in Aristotle, for example, the perfectly serious hypothesis that the brain was nothing more than an organ to 'cool the blood'. Aristotle knew nothing, nor could he have, of the manner of connection of certain sensory organs, e.g. of touch and taste, with the brain. And thus he thought it demonstrable that the brain was *not* involved in sensation: "This brain ... has a character peculiar to itself, as might indeed be expected. That it has no continuity with the organs of sense is plain from simple inspection, and is more clearly shown by the fact, that, when it is touched, no sensation is produced. ([12], book II, 652b1-10) ... Nature has contrived the brain as a counterpoise to the region of the heart with its contained heat, and has given it to animals to moderate the latter ... The brain, then, tempers the heat and seething of the heart" (652b20-7).

Did Aristotle – knowing nothing of modern neurophysiology – have a concept of *pain* different from ours? Certainly we may suppose that he, like us, had experienced pains. He, doubtless, from time to time, had pricked his finger, cut his hand, stubbed his toe, suffered a toothache, and endured a headache. He was, we may be sure, familiar with pain in many of its forms. But he knew nothing of peripheral nerves, of Ad- and C-fibers, of electrical pathways in the spinal cord, of the firing of nerve cells, or even for that matter, of the existence of nerve cells. As a matter of fact, he did not even have the concept of *nerve*, of *cell*, of *electricity*, of *endorphin*, etc. Could he, then, have had *our* concept of pain? I want to suggest that he did, that he could have understood, as well as any of us, claims about persons being in pain, about certain pains being more intense than others, about certain medications' ability to relieve pain, about most persons trying to avoid pain, etc. All he would lack is a twentieth-century scientific explanation of the physiology of pain. But that information ought not, I suggest, to be regarded as part of the *concept* of pain itself. Scientists, as they pursue neurophysiology, are not refining the concept of *pain*, but are furthering our knowledge of pain, its causes, and its relief.

7.4   Case study: Must pains hurt?

Squares have four sides; the edible parts of pineapples are yellow. But whereas it is part of what we have called the "narrow" analysis (i.e. it is *analytic*) of the concept of *square* that squares have four sides, it is not part of the analysis of the concept of *pineapple* that the edible parts of pineapples are yellow. After all, cabbages may be white or purple; ripe apples may be red, yellow, or green; grapefruits may be white or pink; etc. In this age of hybrid fruits and vegetables, we have grown used to the appearance on grocers' shelves of produce in an ever-increasing variety of colors. To date, all the pineapples on the market have yellow flesh, but few of us would be unduly surprised to discover one day a product identical to present-day pineapples but which differed in hue, being orange or pink perhaps. Given how we have handled analogous cases in the past, we probably would not in the slightest be tempted to argue that these orange-colored fruits were not pineapples; we would simply allow that pineapples could come in more than one color.

Insofar as it is analytic of the concept *square* that all squares have four sides, it is impossible to tell a possible-worlds tale, without contradiction, in which there are squares having other than four sides, e.g. five sides. But insofar as being yellow is *not* analytic of the concept *pineapple*, it is perfectly possible – as I have just done in previewing a possible future state of this very universe – to describe without internal contradiction a situation in which there are non-yellow (orange perhaps) pineapples.

What about pain? Is *being hurtful* or *causing hurt* analytic of the concept of *pain*? Would a sensation even be describable as pain if it did not hurt? Is a non-hurtful pain logically impossible in the way, for example, a five-sided square would be? Or, is a non-hurtful pain rather more like an orange-colored pineapple – unusual to say the least, perhaps never even part of one's own experience, but logically possible nonetheless? Once again we take recourse to telling a possible-worlds tale, this time in an attempt to describe a pain which does not hurt.

> Mr. J.R. had very advanced cancer of the neck and jaw. When pain became unbearable despite huge doses of narcotics, a frontal lobotomy was discussed with his family and finally performed in an effort to make his last few months comfortable. Under local anesthesia, small drill holes were made in the skull

over the frontal lobes, and *the fibers connecting the frontal cortex with the thalamus were severed on both sides by an instrument lowered into the brain.* For several days after the operation he was sleepy and confused, did not know where he was, and had trouble recognizing his family. This cleared, however, and he seemed cheerful and alert. *He did not complain of pain and stopped asking for pain medication, but when asked if he still had pain he said, "Of course I do, it's the cancer, right here", pointing to his diseased jaw.* Examination revealed his perception of temperature and pin [pricking] to be acute – he actually "jumped" [in response] to the pin prick, and complained of being "tortured", something he had never said before.

Most [similarly treated, i.e. lobotomized] patients said, unemotionally, that pressure on the tumor was still painful but they were obviously not disturbed by the pain. There was a chasm between the affective emotional aspect of pain [i.e. its hurting] and the pure sensation of pain.

The sensory and emotional aspects of pain can [also] be dissociated [from one another] by certain drugs. For example, high doses of antianxiety agents such as certain tranquilizers do not seriously impair discrimination between stimuli ranging from painless to extremely painful. However, even though subjects may report certain stimuli as being excruciatingly painful they do not seem to care. The drug appears to leave the sensory aspects of pain intact, while almost completely suppressing the emotional aspects.

Is such a tale really possible? Is it really possible – as this tale alleges – to feel a pain *and* yet not have it hurt? It turns out that it *is* possible, indeed that it can be proven to be possible. And it can be proven in the strongest fashion in which we can prove anything possible: by showing that the alleged possibility is *actual*.

The possible-worlds tale just told – of patients who could feel pain but who experienced no hurt – is not the product of a philosopher's imagination as were the tales of the three preceding sections, but is compiled from actual clinical studies.[6] This assembled story is, of

---

6. The first of the three paragraphs indented just above is a direct quotation from *Basic Human Neurophysiology*, by Lindsley and Holmes ([123], 117); the second, from *The Nervous System*, by Peter Nathan ([142], 105); and the

course, still a possible-worlds tale. Its only difference from the usual possible-worlds tales of philosophical texts is that this one happens to be *true* (i.e. is true not just in some other possible worlds, but is true in this, the actual world, as well).

Someone might object: "Pains which do not hurt are a logical impossibility. There cannot be, in this world or any other, pains which do not hurt. The patients who described themselves as feeling pains which did not hurt had *mis*described the situation. They certainly had some sensation; but just insofar as it did not hurt, then it was not pain. Perhaps we currently lack a term for such sensations in our language, the phenomenon being so rare. Nonetheless, such sensations cannot be described as pains. Whether we have a name for them or not, they must be regarded as something other than pains."

The possible-worlds tale just told, then, will not be convincing to everyone. As we can see, it is possible for someone to reject the apparent conclusion of such a tale by arguing that the persons in the tale are misdescribing their sensations. How, now, can we possibly resolve this latter debate? The possible-worlds tale may at first seem convincing to some persons (it is to me, for one), but others can – if they are inclined – find grounds to reject it.

At this point we must be very careful not to think that there is some one 'right' or 'wrong' answer to the question. There would be only if there were some *independent* way, other than our agreeing to use a concept in a certain way, to ascertain when a concept is used correctly or incorrectly. But there is no such way. Our concepts are our own inventions. We do not discover them. If concepts were not of our making, but the sorts of things we could examine to see what is 'really' entailed by them and what not, then we could – theoretically – discover, for example, that we have had the concept of *square* wrong all these many years. We had thought that all squares are four-sided, but having now examined the concept of square we see that we had made a mistake: squares may have either five or eleven sides. It is clear that such a notion would be nonsense. There is no such independent concept of *square* that, if we are careful and attentive, some of us will get right, but if we are careless, all of us might get wrong. It is impossible for *everyone* to have a mistaken notion of *square*.

The question boils down to this. Virtually any pain any of us has

---

third, from *The Neurosciences and Behaviour*, by Atrens and Curthoys ([14], 93).

ever felt has hurt. Is the hurting to be identified with the pain – in the sense that nothing logically could be a pain if it did not hurt – or might – given the pressures of certain kinds of peculiar circumstances – we want to allow that not all pains hurt?

The cancer sufferers who underwent the frontal lobotomies outlined above described their sensations, at the sites where they formerly had pain, as still being pain. The difference, they alleged, was not in their ceasing to feel pain but in that pain's no longer hurting.

The concept of *pain*, like so many other concepts – e.g. of *person*, of *fairness*, of *duty*, of *consciousness* – is in a state of flux. If we are to judge by the on-the-spot linguistic behavior of medical patients and medical practitioners who are involved with the amelioration of pain, all the indicators are that our language is evolving toward making a distinction between sensing a pain and experiencing hurt. The two concepts are coming apart. If, someday, a safe medication is developed which – unlike the opiates, which suppress the sensation of pain altogether – acts like the chemical equivalent of a frontal lobotomy or like a massive dose of certain tranquilizers in that it (here I must use current terminology) suppresses not the pain, but only the accompanying feeling of hurt, we will be hastened toward making a sharp distinction between the two concepts. It may even happen that persons in the future will wonder how it was that we ever confused the two, so used will they have become to taking a tablet when they have a headache to relieve, not the pain, but the hurt.

What, then, shall we finally conclude? Does the concept of *pain* include the concept of *hurting*? I think the answer must be something like this. So frequently are pains accompanied by hurting that we invariably tend to conflate the two concepts. Even so, they can (in my opinion), reasonably, be regarded as logically, or conceptually, distinct. And given certain as yet unrealized developments in medical research, we would in time virtually be forced to use these concepts separately. We have enough empirical data now in hand to suggest that our language just might evolve in that direction. We cannot foretell with any certainty that it will, however. From a philosophical point of view, all we can do is to prepare ourselves for that eventuality.[7] We must be sufficiently flexible in using our concepts so that

---

7. "When the hypothetical upheaval is sufficiently radical we have to go through the agonizingly innovative process of rebuilding part of our conceptual scheme from the ground up. Genuine conceptual innovation is necessary

we are prepared for the kind of intellectual reorientation that might be required.

Summary of sections 7.1-7.4: For the purposes of illustrating one way in which philosophers probe concepts, I have subjected the concept of *pain* to analysis by invoking it in a number of possible-worlds tales in which some quite extraordinary situations have been described. I have tried to show four things: that although pains typically occur within our skins, that although all pains are felt, that although pains typically are the product of nervous systems, and that although pains typically hurt, none of these features is logically entailed by the concept of *pain*. It is possible, I have tried to show, that pains could (logically speaking) occur outside our skins, and even for that matter might be public in the way in which tables, sounds, and aromas are public, more particularly, might exist unperceived; that pains could (logically speaking) occur in creatures which lacked central nervous systems; and that, finally, pains could (logically speaking) occur without a sensation of accompanying hurt. My expectation is that of the several things being claimed, the last – that pains could occur without there being a sensation of hurt – will be the most difficult for many readers to accept. And yet, of the several, it is the one for which there is the best empirical evidence.

The *point* of pursuing such exercises is threefold. First and foremost, some persons find such conceptual explorations fascinating. For such persons, that alone merits the pursuit. The second justification lies in the sharpening of our conceptual tools. Only in understanding what is and what is not entailed by our concepts can we aspire to use them well. If we are going to think, then our thinking cannot be any better than the tools we use. If the tools are dull, the product will be rough and crude. If the tools are well made, and their interrelations understood, then at least we have a chance of making something beautiful and useful with them. We can no more do philosophy well without critically examining our concepts than we could do genetics without a microscope or physics without mathematics.

The third point of the exercise is to unfetter our imaginations. In

---

and there is no way of predicting its outcome. To the question 'What would you say if ...?' we would in such cases have to reply: 'We just wouldn't know what to say ... We'll just have to cross that bridge when we get there'" (Rescher [169], 114).

arguing that certain concepts are not essential to the concept of pain, I have been attempting to *enlarge* the possible application of the concept. By peeling away inessentials, I have tried, not to narrow our concept of *pain*, but to stretch it. Although pains typically, perhaps always, occur within the bodies of creatures having nervous systems, and although pains usually hurt, might we not want to consider the possibility of pains outside of bodies, in things quite unlike us in structure, and unaccompanied by hurt? Only in imagining possibilities beyond the commonplace have we any hope of understanding this world. For understanding this universe (or any other one) consists in large measure in seeing the difference between what *might be*, what *is*, and what *must be*.

CHAPTER EIGHT

Space and time

> In our conversation, no word is more familiarly used or more easily recognized than "time". We certainly understand what is meant by the word both when we use it ourselves and when we hear it used by others.
>
> What, then, is time? I know well enough what it is, provided that nobody asks me; but if I am asked what it is and try to explain, I am baffled. – St Augustine (AD 354-430), *Confessions* ([15], 264)

Augustine's dilemma is one all of us have experienced frequently in our lives, not only about time, but space, morality, justice, education, art, etc. We are perfectly capable of *using* these concepts in our ordinary affairs; but we seem unable to give an explication, or – better – a theoretical reconstruction, of these concepts. All of us understand the concept of time well enough to schedule meetings, to set alarm clocks, to time a cake's baking, and the like. But if asked "What is time?", most persons – like Augustine – would not know how to answer.

8.1 Is it possible to explain what space and time are?

Time and again when I was a student in public school, my teachers solemnly insisted: "In spite of everything we know about electricity, we do not know what electricity *is*." This verdict about electricity can be found, too, in many textbooks of the period. To use Popper's phrase (he was speaking of objections to Einstein's relativity theories; [159], 34), this was – in the end – just a piece of "popular nonsense".

What made that slogan nonsense stemmed from a certain presupposition that prompted it. When asked to explain what it meant to say "We do not know what electricity *is*", my teachers would often reply with something of the sort, "We know that electrical phenomena arise out of the movement of charged particles, and we know many of the physical laws involved, but however much knowledge we gain of this sort, it will never tell us what electricity *is*." I have no doubt that my teachers were well-intentioned, that they honestly believed that this was a legitimate thing to say and to impart to their students. But in the end, it is nonsense nonetheless.

It is nonsense because as a general principle it would deny that we know of anything at all what it *is*. There is nothing special in this regard about electricity. What my teachers alleged to be a peculiar problem with electricity could just as well have been said about glass, the wind, your nose, profit, or freedom. And quite contrary to their argument, we know what things are precisely by knowing what their makeup is, what sorts of physical laws describe their behavior, how they typically act, and how we make use of them. We know, for example, a great deal about the wind. We understand that the wind is not the exhalation of a god but is movement within the atmosphere in which we live. We have learned, too, that air is made up of a mixture of various gases, that air moves because of differential heating (due to the Sun's heat, ocean currents, concentrated burning of fossil fuels, etc.) and because of the Coriolis force (due to the rotation of the Earth), and that air may move in laminar or turbulent ways. And we have learned, over a period of centuries by trial and error and more recently with the greater efficiency conferred by having mathematical theories of gas dynamics, to harness the wind (in windmills, for example). Once we know these sorts of things, even if our knowledge is incomplete, even if, for example, we cannot predict or explain the behavior of the wind as precisely as we might like, we know what the wind *is*. And the same may be said for electricity: once we know the atomic nature of electrical phenomena, have discovered a great many of the physical laws of those phenomena, have harnessed electricity in our generators, machines, radios, computers, and the like, we may perfectly reasonably say, "For the most part, we know what electricity is." Of course we cannot sum up this extensive knowledge in a brief paragraph. A good understanding of electricity comes about only after several weeks or months of study. But it is something attainable with effort. It is certainly nothing unknowable *in principle*.

The moral should also be applied for space and for time. Just as in the case of electricity, many persons have, like Augustine, convinced themselves that there is something deeply mysterious about space and time and that space and time are so inscrutable as to be *unknowable*. "In spite of everything we know about space and time, we really do not know what space and time *are*", I think many persons are inclined to think to themselves. Certainly there are problems about space and time, but the pessimistic belief that space and time are somehow so enigmatic as to be fundamentally unknowable strikes me as a piece of popular nonsense which ought to be excised just like the nonsense about electricity.

What does coming to know what space and time *are* consist in? The answer, I suggest, is perfectly straightforward: it consists, simply, in our having an account which is, first of all, free of internal inconsistency, and, secondly, robust enough both to make sense of our ordinary uses of these concepts and to allow us to do physics. Common, everyday notions of space and time, as Augustine noted sixteen centuries ago, are in quite good enough shape for ordinary affairs. But they are not in particularly good shape for sophisticated thinking about the universe writ large.

Buber, we have earlier seen, had tried to imagine an edge of space and a beginning and end to time and found that he was unable to imagine that there could *be* such things *and* (unfortunately for him) was unable to imagine that there could *not* be such things. Recall (from p. 10 above): "A necessity I could not understand swept over me: I had to try again and again to imagine the edge of space, or its edgelessness, time with a beginning and an end or a time without beginning or end, and both were equally impossible, equally hopeless – yet there seemed to be only the choice between the one or the other absurdity" ([37], 135-6).

In this passage, Buber, writing years later, correctly – but unwittingly – diagnoses the source of the problem: the very ideas at play are 'absurd'. But he never clearly plumbed the absurdity, either as a teenager or as a mature philosopher relating his youthful experience.

The source of Buber's difficulty is an untenable concept of space. It is deeply and irremediably flawed, for it leads, as we see explicitly in Buber's narrative, to incoherence. In Kant's terminology, this particular concept of space was beset by 'antinomies'. In modern terminology we would deem it 'paradoxical'.

Leibniz, in contrast, had a significantly different concept of space. In spite of certain difficulties[1] in his theory of space, I am tempted to say that in the fundamental insight which informed his theory, Leibniz

---

1. For instance, Leibniz denied both that spatial relations are 'real' and that a vacuum is a possibility. Both of these claims are, however, peripheral to his main thesis, and I wish only to pursue his main thesis.

'got it right'. However, if I were to put my praise in just that way, I would undercut what I said earlier about philosophical reconstructions, viz. that they cannot be judged to be true or false. So, forgoing the claim that Leibniz 'got it right', I am inclined to say that Leibniz's account is vastly superior to the common view and, with some repairs, can be made to work reasonably well. (Hereafter, I will refer to the theory being offered below as the "neo-Leibnizian" theory. The qualification "neo" connotes that what follows adopts the core of Leibniz's original theory, but is not to be thought to preserve the whole of that historical theory.) Let me state the essential element in the neo-Leibnizian theory of space in an initially provocative manner, using a form of words only slightly different from Leibniz's own: Space does not exist.

The neo-Leibnizian theory can equally be characterized as being the 'negative' theory of space. It argues, in effect, that there is nothing more to the concept of *space* than that places are dependent on the existence of physical objects.[2] Take away those objects and there are no 'places'. In imagination annihilate all the matter of the universe. Having done so, in no intelligible sense can you then go on to say: "This is the place where the Andromeda galaxy used to be." Without physical things, there are no places. To say of a world devoid of physical objects that one place might be distinguished from another would be of the same order of nonsense as to say that someone might vacate a room and leave her lap behind. Just as a lap is a spatial feature of one physical object, places are spatial features of two (or more) physical objects. In the absence of physical objects, there are no places. Still less is there a 'physical space' which might be thought to be the conglomeration of all places.

But having now stated the thesis – that space does not exist, that there are only things and their places – in a deliberately provocative way, let me try now both to explain what I mean by this and to defend (what must surely appear at the outset to be) an outrageous claim.

8.2   A neo-Leibnizian theory of space and time

It is a truth of logic that any class of things can be divided, without

---

2. On some contemporary interpretations of modern physics, some writers suggest that physical objects are best conceived of as clumps or distributions of energy. That refinement is inessential for our purposes.

remainder, into two mutually exclusive subclasses. Roses, for example, may be divided into all those that are red and all those that are not red. Mammals, for example, may be divided into those that are marsupials and those that are not. And similarly for theories of space, which may be divided into those theories which posit space as a subtle (ethereal) kind of 'stuff' permeating the universe and those theories which do not so regard space.

Isaac Newton, like most persons, subscribed to a theory of the first kind, although Newton's theory, as we would expect, was considerably more robust than most persons'. Motivated in part by a Cartesian* theory of perception and in part by certain theological beliefs, he posited that space was, in his words, 'the sensorium of God', a kind of 'sense organ' by which God was able immediately to know the place (whereabouts) of anything in the universe. We will not concern ourselves with these latter sorts of subsidiary features of Newton's theory. What is essential in his theory was that it was one of the kind which regarded space as a 'container' of the physical objects in the universe.

Most persons, I am quite sure, subscribe to a 'container' theory of space. When they say such a thing as "There are many galaxies scattered about in space", they will often imagine a picture, just on a grander scale, similar to that imagined when they say, for example, "The Eiffel Tower is located in Paris." Just as the Eiffel Tower and Paris may each be regarded as a kind of spatial object (although of course the latter is a rather large spatial object, occupying some 106 square kilometers), the common view would have it that galaxies, too, are physical objects (very big ones) and that they are located in space, viz. a yet larger container (a kind of 'super-Paris' as it were) which is, nonetheless, a 'somewhat physical' sort of thing. The reasoning is by analogy: the Eiffel Tower (a physical thing having spatial properties) is in Paris (also a physical thing having spatial properties), and thus galaxies (physical things having physical properties), being in space, must be in a thing (i.e. space) which in its turn is a physical thing having spatial properties.

This 'container' model of space is unquestionably the one presupposed by Buber. He conceived of space as a kind of stuff of which it was appropriate (meaningful) to speculate where its edge might lie. For containers, whether they be something as small as jam jars or as large as Paris, have outer bounds: there clearly are places which lie on the 'inside' (i.e. are within) and there are other places which lie on the 'outside' (i.e. are without). But, as we have seen (p. 10 above), Buber nearly went insane trying to reconcile himself to operating with this model of space.

Leibniz strongly attacked the 'container' model of space. His particular challenge was to Newton's particular version, but it need not be regarded as so restricted. His objections, and his alternative theory, can be read as applying to any version of the 'container' theory.

> §2. ... real absolute space ... is an idol of some modern Englishmen. I call it an idol, not in a theological sense, but in a philosophical one. ... §3. These gentlemen maintain ... that space is a real absolute being. But this involves them in great difficulties; for such a being must needs be eternal and infinite. Hence some have believed it to be God himself, or, one of his attributes, his immensity. But since space consists of parts, it is not a thing which can belong to God. §4. As for my own opinion, I have said more than once, that I hold space to be something merely relative, as time is; that I hold it to be an order of coexistences, as time is an order of successions. For space denotes, in terms of possibility, an order of things which exist at the same time, considered as existing together. ([5], Third paper, 25-6)

And in the following paragraph Leibniz talks of the "chimerical [fictitious] supposition of the reality of space in itself" (26). What all of this comes down to is Leibniz's arguing that space does not exist; that there are physical objects which, as we say, are 'in space', but space does not exist as a distinct further kind of thing which 'contains' these objects.

In reading Leibniz's characterization of Newton's theory as one of an "absolute" space, and his own as one of a "relative" space, one must recall that these terms did not mean quite the same to seventeenth-century writers as they have come to mean in the period since Einstein proposed his theories of the relativity of space. When Einstein wrote, early in this century, that space is "relative", he was advancing a thesis which clearly presupposed the neo-Leibnizian concept of space, but which advanced – at the same time – claims about the universe, and in particular about mass, energy, gravity, and the transmission of light, which were never dreamed of by Leibniz. It is no part of my concern here to review Einstein's theories. What I am attempting to do is to propose a theory of space and time which is consistent with modern physical theory and which provides a suitable base on which to erect current theories in physics. I will content myself, that is, with arguing against a common, but woefully confused concept of space and time, a concept totally inappropriate for the doing of modern physics.

When Leibniz contrasts his own theory with that of Newton, saying that Newton hypothesizes that space is 'absolute' and that he, instead, hypothesizes that space is 'relative', we must understand that Leibniz is not saying that each of them is arguing that space is a kind of stuff and that they are arguing about whether it is one sort of stuff or another. Quite the contrary, in his saying that Newton subscribes to a theory of absolute space, Leibniz is arguing that Newton believes that space is a kind of stuff. In contrast, when he himself argues that space is relative, Leibniz is arguing that space is nonexistent, in his own words, that the reality of space is "chimerical".

In the Newtonian world-view, space and its contents are two different sorts of *things*; each exists. And although physical things could not exist except by being (at some determinate point or other) in space, space could exist even if it were devoid (empty) of all physical things whatsoever. This view, as I have said, is more or less the commonly held view of space.

Leibniz's view is far more economical, but distinctly at variance with common, popular views. In Leibniz's view, physical objects do not 'inhabit' space. Physical objects exist; some touch one another; others are separated by various distances from one another; but there is no further kind of 'stuff' (space) filling up the places where there are no physical objects.

There is, of course, one immediate benefit from adopting the neo-Leibnizian theory: it solves Buber's problem at a stroke. If space does not exist, then it neither has nor lacks an edge. If space does not exist, then there is no place which lies 'within' space and some other point which lies 'without'.[3]

Many persons find this particular manner of solving philosophical puzzles deeply disturbing and find themselves resisting the proposal.

---

3. Note too that Lucretius's imagined spear thrower stationed at (in his words) "the last limits" (see above p. 9) simply could not exist, and he could not exist for the same sorts of reasons that a person who factored the largest odd number could not exist. Just as there is no largest odd number and hence there could not be anyone who factored it, there is no space and hence there could not be anyone who stood at its "last limits".

To them it seems something of a cheat to attempt to solve a puzzle by undercutting its presuppositions. Thus, for example, some persons have balked at Russell's solution to the famous Barber paradox. Russell described a male, adult barber, who himself had whiskers, who shaved all *and only* those persons in his village who did not shave themselves ([179], 261). The question arises: Who shaves the barber? Whether one answers that he is unshaved, that he shaves himself, or that someone else shaves him, the answer immediately contradicts one of the explicit claims made in the description of the barber. Russell's solution – and indeed the only solution possible to the puzzle – is to recognize that the very description given of the barber is internally incoherent, i.e. it is logically impossible that there should be such a barber. The puzzle can be solved, in effect, only by 'backing up', as it were, and challenging one of the presuppositions of the very problem itself. One 'solves' such a problem, not by *answering* it, but by *rejecting* the problem, by showing that it harbors an untenable presupposition.[4]

Buber could not solve his problem. That either answer led immediately, in Buber's own words, to "absurdity" is evidence not of the profundity of the problem itself, not of the need for ingenious solutions, but of something fundamentally incoherent in the very problem itself. And what that incoherence consisted in, I suggest, is the popularly held, but ultimately untenable, view that space is a kind of 'stuff' of which it is appropriate to imagine that it has a boundary and of which it is appropriate to ask what lies within it and what lies outside it. This 'absolute' (or 'container') notion of space cannot be freed of incoherence.

There is an altogether different sort of argument which may also be brought to bear against the concept of space as being a kind of 'stuff', an argument from English grammar. Consider the two English sentences,

(S1)   There is water between the chair and the wall.

and

(S2)   There is space between the chair and the wall.

From a point of view of English grammar, these two sentences are identical. From a grammatical point of view, they match word for

---

4. For more on the Barber paradox, see [163] and [34], 117-18.

word, phrase for phrase. But in spite of that, there is something profoundly different about these two sentences. The concepts *water* and
space which occur in them behave unexpectedly differently from a
logical point of view. The remarkable dissimilarity is revealed when
we try to paraphrase these two sentences. For the latter can be given a
paraphrase which is anything but possible for the former. (S2) may be
paraphrased this way:

(S2′) There is nothing between the chair and the wall, and the chair is
       not touching the wall.

In this paraphrase, only two sorts of 'things' (or stuff) are referred to:
the chair and the wall. Talk of space has dropped out altogether. No
such paraphrase is possible for (S1). For in (S1), there really are three
sorts of things involved: chairs, water, and walls. But space is not a
sort of thing, and this is revealed by the remarkable paraphrase possible for (S2). Two points need to be made about this maneuver.

First, and foremost, is the need to address the objection that the
paraphrase does not genuinely eliminate talk of space as a kind of
stuff, it merely substitutes a synonym, viz. "nothing", in its place. For
some persons, in reflecting on the paraphrase (S2′), will believe that
they detect in it a reference to three kinds of things: chairs, walls, and
nothingness. Indeed, some persons quite explicitly regard "empty
space" and "nothingness" as (near-)synonyms.

We have, it seems, offered a solution to one philosophical problem,
only to have it replaced by another. Is "nothing", when used in a sentence such as "There is nothing between the chair and the wall", to be
regarded as referring to a thing in the way in which "the chair" and
"the wall" refer to things? What role does "nothing" play in such a
sentence?

The debate over the question what, if anything, "nothing" denotes
has a long and checkered history in philosophy.[5] Philosophers are split
into two camps: those that regard "nothing" as denoting something
(viz. the nothingness) and those that regard "nothing" as playing a
non-denoting role in our sentences.

Lewis Carroll (1832-98), the author of *Through the Looking-Glass*
(who was by profession a mathematician and by avocation a philoso-

---

5. P.L. Heath's article, "Nothing", in the *Encyclopedia of Philosophy* ([67],
vol. 5, 524-5), exhibits two virtues: it is informative and, at the same time, it
is one of the few intentionally humorous writings in modern philosophy.

pher), spoofs the view which would make of "nothing" (and "no-body") the name of something (or someone).[6]

> "Who did you pass on the road?" the King went on, holding out his hand to the Messenger for some more hay.
> "Nobody," said the Messenger.
> "Quite right," said the King: "this young lady saw him too. So of course Nobody walks slower than you."
> "I do my best," the Messenger said in a sullen tone. "I'm sure nobody walks much faster than I do!"
> "He can't do that," said the King, "or else he'd have been here first." ([46], 196)

Many twentieth-century philosophers, especially those among the Continental schools and the Existential schools, have written of Nothingness, treating it – as the King regards "Nobody" in Carroll's fable – as referring to some actually existent thing. They have talked of the fear of Nothingness and of the anxiety caused by the prospects of Nothingness. Some of these philosophers identify Nothingness with death; and others with 'the void'.

But other philosophers will have nothing (!) of that kind of theorizing. These latter philosophers (myself among them) regard "nothing" as playing a different kind of role in our sentences. "Nothing", according to this theory, is just one among several so-called quantifiers, words which, in effect, serve to indicate the size of the classes one is talking about. Thus, for example, we might say, "Everything troubles me today", or "Practically everything is troubling me today", or "Something is troubling me today", or – finally – "There is nothing troubling me today". What this latter sentence says, I would urge, is that there is not anything that is troubling me, i.e. that I am free of troubles. "There is nothing troubling me today" ought not, I suggest, be thought to be saying that I *am* being troubled and what is doing that troubling is Nothing.[7]

---

6. It comes as no surprise that the same person, P.L. Heath, has written both the articles "Lewis Carroll" and "Nothing" in the *Encyclopedia of Philosophy* ([67]).

7. Strawson has written of the tendency of certain descriptive phrases, e.g. "the round table", 'to grow capital letters' and become converted into names, e.g. "the Round Table". One might notice that there is a tendency, too, in the

Along perfectly similar lines, when we offer a paraphrase of "There is space between the chair and the wall" which reads "There is nothing between the chair and the wall and the chair is not touching the wall", the latter ought to be understood as saying "There is *no* (third) thing between the chair and the wall" rather than as saying "There *is* some third thing between the chair and the wall, namely, Nothing." If "Nothing" named a kind of thing in the world, then – by parallel reasoning, it seems to me – so too would "something", "practically everything", "hardly anything", "most", and "a few", etc. None of these, I suggest, names anything in the world. No more so than does "it" in "It is raining" or "there" in "There is a car in the driveway."

If one identifies space with The Nothing, then one immediately invites back Buber's conundrum, only it now reads: "Where does the Nothingness leave off, and what is on the other side?"

The second concern arising over the maneuver of 'paraphrasing-away', as it were, the reference to space as a kind of thing does not so much question the results of applying that technique, but challenges the very technique itself. Some persons are deeply suspicious and troubled over the technique of solving philosophical problems by grammatical or linguistic means. Even cheerfully admitting the correctness of the paraphrase, some persons will resist seeing it as a genuine solution to the original problem. The objection they make is to the alleged *relevance* of the paraphrase to solving the problem.

Again, just as in the case of Russell's proposed solution of the Barber paradox, persons will have differing attitudes about the philosophical methodology involved. Persons come to philosophy with different expectations. What one person sees as a perfectly cogent solution to a

---

writings of certain philosophers for quantifiers similarly 'to grow capital letters'. If we are not careful to resist the temptation, we may find the innocent, familiar "nothing" mysteriously transmogrifying into a name for the (dreaded) Nothing. Arguments which adopt this latter sort of linguistic fraud fall among what have come to be called 'fallacies of reification'.

As a sidelight, I might mention that Strawson's clever phrase occurs in a reply (1950), "On Referring" ([199]), which was directed against Bertrand Russell's "On Denoting" ([177]) written some forty-five years earlier, in 1905. As a matter of fact, at the time Russell wrote "On Denoting", Strawson's birth lay fourteen years in the future. Russell's eventual reply to Strawson was published in 1957 ([181]). There must be few other instances in the history of thought where an author may be found to be defending one of his/her writings fifty-two years after having penned it.

problem, another person may fail to regard as even being relevant. For some persons, the demonstration that "space" has a quite different 'logical grammar' from ordinary substantive terms, such as "water", "wall", and "chair", does nothing to address the problem of sorting out the concept of *space*. Linguistic maneuvers, of the sort we have just gone through paraphrasing away "space" in (S2), are regarded as mere 'word-chopping' or 'hairsplitting', but not as grappling with the deep conceptual problems afoot.

Other persons, in being presented with precisely the same paraphrase and the accompanying discussion of how "space" and "nothing" do not behave grammatically like (incontrovertible) substantive terms such as "water", "wall", and the like, experience something of a 'Eureka'-flash, and come to regard problems like Buber's as having their source in thinking of space as if it were an (ethereal) kind of thing. In my own classroom, I often see the different attitudes persons have toward these methods. On encountering the method of paraphrase and the claim that it can sometimes reveal important distinctions among our concepts, some of my students will embrace it with zeal and regard it as revelatory while others of them will reject it with open contempt.

Who is right? How does one adjudicate when fundamental conceptions about the very practice itself of philosophy are at stake? How does one argue in support of, or against, the method of paraphrasing as a means of solving some philosophical problems? Certainly great numbers of modern philosophers use such techniques: if not every day, then at least on some occasions. One can hardly pick up a current philosophical journal without finding within it some article in which the writer has utilized it or a kindred technique. But for the person unfamiliar with, or unused to, such techniques, to whom such techniques seem linguistic sleights of hand, who initially regards them as being some sort of cheat, how is one to recommend and justify the adoption of such a technique?

There can, of course, be no definitive answer. There can be no answer which is ultimately assured of winning converts to a methodology which some persons view with suspicion or disfavor. It is no more possible to find a way to convince one's opponents of the rightness or utility of a philosophical methodology than it is to find a way to convince one's opponents of the profit of looking at the world through the eyes of a new scientific theory or adopting a new technology. In spite of the commonly held view that there is some one canonical 'scientific method', its existence is, when all is said and done, mythical. Similarly, there is nothing that can be called 'the' philosophical method, either. Philosophers are bound to disagree among themselves about philosophical methods, just as scientists are bound to disagree over scientific methods.

There is no argument in support of the method of paraphrasing which will be convincing to all doubters. One can do no more than apply that method to various cases, display the results, and invite one's readers to decide for themselves whether they regard the method and its results as acceptable. My own attitude has been to adopt the method as one tool among several to be used in struggling to explicate our concepts. I am happy to utilize it in the present case because its results cohere with the results of other approaches and because its results offer a solution to Buber's problem and because the method offers a concept of space suitable for erecting modern physical theories. This is not to say that I believe that the method of paraphrase is the touchstone for doing philosophy. Quite the contrary, I believe that in some instances it has been used in a jawbone fashion, for example in the analysis of the concept of *causation* where it has been applied – in the hands of some philosophers – to too few examples, and thus been used to advance an overly restricted explication of "cause". In short, I do not rest my case, of arguing that space is nonexistent, simply on the basis of a paraphrase of (S2). I build the argument on that paraphrase, to be sure, but on much else besides, e.g. that such an explication solves Buber's problem and that such an explication coheres with modern physical theories whereas a 'container' notion of space does not.

8.3 Objections and replies to the neo-Leibnizian theory

It has been my own experience that most persons relish a fulsome ontology*. By this I mean that most persons prefer a conceptual scheme in which there figure a great number of *kinds* of things. The term "things" here is meant in a very broad, inclusive sense. On this interpretation, "things" will include, of course, the most familiar things of all, namely physical objects, but will include as well all sorts of nonphysical things, e.g. minds (if indeed they are nonphysical), supernatural beings, numbers, classes, colors, pains, mathematical theorems, places, and events. In short, "things" is being used here as a general name for any sort of thing (!) whatsoever that can be named or described.

Most persons, it seems to me, are willing to prune their ontologies only with reluctance. Few persons cheerfully or readily are willing to discard items from their stock-in-trade ontology. Every philosopher who has ever argued that some item or other in the popularly held ontology is expendable insofar as it is mythical or incoherent has, I am sure, met with resistance from persons arguing that the suggestion is a patent offense against common sense.

There is much to be said for the commonsense view of the world. Foremost is the fact that it works extremely well. One tampers with it only gingerly and always at some risk of damaging it. But commonsensical views of the world are not perfect and are not immune to change and improvement. One can sometimes improve on common sense, but one must take care in trying to do so. For a good deal of suggested repair – e.g. that disease is a myth – is downright dangerous.

The neo-Leibnizian theory I have described above, the theory that space does not exist, i.e. that there is no such thing as space, is guaranteed to elicit from many persons the objection that it does so much violence to common sense that it is simply fantastic. The concept of space as being a kind of thing is so pervasive in our commonsense view of the world that any suggestion that space does not really exist is regarded as a philosopher's fancy not to be seriously credited.

Let me try, somewhat further, to undo this sort of resistance. Let me try both to show how the theory works, and how it succeeds in preserving what is valuable in common sense and how it discards what is problematic in the commonsensical view.

Objection 1: Lord Kelvin once extolled the virtues of measurement this way: "… when you can measure what you are speaking about and express it in numbers you know something about it; but when you cannot measure it, when you cannot express it in numbers, your knowledge is of a meagre and unsatisfactory kind" ([109] 80). Probably he overstated the negative side of the case. There are doubtless all sorts of things – such as beauty in music and nobility of character – which have not succumbed to precise measurement but about which our knowledge cannot, reasonably, be judged to be 'unsatisfactory'.[8] On the positive side, however, Kelvin's point is well taken. Measurement, especially if it is reproducible, public, accurate, and utilizable in

---

8. Abraham Kaplan's views on measurement are even stronger than Kelvin's: "No problem is a purely qualitative one in its own nature; we may

a well-established scientific theory, does provide us with valuable knowledge.[9] More particularly, it provides us with knowledge of *real* features of the world. If something is measurable, then it exists. Non-existent things cannot be measured. Now space surely can be measured. We need not, for example, content ourselves merely with noting that there is some space between the chair and the wall, we can proceed to *measure* quantitatively that amount of space. Using a steel tape measure, we may find that the shortest distance between the two is 55.6 cm. Using more refined laboratory instruments, we can measure space with an accuracy of better than one part in ten million. Surely it must be a mistake, then, given the acknowledged possibility of performing such public, reproducible, and accurate measurements, to argue that space itself is a fiction.

Reply to Objection 1: The theory of space being proposed here must not be thought to deny the possibility of our performing such measurements. Any theory which said that it is impossible to measure the distance between chairs and walls would be at such gross variance with simple physical facts as to be worthy of rejection immediately. The neo-Leibnizian theory, obviously, cannot deny such 'hard facts' if it is to be seriously entertained. And indeed it does not. Quite the contrary, Leibniz implicitly allows that such measurements are possible ([5], Fifth paper, §54, 75).

Certainly it is possible to measure the distances between many physical objects. For ordinary-sized physical things, close at hand, we can use calipers and meter sticks; for greater distances, surveyors' transit theodolites; and for still greater distances, radar, parallax measurements, and Doppler red-shift measurements. All of this simply must be admitted, and indeed all of it is left perfectly intact in the neo-Leibnizian theory.

Even more to the point, this theory makes the picture of physical objects standing in various spatial relationships to one another its *fundamental* notion. According to the neo-Leibnizian theory, it is precisely physical objects and their spatial relationships which are real. What

---

always approach it in quantitative terms. We may; but *can* we always do so? Are there not some things which are intrinsically unmeasurable ... ? For my part, I answer these questions with an unequivocal 'No'" ([108], 176).

9. See also Cassirer: "A fact is understood when it is measured" ([47], 140).

is denied to be real is some sort of pervasive 'stuff' (i.e. space) of which these relations are somehow to be thought of as properties.

In this neo-Leibnizian theory, *from the point of view of physics,* what exists are physical bodies, persisting through time, some very small (including the molecules of the gaseous mixture air), others immense, some touching one another, others at various distances, some at relative rest, i.e. not moving with respect to some object conventionally chosen as the 'fixed point', and yet others in motion with respect to that 'fixed point'. But that's it. There is no further ethereal soup (space) in which all these objects 'float', as it were, like fish in the sea. But if there is no ethereal 'stuff' between objects, then Buber's peculiar views of the world *cannot arise.* What we have in this theory is what is worth preserving, viz. physical objects of various sizes moving about with respect to one another. What falls away is precisely, and only, that part of the picture which was problematic: the idea that space was a further kind of 'thing' of which it was appropriate to imagine that it, too, had an 'inside' and an 'outside'.

Objection 2: It is not simply that we are able to measure the distance between non-contiguous objects. It goes well beyond that. Physicists, astronomers, cosmologists, and geometers attribute *geometrical* properties to space, e.g. they are wont to talk of space being "curved" and of space having "three dimensions". Surely only an *existent* thing can have such physical properties. If there is curvature, then there must exist something to *be* curved; if there are three dimensions, then there must exist something to *be* three-dimensional.

Reply to Objection 2: The definition of "curvature", as a mathematically calculable measure, was invented by Gauss (1777-1855) in two papers of 1825 and 1827 on the geometry of two-dimensional[10] surfaces ([76], 15, 97). The Gaussian measure of the curvature at any

---

10. With the advent, c. 1975, of fractal geometry (launched by Benoit Mandelbrot; see [131], chap. XII, for a history) and its talk of 'fractal dimensions', it is becoming common among mathematicians to replace this historical, unqualified use of "dimension" with "topological* dimension". But since there is no discussion in this book of fractal geometry, I have felt no particular need to adopt the reformed terminology. When I speak of spatial dimensions, I will be referring to the historically familiar dimensions of width, height, and depth.

point is the reciprocal* of the products of the greatest and least radii of curvature at that point. For example, consider the curvature at a point on the 'equator' of a perfect sphere. The surface curves equally in all directions, e.g. along the equator itself and along the line of longitude through that point; i.e. both these circles have the same radius. Let us call that radius "R". The measure of the curvature, then, according to the Gaussian formula would be $1/(R \times R)$. Note that it makes no matter whether "R" is regarded as positive or negative: in being multiplied by itself, the result must be positive. Thus, for a (perfect) sphere, the measure of curvature is at every point the same and is always positive.

Imagine now the sphere growing to infinite size: the surface is (effectively) flat, and the radius is infinite (i.e. ∞). The Gaussian formula tells us that the curvature is $1/(\infty \times \infty)$, i.e. zero. That is, a plane surface, a flat two-dimensional 'space', has a curvature of zero.

Thirdly, imagine a doughnut-shaped surface, or as mathematicians call it, a torus (pl. tori). Imagine it to be oriented as if lying on a tabletop. (See figure 8.1, p. 162) Choose a point on the inner surface, i.e. on the perimeter of the hole in the middle. (In figure 8.1, see the left-hand side of the lower diagram.) There are two circles here, at right angles: a horizontal circle (whose radius is labeled "R") comprising that inner perimeter; and a vertical circle (whose radius is labeled "r"), that of the cross-section through the dough of the pastry. (If you prefer, imagine two interlocked key rings, touching at right angles.) What makes this case importantly different from the preceding two is that the two radii of curvature are in *opposite* directions. If one is assigned a positive value, the other must be assigned a negative value. Assume one is $+r$ and the other is $-R$. Then the Gaussian formula gives a negative value for the curvature, i.e. $1/(-R \times +r)$, which is, of course, equal to $-1/(|R| \times |r|)$. Such negatively curved surfaces are exhibited along the inner surfaces of tori, on saddles, and on the bells (flares) of hunting horns, trumpets, etc. (Incidentally, you might notice that the curvature of the surface of tori changes from place to place. While the curvature is negative on the perimeter of the hole, it is positive on the points farthest from the hole [see the right-hand half of the diagram in figure 8.1]. There the two radii, $\mathcal{R}$ and r, point in the *same* direction, and hence the curvature is positive.[11])

As Gauss originally introduced the concept, to apply to features of

---

11. For more on the concept of curvature, see [3], esp. 261-86 and 356-70.

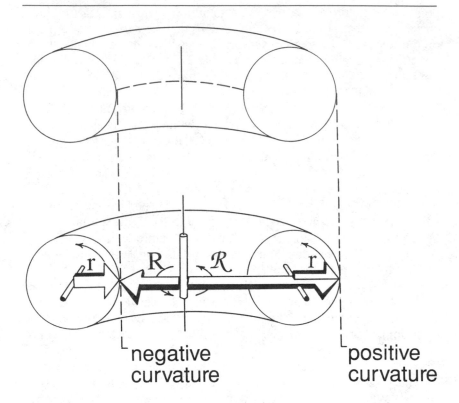

negative
curvature

positive
curvature

Figure 8.1

two-dimensional surfaces, *curvature* is readily grasped. But it was not
long before the concept was extended in 1854, by Riemann (1826-66),
to apply, not to two-dimensional surfaces, but to three-dimensional
space ([173]).

For a mathematician, a 'space' may be of any number of dimensions. Indeed, a 'space' need not refer to anything physical whatever:
it is just a measure of the number of 'dimensions' needed to specify
the 'location' of something of interest. For example, Helmholtz cites
the case of the three-dimensional 'space' of colors: any given color
may be located in the (finite) three-dimensional space of red, green,
and blue, by specifying for each of these 'dimensions' (primary
colors) what percentage occurs in the given color. (He omits intensity;
had he included that parameter, he would have needed a four-dimen-

sional 'space' which was finite in three of its dimensions, and infinite in the fourth.) If someone offered a theory of intelligence, for example, in which there were five independent parameters to be measured – e.g. verbal skills, mathematical skills, physical skills, creative skills, and social skills – then one would have to posit a 'space' of these five dimensions in which to locate any given person. From the mathematical point of view, there is utterly no difference between the 'spaces' of geometry, of color spectra, and of intelligence. All of these, and countless other 'manifolds', are called "spaces". Even philosophers have adopted the concept and sometimes talk (perhaps a bit pretentiously) of such esoterica as "logical" space.

When Riemann *extended* Gauss's original concept of the curvature of two-dimensional surfaces to a three-dimensional space, we must understand that he was proceeding by mathematical *analogy*. He was, in effect, arguing that certain features of three-dimensional geometry (and by extension, four-, five-, six-, indeed any n-dimensional geometry) would be extensions of features of two-dimensional geometry. In any analogy, certain features are preserved and others discarded. And in extending Gauss's original notion, devised for two-dimensional geometry, to three-, four-, or higher-dimensional geometries, we must take care to understand exactly what may be carried over and what is to be discarded.

Riemann discovered that in a 'positively curved' space, many of the familiar theorems of Euclidean geometry do not hold. For example, in such a space, there are no parallel lines and the sum of the angles of triangles always exceeds 180°. But what, exactly, is one to make of this notion of a 'positively curved' space? The intellectual puzzle arises because of the difficulty we have in trying to extend the familiar notions of curvature which were introduced, in the first instance, to apply to two-dimensional surfaces: of the sphere, of the torus, etc. To be sure, the sphere and the torus are three-dimensional objects; but their *surfaces* are two-dimensional 'spaces'. We can intuitively grasp the sense of "curvature" operative in these familiar cases because we can visualize that the curved surfaces are the two-dimensional surfaces of a three-dimensional figure. But when we are then told that our own physical space is (or might be) curved, and we try by analogy to visualize it as being the surface of some four-dimensional solid, our imaginations fail us. The analogy becomes more hindrance than help.

Mathematicians are practiced enough to know how to handle the analogy correctly. Mathematicians, that is, know how to abstract the essential mathematical features from such examples – the plane, the sphere, the torus, etc. Non-mathematicians, however, are done a dis-service by these models, for they are not practiced in focusing in on just the relevant mathematical features at play, and are far too likely, virtually inevitably likely, to be distracted by the robust reality of the physical objects (the Earth, the hunting horn) which 'sport' these curved surfaces. What the mathematician wants to focus on in these models are the surfaces themselves, divorced from the things of which they happen to be the surfaces, i.e. the mathematician is concerned solely with the mathematical, not the physical, properties of these surfaces. But all of this is usually lost in most popular presentations of modern geometry.

Already in the nineteenth century, Hermann Helmholtz recognized non-mathematicians' inability to handle the concept of *curvature* in the manner of physicists and mathematicians, i.e. he recognized that non-mathematicians tried to conceive of the curvature which was said to characterize physical space after the model of curvature which was familiar in the case of the two-dimensional surfaces of three-dimensional objects. Helmholtz advises that one abandon any attempt to conceive of *curvature* in that manner. Instead we should conceive of curvature as the result of a certain kind of *calculation* we perform on quantities we measure with our instruments.

> All known space-relations are measurable, that is, they may be brought to determination of magnitudes (lines, angles, surfaces, volumes). Problems in geometry can therefore be solved, by finding methods of calculation for arriving at unknown magnitudes from known ones. …
>
> Now we may start with this view of space, according to which the position of a point may be determined by measurements in relation to any given figure (system of co-ordinates), taken as fixed, and then inquire what are the special characteristics [e.g. the curvature] of our space as manifested in the measurements that have to be made. This path was first entered by … Riemann of Göttingen. It has the peculiar advantage that all its operations consist in pure calculation of quantities which quite obviates the danger of habitual perceptions being taken for necessities of thought. …
>
> To prevent misunderstanding, I will once more observe that this so-called measure of space-curvature is a quantity obtained by purely analytical [mathematical] calculation, and that its introduction involves no suggestion of relations that would

have a meaning only for sense-perception. ([89], 44-7)

Helmholtz, like Riemann himself, regards this 'new talk' of curvature, not as describing perceivable, or even imaginable, properties of space, but rather as a result to be obtained by mathematical calculation on measured quantities.

In modern science, too, many writers repeat the advice, cautioning readers explicitly about the potentially misleading use of the word "curved". The astronomer Dennis Sciama, for example, writes that it is misleading to talk of non-Euclidean space as "curved". But his point is perfectly general, and does not apply only to non-Euclidean space, for it is, in a way, just as misleading to describe Euclidean space as "flat". I will bracket certain phrases in quoting him, so as to make his point more general. In this instance, bracketing indicates not my insertions, but rather my suggested deletions from the original: "We can easily understand what it means to say that a two-dimensional surface is curved, because we can see this surface lying in three-dimensional [Euclidean] space, and the meaning of the word 'curvature' is quite obvious. But when this same name 'curvature' is also given to a three-dimensional [non-Euclidean] space (footnote: let alone four-dimensional space-time!) it becomes rather misleading. ... All that is meant by the curvature of space, then, is that gravitation affects the motion of bodies" ([186], 146). The essential point is Sciama's last sentence: "All that is meant by the curvature of space, then, is that gravitation affects the motion of bodies." And he might have added, "and affects the path of light rays."[12] (A minor matter:

---

12. The mathematician-astronomer I.W. Roxburgh makes much the same point, but writes at somewhat greater length: "... what is this stuff called space whose curvature is to be determined – how do we measure it? We can, like Gauss, set up a triangulation experiment and measure the angles of a triangle – the answer will not be 180° – but this does not mean space is curved. The experiment is done with light rays and theodolites – the empirical result is a statement about the behaviour of light rays – not about space. It is, as it must be, an experiment about the relationship between objects in space not about space itself. The same is necessarily true about any experiment; from it we learn of the relationship between objects not of the background we call space. ... Space ... is an intermediary that we bring into the formalism [of relativity theory] for ease of representation, but *in any empirical statement about the world the representation* [i.e. space itself] *is eliminated*" ([175], 87; italics added).

The so-called curvature of space varies from place to place. The curvature is more marked, i.e. light rays are more affected, in the vicinity of massive bodies than at places remote from them. And the overall curvature of the entire universe is a function of both the amount and the distribution of mass within the universe.)

Talk of space itself being curved has become commonplace within physics. But one must beware not to interpret such talk too literally, or at least not with the common meanings we assign to the word "curvature". We should no more want to regard the physicist's use of the term "curvature" as being akin to the ordinary use than we should want to regard the physicist's use of the word "field" as being akin to the farmer's.

In suggesting that we should deliberately and consciously try to resist the temptation to conceive of space as a kind of subtle, tenuous, ethereal, or subliminal kind of 'stuff', the sort of thing which begs us to try to imagine where its boundaries might be or what its curvature or geometry might be, I am not suggesting that we reform our language so as to purge it of the *word* "space" or that we cease altogether to talk of space. To try to avoid talking of space strikes me as futile and as foolhardy an enterprise as some have attempted with certain other terms. History provides us with the spectacle of a number of linguistic cultists who have trained themselves to speak without ever uttering words which they regarded as 'corrupt' – not barbarisms like "priorize", "irregardless" and "de-hire", but perfectly ordinary nuts-and-bolts words such as "but" or "not" and even (incredibly) "is".[13] (I have had students, bamboozled by bizarre linguistic theories, try to explain to me that every time one uses the word "but" in describing the behavior of another person, one has insulted that person.[14])

Some proposals to reform language are grounded in good reasons; some are not. Certain proposals – e.g. to use nonsexist pronouns and

---

13. For example, this sort of linguistic nonsense was occasionally peddled in the 1930s by some of the more extreme of the disciples of Alfred Korzybski, founder of the school of General Semantics. General Semantics must not be confused with the modern science of semantics*. Indeed Korzybski himself wrote, "My work in General Semantics has nothing to do with the above-mentioned disciplines [pragmatics, semantics, and logic]" ([113], 282).

14. Counterexamples which refute the theory are easy to find. It is no insult, but rather a compliment, to say, "She had missed a day of work because of an airline strike, but still managed to break all sales records for July."

nonsexist descriptive terms or to eliminate offensive racist and ethnic labels – have powerful ethical warrant. However, there are no similarly good reasons – either on ethical or on any other grounds – for eliminating such words as "is", "but", and "space". These latter sorts of terms, or equivalents, are enormously useful, being well-suited for most contexts. It would be pointless and counterproductive to abstain from using the word "space". All of us, myself included, will surely continue to say such perfectly intelligible and correct things as "There is not enough space on the shelf for this book" or "There is too much space in the garden to conceal with a single rosebush." My suggestion is only that, even though we use the word "space" often and with propriety, we not allow ourselves to think that the term designates some sort of tenuous 'stuff'. When we find ourselves lapsing into the kinds of speculations which so befuddled Buber, and perhaps ourselves earlier, it is at that point that we should remind ourselves that "space" does not function in our language like "water", that any sentence containing the word "space" can be paraphrased so that talk of "space" drops out. ("There's not enough space on the shelf for this book" might become, for example, "If all the objects on the shelf were to be shoved to the left end of the shelf, then the distance at the right end, between the last object and the right edge of the shelf, would be less than the width of this book.")

George Berkeley (1685-1753), perhaps paraphrasing Francis Bacon, wrote: "… we ought to 'think with the learned and speak with the vulgar [ordinary persons]'" (*A Treatise Concerning the Principles of Human Knowledge*, [27], 45-6). Although I certainly do not share the views he was advancing in the context in which the quotation appears (he was arguing against the reality of material objects), the maxim, divorced from that particular application, remains good advice. The word "space" is here to stay. Nonetheless, there is nothing to prevent our adopting a refined understanding of the concept invoked by that word. Although we persist in using the word, we can certainly adopt the sort of conception counseled by the learned: by Leibniz, by Helmholtz, and by modern cosmologists. We are free to abandon the incoherent notion of space which would make space a kind of 'stuff', or, even worse, a kind of 'curved stuff'.

Objection 3: The idea that space exists derives not just from common sense, or even, for that matter, from physics, but from perception. Space is not a theoretical posit, or hypothetical entity, in the way in which the 'collective unconscious' might be thought to be. Quite the contrary, space is every bit as perceivable as are physical objects. For I do not see only physical objects, I can also see *the space between them*. On clear moonless nights, I can look up at the sky and see the very blackness of space itself. In short, I can *see* space. Since I can see space, and since I am experiencing neither an illusion nor a delusion, space must, then, exist.

Reply to Objection 3: It is perfectly clear what the reply must be to this last objection. Someone holding to a neo-Leibnizian theory of space, who thereby wishes to deny the reality of space, must counter-argue that space is *not* visible. But can one reasonably do this? Is not space visible in just the same sort of way, for example, that my hand is visible when held up before my eyes in a well-lighted room? There are, I think, two different sorts of cases where one might think one is perceiving space itself, and we would do well to examine both of them.

The first sort of case involves ordinary, daylight perception, the kind you and I regularly experience as we look about ourselves in well-lighted places. What do we see? Typically, all sorts of physical objects – tables, chairs, pictures on the walls, carpets, human beings, etc. (if we are indoors); buildings, trees, roads, flowers, clouds, human beings, etc. (if we are outdoors) – lying at different distances from our vantage point. These many things are scattered about in different places, and often there are few if any other things occupying the places between them. About this we can all agree, and up to this point we give identical reports. But is there something more to be seen? Is there, in addition to the sorts of things just mentioned, space as well? Do we *see* space between the objects?

To be sure, we *say* such things as "I can see space between the wall and the chair" or "I can see that there is a space between the wall and the chair." But – as before – we must treat such locutions very carefully. If you could really (or genuinely or authentically) *see* space, then you ought to be able to answer the question, "What color is that space?" Immediately, you are brought up short. What color *is* the space between the chair and the wall? If you try to answer that it is colorless, then you might rightly be asked how you could possibly see something which is colorless. In more familiar cases where we use the term "colorless", we can talk of seeing the colorless item, a liter of distilled water for example, because the object refracts light (other objects look distorted in various ways when viewed through the object) or because the colorless object exhibits reflections on its surface. But space is supposed to be even more colorless than the most perfectly distilled water. Locally, in our living rooms and on the street in front of our homes, space does not refract the images of objects and space does not boast a surface which sports reflections. Space is thought to be non-refractive and non-reflective. If so, then it must be *perfectly* invisible. What 'seeing space' amounts to, then, is looking at the places between visible things and failing to see anything there. 'Seeing space' is not the successful seeing of something which exists, but is instead the looking at a place and the failure to see anything there. We do not *see* space; what we see – and describe in a slightly misleading way – are places devoid of things.

This leaves the other case which I mentioned a moment ago. Can't we see space when we look up at the sky on a moonless night? Can't we see the inky blackness of space itself? "Space is not colorless after all; phenomenologically space is black, and can be seen," our critic might object.

Often, persons who hold to the theory that space is a kind of thing are not consciously aware that they hold two inconsistent views about space: both that space in our living rooms is colorless and space between galaxies is black. But they cannot have it both ways. And they must be challenged: "Well, which is it, colorless or black, and why the difference?"

The simple answer is that it is neither. The tension between the conflicting answers arises out of a misbegotten concept of space. The places between objects, where there are no other objects, are not 'things' of which one can ask, "Are they colored or colorless?" Empty places are not things: they are neither colored nor colorless; they are not black, and they are not any other color either.

"Why, then, is the space between the chair and the table, unlike the space between Mars and Venus, not black?" This way of putting the question persists with the confusion. The 'space' between Mars and Venus is *not* black. We do not see blackness between the chair and the table, not because the space 'there' is some other color, but because we can see, by looking through that place, the illuminated wall beyond. If space existed and were colored, then I could not see my hand when held up a few inches from my nose: the intervening space would block my view. The sky is black between Mars and Venus, not because (interplanetary) 'space' is black, but rather because there is nothing to be seen there (between the planets) and nothing (except for an occasional distant star) to be seen further on, either.[15]

When we look up at the sky on a moonless night and get an impression of black, we are not seeing a black 'thing'. We are not seeing anything at all, and our nervous system fools us, by presenting it to our consciousness as if it were a gigantic piece of coal. Sometimes we get an impression of black from genuinely black physical objects, e.g. lumps of coal and the like. But our nervous system presents (much) the same visual impression when there is nothing there whatsoever. We must take care not to think that if there is a visual impression of black, then there is something there which *is* black.

The ancients used to think that the (night) sky was the interior of a hollow black globe and the stars were tiny holes in that globe through which light shone. We should not want to replace that defective notion with one which would substitute for the black globe an infinite, tenuous, subtle 'container', either black *or* colorless. Physical things exist,

---

15. From a phenomenological point of view, i.e. from the point of view of the sensory quality of the experience rather than the physics of its cause, we should realize that black is a color, on an equal footing with red, blue, yellow, etc. The often-heard slogan "black is not a color" is an article of physics, not of the phenomenology of sense perception. Black happens to be the color we perceive within our visual fields in those areas which are negligibly illuminated. It is possible, of course, to imagine that such minimally illuminated areas might have been perceived as red or yellow, or some other color. That we perceive such areas as black just happens to be a product of the way we are wired.

It is not surprising, then, that when at first robbed of illumination, our visual sense offers up to us a visual field which is black. But, as we know, after a while, the blackness 'fades' from our consciousness. When seated in a darkened room for several minutes, most of us become oblivious to the black visual field in just the way that we become oblivious to the kinesthetic sensations of our body pressing against our chair. We come gradually not to see anything: there is no color sensation at all, not even of blackness.

What is it like to be born blind? Is it to experience an infinite, black featureless visual field? I think not. I sometimes try to imagine blindness by moving my hand from clear view in front of my face around to the back of my head. At no point does my hand enter 'the inky blackness'. It simply disappears from view. That is what, I imagine, it must be like to be blind: just what it is like for me not to be able to see something positioned directly behind my head. I am, like everybody, blind in that direction. To be completely blind is to be unseeing, not as we all are in *some* directions, but to be unseeing in *all* directions. It is not to perceive an inky blackness.

and because there are physical things, and only because there are physical things, there are also places. There is no need to posit an antecedently and independently existing physical space, a container, as it were, in which to imbed these physical objects. Neither physics nor our logic requires such a posit. Indeed, the very idea itself is, ultimately, internally incoherent.

8.4 Interlude: The expression "*x* does not exist"

Doubtless one of the things which bemuses, indeed even baffles, persons new to philosophy is metaphysicians' proclivity to pronounce of all sorts of things which non-philosophers regard as relatively familiar that they are, in the end, nonexistent. Metaphysicians have often been known to deny the very existence of such (seemingly) obvious things as space, time, minds, material objects, superegos, evil, miracles, causes, physical laws, free will, and objective truth. Sometimes their negative pronouncements have the result of inducing great curiosity in their hearers, but sometimes the effect is entirely opposite to that intended, inducing, instead, great impatience, even outright alienation. The audience for such claims may find themselves initially protesting: "But surely that cannot be right. It is patently obvious that such a thing really does exist." Such persons may come to regard metaphysics as the wholesale rejection of common sense.

Generally metaphysicians know very well that in denying the existence of certain things we are bucking common sense. Metaphysicians are not a species apart. Virtually all of us grow up among the very persons to whom we direct our writings and speak (more or less) the same language as the proverbial 'man in the street'. What explains our talk about "*x* does not really exist" is our indulging in a kind of literary license, a minor – but possibly potentially misleading – piece of professional hyperbole. Usually such locutions are meant as attention-getters, as a means of highlighting dramatically and forcefully the focus of our concerns. In most cases (but certainly not quite all), the metaphysician who writes "*x* does not exist" may be found to be advancing a rather more complicated theory, viz. "*x* does not exist, if by '*x*' one means '*y*'; and while *y* does not exist, something else, viz. *z* does; and taking the latter to be what is denoted by '*x*' is a better theory." Put less formally, generally what is involved in the metaphysician's denying that *x* exists is really the offering of an alternative theory, to be substituted in place of the prevailing, and allegedly defective, theory about the nature of *x*.

In denying, as I have just done in the previous section, that space exists, I did not stop simply with making that denial. What was involved in denying that space exists was the elaboration that what was being challenged was a particular concept of space, a concept which would portray space as being itself something like a spatial object. And it is that particular concept, I argued, which is incoherent and in need of replacement. What was not being challenged, indeed what was being insisted upon, is most of what occurs in the ordinary concept, e.g. that there are physical objects, that they are strewn about the universe in different places at varying, and indeed measurable, distances, and that physics can tell us a very great deal about how material objects can interact gravitationally and can tell us the geometry of the path of radiation in the vicinity of massive bodies. In denying that space exists, not only was none of this latter denied, it was positively insisted upon. The claim that space does not exist is my (and several other philosophers') way of calling attention to the fact that space *conceived after the fashion of a quasi-physical object* is an untenable notion.

And thus it goes. Typically when metaphysicians deny that something exists, we do not just leave it at that. What we are in fact doing is offering an alternative theory; we are trying to show that there is something defective in the ordinary notion and are offering a repair. Only rarely, if ever, do we suggest that a concept should be discarded without being replaced by anything at all.

In the following section, we will, for the first and only time in this book, encounter a theory, McTaggart's theory of time, which is of the latter sort. McTaggart argued that neither of the two principal theories of time is tenable, and that time does not exist. Few other metaphysicians are disposed to accept his arguments.

8.5   Positive and negative theories of time

Just as there are two major theories of space – the 'container' theory and the relational (or Leibnizian) theory – there are two major theories of time. Indeed, I regard it as one of the most important successes of modern metaphysics to have discovered just how *much* similarity there is, in their formal aspects, between space and time. (We will devote sections 8.7 through 8.10 to the topic of spatial and temporal analogies.)

There is a certain problem in what we are to call each of these theories. The first is sometimes called the "absolute", "dynamic", "Augustinian", or, simply, the "*A*-theory". The latter name, "*A*-theory", does not stand either for "absolute" or for "Augustinian", but derives from J.M.E. McTaggart (1866-1925), who distinguished two sets of temporal terms, one he designated the "*A*-series" and the other, the "*B*-series". The second, opposing, theory is sometimes known as the "relative", "static", or "*B*-theory" of time.

In its way, the Augustinian theory of time is the temporal analog of the 'container theory' of space and, not surprisingly, it prompted in Augustine himself much the same sort of bewilderment that we have already seen in Buber: "Time ... is never all present at once. The past is always driven on by the future, the future always follows on the heels of the past, and both the past and the future have their beginning and their end in the eternal present" ([15], §11). Hardly are these words down on paper than Augustine has second thoughts and retracts, or contradicts, what he has just said about the present being 'eternal': "Of these three divisions of time ... how can two, the past and the future, *be*, when the past no longer is and the future is not yet? As for the present, if it were always present and never moved on to become the past, it would not be time but eternity" (§14). But this is only the start of his problems. For now he goes on to write:

> If the future and past do exist, I want to know what they are. I may not yet be capable of such knowledge, but at least I know that wherever they are, they are not there as future or past, but as present. For if, wherever they are, they are future, they do not yet exist; if past, they no longer exist. So wherever they are and whatever they are, it is only by being present that they *are*. (§18)

> ... it is abundantly clear that neither the future nor the past exist, and therefore it is not strictly correct to say that there are three times, past, present, and future. It might be correct to say that there are three times, a present of past things, a present of present things, and a present of future things. Some such different times do exist in the mind, but nowhere else that I can see. (§20)

What Augustine is finally driven to, we see, is a 'psychological' theory of time: the past and the future exist (mysteriously) 'in the mind', but not in objective reality. Any such theory must immediately face the problem how it is possible to measure time. This would be an especially acute problem in modern physics where it is commonplace, using exquisitely crafted instruments, to resolve time intervals into million-millionths of seconds. Such remarkable precision seems orders of magnitude beyond what any of us is capable of by psychological reckoning. But even in the far cruder physics of the fourth century AD, a psychological theory of time faced a hopeless uphill battle. Augustine's claim – "It is in my own mind, then, that I measure time. I must not allow my mind to insist that time is something objective" (§27) – is a virtual non-starter when it comes to explaining several persons' common measurements of time. Augustine would have us believe that memories and expectations are the actual objects of our temporal measurements: "... it is not future time that is long, but a long future is a long expectation of the future; and past time is not long, because it does not exist, but a long past is a long remembrance of the past" (§28). Memories of the past and expectations of the future are no substitute for actual physical measurements of temporal intervals *as they occur*. My memory of my son's birthday celebration, for example, may last only a fleeting moment, although the celebration may have gone on for hours. Presently held memories and expectations simply do not have the temporal extents of the events remembered or expected and cannot be used as their proxies in our trying to determine their durations.

How can we summarize the core of Augustine's theory? Augustine, himself, provides a useful characterization: "[Time] can only be coming from the future, passing through the present, and going into the past. In other words, it is coming out of what does not yet exist, passing through what has no duration, and moving into what no longer exists" (§21). You can see here why Augustine's theory has sometimes been called the "dynamic" theory. He posits, not things or events evolving through time, but time itself as moving from the future, through the present, to the past. And you can also see why one might regard such a theory as the temporal analog of the spatial theory which regards space as a 'container'. For just as the absolute theory of space treats space itself (as we have seen) as a quasi-spatial thing, Augustine's theory of time treats time itself as a quasi-temporal thing, i.e. as a sort of thing which "passes" and "moves". And you can see, too, why Augustine's is sometimes regarded as a 'positive' theory of time: because it asserts that there is *more* to time than just events standing in temporal relations. It may be contrasted with so-called 'negative' theories which assert that there is nothing more to time than events standing in temporal relationships.

Augustine, to be sure, is not wholly happy with his own theory, and seems constantly to be troubling himself with peculiar questions – ones which arise naturally for a positive theory – such as "While we are measuring it, where is it coming from, what is it passing through, and where is it going?" (§21). But where Buber was driven to despair, Augustine – cleric that he was – was driven to prayer. Throughout his chapter on time, Augustine beseeches God for divine illumination on these mysteries.

At the beginning of the twentieth century, McTaggart may be found to be promoting arguments virtually identical to Augustine's. But where Augustine confessed his bewilderment at the results of his own researches and seemed distressed by them, McTaggart unabashedly concludes that time is, in his words, "unreal".

It may seem strange that I will take McTaggart to task for this latter conclusion. After all, have I not just finished a moment ago, in this very chapter, a lengthy argument to the effect that space is nonexistent? Why should I be sanguine about my own denial that space exists, and then take exception to McTaggart's claim that time does not exist?

There is an important distinction between the sort of theory about space which I have just advanced and the sort of theory about time which McTaggart advances. In denying that space exists, I tried to explain that what that short proposition was to be understood to be asserting was that there is nothing in Nature like what is described by the theory of absolute space. I was denying one particular theory of space, only to be offering what I take to be a better theory, that of relative space, in its stead. And what makes the foregoing enterprise so different from McTaggart's theory of time is that McTaggart, in arguing for the unreality of time, is *not* offering a theory of relative time to replace or supersede a theory of absolute time, but is arguing against the viability of *either* theory. McTaggart is not saying, "Time does not exist, if you mean by 'time' *y*"; he is saying, "Time does not exist, period."[16]

McTaggart begins by directing attention to two different ways we

---

16. A certain qualification is in order. In the latter half of *The Nature of Existence* ([130]), McTaggart makes a concerted effort to explain how, if time does not exist, then there is at least the *appearance* of time. So while it is strictly correct to say that McTaggart argues that time does not exist, he at least tries to preserve something of our ordinary account, viz., if not the actuality, then at least the appearance, of temporality.

commonly refer to positions in time. Right at the outset, he qualifies his introduction to this topic by writing "as time appears to us *prima facie*". He can hardly begin by saying that time *is* one way or another, for he is setting out to prove that time does not exist. Hence he talks of the "appearance" of time, so as not to admit that time does in fact exist: "Positions in time, as time appears to us *prima facie*, are distinguished in two ways. Each position is Earlier than some and Later than some of the other positions. ... In the second place, each position is either Past, Present, or Future.[17] The distinctions of the former class are permanent, while those of the latter are not. If *M* [some event] is ever earlier than *N* [some other event], it is always earlier. But an event, which is now present, was future, and will be past" ([130], §305).

The latter of these series, McTaggart calls the "*A*-series", the former, the "*B*-series": "For the sake of brevity I shall give the name of the *A* series to that series of positions which runs from the far past through the near past to the present, and then from the present through the near future to the far future, or conversely. The series of positions which runs from earlier to later, or conversely, I shall call the *B* series" ([130], §306).

McTaggart then proceeds to argue that it is the *A*-series which is metaphysically more fundamental, for it is the *A*-series alone which can account for *change*, not the *B*-series. The *B*-series is, in a certain sense, *static*: it cannot account for an event's *changing* from having been future, to becoming present, and, finally, becoming past.

> Take any event – the death of Queen Anne, for example – and consider what changes can take place in its characteristics. That it is a death, that it is the death of Anne Stuart, that it has such causes, that it has such effects – every characteristic of this sort

---

17. Later, in a footnote to §329, McTaggart qualifies these statements a bit. On the supposition that there is a first moment of time, then there is no moment Earlier than that moment and there is nothing Past to that moment. Similarly, if there is a last moment of time, there is nothing Later than that moment, nor is there anything Future to that moment. So when he writes that *each* "position is Earlier than ... some other position", etc., he wants to be understood as making this claim for all positions in time except for the first and last moments, if such exist at all. This minor correction is inessential for his ensuing arguments.

never changes. ... At the last moment of time – if time has a last moment – it will still be the death of a Queen. And in every respect but one, it is equally devoid of change. But in one respect it does change. It was once an event in the far future. It became every moment an event in the nearer future. At last it was present. Then it became past, and will always remain past, though every moment it becomes further and further past.

Such characteristics as these are the only characteristics which can change. And, therefore, if there is any change, it must be looked for in the *A* series, and in the *A* series alone. If there is no real *A* series, there is no real change. The *B* series, therefore, is not by itself sufficient to constitute time, since time involves change. ([130], §311)

Notice how McTaggart's account of time is reminiscent of Augustine's: the future 'changes' into the present, and the present 'changes' into the past. Once an event is past, then it 'recedes' further and further from the present. According to this account, it is *time itself*, or positions in time, which undergo change.

Various critics have strenuously objected to this account, since it seems to temporalize time itself. Time itself seems to be moving through time: the future 'becomes' the present, and the present 'becomes' the past. The picture seems to presuppose a kind of super-time, against which the flow of 'ordinary' time might be measured. Needless to say, many philosophers have attempted to create theories of time in which such an awkward, and probably unintelligible, notion is not introduced at all. In chapter 11, we will examine a totally different sort of theory, one in which time itself does not change, but it is objects, or things, which change in time. (McTaggart, in §315, explicitly rejects this alternative theory.) But this is to get ahead of ourselves. For the moment, we must see what McTaggart concludes from his argument that the *A*-series is metaphysically more fundamental than the *B*-series.

He continues by arguing that time itself can exist only if there is something in reality which has the properties of the *A*-series. That is, he argues that time is real only if there are events which are future, become present, and recede into the past. But there can be no such events. For nothing whatever can have these properties since they are, as he attempts to show, logically inconsistent with one another, and no real (existent) thing can have logically inconsistent properties. Just as a five-sided square would have logically inconsistent properties and hence could not possibly exist, McTaggart tries to demonstrate that a time which was future, became present, and receded into the past would have logically inconsistent properties and hence could not possibly exist:

> Past, present and future are incompatible determinations. Every event must be one or the other, but no event can be more than one. ... But every event [except the first and the last, if there are first and last events] has them all. If *M* is past, it has been present and future. If it is future, it will be present and past. Thus all three characteristics belong to each event. ([130], §329)

In short, every event has incompatible determinations: it is past, present, and future. The case is analogous to a figure having exactly four and having exactly five sides. The characteristics are incompatible, and no such figure could possibly exist.

McTaggart anticipates the obvious objection that he has neglected the *tenses* of the various verbs.

> It may seem that this [claim that there is an incompatibility of determinations] can easily be explained [i.e. exposed to be an error]. Indeed, it has been impossible to state the difficulty without almost giving the explanation, since our language has verb-forms for the past, present and future, but no form that is common to all three. It is never true, the answer will run, that *M is* present, past and future. It *is* present, *will be* past, and *has been* future. Or it *is* past, and *has been* future and present, or again *is* future, and *will be* present and past. The characteristics are only incompatible when they are simultaneous, and there is no contradiction to this in the fact that each term has all of them successively. ([130], §330)

But McTaggart has raised this objection only, in turn, to dispute it. His ensuing counterobjection, i.e. his defense of his theory, lies in his asserting that every moment of time "is both past, present, and future" ([130], §331). As I reconstruct his rebuttal (§331), it seems to me to be something of the following sort. Consider the present moment: it is of course present; but equally, if we were to pick a past moment, then the present moment is future; and equally, if we were to pick a future moment, then the present moment is past. Thus, the present moment is not only present, but past and future as well.

This reply in defense of his theory strikes me as wrongheaded in the extreme. It strikes me as analogous to, and as unacceptable as, the following argument (where Carol plays the role of Future, Betty of Present, and Alice of Past).

> Carol is taller than Betty, who in turn is taller than Alice. Focus your attention on Betty. Now, pick someone who is shorter than Betty, e.g. Alice. Compared to Alice, Betty is tall. Now pick someone who is taller than Betty, e.g. Carol. Compared to Carol, Betty is short. Betty is thus both short and tall. But *being short* and *being tall* are incompatible determinations. Thus Betty could not possibly exist.

I suggest that McTaggart has made the equivalent error. That any moment of time may be present, and equally may – relative to some other moments of time – be future, and equally may – relative to still other moments of time – be past, does nothing to show that any moment of time is both past, present, and future. No more than does your being taller than some persons and shorter than still others establish that you are both tall and short. One need not, then, conclude – as did McTaggart – that time is self-contradictory, and hence, that its very existence is logically impossible.

McTaggart's theory of time, which virtually all commentators have subsequently found curious, unorthodox, and – in the end – quite unacceptable, was not just an isolated or insignificant fragment of his philosophizing. It stemmed in large measure from his inability to shake off the Augustinian concept of time, in which time was conceived as something 'moving' from the future, through the present, and into the past. McTaggart marked the culmination, if not quite the end, of a long era of conceiving of time in this familiar, even though confused, manner. The modern approach is, in a way, the very antithesis of McTaggart's.

McTaggart's theory, like Augustine's, was a positive theory: it argued that there was something more to time than merely events standing in temporal relations. (Other writers have called this additional feature 'becoming', and argued that *becoming* could not be accounted for within a negative theory, e.g. within a bare *B*-series.) Negative theorists propose, in contrast, that temporal relations can be treated analogously to spatial relations and that adequate theories of time can be constructed by regarding time as nothing over and above the temporal relations events have to one another.

What is currently regarded as being needed, both for metaphysics and for science, is a theory of time which is free of internal inconsistency and which is able to accommodate a variety of facts: (1) that temporal events form a series, i.e. that events may be earlier than, simultaneous with, or later than other events; (2) that there is a present, a future, and a past; (3) that things change, evolve, grow, degenerate, etc.; and (4) that temporal relations – as attested to by the fact that they can be measured by scientific instruments with accuracies far beyond what are psychologically possible – are not 'just in the mind', but are objective facts of Nature.

8.6   The generalized concept of *space*

Descartes and a number of subsequent philosophers, e.g. Locke, have argued that it is of the essence of material objects to be *extended in space*, i.e. to 'take up room' as we might say more colloquially. Descartes wrote: "... nothing whatever belongs to the concept of body [i.e. material object] except the fact that it is something which has length, breadth and depth and is capable of various shapes and motions" (*Replies to the Sixth Set of Objections* in [55], vol. II, 297). Nothing is a *material* object, we are inclined to assert, if it is not 'extended' in these three dimensions. Shadows cast by our bodies and images projected on movie screens, while extended in two spatial dimensions, specifically, while having width and height, lack the third spatial dimension, viz. depth, and are thus not accorded the status of materiality, are not, that is, regarded as being material objects.

Being extended in three dimensions is not, however, a sufficient condition for being a physical object. It is merely a necessary condition. Reflections in mirrors are three dimensional; so are well-crafted projected holographic images. And yet neither reflections in mirrors nor projected holographic images are material objects. Clearly something more, besides being extended in three spatial dimensions, is required for something to count as being a bona fide material object.

What is the difference between – let us use as our example – a real (physical or material) chair and its reflection, both of which are extended in three dimensions? The crucial difference is that although the real chair and its reflection in a mirror are both visible, only the former is tangible. Put another way, we can say that although both the real chair and its reflection exist in *visual space*, only the real chair, not its reflection, exists in *tactile space*. There are in this example two conceptually distinct *spaces*: that of sight and that of touch. There are, to be sure, remarkable correlations between the two, but the two spaces remain, nonetheless, conceptually distinct. Indeed each and every sensory mode may be regarded as giving us access to a 'space': there is the space of sight; of touch; of hearing; of temperature; etc.[18]

Whatever correlations there are in the data across sensory spaces (visual-auditory; visual-tactile; etc.) are both contingent and knowable only by experience (i.e. knowable only *a posteriori**). As infants we had to *learn* by trial and error the connection between the visual and the tactile.[19] We had to learn that if something felt a certain way, then it would (probably) look a certain way, and that if something looked a certain way, then it would (probably) feel a certain way. Persons born blind who, by surgery, have acquired sight as adults find that it takes them some months before they are able, using their eyes, to recognize objects which are perfectly familiar to their hands.[20] As adults, they have had to learn over a period of months, as the rest of us did as

---

18. "Older babies live more and more in a world in which the information from the senses is separated into a visual world [i.e. a visual space], an auditory world [space], and a tactual world [space]" ([32], 47).

19. One of the most surprising findings of experimental psychology is that newborns, in contrast to six-month-old infants, have an ability to reach directly for objects in their visual and auditory fields. Even blind newborns "stare at their hands, tracking them with their unseeing eyes" ([32], 69). But these sorts of innate abilities, strangely, seem to fade as the child grows during the first year, and come to be replaced in the second half-year after birth by learned hand movements guided initially by eye, and later, kinesthetically. These totally unexpected findings provide a good object lesson against trying to do science in an a priori manner. Once again, we see how the world often frustrates our naive anticipations of its manner of working.

20. In 1693, William Molyneux (1656-98) wrote to John Locke posing the following question (which has since come to be known as "Molyneux's problem"): "Suppose a man born blind, and now adult, and taught by his touch to distinguish between a cube and a sphere. ... Suppose then the cube and sphere placed on a table, and the blind man made to see. ... [I pose the following question:] whether by his sight, before he touched them, he could now distinguish and tell which is the globe, which the cube?" ([124], book II, chap. IX, §8). Molyneux and Locke both agreed the newly sighted adult would not be able immediately to make the connection between his visual

infants, how to map the data of the visual and the tactile sensory modes back and forth.

In talking and writing uncritically of *space*, we habitually overlook the differences between visual space and tactile space. But occasional exceptions remind us that there really is not just a theoretical difference between these two spaces, but a real one. Persons born blind have no experience of the features of visual space. But they can detect the features of tactile space. They can tell, by feeling physical things, what their shapes are, how large they are, whether they are rough or smooth, hard or soft, and where they are positioned in relation to other physical objects.[21] For the sighted, shadows and holographic images occur in visual space but not in tactile space. And for all of us – sighted and sightless alike – there is at least the logical possibility, as is so often featured in fiction, of invisible objects: things which are detectable tactilely but not visually.

Nonetheless, in spite of the real differences between visual and tactile space, there is – for the normally sighted among us – such a good mapping between the contents of these two spaces that we tend naively to regard these two spaces as one, real, unified, objective public space. We operate with the assumption that if something appears in visual space, then it occurs in tactile space as well, and conversely.

But it must be understood that this assumption of a single, unified space of sight and touch, handy as it is, is warranted by *contingent* facts about this particular possible world. It is not especially difficult to imagine how those facts could be otherwise. With a little ingenuity, we can invent possible-worlds tales in which the enormously useful correlation we find between the visual and tactile in this world simply does not exist. We can describe possible worlds in which your visual data bear little if any detectable correlation with the data furnished by your tactile senses. We can imagine a world, for example, where your hands inform you that you are feeling a teakettle in the cupboard beside the stove, but where your eyes, at that very moment, tell you that you are looking at a distant catamaran hauled up onto the sand of

---

and tactile data. Their scientific instincts were to prove correct. Modern empirical research has confirmed their prediction (see, e.g. [218], 204, and [83]).

21. They can also tell, with their fingers, whether something is hot or cold. But the temperature of things is not usually considered to be a *tactile* property, even though the nerve endings which are sensitive to temperature are located within our skins alongside our organs of touch.

a windswept beach. Such a tale is merely an extension of the sorts of stories which are actually true of our visual and auditory senses. I am now looking through an open window and can see rain falling outside. At the same time, I am also hearing Beethoven's *Archduke* Trio (there is a recording playing in the adjoining room). I – like you – have no difficulty living simultaneously in the two, often disparate, sensory spaces of sight and sound. The correlation between the two is often exceedingly poor. And from such an example, we can see how it could be (i.e. how it is logically possible) that the correlation between the visual and the tactile might be equally poor.

The things we standardly regard as being material objects typically exist in (at least) two sensory spaces: the visual and the tactile. Is one of these two spaces more fundamental in our attributing materiality to a thing? Would we be inclined to attribute materiality to something which was visible but not (even in principle) tangible? Would we be inclined to attribute materiality to something tangible but which was invisible? I think the answer is fairly clear. 'Merely visible' things, e.g. shadows, reflections in mirrors, projected holographic images, are standardly regarded as nonphysical.[22] In contrast, were we to find a region of space where our hands, sonar, etc. told us there was an object, but where our eyes were unable to detect anything, we would come, especially if the same results were obtained by other persons as well, to regard that place as being occupied by an invisible physical object.

Granted, I may be misjudging the pre-analytic inclinations of other persons. I am, to be sure, depending heavily on assessments of how I actually use the concept of *material object* in typical cases and of how I would use that concept in unusual cases. I am assuming, as a speaker and writer of a commonly shared language and of a more-or-less commonly shared conceptual scheme, that my own use is fairly typical and that my own leanings in this matter are reasonably representative of

---

22. The list of my examples may be contested. Some writers place reflections in mirrors in a different category than shadows and holograms. They argue that in viewing a reflection in a mirror, e.g. of a chair, one *is* seeing a material object, viz. the chair, only one is seeing it in a somewhat misleading way, i.e. as if it were in a place where it is not in fact. Nothing I am saying depends on how we choose to describe reflections in mirrors. Reflected images are merely presented as a putative example of intangible visual data. If reflections are not to be accorded this status, then – for the purposes of illustration – there are others: holograms and afterimages might serve nicely.

those of most other persons. Suppose, for the sake of argument, that I have diagnosed correctly both my own and other persons' weighting of the various criteria for invoking the concept of *material object*: that most of us, if it came to having to choose between the tactile and the visual as being more fundamental to the concept of materiality, would choose the former. If this is in fact true, might there be any explanation for it? Or, is it purely arbitrary which way we choose?

I think it is not. I think there is a profound reason why we regard the tactile as the more fundamental. And this reason has to do, once again, with the particular way this world is constructed. In some other possible worlds, the conscious creatures therein might, given the way their worlds are constructed, have good reason to regard the visual as more fundamental than the tactile.

I have in mind such facts as the following. Visual buses speeding toward oneself, e.g. images on movie screens, do not (with rare exception, viz. for the fainthearted) injure or kill us; tactile buses do maim and kill. If you lived in a world whose visual images were like those of this world, and whose tactile images were like those of this world, but whose visual and tactile images bore no correlation one to another, then you would quickly have to learn to act in accord with the tactile data if you were to survive in that world and to disregard, save for its entertainment value, the visual data. In this world, tactile knives cut our flesh and cause pain; visual knives do not. Tactile water slakes our thirst; visual water does not. Tactile heaters warm our homes; visual ones do not.

All of the immediately foregoing data are contingent. The reported facts, e.g. about the respective dangers of visual and of tactile buses, hold for this particular possible world (and for some others), but not for all. We can imagine possible worlds where precisely the opposite would hold true: where visual buses, but not tactile ones, could kill; where visual water slaked thirst, but not tactile water; etc. In these latter worlds, you would be well-advised to ignore what your fingers and hands were telling you and to pay close attention to what your eyes revealed.

It is a matter of course to believe uncritically that the data furnished by our eyes and by our fingers must coincide, that there is a single, unified world external to our skins, and that we have access to that unified world through several sensory modes. But to the extent that this is true, it is not true of logical necessity, it is true sheerly as a matter of contingency. The world did not have to be of this remarkably convenient sort; it did not have to accommodate itself so handily to our several sensory modes so as to allow shared access by sight, by touch, and (to a lesser degree) by hearing and smell. We can readily describe worlds in which such redundancy is not the order of the day, indeed in which such redundancy does not exist at all. We take so much for granted. We casually and naively assume that our sight and our touch must reveal pretty much the same data about the world. But the truth is that there is no necessity in this happy fact at all. The world could have been vastly different. That it is this way, and not far less congenial, is really quite dumbfounding and wholly without natural explanation.[23]

It is not only the coincidence of the visual and the tactile which is remarkable in our pre-analytic concept of physical bodies. It seems not to have occurred to Descartes at all that it might be possible for a physical object to have fewer or more spatial dimensions than three. But by the end of the nineteenth century the idea was being actively explored. In 1884, Edwin Abbott (1838-1926) published an entertaining, and at the same time uncommonly ingenious, book *Flatland* ([1]) describing a possible world in which physical objects are two-dimensional. The theme has been taken up again, and much expanded, in Alexander Dewdney's recent (1984) book, *The Planiverse* ([56]).[24]

---

23. One might think that the coincidence of our visual and tactile senses is no coincidence at all, that it can be explained as a product of evolution. But to argue in that fashion would be to miss the point. For it even to be possible for evolution to throw up visual and tactile senses which furnish correlative data, there must antecedently *be* correlative features in objects which can be accessed by different sensory modes. It is the very existence of such correlative features, even before evolution comes into play, that is the source of the marvel of this particular world.

24. Stephen Hawking, in *A Brief History of Time*, argues against the possibility of there being two-dimensional creatures: "If there were a passage [alimentary canal] right through its body, it would divide the creature into two separate halves; our two-dimensional being would fall apart ... Similarly, it is difficult to see how there could be any circulation of the blood in a two-dimensional creature" ([87], 164). Neither of these arguments is particularly effective.

Some paths through two-dimensional entities do allow for the separation of the two regions, e.g. a cut with scissors straight across a piece of cardboard. But other paths, even though they create two (topologically) unconnected regions, do not allow for the separation of those two regions in a

Once one begins to speculate how different from this another world might be, and thus begins to realize the countless number of ways this world might have been less congenial and the countless number of ways it might have been more, the sheer *contingency* of our world looms as the most baffling, and in principle the most inexplicable, datum in all of Nature. Anyone who minimizes this aspect of metaphysics has depreciated its essence.

8.7   Extension in time

In seventeenth-century physics, there was a quaint expression, "punctiform mass" (sometimes "punctual mass"), which derived from the Latin "punctum", for "point". A punctiform mass was, thus, a mass (i.e. a physical body) which existed entirely 'at a single point'; it was, that is, a zero-dimensional body. The notion of a punctiform mass was invented because it provided a convenient means of solving certain, otherwise intractable, problems posed by the then-current state of physics (footnote 10, p. 52). Even so, in spite of its usefulness in computations, physicists who adopted the concept did so reluctantly and hastened to point out that it was to be regarded as nothing more than a convenient *fiction*. No real body was conceived to exist only at one point: it was, they all insisted, in the very nature of physical bodies to be *extended* in space.

With the hindsight of modern developments, both in physics and in philosophy, we perceive a curious imbalance in such earlier pronouncements. For if it is in the nature of physical bodies to be ex-

---

two-dimensional space, e.g. recall jigsaw puzzles. The pieces of assembled jigsaw puzzles, although distinct from one another, move about together because they are *interlocked*. One can gently tug sideways on the corner of such a puzzle, and all the interlocked pieces will move laterally together. To disassemble such a puzzle (without destroying it), you must lift the pieces, one by one, up out of the plane of the puzzle, i.e. into the third dimension. But so long as you confine movement to a two-dimensional space, the assembled puzzle remains intact. In short, a simple way for a two-dimensional being to hold together, even though traversed by a canal, is that the canal separating the parts be (roughly) Omega(Ω)-shaped. And Hawking's argument about the circulation of blood is no better. One easy way around the difficulty is to posit separate, self-contained circulatory systems in each 'segment' of the creature. Another way is to posit a creature (like countless primitive organisms on Earth) which have no circulatory systems at all.

tended in space, then surely it must also be in their nature to be extended in time. An instantaneous object, one that exists solely for an instant of time, i.e. does not endure for any fraction, however small, of a second, is no physical object at all. Even the most ephemeral sub-atomic particles of modern nuclear physics, particles which might have an entire lifetime of no more than one trillion-trillionth of a second, at least have *some* finite temporal duration. But truly instan-taneous 'things' cannot be regarded as having real existence.

If one is going to opt for the theory that it is of the very nature of physical bodies to be extended in space, then by parallel reasoning (or by invoking analogous intuitions) one similarly ought to propose that it is of the very nature of physical bodies to be extended in time.[25] There are perhaps many psychological theories why we human beings have tended to regard space as more 'real' than time and to conceive of physical objects necessarily being extended in space but overlook-

---

25. At the risk of confusing you, let me mention that time is a kind of 'space'. In just the way we saw in the previous section that things may be ordered in a tactile space, or in an auditory space (some 'things' are heard to be near, others far; some soft, others loud; some low-, others high-pitched; etc.), things may also be ordered in time. Time is a one-dimensional space. (Recall McTaggart's *B*-series.) Unfortunately, the potential for confusing matters is so great in talking of time as being a kind of 'space', that, having now made the point, I will drop it. I certainly do not wish to be thought to be arguing that time is the 'fourth' dimension in the set {length, height, depth}. Far too much nonsense of this latter sort has already been promoted in this century by misrepresentations and crude caricatures of relativity theory, and I have no wish to contribute further to it. The only point is that we can talk both of the general concept of *a space* (e.g. tactile, auditory, olfactory spaces) and of *the space* of length, height, and depth. It is just a sorry fact of English that the identical word "space" is used both for the generalized concept and for a specific instance of that concept. It is almost as if we used the general-ized word "figure" for both shapes in general and for some specific shape, e.g. squareness.

Some writers use the term "space" in an even broader sense than that adopted in this book. For example, in their discussion of persons searching for an explanation how a certain programmable electromechanical device works, Dunbar and Klahr ([61]) describe their subjects as 'searching the hypothesis space' and 'exploring the experiment space'. Their appeal to a 'space' in this latter context – rather than to merely a collection or set – is apt to the degree that the contents (hypotheses and experiments, respectively) of the 'spaces' referred to are capable of being ordered.

ing that they are equally necessarily extended in time. Whatever the psychological explanation may be, it is irrelevant for our purposes. It suffices simply to call attention to our historical conceptual lopsidedness about this issue.

Some persons will try to explain the felt difference in our naive attitudes toward space and time in this way: "Look at any physical object you like. The pencil in your hand will do as an example. Its entire spatial extent is given in your perception; you can see the whole spatial extent of the thing. But you cannot similarly see its entire temporal extent. You see only a brief segment of its total extent in time. The entire spatial extent is present at once, but not its temporal extent." As intuitively appealing as such a line of argumentation may be, it is curiously circular. In a way, it presupposes the very thing that needs explaining.

What does it mean to say that the entire spatial extent of the pencil is given in your perception? In looking at the pencil today, we certainly do not perceive what spatial extent that pencil may have had yesterday or may come to have tomorrow. The pencil may have been somewhat longer yesterday (it may have been sharpened and hence shortened last night); similarly it may be shorter again tomorrow. In seeing its so-called entire spatial extent we are seeing only what spatial extent it has *now*. In looking at the pencil *now*, what we see is one 'snapshot', if you will, in the entire 'lifetime' of that pencil. The entire lifetime is composed of a continuous series of snapshots. If a physical object ever in its lifetime changes in size or shape, then at no moment of observation can we ever see 'the entire spatial extent' of that object. What we in fact see in one episode of observation is but one thin 'slice' of its existence.

Some objects, however, are vastly larger than pencils. Some objects are so immense in their spatial extent that we cannot, normally, perceive that expanse in any 'snapshot' view. The Great Wall of China, for example, meanders for a distance of more than 2400 kilometers (a distance equal, roughly, to that between Paris and Moscow). There is no place on the face of the Earth where one can see both the eastern and the western termini of the Wall. And yet visitors to Beijing do often report that they have 'seen the Wall', have walked upon it, and have photographed it. The Great Wall is extravagantly extended in *both* space and time; and what counts as 'seeing the Wall' is seeing *part* of its colossal spatial extent and seeing *part* of its millennial temporal extent. One does not have to have seen the entire 2400-kilometer length, nor to have been eyewitness to the unfolding of its thousand-year history, to be entitled to claim having seen the Wall.

Physical objects are multidimensional entities. In this world they are extended in three 'spatial' dimensions, i.e. have width, height, and depth. They are also extended along one temporal dimension, i.e. have some definite (finite or perhaps infinite) duration. Moreover, each is positioned somewhere within the space (or along the continuum) of mass, i.e. each physical object has some nonnegative mass. And in addition each is positioned somewhere within the discrete (i.e. quantized) space of electrical charge, i.e. each physical object has an electrical charge which is some integral multiple of a unit charge. Thus, to say, as is often said nowadays, that physical objects are 'four-dimensional' is actually to understate the case. Physical objects have a number of dimensions beyond their spatial and temporal ones.

For our purposes, we will not pay much attention to such further dimensions as mass and electrical charge. It is not that these are unimportant. It is simply that they are not of central concern for the purposes of this chapter.

Once one has expanded one's horizon so as to conceive of physical objects, not in the seventeenth-century manner as things extended merely in width, height, and depth, but in the modern fashion as things extended in width, height, depth, and time, then some quite remarkable benefits accrue.

One particular benefit, which we will explore in the next section, is the startling insight we are given into the profound analogy between space (i.e. the space of width, height, and depth) and time. Many ancient beliefs – such as that it is possible to move about in space but not in time – are exposed as being straightforwardly based on a confusion and are simply mistaken.

The second benefit, to be explored in chapter 11, is that we have a means to solve McTaggart's puzzle about change. Or, if you happen to think McTaggart's puzzle is bogus to begin with and not in need of 'solving', then at least we have a means to address seriously the problem of change without having to posit a super-time against which time itself is moving. By conceiving of physical objects as being things extended in time, we have the conceptual equipment needed to explain change, by identifying change not as a movement of time, but as things having different properties at different times. It is things which change their properties in time; not time itself which changes relative to a super-time.

Let us turn, then, to examine the first of these alleged benefits, the revealing of the nature and extent of the formal similarity between space and time.

8.8   Taylor on spatial and temporal analogies

Over the course of your intellectual life, there will be, if you are fortunate, a number of occasions where a particular lecture, article, or book will prove revelatory. You will happen upon an outstanding piece of work which will open your eyes to a new way of seeing the familiar or seeing through the confusing. In my own career, such a piece of philosophy has been Richard Taylor's 1955 paper "Spatial and Temporal Analogies and the Concept of Identity" ([203]). I regard his paper as one of the classics of modern philosophy.[26]

Taylor undertakes to prove that there are many more *formal** similarities between space and time than are usually recognized; he does this by showing that several of the alleged differences between space and time are just that, alleged, not real.[27] To argue for these similarities, Taylor begins by pointing out that many temporal concepts have 'counterparts' (or analogs) among spatial concepts, e.g. the temporal concept *now* has an obvious spatial counterpart, *here*. So numerous are these pairings, that we can set up a mapping, or lexicon (see p. 191), for 'translating' between temporal concepts and their spatial analogs. The terms "T_1", "T_2", etc. designate specific moments of time, e.g. 14:31 Eastern Standard Time on 12 August 1948, or the moment when Columbus first set foot on the continent of North America, etc.; while "P_1", "P_2", etc. designate specific places, e.g. the northeast corner of the Acropolis, or sixty kilometers due east of the geographical center of Ottawa, Ontario.

There is, of course, one striking *dis*analogy between temporal and spatial terms: although there is but one temporal dimension, there are

---

26. Taylor credits Donald Williams ([213]) and Nelson Goodman ([81]) with having laid the groundwork for his own inquiries.

27. The qualification "several" is important; so is the characterization "*formal* similarities". Taylor is not arguing for the perfect (i.e. complete) similarity of space and time; still less that space and time are 'one and the same thing' (see footnote 25, p. 187). He is arguing only that space and time share more formal analogies than had previously been believed. In the next section, 8.9, I will explore one way in which time is not analogous to space.

Lexicon

Time	Space
"at a time T_1, T_2, …"	"at a place P_1, P_2, …"
"is earlier than"	"is north of"
"lasts (endures) for 1 minute"	"stretches for 1 meter"
"occupies (lasts throughout) the interval T_1-T_2"	"occupies the region between P_1 and P_2"
etc.	etc.

three spatial ones. To map the temporal "earlier/later", we must choose one of the three spatial candidates: I have chosen "north/south". (We simply ignore in this exercise "east/west" and "up/down"; these latter spatial terms will not be assigned temporal counterparts. And we will ignore, too, that the dimension "north/south" has endpoints [the poles] while "earlier/later" may not.)

A crucial concept in this exercise is that of *part*. Normally, when we think of the parts of things we think of their *spatial* parts. If a thing, e.g. the Trans-Canada Highway, stretches across the continent through Canada, then that part which stretches from the border of British Columbia and Alberta to the border of Manitoba and Ontario may be considered a spatial part of the highway. But insofar as physical things are extended both in space and in time (see section 8.7), we may speak of their temporal parts with as much propriety as we do of their spatial parts. If an object endures, let us say from 12 October 1928 to 19 February 1998, then the temporal interval 23 July 1933 through 5 September 1941 may be regarded as a *temporal part* of the object.

Looking at the last item in our lexicon, we can explain readily the concept of an object O 'lasting throughout' a temporal interval T_1-T_2: at every moment (instant) between T_1 and T_2, including the two instants T_1 and T_2 themselves, there exists some temporal part (called a "T-part") of the object O. Similarly, for an object to occupy the (or better "a") region between P_1 and P_2 means this: at every point along some continuous spatial path (there are of course an infinite number of such paths) connecting P_1 and P_2 there exists some spatial part (*S*-part) of the object *O*. (Note that the path need not be a straight line. Boomerangs [at rest] occupy a continuously connected region of space without occupying the region along the straight line connecting their ends.)

With the Lexicon in hand, we can proceed to examine several of Taylor's quite remarkable and startling theses.

Thesis: *Just as an object may be at one place at two different times, an object may at one time be at two different places.* This thesis is surprising just because it has been so often denied. Indeed it is virtually axiomatic in many persons' thinking about space and time that one object may be at one place at two different times, but that one object *cannot* be at one time in two different places. Their argument might be something of this sort: "This pen which I have carried about in the city today, last night sat on my desk here at home. I am now putting it back on my desk precisely where it had been last night. Yesterday it was in a certain place; today it is back in that very same place. At two different times it has occupied the same place. But no one thing can be in two different places at the same time. If the pen is now on the corner of my desk, it cannot also now be five kilometers away, on the floor of the public library." So familiar is this sort of argument, that one wonders how it is even possible to challenge it. But Taylor does so, and does so successfully.

The problem with the argument just given is that it omits to mention one exceedingly important fact. It will not do, for the purposes of arguing that one object can be in the same place on two different occasions, to talk about a certain pen last night and about a *different* pen (however similar) which occupies that place today. It must be one and the same pen. But how is the identity of today's pen with the pen which existed last night to be accounted for? The usual way for the pen which exists today to be reckoned as being the same pen as one which existed last night is for the pen of last night to have remained in existence until the present moment.[28] But once that presupposition in the description of the situation is made explicit, then the argument –

---

28. Whether existing throughout the interval is the *only* way for the pen which exists today to be reckoned as being the same pen as the one which existed last night is a question which is postponed until chapter 11. There (in

when repaired – proves not what it is usually thought to prove but precisely its contrary. Let us see why.

The standard way in which it is possible for an object O to exist in one place at two different times comes about through that object's existing at all times throughout that temporal interval. Using symbols, we may express the point this way:

O is at P_1 at T_1

O is at P_1 at T_2 (where $T_1 \neq T_2$)

O exists throughout the temporal interval T_1-T_2

If this is what is typically involved in an object's being at one place at two different times, then we may state the analogous thesis – for an object's being at one time in two different places – by using the Lexicon to translate all of the temporal terms to spatial terms and all the spatial terms to temporal. The correct, or fully stated, analog thus becomes:

O is at T_1 at P_1

O is at T_1 at P_2 (where $P_1 \neq P_2$)

O exists throughout the spatial interval P_1-P_2

Is it possible for anything to satisfy these latter conditions? If there is any such thing, then it is a thing which at one time is in two different places. As it turns out, there are countless numbers of actual things satisfying precisely these conditions. There is no need in this instance to take recourse to possible-worlds tales. The actual world provides us untold numbers of examples. The Mississippi River, for example, satisfies the just-stated conditions. At any one time it exists in two different places (e.g. in Memphis and in New Orleans) and exists throughout a spatial interval between those two places (viz. along a path through Vicksburg, Natchez, Baton Rouge, etc.).

What is commonly found in cases where an object (e.g. the pen) exists at two different times in the same place is that the object is temporally large enough to span the temporal interval from the one time to the other. In similar fashion, an object (e.g. the Mississippi River or

---

footnote 11, pp. 344ff., and again in section 11.6.5) we will examine the possibility of identity at two different times without identity through all intervening intervals. But for the moment we ignore that complication.

the Great Wall of China) can exist at two different places at the same time by being spatially large enough to span the spatial interval from the one place to the other.

There is an obvious objection to be anticipated. Someone might protest that in the case of the pen being on the desk last night and being there again today, the *entire* pen is present on both occasions; but in the case of the Mississippi River's being present in both Memphis and New Orleans, the entire river is not present at either place, only a relatively short stretch of the river's very considerable length is present at either place. But this objection fails to carry through the analogy in its full. What exactly is present, at any given time, when the pen is on the desk? Certainly not the complete temporal extent of the pen, but only a temporal part. What exactly is present, of the Mississippi River, at any given place, e.g. at Memphis or at New Orleans? Not the entire spatial extent of the river, certainly, but only limited spatial parts.

It is by identifying "parts" with "spatial parts" and overlooking "temporal parts" that one falls into the mistaken belief that the pen is wholly present at any particular time. But once one recognizes that objects are extended both in space and in time, and that at any one place there exists only a spatial part of an object, and that at any one time there exists only a temporal part of an object, then one can finally understand how objects can be both in one place at two different times and at one time in two different places. An object can be in one place at two different times if it is (temporally) long enough to extend (in time) from the one time to the other; an object can be at one time in two different places if it is (spatially) long enough to extend (in space) from the one place to the other.

What, finally, are we to say, then, of the often-proclaimed dictum that it is impossible for one object to be in two places at the same time? Taylor has shown us one way in which an object *can* be in two places at the same time. My right arm is too short (in its spatial extent) to allow it at any one time to be both in my office and in my living room. (Some three kilometers separates the two places.) But that same right arm is quite long enough to be both on the armrest of my chair and on my desk. As a matter of fact it *is* in both places now, as I write these very words.

This is as far as Taylor's first thesis takes us. But we would do well to linger a moment to ask one more question before moving on to his next thesis. Is the way described in Taylor's first thesis the *only* way for an object to be in two places at the same time? Must every object which is in two places at one time span a path between the two places? It turns out, surprisingly, that there are certain sorts of objects which can occupy two or more places at once *without* occupying any intervening places. For there are certain things which we count as 'objects' and yet which may be scattered about at a variety of places. Such 'scattered objects' are sometimes called "assemblages" or "collections". The items of clothing which make up my wardrobe, the individual books which make up my personal library, the ships comprising the u.s. Sixth Fleet, are all examples of such 'scattered objects'. Where, exactly, is my wardrobe? Most of it is in my bedroom closet; some of it is on my body; some of it is in my dresser; some is in the laundry room; some is at the dry cleaners; and some is hanging on a hook in my office at the university. My wardrobe is, thus, now at several different places. More exactly, spatial parts of my wardrobe are at several different places. But what makes my wardrobe different from other objects which are also at different places at one and the same time is that the various spatial parts of my wardrobe are not spatially connected one to another; they exist at different places *without* occupying the intervening places.

We often overlook the category of 'scattered objects', believing uncritically that all objects must have spatially connected parts. But there are too many counterexamples to allow us to sustain this naive belief. Where, for example, is Indonesia? or Michigan? or Hawaii? There is no land route through Hawaii connecting Lihue with Hilo. The northernmost island in the chain (where Lihue is located) is unconnected by land to the southernmost island (where Hilo is). (See figure 8.2, p. 196) Yet, if we want to believe that Hawaii is somewhere, i.e. has a place, then we are forced to recognize that some spatial objects (in this example, a large geographical object) do have spatially disconnected parts. And thus not only is it possible for an object to be at different places at the same time, some quite familiar objects *are* at different places at the same time; moreover, some of these latter objects (e.g. your wardrobe, the state of Hawaii) have spatial parts which are disconnected from one another.

Thesis: *Time need not be regarded as essential to change. Things may change in space just as well as in time.* If by "change" we stipulate that we *mean* temporal processes, then this claim is legislated to be false by definition. But should we be hasty to make the stipulation?

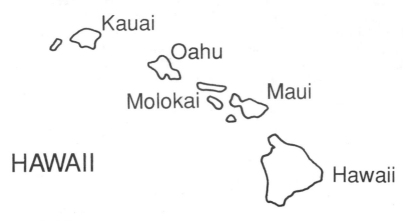

Figure 8.2

What does it mean for some object to change in time? There are at least two things that might be meant: (1) that the object changes its place, or (2) that the object changes its properties.

If being at different places at different times counts as a 'change in time', then the spatial analog is trivially satisfiable. Using the Lexicon, the analogy becomes, 'being at different places at different times'. But this latter is *precisely* the identical condition, simply restated equivalently. In short, change of place through time just *is* change of time from place to place. Things which move about in time from place to place also move about in space from one time to another. Movement in place through time is as much movement in time as it is movement in space.

What about 'change in properties' through time? An iron object may start out in a glistening, polished state at T_1. But over time, without changing its place, it may gradually rust, so that at T_2 it is considerably rusted. Is there a spatial analog? Can an object change its properties through space, i.e. at one time have different properties in different places? It is easy to describe such cases. One end of an iron object, at P_1, may be in a glistening, polished state. But at the very same time, along the spatial extent of the object, there is more and more rust. At its other end, at P_2, it is considerably rusted. The degree of rust progresses, not through time, but through space. This certainly presents itself as a change, only a change in space, not in time.

From a formal point of view, objects can 'change' as easily in space as they can in time. There seems to be no good reason to restrict the concept of *change* solely to *change in time*.

Thesis: *In just the way in which it is possible for things to change their spatial positions and relations, it is possible for things to change their temporal positions and relations.* Change in spatial position is familiar: an object O_1 which had been north of another, O_2, may later come to be south of that object. But can an object O_1 which had been earlier than O_2 come to be later than O_2? Taylor argues that the answer is Yes, if we take care to spell out the analogy in full. We begin by stating the conditions for change in spatial positions:

> O_1 at T_1 is north of O_2
>
> O_1 at T_2 is south of O_2

Using the Lexicon, we create the temporal analog:

> O_1 at P_1 is earlier than O_2
>
> O_1 at P_2 is later than O_2

Is this possible? Can an object (or event) occur before another at some place P_1 and after that other at a different place P_2? Yes, there are indeed such events.

Imagine four persons positioned at equal intervals along a straight line. (See figure 8.3, p. 198.) Alice is at position zero; Betty, one-third of a kilometer further along; Carol, at two-thirds of a kilometer from position zero; and Diane, fully one kilometer beyond position zero. They all have synchronized watches, and at 12 noon, Alice fires a starter's pistol and Diane strikes a drum once. Since sound travels through air at 331 m/sec, just about one second later, at 12:00:01 PM, Betty hears the pistol shot and Carol hears the drumbeat. And one second after that, at 12:00:02 PM, Betty hears the drumbeat and Carol, the pistol shot. Where Betty is standing, the sound of the pistol occurs one second earlier than the sound of the drum. Where Carol is standing, the order is reversed: the sound of the drum occurs one second before the sound of the pistol.

A now-familiar objection may be expressed: "When we speak of an object changing its position in space, the *entire* object is present first at one and then the other location. But in this example, the 'entire' event – the gunshot or the drum stroke – is not present at either place." But, in light of the earlier discussion, the counterobjection

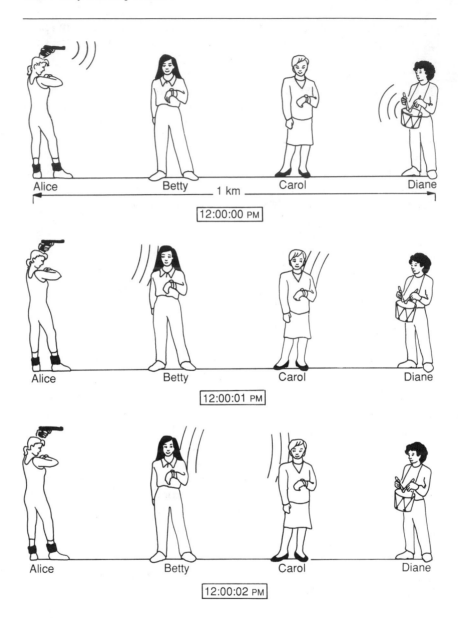

Figure 8.3

should be clear. As objects move about in space, at any given time what is present at a given place is only a temporal-part (*T*-part) of that object. In the example of the gunshot and the drumbeat, what is required for the analogy to be complete is that at any given place what is present at a given time is only a spatial-part (*S*-part) of the object. And this latter condition is precisely satisfied. As each of the two 'objects', the gunshot and the drumbeat, spread out through space (at 331 m/sec), spatial-parts occur at given places at given times. The analogy is thus complete.

McTaggart, we will recall (see above, p. 176), had explicitly denied that events can change their temporal relations: "If *M* is ever earlier than *N*, it is always earlier" ([130], §305). The present example shows that McTaggart's claim is not unconditionally true. McTaggart had overlooked the fact that certain events are of a sort which propagate through space. For such events, their order of occurrence can, and will, vary from place to place. For McTaggart's claim to be made true, it will have to be qualified in this way: "If *M* is ever earlier *at some given place* than *N*, it is always earlier *at that place* than *N*."

Thesis: *To the extent that things can 'tarry' in space, they can as well in time.* This thesis has often been denied. Things need not move about in space, it is alleged, but nothing can fail to move forward in time. Everything 'grows older', i.e. moves through time.

If, as has often been alleged, things need not move about in space, i.e. can tarry in space, can we construct an analog for something's not moving about in time? For an object to tarry in space means simply that it remains at one place during some temporal interval. Formally, this may be expressed this way:

O_1 is at P_1 throughout the temporal interval T_1-T_2

Using the Lexicon it is easy to construct the spatial analog:

O_1 is at T_1 throughout the spatial interval P_1-P_2

Rewriting to make the English slightly more idiomatic, we get:

At T_1, O_1 exists throughout the spatial interval P_1-P_2.

These latter conditions are trivially simple to satisfy. Any object O_1 which, at some particular moment of time T_1, extends from place P_1 to P_2 is occupying a given time throughout some spatial interval. Far from tarrying in space being impossible, it would seem that every physical object which takes up any space whatsoever must satisfy these conditions. The spatial analog of 'moving through time' is nothing more, or less, than being extended in space. To 'grow older' is to move through time, i.e. to occupy successive points of time. The spatial analog is simply occupying successive points of space.

Thesis: *In just the way in which things may move back and forth in space, they may also move back and forth in time.* This thesis is the highlight of Taylor's paper. It is the most startling and provocative thesis of the lot.

We must begin by attending to the formal conditions for moving forward and backward in space. Obviously, we will have to refer to three different times. We will talk of T_1, T_2, and T_3, where T_1 is the first in the series and T_3 the last. In English, we can state the conditions this way: "At first, at T_1, the object is at place P_1, but not at place P_2. Sometime later, at T_2, the object is at (i.e. has moved to) place P_2, and is, of course, no longer (i.e. at T_2) at its original place P_1. At a still later time, T_3, the object has moved back to its original place, P_1, and is (of course) no longer at P_2."

At T_1: T-part$_1$ of O is at P_1; and [at T_1]
                  no S-part of O is at P_2.

At T_2: T-part$_2$ of O is at P_2; and [at T_2]
                  no S-part of O is at P_1.

At T_3: T-part$_3$ of O is at P_1; and [at T_3]
                  no S-part of O is at P_2.

The temporal-counterpart may now be constructed. We will let P_1, P_2, and P_3 be any three ordered positions in space.

At P_1: S-part$_1$ of O is at T_1; and [at P_1]
                  no T-part of O is at T_2.

At P_2: S-part$_2$ of O is at T_2; and [at P_2]
                  no T-part of O is at T_1.

At P_3: S-part$_3$ of O is at T_1; and [at P_3]
                  no T-part of O is at T_2.

A bus shuttling back and forth between Vancouver and Burnaby satisfies the former of these two sets of conditions, i.e. it is moving back and forth in space. What is an example of something which satisfies the latter set of conditions?

To find such an example, we need to look more closely at what it is to move back and forth in space. If we examine the first set of conditions very closely, we see that they satisfy the following, alternative, description: "Consider three ordered moments of time, T_1, T_2, and T_3. If we trace the path through these three points, we discover that at the first time, the object is at P_1, at the second time the object is at a different place P_2, but when we get to the third and last time, we discover that the object is 'back at' P_1 again."

Applying the Lexicon to this latter description, we can state the formal conditions for moving back and forth in time in this equivalent, more intuitive fashion: "Consider three ordered points of space, P_1, P_2, and P_3. If we trace the path through these three points, we discover that at the first place, the object is there at T_1, at the second place the object is there at a different (later) time T_2, but when we get to the third and last place, we discover that the object is there at T_1 (i.e. has already been there at the same time it was at P_1)." In short, what is required for something's moving back and forth in time is for a thing to be simultaneously at places P_1 and P_3 and to be at P_2 (between those two places) at some other time. Could anything possibly satisfy these conditions?

Any ∨-shaped object possesses the necessary spatial features to be able to move back and forth in time. Consider a ∨-shaped object O, moving northward. (See figure 8.4, p. 202.) If we choose three places, P_1, P_2, and P_3 [Weston, Centralia, and Eastwich], lying along a west-east axis, the tips of the ∨ will pass at T_1 (viz. simultaneously) over P_1 [Weston] and P_3 [Eastwich], while the cusp of the ∨ will lie to the south of P_2 [i.e. south of Centralia]. Sometime later, at T_2, the tips of the ∨ will have passed beyond P_1 [Weston] and P_3 [Eastwich], but the cusp of the ∨ will be at P_2 [Centralia]. If one traces the spatial path from P_1 to P_2 and from P_2 to P_3, one will discover that as one progresses, O will be at P_1 [Weston] at T_1; at P_2 [Centralia] at T_2; and – surprisingly – as one gets to the third and final point, P_3 [Eastwich], one discovers that O has already been there, simultaneously with its earlier occurrence at P_1 [at Weston]. Thus this object has satisfied perfectly the formal conditions for 'moving back and forth in time'.[29]

---

29. My thanks to Professor Leslie Ballentine for calling my attention to a special feature of this and all other known examples of things which travel back and forth in time. Notice how, in this example, the object O is 'bent'

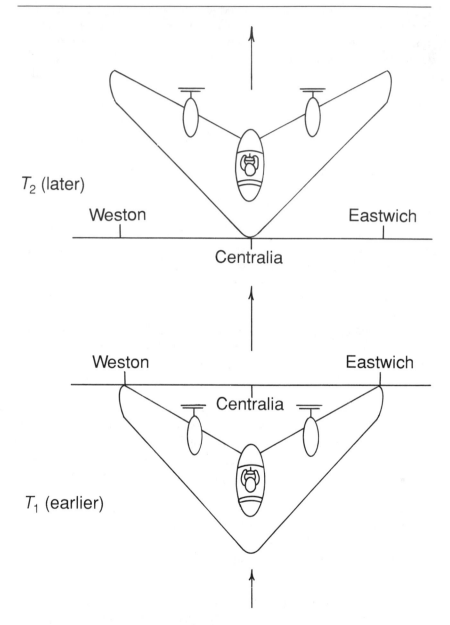

T_2 (later)

Weston   Eastwich

Centralia

Weston   Eastwich

Centralia

T_1 (earlier)

Figure 8.4

The pivotal point in this last thesis – "In just the way in which things may move back and forth in space, they may also move back and forth in time" – is, of course, in the qualification, "in just the way". For it is not being claimed, for example, that you can now, as an adult, travel backward in time and shake hands with yourself as an eight-year-old, or that you can travel forward to the future and attend your own funeral.[30] The claim here is far more modest. It is being claimed only that in the way in which it is possible for (a temporal-part of) an object first to be at one place, (a temporal-part) to be later at another place, and still later (a temporal-part) to be back at the first place, then in a parallel way it is possible for (a spatial-part of) an object at one place to occur at a certain time, (a spatial-part) to be present at a further place at a later time, and (a spatial-part) to be present at a still further place at the same time as (a spatial-part of) it occurred in the first place. If the former of these situations is to count as 'moving about in space', then the latter is entitled to be regarded as 'moving about in time'.

8.9   Is there a temporal analog of the "right/left" problem?[31]

Immanuel Kant seems to have been the first philosopher to have been intrigued by the differences between what, in modern terminology,

---

in two spatial dimensions, viz. it was ∨-shaped. In order to cite an actual example, it was necessary to invoke a spatial object having (at least) two spatial dimensions. It is *theoretically* possible that movement back and forth in time should occur for an object which is not 'bent' in space. But it seems to be a contingent fact of this world, however, that the only objects which do move back and forth in space are of the sort described, i.e. are objects which are curved in two or more spatial directions.

30. What characterizes these latter two examples is that two temporal stages, or *T*-parts, of an object are simultaneously present at a place. Nothing in Taylor's argument permits such an occurrence. Whether 'moving about in time' in this *latter* sense – in which two distinct *T*-parts of an object may be simultaneously present – is coherent will be examined later (in section 8.11).

31. This section is a slightly revised and expanded version of the article, "Is There an Ozma Problem for Time?" which originally appeared in *Analysis* 33, no. 3 (Jan. 1973), 77-82. I am pleased to acknowledge my indebtedness to J.F. Bennett's fine paper "The Difference between Right and Left" ([26]) which examined the spatial version of the problem which provokes this present discussion.

have come to be called "incongruous counterparts" or – more technically still – "enantiomorphs". Enantiomorphs are mirror images of one
another, although not all mirror images are enantiomorphs. The mirror
image of the letter "A" is not an enantiomorph; the mirror image of
the letter "Z" is. The difference is that there is a (vertical) axis of
symmetry in the letter "A", i.e. the letter is *symmetrical* about its vertical axis: A. The letter "Z" has no axis of symmetry, either vertically or
horizontally: ƻ, ⱬ. Hence the letter "Z" and its mirror image form a
pair of enantiomorphs.

Enantiomorphs may be pairs of one-dimensional figures, pairs of
two-dimensional figures, or pairs of three-dimensional figures. The
one-dimensional figures

$$\boxed{-\ -\ -} \qquad \boxed{-\ -\ -}$$

are enantiomorphs. Neither one can be moved in a one-dimensional
space (i.e. slid sideways) so as to be made to coincide with the other.
Of course, if either one were to be rotated in a two-dimensional space,
e.g. in the plane of this page on which they are printed, they could be
made to coincide. The two-dimensional figures $\boxed{b}$ and $\boxed{d}$ are enantiomorphs: neither can be moved about (including being rotated) in
two-dimensional space so as to allow it to coincide with the other. But
while $\boxed{b}$ and $\boxed{d}$ are enantiomorphs, $\boxed{b}$ and $\boxed{q}$ are not: either one
can be moved (rotated) so as to permit it to coincide with the other.
Similarly $\boxed{d}$ and $\boxed{p}$ are non-enantiomorphs, i.e. are congruous figures.

Kant's examples (1783) were of three-dimensional enantiomorphs:
"... the left hand cannot be enclosed in the same bounds as the right
one (they are not congruent); the glove of one hand cannot be used for
the other" (*Prolegomena* [107], §13). A right-handed glove cannot be
rigidly moved about in three-dimensional space so as to be made to fit
a left hand. It can, of course, be turned inside out, and that will do the
trick. But turning a glove inside out is not a rigid movement through
space. It involves stretching or bending the object. For two objects to
be regarded as enantiomorphs, it is necessary that they cannot be
brought into coincidence (i.e. cannot be made congruent) without
bending or stretching.

What is there about the right- and the left-handed gloves which
accounts for their being enantiomorphs of one another? Each glove we
may suppose is made of the same sort of material as its mate, each
weighs the same as the other, each has the same total volume as the
other, and each has a thumb, followed in order by four fingers: the

index (or forefinger), the middle, the third, and the so-called little finger. Even so, for all these similarities, there is a profound difference, as all of us who have ever mistakenly tried to fit a left-handed glove on our right hand know very well. Of course we can put labels to these differences: we can say that one of these gloves is "left"-handed and the other "right". But the important question – for Kant and subsequent writers – has been whether or not these terms "right" and "left" could ever be *learned* by someone who had not *experienced* the sort of difference exhibited by the pair of gloves.

A century later, Kant's problem about the difference between "right" and "left" appears in William James's *Principles of Psychology*, where it can be seen to be evolving into a problem about *communication*: "If we take a cube and label one side *top*, another [presumably the side parallel to it] *bottom*, a third *front* and a fourth [again, presumably, the side parallel to the latter] *back*, then there remains no form of words by which we can describe to another person which of the remaining sides is *right* and which is *left*" ([103], vol. II, 150). James's claim, obviously, needs to be qualified. For there is one, trivial, way in which we can describe the difference. We can call the one "right" and the other "left". But we see what James was getting at, even if he managed to express himself poorly.

Suppose you are in telephone contact with someone and are trying to get her to duplicate a certain cube whose faces you have labeled in a particular fashion. (See figure 8.5, p. 206.) You want the front labeled with a single dot; the back labeled with two dots; the top, with three; the bottom, with four; the left, with five; and the right, with six. You begin by telling her to pick *any* side and label it with one dot; to move to the parallel (opposite) side and label it with two dots. Then she can choose any one of the remaining four sides and label it with three dots; and fourthly she is to label with four dots the side parallel to the one bearing the three dots. But now there is a problem (James's problem). In assigning the next two sets of dots, she cannot just arbitrarily pick one of the two remaining sides and label it with five dots, and the sixth, the last, remaining side with the set of six dots: she has got to get the fifth choice, the left-hand side, correct. She has to put her five dots on the same side, the left-hand side, as you have put your five dots. You have, that is, to make sure that she is using the terms "left" and "right" in the same way you are, and has not – somehow – got them reversed. (Some persons, we know all too well, frequently mistake the two directions, right and left. Perhaps your telephone correspondent is confused or, even worse, was taught to speak

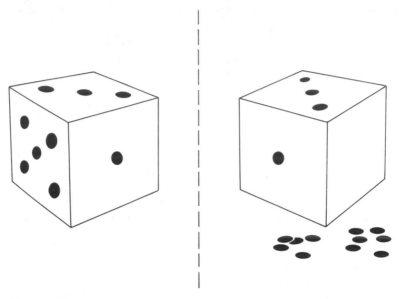

Figure 8.5

English by someone with a perverse sense of humor.) How can you make sure that she is using the terms "left" and "right" as you do?

You realize that you can solve the problem if you can figure out in which hand she is holding the telephone headset. You ask her, and she replies "my right hand". But still you are not sure that she is using the terms "right" and "left" just as you do. There are various ways you might go about trying to determine whether she is using the words in the same way as you, or in the reverse manner. You might ask her, further, whether she was holding the headset in the hand which is on the same side of her body as her appendix. In this latter instance, you would be assuming that her body was anatomically similar to that of nearly every other woman. Or, again, you might ask her to look up in the night sky and describe, using the terms "right" and "left", the spatial relations of various constellations to one another. So long as you could see those constellations, then you could quickly tell whether she was using the terms "right" and "left" as you do, or whether she had got them 'reversed'.

It is clear that there *are* a variety of ways to tell whether someone, out of sight, with whom you are communicating uses the terms "right" and "left" in the same, or a reversed, manner. But all of these ways, it seems, involve presupposing that you and the other person have access to one or more shared enantiomorphs: the asymmetrical disposition of internal organs (e.g. the appendix) in the human body, overhead stellar constellations, etc.

The problem is 'cranked up a notch' when these latter, obvious, solutions are explicitly disallowed. Suppose in the Search for Extra-Terrestrial Intelligence (see the discussion of SETI in section 5.2, pp. 80ff.), you are in communication with a distant intelligence, on a planet so shrouded by a dense cloud cover that there is no opportunity for you and her to observe any physical object in common. Moreover, her own body is not at all humanoid. She does not even have an appendix. Of course she does not speak English or any other Earth-based language. You communicate via a code, similar to Morse code, i.e. of pulsating signals. Presuming you could even get to the point of intelligible conversation (again, see section 5.2), could you figure out which term in her language meant "right" and which "left"?

Martin Gardner, in his *Ambidextrous Universe*, states the problem in this manner:

> Is there any way to communicate the meaning of "left" by a language transmitted in the form of pulsating signals? By the terms of the problem we may say anything we please to our listeners, ask them to perform any experiment whatever, with one proviso: *There is to be no asymmetric object or structure that we and they can observe in common.* ([75], 160)

Gardner calls this the "Ozma problem". (He has borrowed the name from the Ozma project, a 1960 project of SETI, whose director, Frank D. Drake, in turn had borrowed the name from a character in a book by L. Frank Baum.)

The Ozma problem has never been raised in regard to any but spatial relations. Is this just lack of imagination? Richard Taylor, we have already seen (section 8.8), has argued persuasively for a very much more thorough analogy between spatial and temporal relations than had previously been thought possible. How much further can we press the analogy? Specifically, can we construct an Ozma problem for time? Is there, that is, a problem with "earlier/later" analogous to "right/left"? The task divides into two stages. First we must formulate the proper analogy, and second we must investigate whether the problem is solvable.

For current purposes, the Lexicon given above (p. 191) is inadequate. We will require one modification and two additions. Where we had earlier mapped "earlier/later" onto "north/south", we will now map the former onto "left/right". And in order to translate Gardner's statement of the spatial Ozma problem into its temporal equivalent, we will have to have dictionary equivalents for both "pulsating signals" and "asymmetric object".

"Pulsating signals" may be taken to mean something like "a series of markers (e.g. audible beeps and their absences) arranged in a temporal order". Implicit in Gardner's story is that the signals or messages should be received during a time, i.e., consecutively, but at one place. A Taylor-analog could, then, be something of this sort: "a series of markers arranged in a spatial order". To ensure the completeness of the analogy we must add the rider that this message should be received within a spatial extent but all at one time. A notched iron bar, for example (where the notches are the coded message), would satisfy the description. The message is extended over a space (i.e. the length of the bar) and is all of it simultaneously present.

The temporal analog of a spatially asymmetric object is easy to name but perhaps slightly more difficult to explain. A temporally asymmetric object is one for which there is no moment such that the history of the object up to that moment is the 'reflection' of the future of that object subsequent to that moment. Noticeably the explanation seems to be infected with a slight residue of spatial terminology, viz. "reflection". The term is, however, a mere convenience. We have many more occasions to speak of spatial reflections than of temporal ones, but the suitability of the term for both contexts should be obvious. Most objects are temporally asymmetric, but not quite all. With a little ingenuity we can actually make a temporally symmetric object. For example, a pure pitch of constant volume, physics tells us, would sound exactly the same if recorded and played backward. There is in such an example a temporal axis of symmetry: there is some moment, the midtime of its duration, about which the sound is temporally symmetric, i.e. reflected.

It is important to note for our discussion below that physical objects, too, are very often temporally symmetric within selected time intervals. For example, the notched iron bar which we have alluded to may for years undergo no internal physical change whatever. During that segment of its total history it is temporally symmetric. If nothing is happening to it over a course of, let us say, two centuries, then the description we give of what happens to it from the first year to the end of the one hundredth year is precisely the same as any description we give of it from the end of the two hundredth year (backward) to the beginning of the one-hundred-and-first year. Putting the matter perhaps a bit cryptically: we cannot tell by examining the bar during that two-hundred-year interval whether it is growing older or younger. In this respect it is the temporal analog of a spatial object which has no preferred direction, e.g. William James's cube.

For fairly obvious reasons in the statement of the temporal Ozma problem only temporally symmetric objects are to be mutually accessible to both of the communicators. Allowing a bit of judicious editing, the problem emerges thus:

> Is there any way to communicate the meaning of "earlier than" by a message transmitted all at once by a series of spatially arranged markers? By the terms of the problem we may send any message we please, with one proviso: There is to be no temporally asymmetric object or structure to which the sender and receiver have mutual access.

Does this problem really make sense? Can there be a problem about communicating the meaning of "earlier than" at all analogous to the problem of communicating the meaning of "left of"? We understand how one person communicating with another by telephone should be frustrated in trying to tell the other person, who did not already know, which was her left hand and which her right. Could there really be a problem in trying to instruct the other what the difference between earlier and later is? The very fact that they are communicating at all, that one is saying *now* this and *then* that, would seem to solve the problem. Even if, by the terms of the problem, the message must be received in its entirety all at once so that conversation between the two parties over a period of time is explicitly excluded, the *reading* of the message, unlike the mere receiving of the message, is emphatically *not* instantaneous but must take some amount of time. We can imagine the sender forwarding the following sort of message:

> Dear reader: I should like to explain to you how I am using the terms "earlier" and "later". The reading of this message, we both know, takes time. We further know that events are ordered in time. You can understand what I mean by "earlier" and

"later" by reflecting on the point that as I use the term "earlier"
you will have read the word "Dear" *earlier* than you will have
read the word "reader". You will have read "reader" *later* than
you will have read "Dear".

This ready solution to the temporal Ozma problem is, however,
mere illusion. The argument harbors an important implicit assumption
which, when exposed, undermines the conclusion. To reveal this
assumption I propose to pursue the problem in a slightly altered, but
equivalent, way.

Let us imagine the original (spatial) version of the Ozma problem
as concerning not the instructing of a remote listener as to which is
right and which left, but rather the attempt to discover, by means of
the communication link we have described, which items on the distant
planet are incongruous counterparts or enantiomorphs of items here on
Earth. The two versions of the spatial Ozma problem are equivalent in
this respect: a solution to either one would provide a means to solve
the other. As we have seen, if we knew that the intelligence with
whom we were talking on the telephone had a body spatially congruent to our own, i.e. was not enantiomorphic relative to us, we could
simply tell her that her right hand was the one which was on the same
side of her body as her appendix. The solution to the first problem
provides a means of solving the second, and (it should be obvious)
conversely.

In the light of this alternative description of the spatial version of
the Ozma problem, we can construct a second formulation of the temporal Ozma problem. Under this revision we can conceive of the problem, equivalently, as concerning the attempt to inform the receiver
whether the region in which the message originated shares a time
direction congruent with that of the receiver or whether the two regions are temporal enantiomorphs of one another.

Stating the problem in this way, we can readily see what is wrong
with the suggested solution to the temporal Ozma problem: it helps
itself gratuitously to one of the two possibilities which are to be
decided between. For consider: if the region in which the message is
received is suffering a local time reversal, then the test forwarded by
our misguided sender will have precisely the opposite effect to the one
intended. If we were to observe that strange planet directly it would
appear to us to be running backward. Creatures would grow younger
instead of older, golf balls would fly out of holes and stop abruptly at
the head of a putter, which is then cocked upward, etc. Similarly for

the reading of the message. Relative to *our* time, the receiver would "start" reading at what we take to be the end of the message and would finish reading some time later with the word "Dear". "Dear" (contrary to our expectations) would be read later than "reader", not earlier.

The analogy with the spatial Ozma problem thus emerges rather more live than the first solution would have led us to think it might. But if this solution does not work, is there any that does? Is there any message conceivable, subject to the constraints given, which would allow the passing of decisive information concerning the relative directions of time in the regions of the sender and of the receiver? The original spatial Ozma problem, the problem of finding out whether our correspondent is like or oppositely handed, is generally acknowledged to be *insolvable* short of performing certain quite technical (and expensive) experiments in particle physics.[32] At the level of ordinary experience, the spatial version of the Ozma problem remains insolvable (see [26]). Is the temporal Ozma problem similarly insolvable? An argument can be given that the latter, temporal, version is also insolvable.

Suppose we were able to observe directly two planets which are temporal enantiomorphs of one another. (If we were to film the histories of both of these planets and then run *one* film backward, the scenes projected would be indistinguishable.) On one of these planets, the one in which time runs the same way as ours, we see a woman pick up an iron bar, clamp it in a vice, and studiously proceed to file a series of notches in it. For a while filings fall to the floor. At last she is finished, she unclamps the bar, and places it away on a shelf where it sits for a very long time.

---

32. In 1956-7 it was shown in a series of landmark experiments – which were to win a Nobel Prize for Chen Ning Yang and Tsung Dao Lee, who had proposed that such experiments be undertaken – that there is a fundamental asymmetry in the manner in which certain subatomic particles decay [disintegrate]. Anyone, anywhere in the universe who duplicated these experiments – provided that the laws of Nature are uniform throughout the universe – would, theoretically, then be in a position to be instructed how to apply the terms "right" and "left" unambiguously. But to date, this seems to be the *only* way to solve the spatial version of the Ozma problem. Anyone operating with the 'normal' artifacts of everyday experience would be totally unable to solve the problem.

As we look in on the second planet, we see a similarly notched bar sitting on a shelf. At first all appears normal. After a while, however, strange things begin to happen. A woman walks backward into the room, takes the bar from the shelf and clamps it in a vice. A file rises abruptly from the workbench to her waiting hand. She places the edge of the file into one of the notches in the bar. Suddenly some filings leap from the floor to meet the file which is abruptly drawn across the bar, welding these flying particles into the notch in the bar. And so the story goes on.

But what about the bars during these longish periods when they sit unchangingly on their shelves? If we look at one of the bars during just that time, we cannot tell on which of the two planets it resides. We must wait to see what happens *on that planet*. The Ozma problem asks us to imagine such a bar removed from its planet of origin, to imagine it wrenched from its surroundings with their telltale clues and delivered naked to us. Can we tell by examining the bar on which planet it originated? The conclusion we are driven to is that there is *no* way to tell. Anything that the writer on the first planet could have written could, with equal likelihood, appear verbatim in a message from the second planet. We would be totally unable to assign such a message to one planet or to its temporally reversed counterpart. Thus the analogy between the spatial and temporal versions of the Ozma problem seems complete.

Surprisingly, this conclusion too, just like its erstwhile opposite, follows from a defective argument and must be rejected. Let us see why.

This latter argument, an argument for the insolvability of the problem, assumes that we can transport the iron bars in question off of each of the two planets described. There is, of course, no problem for the planet in which the direction of time is the same as that of Earth. We can imagine the machinist in the first case returning eventually, taking the bar down from the shelf, ensconcing it in a rocket, and launching the rocket heavenward. Years later the rocket in its aimless flight is intercepted quite accidentally by some earthlings who, knowing nothing of its place of origin, take its cargo home to study.

But what story shall we tell for the second case? What sort of *causal* chain of events can deliver a bar to us from a planet where time is oppositely directed? There would seem to be a profound difficulty in there being communication, or causal interaction, between two planets so related. For the second planet, the rocket-ship account simply will not work. For the woman in our second story to take the bar, place it in a rocket, and launch it off into space would *for her on that planet* be a case of her operating contrary to the laws of thermodynamics. We would expect on this second planet – since time there is running in the reverse direction to our time – that rocket ships would land while sucking in flames and smoke, but not that they should lift off spewing out flames and smoke.

How then *are* we to get possession of the bar? It would appear that the only way for us to receive the described sort of message from a planet whose time direction was opposite to ours would require that there be a violation of some causal laws on one or both of the two planets.

So far-reaching is this point that it even requires that we retract the thought experiment which originally set the stage on which the problem was to be played out. We have uncritically imagined someone looking in on both of two planets having opposite time directions. But even this amount of causal interaction is in violation of causal laws. Part of the story we tell of the process of seeing involves the emission of photons from objects and the *subsequent* impinging of these photons on our retinas. But this process is obviously directed in time. On a planet where time ran oppositely to ours, *we* could not see objects at all: objects would not be photon-emitters, but would be photon-sinks (i.e. would 'suck in' photons).

In sum, the analogy ultimately flounders. The Ozma problem for spatial relations is genuine for all regions of the universe where time is directed as it is on Earth. No causal laws need be violated for two spatially incongruous planets (e.g. where humanoids have their appendixes on the left, rather than the right, sides of their bodies) to be in temporal communication with one another. The analogous situation does not hold for temporally incongruous planets. For two temporally incongruous planets to be in communication by means of a spatially extended message does require the violation of causal laws on one or both of the two planets concerned.

Taylor-type analogies between spatial and temporal relations do, apparently, have their limits. The Ozma problem is one feature of spatial relations which is without counterpart among temporal relations. While we can construct an Ozma problem for spatial relations, given things as they stand here and now, we can construct an analogous Ozma problem for temporal relations only if time 'runs backward' in some regions of the universe.

8.10   On the connectedness of space and the connectedness of time[33]

Once again, the problem derives from Kant. In the *Critique of Pure Reason*, Kant argues that we must conceive of space (i.e. the space of length, width, and depth) and of time as each being unified, i.e. that there cannot be several spaces or more than one time.

> ... we can represent to ourselves only one space; and if we speak of diverse spaces, we mean thereby only parts of one and the same unique space. ... These parts cannot precede the one all-embracing space, as being, as it were, constituents out of which it can be composed; on the contrary, they can be thought only as *in* it. Space is essentially one. ([106], A25)

> Different times are but parts of one and the same time. ... The infinitude of time signifies nothing more than that every deter-minate magnitude of time is possible only through limitations of one single time that underlies it. ([106], A32)

Kant believes that the human mind is constrained to operate in this manner, that we cannot coherently think of (actually existing) objects which are spatially inaccessible to one another, or of incidents in time which do not stand in unique positions in a single temporal con-tinuum.

In effect, Kant's claim about space is that it is a priori necessary for

---

33. This section is a revised version of "Spatial and Temporal Worlds: Could There Be More Than One of Each?" which appeared in *Ratio* 57, no. 2 (Dec. 1975), and in the German edition, as "Räumliche Welten und zeitliche Welten: Könnte es mehr als je eine geben?" In this present version, much of the original terminology has been altered to accord with that adopted in this book.

I would particularly like to re-express my gratitude to Jonathan Bennett, who painstakingly read two early versions of the original paper and offered invaluable advice, some of which I declined on the first occasion of publica-tion, but which I am now happy to follow. I would also like to express thanks to Raymond Bradley and the participants in the Faculty and Graduate Semi-nar at Simon Fraser University for their helpful comments. Eike-Henner Kluge found an error in the original published version. I have addressed the matter he raised, and tried to correct it, in footnote 34 (p. 217) below.

any two spatially extended objects to stand in some determinate spatial relations to one another. It is impossible for (the spatial parts of) either object not to be in some spatial direction (south, north-by-northwest, etc.) to (the spatial parts of) the other. Similarly, his claim about time is that it is a priori necessary for any two temporally extended objects to stand in some determinate temporal relations to one another. It is impossible for (the temporal parts of) either object not to be in some temporal relation (i.e. earlier than, simultaneous with, or later than) to (the temporal parts of) the other. All of this is, of course, just another way of saying that space and time are each unified, that the regions of space are not disconnected from one another, and that incidents in time are not disconnected from one another. Like Taylor (see section 8.8), Kant can be seen to be arguing that there is an important *analogy* between space and time. In this instance, that both can be conceived of only as being unified.

Anthony Quinton has challenged Kant's claims about this particular analogy between space and time. Quinton argues ([164]) that Kant is right about time, that time must be unified, but argues that Kant was wrong about space. He argues that space (the space of length, width, and depth) need *not* be unified.

I think that Quinton has made a mistake. I will try to show that Kant was correct in arguing that there *is* an analogy between space and time in respect of connectedness. That is, I agree with Kant that if either space or time is unified, then so, too, is the other. But where I differ from Kant is in arguing that neither space nor time need be conceived of as unified, that we *can* conceive of both space and time as being unconnected. In short, Kant was right in arguing that there is an analogy; but he was wrong about what that analogy actually is.

Quinton begins by trying to show that space need not be thought to be necessarily connected. (His first argument needs some minor repair, which I will make below; but on the whole it is correct.) Quinton then attempts to construct a parallel argument in an attempt to prove that time need not be thought to be necessarily connected, but finds he is unable to do so. From this, Quinton concludes that Kant was right about time, that time must be unified. I will try to show that Quinton's second argument – for the unity of time – rests on two mistakes, and that his conclusion is not warranted. I will try to show that time, like space, need not be thought to be necessarily connected.

Quinton approaches the problem through the now-familiar method of telling a possible-worlds tale. In an attempt to prove that two spatial regions may be totally unconnected to one another, Quinton describes a man living in England who when he falls asleep finds himself at a lakeside in a tropical setting. His experiences at the lakeside, unlike many dream-sequences, are as ordinary, as matter-of-fact, and as uneventful as are his everyday English experiences. Nothing dream-like, fantastic, or wildly unlikely occurs in the tropical environment. The hero passes the day in the tropics and when he falls asleep there immediately finds himself in England. And these English and tropical experiences regularly alternate.

Faced with these two sets of experiences both of which are non-dreamlike, both of which seem to be waking experiences, how do we determine which is dream and which is reality? Quinton fills in his tale in such a way as to make the decision arbitrary and hence impossible. To the objection that the lakeside experience is not public, he lets it be public: various other persons in England on going to sleep similarly find themselves in the tropical setting; they meet their English acquaintances there ([164], 142), etc. As the details get filled in, it becomes more and more unreasonable to say of either set of experiences that it is a dream and the other is genuine. Rather, from the contrived similarity of the experiences we would want to say that they are both genuine. They are very unlike dreams: they are not fantastic, they are public, scientific principles work in both, etc. In a word, we would have to say that Quinton's hero inhabits *two* places.

Having effectively argued that it is possible that a person should inhabit two places, the next step of the argument involves determining whether these two places must be located within the same physical space or not. At this point, Quinton's argument falters a bit: "Suppose that I am in a position to institute the most thorough geographical investigations and however protractedly and carefully these are pursued they fail to reveal anywhere on earth like my lake. But could we not then say that it must be on some other planet? We could but it would be gratuitous to do so. There could well be no positive reason whatever, beyond our fondness for the Kantian thesis, for saying that the lake is located somewhere in ordinary physical space and there are, in the circumstances envisaged, good reasons for denying its location there" ([164], 143). To be frank, I do not see what 'good reasons' Quinton has in mind when he says that there are good reasons for denying that the lake is located in ordinary physical space. His assertions to the contrary notwithstanding, as he has described the circumstances, it *is* perfectly possible that the lake should exist on some other planet in 'ordinary physical space'. Nevertheless his possible-worlds tale can be enhanced in such a way as to yield the results he seeks. Rather than simply having his hero 'institute the most thorough geographical investigations' on Earth, let us add to the tale that the hero carries out a thorough exploration of his *entire* spatial world. Admittedly this is a trifle hard to imagine, but it is not at all logically impossible. At best it is physically* impossible. But since we are telling a possible-worlds tale anyway, a tale which may depart, short of logical inconsistency, as much as we wish from the facts of this world, there is no particular difficulty in adding to the story the information that the hero completes an infinite number of explorations in a finite time. (Perhaps he has a kind of radar-like device whose signal traverses space instantaneously.) In any case, we simply build it into our tale that a *complete* examination of the space in which either locale is situated fails to reveal the other locale. And with this repair to his tale effected, we can proceed to Quinton's first set of conclusions: the two places are in different spaces, i.e. are spatially unconnected, and Kant's thesis that at most one space is possible is refuted.[34]

Quinton's possible-worlds tale has one particularly odd feature which he does not comment on, but which, because it may appear to undermine his case, deserves to be made explicit and defended. It is often claimed that a person cannot be in two places at one time. Quin-

---

34. There is a residual problem: perhaps the lakeside is located not at an unconnected place in space, but is at a connected place, only it is in the future or the past. Can we adjust for this complication? I think we can. We are given that the marvelous radar-like device can furnish an instantaneous snapshot picture of all of space accessible from England. Suppose, further, that the region of space which contains England is a reasonably deterministic one in which extensive prediction and retrodiction* are possible. And finally suppose that the best scientists know enough of the laws of nature to be able to perform remarkably complete predictions and retrodictions. Under these circumstances, scientists might be able to deduce that the region of space which contains England never has, and never will, contain the lakeside setting. Such empirical evidence would indicate that the lakeside is not connected both in time and in place to England, i.e. (1) that if the space which contains England is unified, then the lakeside stands in a time stream outside of that of England; (2) that if time is unified, then the lakeside resides in a space unconnected to the space which contains England; or (3) that the lakeside is neither temporally nor spatially connected to England. Each of these results challenges at least one of the two Kantian theses. Taken altogether, they would indicate that there are no grounds to regard either of his theses as being a priori necessary.

ton's tale seems to run afoul of this prohibition, for the fellow he describes while asleep in England is simultaneously awake in the tropical setting. He would appear then to be in two places at the same time.[35] But while this is true – and undeniably odd in the extreme – it does not, by itself, serve to undermine Quinton's tale. For, as he has described the situation, with there being no causal interaction between the two places, nothing untoward or incoherent follows from the hero's being in two places at the same time. The hero's being in two places at the same time seems to work no mischief in this context and the tale remains innocent. Perhaps the impossibility claim ought to be tidied up to read, "No person can be *awake and* in two places at the same time", but it is not clear that even this repaired claim is true. In any case we need not pursue it, for – as Quinton first tells the tale – the hero is never awake in two places at the same time. Whenever he is awake in one, he is asleep in the other.

Having constructed his first possible-worlds tale in which he argues for the possibility of there being two distinct spaces, Quinton asks whether we can construct an analogous tale showing the possibility of there being two times. Surprisingly he argues that time, unlike space, is unitary, that there can be only one time.

Quinton does not seem to realize, however, that the technique of possible-worlds storytelling is ineffectual for his purposes. Rather than, as in the first tale, trying to establish the logical possibility of a certain proposition (viz., "There are two spatially unconnected places"), he is trying to establish the logical *im*possibility of a certain proposition (viz., "There are two temporally unconnected events"). It suffices in the first case simply to show that there exists some fairly expansive, consistent description of some possible world or other in

---

35. Remember, Taylor's first thesis (pp. 192ff.) states only a sufficient condition for an object's being in two places at the same time, viz. by being spatially large enough to span a path between the two. But that thesis does not claim that this is the *only* way for a thing to be in two places at the same time. Taylor's thesis leaves open the possibility that a thing may exist in two places at the same time *without* occupying each point along a spatial path connecting the two.

That Quinton's hero is simultaneously in two different places is a corollary of his second thesis, to wit, that there cannot be more than one time. When we get to that discussion, in a moment, I will argue against the propriety of Quinton's using that description of his hero. But for the moment, it does no damage to accept it.

which the proposition in question ("There are two spatially unconnected places") occurs. But to show, as Quinton wishes, in the second case, that some given proposition is logically *im*possible, it is insufficient to author *one* tale in which the proposition ("There are two temporally unconnected events") occurs and to show that that tale is logically inconsistent. Rather, in order to prove the proposition to be logically impossible, Quinton must show that any tale whatever which includes the proposition under survey would be logically inconsistent.

The method of possible-worlds storytelling is well-suited for showing that certain propositions (of the form "There is an *x* such that *x* is *y*") are logically possible. All one must do is to find one such story in which the claim occurs and which is free of self-contradiction. But the method is ineffectual when it comes to proving the negation, i.e. when it comes to proving the impossibility of propositions of that form. For now the job becomes, not one of showing that some *one* story which includes the proposition is free of inconsistency, but rather that *every* story which includes the proposition is self-inconsistent. What the latter really amounts to is not storytelling at all, but rather explaining why it is impossible to tell a self-consistent possible-worlds tale in which the proposition at issue is included.

But this is not what Quinton undertakes. Instead, he proceeds as he did in the first instance. He attempts to tell a possible-worlds tale in which the claim that there are two temporally unconnected events occurs; he argues that this latter story entails a contradiction; and concludes that it is impossible that there should be two temporally unconnected events. Just from considerations of methodology alone we can argue that he has failed to establish his negative thesis. Finding one case in which the supposition that there are two temporally unconnected events leads to an inconsistency does *nothing* to establish the impossibility of there being temporally unconnected events. His approach to the question can yield only inconclusive results. The method of possible-worlds storytelling cannot establish the negative results he desires.

But questions of methodology aside, Quinton commits a second error. There is an internal flaw in the latter possible-worlds tale he tells. Even though, were it successful in entailing an inconsistency, it would still be insufficient to justify his negative thesis, I will try to show that it fails at the more limited task of entailing an inconsistency. For Quinton's latter tale, when shorn of a question-begging assumption, in fact demonstrates precisely what Quinton is trying to deny, viz. that it is logically possible that there should be two temporally unconnected events. Quinton produces two arguments ([164], 145 and 146) to show that every lakeside event can be dated in England. I will examine only his first argument. (I think the flaw is virtually identical in both cases.)

He asks us to imagine that the fellow who is alternately in England and in the tropics cannot remember whether lakeside events occurred earlier or later than the events he remembers in England. But, says Quinton (switching again into a first-person narrative): "The trouble with this obstacle to unitary dating is that it is too easily circumvented. At the beginning of day 1 in England I write down in order all the lakeside events I can remember. On day 2 in England I cannot remember whether the events of day 1 follow or preceded the lakeside events in the list. But the list will be there to settle the matter and I can, of course, remember when I compiled it" ([164], 145). The error here is subtle. Quinton argues that unitary dating (i.e. the intercalating) of events in the two sequences can be obtained by the simple expedient of daily writing down in one sequence the events one remembers from the other. I agree that this device will work, provided one is writing down one's *memories*. But how, in a non-question-begging way, is this matter to be decided? How does Quinton's hero know that he is writing down memories (of past events) and not, for example, precognitions (of future events)? Let it be granted that each time the hero of the tale awakes in England he *knows* one day's worth (or twelve hours' worth or whatever) more information about the lakeside events. I am not calling into question that his writing down of his experiences is the chronicling of genuine occurrences and that he can be said to know that such-and-such events truly are incidents occurring at the lakeside. What I am challenging is his right to describe this knowledge, these daily cognitions in England, as *memory*.

What criteria need be satisfied to entitle us to say of a cognition that it is a case of memory? Are these criteria satisfied or even satisfiable in the case under examination? In order to see what is involved in making the decision between memory and other modes of cognition, let us ask ourselves how we make the decision in the ordinary case, in our normal, ordinary series of wakeful experiences. For convenience' sake, let us for the moment restrict our attention to a single alternative mode of cognition: precognition. Precognition (foreknowledge or prescience), if it occurs at all, occurs so rarely that we need hardly ever trouble ourselves over the matter of distinguishing it from memory. But if it did occur more often and we did have to distinguish it from memory, we could not do so on any intrinsic feature of the experience itself or on any introspective basis. No mental phenomena carry with them an identifying mark of memoryhood. Some of the things we think we recall never happened at all, yet introspectively these thoughts (images, beliefs) are indistinguishable from genuine memories. Merely being memorable or, more exactly, having the felt quality of a memory is no guarantee of the truth of that which has that quality. Our mental faculties can be faulty or deceived. We can believe that we remember events and it turns out that these events did not occur, and similarly we can fail to remember events that did occur. That a thought or mental image is really of a past occurrence and not perhaps a precognition of a future one is guaranteed by nothing in the thought or the image itself. The manner in which memories and precognitions present themselves to consciousness seems to be all of a piece. To learn that a memory-like thought is really a memory and not a precognition we must depend ultimately on objective criteria and more exactly on *physical* criteria.

Generally we do not have to depend on physical criteria, for we quickly come to learn by experience that in virtually all cases when we have memory-like experiences we are having genuine memories. But if precognition were a common occurrence we would then have to rely not on this (just mentioned) statistical generalization but on the 'testimony' of singular physical facts. We can understand that, under these latter circumstances, we would have to ask ourselves, "Look, self, I seem to recall writing a contract with Jones. Am I remembering or precognizing?" It would do little good to attempt to secure the corroborative testimony of another person, Jones himself for example, for he would presumably have precisely the same quandary. The answer to the question whether I (or we) are remembering or precognizing is decidable only by looking to see whether the contract exists now. If it does, we are remembering; if it does not, we are precognizing. Ultimately, if the question of deciding between memory and precognition seriously arises for a group of persons all of whom share the same cognition, then it is answerable only by the testimony of *physical* facts.

If we lived in a world where precognizing was as common as remembering, then Quinton's argument would be all-too-obviously question-begging. But even if it is not *obviously* question-begging, it is question-begging nevertheless. We need only raise the question of the possibility of precognizing as an alternative description of what Quinton's hero is doing, to see that the question is unanswerable in his tale. What right, we should want to know, does Quinton's hero have to assume that he is remembering rather than precognizing? The answer: None. In a world where precognizing is an acknowledged possibility, even the corroboration of others who shared similar lakeside experiences would be inadequate to decide between a case of memory and one of precognition.

If England and the tropical lakeside were spatially and temporally connected, we could appeal to physical records, to the causally linked remnants of past events – photographs, memoranda, burnt embers, contracts, and the like – to settle whether the 'memories' one has in England of the lakeside were genuine memories or precognitions.

> If a man could pass through Paradise in a dream, and have a flower presented to him ... and if he found that flower in his hand when he awoke – Aye! and what then? (Samuel Taylor Coleridge [50], 282)

But Quinton's tale of the two spatially unconnected places is so constructed as to preclude the very possibility of there being physical records shared in the two worlds ([164], 143). There are no physical objects common both to England and to the lakeside environment. There are no clocks, starscapes, written memoranda, or even rocks that occur in both worlds.

But what about persons' bodies? Cannot the required records be made on them? Suppose Quinton's hero were to write down on his own skin a diary of events as they occurred in the tropics. Wouldn't the hero then know, when in England, that the events recorded on his skin happened *earlier*? Since causes always precede their effects, the requisite proof would seem literally to be in hand.

This latter repair will not do. For as Quinton tells the tale, his hero does not have one body in two places or even one body now in England and later in the tropics: his hero has (or inhabits) *two* bodies.[36] The English body (we can guess) is a pallid white wracked with chilblains; the tropical body is a sunbathed bronze infused with robust good health. The English body does not become tanned, and the tropical body does not grow pale.

The 'linkage' between the two worlds is experiential, not *physical*;

---

36. Later, in chapter 12, I will argue (as does Quinton in his *The Nature of Things*, [165], 95-6, 99-102), that it is logically possible that a person should serially inhabit any number of different bodies.

persons reside in both worlds but not physical objects. And the testimony of persons in the absence of corroborating physical evidence is indecisive in the matter of deciding between memory and precognition. Quinton's 'traveler' is not entitled to describe his cognitions in England of his lakeside experiences as being memories. That they merely 'feel like' memories is simply not good enough evidence in the face of a serious challenge to the claim that they are memories. Thus, we must give a different description of the hero's memory-like thoughts. But what description?

Having gone to some trouble to expose one question-begging way of telling the possible-worlds tale, we must be especially careful not to fall into the trap of replacing it with another. It would be all too easy to argue that since we are not entitled to say that the hero remembers the lakeside events, we must say instead that he either remembers, simultaneously cognizes, or precognizes those events. In effect, we replace a single description (viz. "remembers") with three seemingly exhaustive possibilities (viz. "remembers or simultaneously cognizes or precognizes"). But to make the claim that these three alternatives exhaust the possibilities is just to *presuppose* the truth of precisely what is in question, namely, the Kantian hypothesis that all events are temporally related to one another. If we are to avoid prejudicing our tale a second time, we must take care to drive a non-Kantian wedge at this point. We must, at the very least, seriously entertain a fourth possibility, to wit, the possibility that our traveler, upon awakening in England, genuinely cognizes lakeside experiences, but the lakeside experiences themselves are neither earlier than, simultaneous with, nor future to the time of cognizing them in England.

To say of something that it is a memory logically guarantees that it is true of a past event. If the hero of Quinton's tale when in England were able to identify his seeming memories as genuine memories, then Quinton's and Kant's claim that all temporal events may be organized into a single temporal sequence would be reinforced. But this is precisely what is impossible in Quinton's own tale. There is no way whatsoever in Quinton's tale for the hero to ascertain what the status is of his seeming memories of the lakeside. There is nothing whatsoever to indicate whether they are memories, simultaneous cognitions, precognitions, or – even more drastically – none of these. In short, contrary to Quinton's own conclusion, the events of the lakeside *cannot* be intercalated with those of England. It would seem, then, that there is no reason whatever to persist with the Kantian thesis that time must be unitary and that such a property of time is known a priori.

Space and time may in fact *be* unified. But if they are, then – contrary to Kant – this is no a priori truth. We are not constrained to think of all regions of space as being connected and all events in time as being connected. This conclusion holds not just for the space and time of physics or natural science. What I have tried to show is that it is possible that the space and time of human experience may have unconnected elements. With some imagination, we can describe possible experiences which, if they were to occur, would warrant our insisting that *experiential* space and time are not unified.

8.11   Time travel

One kind of time travel is so common, so familiar, that it is rarely ever recognized for what it is. All of us – except those at death's door – have an ability to travel forward in time. All we have to do is wait. Waiting is the simplest and most direct form of time travel. Most parents know this intuitively, although perhaps without ever having realized that they do. When youngsters, filled with the anticipation of a birthday party, say impatiently, "I wish it was tomorrow",[37] their parents will often counsel them by saying, "Just wait; it will be."

But waiting has two drawbacks. First, it is strictly forward-directed: one can travel into the future by waiting, but not into the past. Moreover, there does not seem to be any analogous 'operation' which will take us backward in time. There is no such thing as 'reverse-waiting' or 'unwaiting'. The second drawback to waiting as a mode of time travel is that it proceeds in lockstep with the ticking of the clock. To get from noon today to noon tomorrow takes twenty-four hours of waiting. What persons who are seeking 'better' methods of moving about in time clearly want is a way of getting from noon today to noon tomorrow without having to spend twenty-four hours in the process. A minute or two of traveling time is far more attractive to them.

Taylor has shown us *one* way of traveling forward *and backward* in time. Objects which are curved in space can, as we have seen, perform the temporal equivalent of objects moving back and forth in space (see pp. 200-3). But that is of scant use to the person wanting unlimited capacity for time travel. By bending my body into a ∨-shape – head and toes forward, hips to the rear (i.e. similar to that of the object pictured in Figure 8.4, p. 202) – and by moving forward at 1 m/sec, then

---

37. The subjunctive mood seems to have disappeared among today's youth.

along a certain path my toes will travel backward in time from my hips by a fraction of a second. But I cannot use Taylor's method to transport my present body from now to yesterday, still less to the year 1750.

The concept of moving forward or backward in time by great leaps is intelligible. Suppose it takes me eight hours to digest a meal and suppose that in one day my hair grows 0.06 cm. Now suppose that I am placed into a 'time machine'. I sit in the machine for the time it takes me to digest the meal I just ate. In this same time my hair grows 0.02 cm. In short, my body has aged eight hours. But suppose when I step out of the machine it is one year later (or earlier) than when I stepped into the machine. This would be a case of the sort of time travel which is depicted in countless science-fiction writings. We will call this 'accelerated' time travel.

Is accelerated time travel possible? Forward-directed accelerated time travel is certainly logically possible. It may even be physically possible. Indeed the technology may be imminent. If cryogenic freezing (low-temperature 'suspended animation') can be realized for human beings, it would certainly qualify as forward time travel. We already possess the technology to forward accelerate in time certain creatures (e.g. the fish *Dallia pectoralis* [145], 19), which can be frozen alive and subsequently thawed and revived with little or no permanent damage.[38]

But the real problem has always been with the notion of backward-directed time travel. Is accelerated backward time travel physically possible? There is a certain amount of empirical evidence that it is not. The best of this evidence is simply the fact that, so far as we can tell, no one has traveled to the here and now from any time or place in the future. Of course such evidence is not conclusive: it may be that future generations will have destroyed themselves in a war or environmental disaster; or it may be that they will have enacted legislation with sufficiently severe sanctions and policing to prevent time travel to our century; etc. Nonetheless, the very fact that there are no visitors here and now from the future strongly suggests that at no time in the future will a means be found to permit traveling backward in time. And the fact that it will never be done in turn suggests that it is physically impossible.

But even if backward time travel were to be physically impossible,

---

38. For a bibliography on 'freeze tolerance' see [198], 79-84.

might it still be logically possible? Even if this world is of such a sort that traveling backward in time cannot be realized, might there be other possible worlds where traveling backward in time does occur?

Many persons have thought that traveling backward in time is logically impossible. Their arguments typically are of this sort: "If you could travel backward in time, then you could encounter yourself when you were a youngster. Even if you are not normally homicidally inclined, it is at least theoretically possible that you kill that youngster. But if you did, then you would not have grown up to have reached the age when you traveled back in time. Thus there would be a contradiction: you both would and would not have traveled backward in time. Since the story involves a contradiction, it is logically impossible to travel backward in time." Such arguments have been around for years. They are especially tricky because they involve what are called *modal** concepts, in particular the notions of *possibility* and *impossibility*. Does the very concept of travel into the past entail contradictions? Does the possibility of murdering yourself as a child show that backward-directed time travel is an impossibility?

The answer is: there is no possibility, if you travel into the past, of murdering yourself as a child. The very fact that you are here now *logically* guarantees that no one – neither you nor anyone else – murdered you as a child, for there is no possibility of changing the past.

This notion that one cannot change the past needs careful attention. There is nothing special about the past in this particular regard. For you can no more change the past than you can change the present or change the future. And yet this is not fatalism. I am not arguing that our deliberations and actions are futile.

I cannot change the future – by anything I have done, am doing, or will do – from what it is going to be. But I can change the future from what it might have been. I may carefully consider the appearance of my garden, and after a bit of thought, mulling over a few alternatives, I decide to cut down the apple tree. By so doing, I change the future from what it might have been. But I do not change it from what it will be. Indeed, by my doing what I do, I – in small measure – contribute to making the future the very way it will be.

Similarly, I cannot change the present from the way it is. I can only change the present from the way it might have been, from the way it would have been were I not doing what I am doing right now. And finally, I cannot change the past from the way it was. In the past, I changed it from what it might have been, from what it would have been had I not done what I did.

We can change the world from what it might have been; but in doing that we contribute to making the world the way it *was*, *is*, and *will be*. We cannot – on pain of logical contradiction – change the world from the way it was, is, or will be.

The application of these logical principles for time travel becomes clear. If one travels into the past, then one does not change the past; one does in the past only what in fact happened. If you are alive today, having grown up in the preceding years, then you were not murdered. If, then, you or anyone else travels into the past, then that time traveler simply does *not* murder you. What *does* that time traveler do in the past? From our perspective, looking backward in time, that traveler does whatever in fact happened, and that – since you are alive today – does not include murdering you.

Time travel into the past involves no intrinsic contradiction. The appearance of contradiction arises only if one illicitly hypothesizes that the time traveler can change the past from what it was. But that sort of contradiction has nothing whatever to do with time travel per se. One would encounter the same sort of contradiction if one were to hypothesize that someone now were to change the present from the way it is or someone in the future were to change the future from the way it will be. All these latter notions *are* logically impossible. But none of them is intrinsic to the concept of time travel.

One should take care in describing time travelers not to give them logically impossible capabilities, e.g. the capacity to change the past from the way it was, the present from the way it is, or the future from the way it will be. But once one has done that, then there is no need to think the concept of time travel to be logically impossible. It just turns out to be a contingent fact about this actual world that accelerated backward travel in time does not occur.

CHAPTER NINE

Properties

9.1   The one and the many

Certain philosophical questions arise on their own quite naturally. Few persons have to be prompted to ask such questions as "Are there souls?", "Is there a God?", "What is the basis of good and evil?", or "Why do ethical and moral values seem to change from culture to culture and from time to time?" Other philosophical questions are slightly more remote, and occur to some, but not nearly as many, persons. A few of these we have already mentioned, e.g. "Is there an edge to space?" and "Are persons distinct from human bodies?" But some other philosophical questions are so recherché as to be distinctly 'philosopher's questions'. They are the sorts which occur naturally to very few persons. They are the sorts of questions which one must be induced, under provocation or tutelage, to come to see as posing genuine problems worthy of pursuit and whose answers are both subtle and central. One of these latter problems is the problem of 'the one and the many' introduced, virtually at the dawn of the philosophic enterprise, by Plato (427?-347 BC).

Plato asked a deceptively simple question: How is it possible for there to be two or more things of the same sort? How, for example, is it possible for there to be two 'identical' clay vases?

At one level, the answer might simply be: there are two identical clay vases because one is a good copy (replica) of the other. Or, we might say: there are two identical clay vases because they were both cast from the same mold. But Plato's original question was not the kind of question to which these latter would be proper answers. Plato's question was intended to go much deeper. It is not about any two (or three, or more) examples we might care to single out; his question is one of overarching generality: How is it possible for there to be more than one thing of any kind whatsoever, regardless what kinds of things (vases, persons, clouds, mountains, etc.) there are? In short, what sort of theory must we propose to explain *multiplicity itself* in the world?

Why is the very occurrence of multiplicity (in Plato's terminology, 'the many') thought to be a problem? Let us see.

Perform the following thought-experiment. Imagine any two things, e.g. two vases or two pens or two apples. Now imagine them *perfectly alike*: they have the same weight, same physical dimensions, same color, same temperature, same texture, same physical constitution, etc. etc. It is not just that they have no perceivable or detectable difference, something that might reveal itself to your eye or to your measuring instruments; you are being asked to imagine that the similarity goes beyond undetectable difference to there being absolutely no difference whatsoever. If you have trouble stretching your imagination in this way in regard to ordinary material objects, imagine some of the more arcane products of science, e.g. microscopic perfect crystals which really do seem to exhibit the perfect sameness just posited, or a DNA molecule which replicates itself with no mutation. The problem can now be put: What accounts for the *difference*, the very fact that there are *two* or more of these things, when *by hypothesis* everything that is true of one – e.g. its being red, or its having a mass of 15.65 g, or its being made up of a number of specific atoms in some determinate spatial configuration – is likewise true of its mate? In short, what accounts for sheer difference, given identity of features?

Modern philosophers use a technical vocabulary to frame these questions and to discuss possible solutions. Things which share all their features in common, e.g. the perfectly similar vases, apples, cloned DNA molecules, which we have just described, are said to be *qualitatively identical*. They are identical, that is, in sharing one another's *properties* in common.

Obviously every one thing is qualitatively identical to itself, in just the same manner as, for example, every woman is as tall as herself. But while every thing is qualitatively identical to itself, only some things are qualitatively identical to other things. The hand calculator sitting on my desk right now is (to the best of my knowledge) not qualitatively identical to any other calculator in existence. The unique damage to one corner of its case, having been caused by its getting caught in the drawer in my desk, accounts for the difference. The fact that no other calculator, however similar otherwise, bears precisely the same sort of physical damage to its own upper-right-hand corner assures that my calculator is *qualitatively distinct* from every other thing in the world. (Chipped plastic cases are as unique as fingerprints.)

This very calculator, the one with the damage to its corner, which is qualitatively distinct from every other thing in the world, is nevertheless *numerically identical* with the calculator which is positioned on my desk next to the telephone. That is to say, my calculator with the chipped case just *is* the selfsame, or very same, calculator that is positioned next to my telephone. When one speaks of *numerical* identity, one is speaking of a single thing. The single thing being spoken of is *both* the calculator having the damaged case *and* is (at one and the same time) the very thing which is positioned next to the telephone on my desk.

It is obvious, then, that certain *logical* relationships hold between the concepts of *qualitative identity* and *numerical identity*. These relationships may be stated in three axioms (theses or principles):

---

1. Each and every thing is qualitatively identical to itself.

2. Each and every thing is numerically identical to itself.

3. Whatever are numerically identical are qualitatively identical.[1]

   Figure 9.1

It is somewhat barbarous, and indeed even somewhat logically misleading, to talk of two things being numerically identical. The very concept of *numerical identity* implies singularity of reference. To avoid such clumsiness, and indeed literal incoherence, philosophers typically take recourse to using variables, e.g. "x" and "y", in talking of qualitative and numerical identity so as not to give the mistaken impression that they are presupposing that they are talking of exactly one or two things. We are already familiar with the use of variables in algebra, where difference in iconography, the visual appearance of symbol, does not invariably mean that the things referred to also are different. Consider, for example, the relatively trivial pair of equations:

---

1. This third axiom will be refined in chapter 11.

$$x + y = 14$$

$$x \times y = 49$$

The only values which satisfy both these equations simultaneously (i.e. together) are $x = 7$ and $y = 7$. Although the two *symbols*, "x" and "y", certainly differ, that difference does not carry over to a difference in the things referred to. Both symbols, in spite of their difference, refer to one and the same thing, viz. the number seven. When, then, philosophers use variables, e.g. "x" and "y", in stating theses about qualitative and numerical identity, their use of different symbols explicitly leaves it as a wholly open question whether one or more things is being referred to. That is, difference of symbols does not suffice to imply difference of referent.

Using variables, the theses, or principles, stated a moment ago can be restated somewhat more perspicuously. We will also introduce a bit more symbolism.

- Numerical identity will be symbolized with the familiar equals-sign, "=".

- Qualitative identity will be symbolized by "Q".

- The relation of *implies* will be symbolized by "$\rightarrow$".

- The so-called *quantifier*, e.g. "for any x", will be symbolized as the prefix "(x)".

Thus in figure 9.2 (p. 232), we get the symbolic renderings of the principles of figure 9.1 above.

The third of these principles (in figure 9.2) bears the name "The indiscernibility of identicals."[2] It is one of the few undisputed theses of metaphysics.[3] After all, it says nothing more startling than that each

---

2. The name was coined by Quine ([162], 139). The term "indiscernible" is principally one of psychology: there it refers to what we cannot *perceive* to be different. But as used here, in these metaphysical principles, the term is intended in a *stronger* sense, viz. it is to be taken to mean "indiscernible *in principle*", i.e. to mean that there is no difference at all in properties, not just that there are no perceivable differences. "Indiscernible" in metaphysics is thus a synonym for "qualitative identity".

3. An apparent exception may be found in the writings of Alfred Korzybski (see above footnote 13, p. 166). On the face of it, Korzybski seems to deny the very possibility of numerical identity: "a principle or a premise that

1. Each and every thing is qualitatively identical to itself.
   (For any x, x is qualitatively identical to itself.)

   $(x)(x \mathrel{Q} x)$

2. Each and every thing is numerically identical to itself.
   (For any x, x is numerically identical to itself.)

   $(x)(x = x)$

3. Whatever are numerically identical are qualitatively identical.
   (For any x and for any y, x's being numerically identical to y implies that x is qualitatively identical to y.)

   $(x)(y)(x = y \rightarrow x \mathrel{Q} y)$

   Figure 9.2

single thing shares with itself whatever properties it happens to have.

Far more controversial and far more problematic, however, is the converse thesis which was originally introduced by Leibniz. This latter principle conveniently bears the converse name, viz., "The identity of indiscernibles", and it says that if any x and any y share *all* their features or properties in common, then there is but one thing, i.e. then x and y are not two objects, but are the selfsame object. In symbols, this latter, fourth, principle may be stated this way:

$(x)(y)(x \mathrel{Q} y \rightarrow x = y)$

Immediately, this latter principle seems to be in direct conflict with the result of our thought-experiment of a moment ago. We had posed

---

'everything is identical with itself' is *invariably false to facts*" ([114], 194). But his ensuing explanation suggests that he is not denying the principle of the indiscernibility of identicals, indeed is not even discussing that principle. He is, rather, calling attention – in a somewhat misleading manner – to his theses that all things change over time (194) and that no two persons react to any one thing in precisely the same way (194-5). Neither of these latter two claims, whether true or false, contradicts the principle of the indiscernibility of identicals. (We will devote the whole of chapter 11 to an examination of the problem of change over time.)

ourselves the task of trying to imagine two numerically distinct, qualitatively identical objects: two apples; two vases; even a DNA molecule and its perfect clone. But if this latest principle of the identity of indiscernibles were to be accepted as true, if, that is, indiscernibility (i.e. qualitative identity) were conceded to confer numerical identity, then the results of our thought-experiment ought to have been at least mistaken if not outrightly impossible.

Obviously, this relationship between qualitative identity and numerical identity requires closer examination. Plato certainly believed that qualitative identity was possible without numerical identity, that it is possible, for example, for two or more things to share all their properties in common. But if two things really do share *all* their properties in common, what, then, could possibly account for there being *two* of them? How is it possible for there to be multiplicity without qualitative difference?

Leibniz himself thought that there *could not be* two numerically distinct but qualitatively identical things. But he believed that this impossibility flowed, not from logic, not from metaphysical principles, but from the perfection of God. Leibniz acknowledged that there was no *logical* bar to there being qualitatively identical, but numerically distinct, objects. If such existed, however, there would seem to be a curious redundancy, a gross imperfection, in Nature. And thus Leibniz hypothesized that the reason there are no such actual oddities in Nature is because Nature is the handiwork of God and God is perfect. God, he argued, could have 'no sufficient reason' for introducing a redundancy into the world. If He made two of the same things, then that would be evidence that He had not 'got it right' the first time: an unacceptable imperfection in a Perfect Being ([5], Third paper, §§5, 13, and 19). In short, even though it is logically possible that there could be numerically distinct, but qualitatively identical, things, their existence would be a blot on God's perfection and hence Leibniz steadfastly believed that no such things in fact existed. So sure was he of this latter conclusion that he ridiculed an acquaintance who actually tried, empirically, to find two qualitatively identical fallen leaves in the autumn garden ([5], Fourth paper, §4). Without venturing outdoors, Leibniz was convinced of the folly of the exercise.

Virtually no philosopher since Leibniz has given any credence to Leibniz's 'theological solution' to the puzzle about how qualitative identity does not automatically confer numerical identity. Better theories are needed to explain the real possibility, indeed the actuality, of the numerical difference of qualitatively identical things.

The solution to the puzzle about the exact nature of the relationship between qualitative identity and numerical identity turns on the degree of inclusiveness, or the compass, we are to understand when we describe qualitative identity as the sharing of *all* properties in common. What *are* the properties we are here talking about? What are the properties which make up a thing? For example, is my being born several years after Bertrand Russell a *property* of mine? Is it one of Russell's? If the calculator on my desk happens to have been the 234,921st one to roll off the assembly line, is that one of its *properties*? If a distant relative, totally unknown to me, happens to die and leave me a fortune which his lawyer steals without ever having informed me of the inheritance, do I have the *property* of being a legatee, although I am in total ignorance of the situation? Might we want to make a distinction between intrinsic (or real) properties and extrinsic (or accidental) properties? If so, what might such a distinction amount to?

Such examples, and the questions they raise, show that the very notion itself of *having a property* is not pre-analytically precise. We have an unrefined concept which serves admirably for ordinary purposes, but it is not sophisticated enough to guide us through these current perplexities. To advance, we shall have to examine, in considerably more detail, just what the concept of *having a property* amounts to.

9.2   Cataloguing properties and relations

So central is the concept of *property* not only to our doing of philosophy, but to our very ability to communicate in language one with another, that it itself has been the object of much research and speculation. Just reflect for a moment on how very much of our ordinary conversation, the news we hear, and the instructions we are given, consists of someone's picking out a subject and then proceeding to specify one or more of its properties: "The toast is burned"; "Sylvia is at the door"; "The Free Trade bill was given third reading in Parliament today"; "You can thin the shellac by adding 50 cm^3 of denatured alcohol"; "DNA is a helical molecule"; etc.

There is no one way, nor probably even just a few, to catalogue properties. One might, for certain purposes, want to classify properties according to whether their presence in physical objects is detectable by direct sensory experience. For example, we might want to contrast such readily observable properties as size, shape, weight, and color with more remote properties of the sort detectable only with scientific instruments, e.g. electrical resistance, conductivity, inductance, atomic number, and magnetic permeability, to name just a few. Or, again, we might want to classify properties according to whether they are relatively familiar (e.g. toothache, worry, fear) or whether they are comprehensible only in light of a sophisticated theory (e.g. capital, debenture, cash flow, psychosis, superego, male bonding, disfellowship).

For the purposes of doing philosophy, certain ways of cataloguing properties have proved useful for shedding light on some philosophical problems. No one way of cataloguing properties can be regarded as definitive. The following catalogue is devised, then, with an eye on its eventual use in philosophy. It is in no sense the only, or the 'best', way to classify properties. What warrants its introduction here is the use to which it will subsequently be put.

9.2.1 Primary versus secondary properties

One of the most fundamental notions many persons operate with is that some properties (features) of things are 'out there', in the world, as they say, while others are 'in us', in our minds, they might put it. For example, some persons are wont to subscribe to the dictum "Beauty is in the eye of the beholder", by which they mean that the 'external' physical world is not literally beautiful or ugly; it is, in the final analysis, merely a display of shapes, noises, and colors, and any beauty or ugliness associated with the scene is literally located within us. Beauty or ugliness – on this account – is our individual (or in some cases, perhaps, our collective) way of *reacting* to certain external stimuli.

Persons who adopt the sort of dichotomy between what is 'out there' (the stimulus) and what it causes in us (the response) are, knowingly or not, operating with a pair of distinctions, if not originally due to, then at least actively promoted by, John Locke. Locke believed that the external physical world, the world, that is, outside our minds, is populated (furnished) with objects having very few properties indeed ([124], book II, chap. VIII, §§7-26). These external objects have but five properties. Locke was, one must recall, operating with seventeenth-century physics which knew nothing of modern atomic physics, electricity, magnetism, chemistry, and biology. These five properties he called "primary properties". They comprised: (1) extension (i.e. the object's taking up space); (2) figure (roughly, its shape); (3) motion or rest; (4) number; and (5) solidity (or impenetrability).[4] Together these primary properties had the 'power' to cause *in us* not only perceptions ('ideas'[5] he called them) of shape, motion, etc., but as well perceptions of color, sound, warmth or cold, odor, etc. These latter perceptions which did not 'correspond' to the primary properties of material objects were said to be of 'secondary' qualities.

I think it safe to say that most persons, particularly those who are products of Western culture, habitually vacillate between two incompatible theories of perception. If not pressured by odd cases, many of us go about our lives believing that the things we see really do have the properties they appear to have: the wall is yellow; the piano is dark brown; and the apple is red. But if someone reminds us that the yellowness of the wall, the brownness of the piano, and the redness of the apple cannot be seen when the illumination is extinguished, and yet nothing much seems to have happened to the wall, the piano, or the apple themselves, many of us will immediately switch to a Lockean-type theory and will then be inclined to place the color of these objects, not in the things themselves, but in our reaction to them. We may, under these latter circumstances, find ourselves saying: "The yellowness of the wall is my way of reacting to some physical feature of the wall. When the wall is illuminated, it gives off electromagnetic radiation (visible light) which is focused on the retina of my eye, which in turn causes a signal to pass along the optic nerve to my brain. And by some process, not yet understood, it eventuates in my seeing yellow. According to this scientific explanation, then, yellowness is not a property of the wall, but a property of my mind (brain?). What property the wall actually has is the physical 'power' to cause *in me* (and in the rest of us) a certain kind of reaction."

I am sure that this latter sort of response is familiar to nearly every reader. It is virtually an icon of modern science. But it is also, perhaps very much less obviously, more a product of metaphysics. It is, after all, not the sort of theory which is even amenable to laboratory testing. It is, rather, a philosophical edifice mounted upon certain scientific

---

4. Sometimes Locke added another to this list: texture. (See, for example, [124], book II, chap. VIII, §§10 and 14.)

5. The word "ideas" in seventeenth- and eighteenth-century philosophy was more multipurpose than it is today. Then it was used to refer not only to beliefs but to perceptions and memories as well.

data in an attempt to explain, to make sense of, that data. It is no product of experience, but clearly goes beyond experience.

At first it may seem that the Lockean theory cannot be of the latter metaphysical sort. It might be supposed, as I think it often mistakenly is, to be a straightforwardly scientific theory whose credentials have been so well established in the psycho-physiologist's laboratory as to be beyond reasonable doubt. But the situation is not at all so simple. Our sensations of secondary properties are supposed, on this theory, to be *caused* by primary ones. But all of the data 'furnished' to our minds, whether of alleged primary or secondary qualities in the things themselves, turn out – on such a theory – to be secondary, caused by, but once-removed from, as it were, the primary properties of things out there in the world external to our minds. We have no direct access, except through the mediation of our senses, to the external world itself. We can no more sense directly in things themselves the power which causes in us perceptions of length or of solidity (supposed primary properties) than we can sense in things the power which causes in us, for example, feelings of warmth, images of color, or episodes of musical tones (supposed secondary properties). But if so, if in principle there is no direct access – save through their effects – of the primary properties of external objects, how can we know that such things really exist and how can we know anything of their 'real' nature? Locke thought that the relationship between, on the one hand, our perceptions of primary properties and, on the other, the primary properties themselves was that of resemblance, while our perceptions of secondary properties bore no resemblances to anything 'in' material objects themselves ([124], book II, chap. VIII, §15). But this belief is at the very least unprovable. There is certainly no conceivable experiment which could ever show that our perceptions of primary properties 'resemble' real properties in material objects and that our perceptions of secondary qualities do not.

Locke's theory soon encountered still worse problems at the hands of Bishop George Berkeley. Locke's theory, which was motivated to accommodate the burgeoning empiricist movement in the new science of the day, ironically was to furnish the groundwork for Berkeley's theory that there was no good evidence of any external, or material, world whatsoever ([27]). It is easy to see how the seed of such a radically opposing theory lay within Locke's theory. There was no convincing way, or suggestion of a mechanism, within Locke's theory to bridge the gulf between the knowledge of the contents of one's own mind and the supposed correspondence of these contents with something external to one's mind, i.e. a physical, material world independent of mind. Berkeley took the audacious leap of pressing the seventeenth-century version of empiricism to its limits and thus – paradoxically – coming to deny what had up until then seemed to be a bedrock of empiricism. Berkeley insisted that only what is perceived can be regarded as proven to exist. Such a dictum might be thought to be necessary to the pursuit of an objective science. Mere opinion and flights of fancy are to be banished. No more would one invoke such unempirical, untestable existents as Aristotle's 'natural place' or 'unperceivable substance' (more on the latter in chapter 10). For science to be properly grounded, it must be grounded – Berkeley and most of his empirically minded contemporaries similarly believed – in *proofs* stemming from that which was perceivable, demonstrable, and reproducible.

But like so many principles which on first enunciation seem so promising, and indeed even self-evidently true, Berkeley's uncompromising insistence on the centrality of the role of perception in determining what was to be regarded as real and what was to be relegated to the storehouse of mythology soon had some extremely counterintuitive implications. Having adopted Locke's notion that secondary properties have bona fide credentials of reality (no one could possibly doubt that he/she was in pain), Berkeley was driven, ineluctably, to the conclusion that material objects, existing independently of their being observed, not only did not in fact exist, but were a logical impossibility. In pursuing to its inevitable conclusion a particularly hard-nosed (or perhaps less charitably described, ham-fisted) version of empiricism, Berkeley found himself driven away both from Cartesian dualism and from materialism*, to idealism* – to the theory that only minds and their contents exist. So startling and unacceptable was such a conclusion, however, that Berkeley 'saved the day' by having God observe everything constantly and by His so doing keep the external world in continuous existence. Needless to say, Berkeley's theological way out of his own dilemma about the existence of the external world (just like Leibniz's earlier theological solution to the dilemma about qualitative identity [see above, p. 233]) would turn out to be one which would be shunned by his successors. Theological solutions to metaphysical puzzles have not been much in vogue for centuries. Indeed, even in those periods in history when they were rather more acceptable, they were always adopted only as a last resort. Metaphysics has always preferred natural explanations to supernatural ones. And in recent centuries, the tolerance for the latter has declined headlong.

In the two centuries since Berkeley, scores of philosophers have tried to construct philosophical accounts which at once will do justice to empiricism and the important role therein of theorizing combined with deliberative, controlled observation and experimentation, but without at the same time carrying Berkeley's conclusion that the external world is a myth.

Kant's efforts in this regard were both monumental and heroic ([106]). But his particular solution, although eliciting extraordinary numbers of responses and reactions, has not earned a contemporary following. Half a century ago, the redoubtable G.E. Moore (1873-1958) tried his own hand in a remarkably curious and highly original article, "A Proof of the External World". It is, at the very least, entertaining – and perhaps a bit eye-opening – to sample the method of his argumentation and the style of his unique prose.

> ... if I can prove that there exist now both a shoe and a sock, I shall have proved that there are now "things outside of us"; ... and similarly I shall have proved it, if I can prove that there exist now two sheets of paper, or two human hands, or two shoes, or two socks, etc. ... Cannot I prove any of these things?
>
> It seems to me that ... I can now give a large number of different proofs, each of which is a perfectly rigorous proof ... I can prove now, for instance, that two human hands exist. How? By holding up my two hands, and saying, as I make a certain gesture with the right hand, "Here is one hand," and adding, as I make a certain gesture with the left, "and here is another." ...
>
> But did I prove just now that two human hands were then in existence? I do want to insist that I did; that the proof which I gave was a perfectly rigorous one; and that it is perhaps impossible to give a better or more rigorous proof of anything whatever. ([136], 144)

Moore, himself, was under no illusions about the expected reception for his 'proof'. He knew that such a proof would be bound to elicit dissatisfaction, indeed even ridicule, from some other philosophers. Even so, Moore was convinced that he was on the right track. Be that as it may, controversy still continues over the cogency of such an approach. Some philosophers regard Moore's work as a needed breath of fresh air on a stuffy topic; others think it totally off-base, that it misses entirely the very problem facing Locke, Berkeley, and Kant.

My own opinion as to the place to find a solution leans heavily toward the revising of empiricism which has taken place in more recent decades.

When I went for a walk recently, I passed a parked car sporting a bumper sticker reading: "When all else fails, lower your standards." Although I would normally simply smile at such an unabashedly unreserved slogan and would dismiss it as being too sweeping, I recall it here because it has a particular relevance. It sums up succinctly what was wrong with Locke's and Berkeley's empiricism and points to the way out of their dilemma.

Locke's theory contained implicitly the requirement that the existence of external objects could be known only through sensory experience, or as it is sometimes called, the data of sense. But sensory data are intrinsically 'in the mind'. Berkeley probed this feature of the then-current version of empiricism remorselessly and saw, correctly, that it leads to a skepticism about the external world. The only way he was able to see to escape his conclusion was to posit a God who kept a constant vigil on the world.

Late-twentieth-century metaphysics pursues another course. In particular, modern philosophy has dropped the inordinately high, unrealizable requirement that sensory data be required to *prove* that the external, public, objective world is of one kind rather than some other. The demand for *proof* (understood in the sense of "certainty") has given way to the more realizable, tractable, and practicable demand for reasonable, although not necessarily conclusive, evidence for whatever is being hypothesized. The modern view is not that sensory data prove, or ever could prove, the existence of a physical, external world, but that sensory data provide good grounds for regarding the hypothesis of the existence of a physical, external world as a reasonable posit, indeed as the *best* of the (currently) available alternatives. Moreover, there are two powerful incentives for adopting this particular posit. One, it matches the common, ordinary view of the way the world is; and two, it matches the scientific view of the way the world is. But neither of these two benefits can be regarded as establishing the hypothesis as being *demonstrably true*. We cannot, in any absolutely conclusive way, prove that an external world exists. The hypothesis that it does exist is a *metaphysical posit*, probably the most common metaphysical posit of our entire civilization. But for all that, it is a piece of metaphysical theorizing nevertheless and not an incontrovertible 'fact'. It is after all possible, with some effort, to deny the existence of an external world; it is possible, for example, to believe that the only things that exist are mental things. To cite a near, but not so extreme, parallel: we have seen Christian Scientists, with perfect consistency both in word and in deed, deny the existence of disease.

9.2.2 Manifest versus dispositional properties

Consider the contrast between the two properties *is broken* and *is breakable*, or between *is burning* and *is flammable*. The first of each of these pairs, *is broken* and *is burning*, seems readily comprehensible. We recurrently encounter both broken and burning items. Indeed these properties of things can literally be *seen*. Their existence can be ascertained by direct observation. But what about the latter pairs of properties, *breakable* and *flammable*? What sorts of properties are they? We cannot in general tell whether something is breakable simply by looking at it; and only rarely – for some few selected kinds of things – can we tell, without putting a flame to it, whether something is flammable. These latter sorts of properties bear the technical name "dispositions". In a sense, they are properties in potentiality; they are properties waiting, as it were, to break out into actuality. The flammable thing has the potential to become burned; the breakable thing has the potential to become broken.

The properties of *being broken* and of *being burned* are standardly said to be "manifest" properties. To be sure, this nomenclature is somewhat ill-chosen, since "manifest" often carries the connotation of being apparent or obvious. In the technical sense in which certain properties are spoken of as being "manifest", there is no suggestion that they are apparent or obvious. For example, the charge on an electron or the peculiar structure of a carbon diamond crystal are anything but 'obvious'; and yet, in the technical sense being spoken of here, these properties are said to be manifest.[6] For technical purposes, then, a "manifest property" means nothing more, or less, than a nondispositional property of a thing.

On an intuitive, pre-analytic basis, the distinction between manifest and dispositional properties seems both clear and firm enough. But on

---

6. A term which is sometimes used in place of "manifest" is "occurrent", but it too carries its own peculiar problems, and will not be used here.

careful probing, the distinction seems in danger of evaporating. Properties like *being square* seem paradigmatically to be manifest, while *being fragile* or *being flammable* seem paradigmatically to be dispositional. But what about *being red*? Do physical objects, e.g. ripe strawberries, manifest the property of redness, or, as Locke hypothesized, do they merely have the 'power' (i.e. the potential or disposition) to cause in us a sensation of redness under certain circumstances (e.g. the lighting being of a certain wavelength and intensity, our eyes and optic nerves, etc., being in proper working order)? With examples such as the latter, the very distinction, or at least the criterion for applying the distinction, seems in imminent danger of collapse. Karl Popper has even gone so far as to argue that all properties are, in the final analysis, dispositional: "If 'breakable' is dispositional, so is 'broken', considering for example how a doctor decides whether a bone is broken or not. Nor should we call a glass 'broken' if the pieces would fuse the moment they were put together: the criterion of being broken is behaviour *under certain conditions*. Similarly, 'red' is dispositional: a thing is red if it is able to reflect a certain kind of light – if it 'looks red' in certain situations. But even 'looking red' is dispositional. It describes the disposition of a thing to make onlookers agree that it looks red" ([159], 118). Popper's suggestion that even the property of *being broken* is dispositional may need a moment of clarification. How does a doctor tell whether a bone is broken? Presumably by administering some test: asking the patient to describe his/her sensations; manipulating the limb; looking for telltale swelling and hematoma; taking an X-ray; etc. In other words, the property *being broken* has the disposition to produce certain results in certain test situations, including – in the case of the broken glass – the property of *not* fusing back together when reassembled. In Popper's view, then, the distinction between manifest and dispositional properties is nothing absolute, but merely one of degree. (We can anticipate that devising a scheme to measure such a degree of difference will prove extremely difficult.)

There is a temptation to locate dispositional properties in a peculiar niche in the scheme of things. On some accounts, dispositional properties are portrayed as halfway houses along the road between nonexistence and full-blown actuality. Solubility, for example, on this view, would be regarded as a property intermediary between being undissolved and being dissolved. Such a theory is to be avoided, if possible. Normally we think of existence as a strictly all-or-nothing affair. There are no degrees of existence: either something exists, or it does not. There is nothing which half or partially exists. Of course it may happen that some part of a thing exists while some other part does not. The east wing of an office building may have been demolished and removed, and only the west wing remains. But it would be incorrect to say that the office building now half exists. What makes better sense is to say that half the office building has gone out of existence, while half the office building still exists.

Having eschewed a notion of 'partial existence' elsewhere in metaphysics, we should be extremely reluctant to invoke it in explicating the nature of dispositional properties. But if dispositional properties are not partial-existents, what might they be?

Some metaphysicians regard irreducible potentialities as anathema: they will have no truck with them in their theories. Dispositions, according to these philosophers, are metaphysical misbegottens. Such philosophers adopt what is called a philosophy of *actualism*. The only properties which they will recognize as being "real" are actual, or manifest, properties. But how, then, is one supposed to be able to account for the real difference between, let us say, a clay brick which is not burning and is nonflammable, and a paper book which also may not be burning but which indisputably is flammable? If neither is now (actually) burning, how are we to account for the fact that one is non-flammable and the other flammable? What does the latter distinction amount to if not that one is not actually burning and the other one is? In short, how can dispositional properties be accounted for in terms of actual (or manifest) properties?

Actualists will have to maintain that in the case of the brick and the book, for example, there is some actual property other than its non-burning or burning which each has and which marks the difference. There will have to be, on their theory, some actual property which the brick has which prevents its burning, while there will have to be some (other) actual property which the book has which allows for its burning. In neither case are there any merely 'possible' properties lurking behind the scenes, as it were, waiting to break out into full actuality.[7]

If dispositional properties ("fragile", "semipermeable", "heliotropic", etc.) figure prominently in natural science, they seem to be at least as, if not more, prominent in our explanations of human behavior. Our descriptions of personality seem invariably to be couched almost exclusively in terms of dispositional properties. A given person may be honest, sentimental, loving, caring, punctual, hardworking,

---

7. For more on this issue, see Elizabeth Prior's monograph, *Dispositions* ([161]).

fastidious, and slow to anger. All these properties, we note, are to be regarded more as dispositional than manifest. But how are we to account for persons having such properties? There seem to be some prospects for our coming to understand, from a physical point of view, how a person feels a pain. We might even, that is, reach the point in the foreseeable future of physico-psychological research where we will be able to 'pin down' the source and mechanism, as it were, in our physical bodies of our pains. But will we be able, similarly, to account for dispositions such as a person's being honest? There is no reason to think that the task is in principle impossible. But neither should we underestimate its magnitude. To see how formidable is the task of accounting for dispositions in terms of manifest (actual) properties, just ask yourself what manifest property of a person could possibly account for his (having a tendency toward) being stingy or (a likelihood of) being self-deprecating. Physico-psychological theories which would permit the reducing of human dispositions to manifest properties of physiological states are not even in their nascency.

In light of what has just been said, it may appear that the entire theory of dispositional properties is so rudimentary as to be unworthy of notice. But such a conclusion would reflect a misunderstanding of the philosophic enterprise. A philosopher's progress toward a theory is at least a two-step, often an iterated, procedure. When Carnap tried to explicate the curious practice we call "philosophical analysis" (see above, pp. 102-8), he emphasized the importance of the role of elucidating the explicandum, the pre-analytic concept, which is eventually to be replaced by an improved concept, the explicatum.

> There is a temptation to think that, since the explicandum cannot be given in exact terms anyway, it does not matter much how we formulate the problem. But this would be quite wrong. On the contrary, since even in the best case we cannot reach full exactness, we must, in order to prevent the discussion of the problem from becoming entirely futile, do all we can to make at least practically clear what is meant as the explicandum. ... It seems to me that, in raising problems of analysis or explication, philosophers very frequently violate this requirement. They ask question like: 'What is causality?', 'What is life?', 'What is mind?', 'What is justice?', etc. Then they often immediately start to look for an answer without first examining the tacit assumption that the terms of the question are at least practically clear enough to serve as a basis for investigation, for an analysis or explication. Even though the terms in question

are unsystematic, inexact terms, there are means for reaching a relatively good mutual understanding as to their intended meaning. An indication of the meaning with the help of some examples for its intended use and other examples for uses not now intended can help the understanding. ... By explanations of this kind the reader may obtain ... a clearer picture of what is to be included and what is intended to be excluded; thus he may reach an understanding of the meaning intended which is far from perfect theoretically but *may be sufficient for the practical purposes of a discussion* of possible explications. ([45], 4-5; italics added)

What we have here been doing is laying the necessary groundwork for any eventual, viable theory of dispositional properties. We should not be disheartened that we are unable to propose finished theories. Having introduced the distinction between manifest and dispositional properties, and having explored some of the problems (e.g. whether the distinction is absolute or merely one of degree, and whether potentialities are reducible in principle to actual properties), we can content ourselves with intuitive notions of these concepts. We need feel no particular diffidence about our stopping at this point. As I explained earlier, in the case of the concept of *possible world*, not every concept needs to be clarified in order for us to be able to use the concept and indeed to get much mileage out of it. (Two thousand years of mathematics proceeded apace with no viable explication of *number* at all.) For present purposes, the concepts of *manifest* and *dispositional* property have been elucidated sufficiently for us to proceed.

9.2.3 Binary properties; comparative and quantitative properties

It is a poor joke which describes a woman as "half-pregnant". Being pregnant is one among a class of properties which are strictly binary, i.e. such properties occur in an all-or-nothing manner. Either a woman is, or she is not, pregnant: there is nothing halfway, as it were, between nongravidity and pregnancy. Similarly, a given combination of playing cards in a game of gin rummy either has, or does not have, the property of being a meld. Binary properties, we say, "do not come in degrees".

Many properties do, however. Your car may be heavier than mine: its weight is greater than, or exceeds, the weight of my car. Or, again, my piano may be more out of tune than yours: its dissonance is greater than, or exceeds, that of your piano. These properties – weight, dissonance, intelligence, hardness, etc. – permit of *ordering*. Such properties, which do come in degrees, are sometimes spoken of as being 'qualitative' properties. But since we will use the word "quality" in a specialized sense in a moment (in section 9.2.6), we will not adopt that particular nomenclature, preferring instead to call properties which come in degrees 'comparative' properties. Accordingly, pregnancy is a binary property; but length of pregnancy is a comparative property: one woman may be in her fourth month of pregnancy while another is in her third. The former, although being no more pregnant than the latter, will have been pregnant for a greater length of time.

Certain comparative properties themselves feature a further property.[8] Some comparative properties – weight, for example – occur in quantifiable amounts in such a way as to permit us to say that one thing exceeds another in that property by some specifiable factor. Intelligence, for example, although, like weight, a comparative property, lacks this further feature. A person with an intelligence quotient (IQ) of, let us say, 150, is not twice as intelligent as a person with an IQ of 75. The joint intellectual efforts of two persons each with an IQ of 75 will not match that of a person blessed with an IQ of 150. But the combined weight of two persons each with a weight of 75 kg will equal the weight of a person of 150 kg. The property of weight, then, is quantifiable in a way in which intelligence quotient is not. Weight is said to satisfy 'the law of addition'; intelligence not.[9]

Such obvious differences, and their causes, explanations, and peculiarities, have been the subject of much research in the past one hundred years. One of the most telling differences between the modern period of physics (i.e. since the seventeenth century) and its precursor has been the emphasis on quantitative measurements of the sort we see possible in the example of weight. And one of the most

---

8. This claim is no mistake. Properties may themselves have properties. This hierarchical structure of properties has been implicit throughout this entire discussion. The property of pregnancy, for example, is binary, we have already said. Spelled out in greater detail, what we have said is that the property of being pregnant itself has the *property* of being binary. Etc.

9. The classic study of the distinction being alluded to here is Norman Campbell's *Foundations of Science* ([43]; see esp. chap. 10). More recent 'classic studies' include S.S. Stevens's "On the Theory of Scales of Measurement" ([197]). Brian Ellis's *Basic Concepts of Measurement* ([66]) includes a good bibliography through 1966.

enduring debates in the philosophy of science has been on the question whether the sorts of measurements which are common within physics, and consequently the sorts of scientific laws it is possible to adumbrate within physics, should be thought to be the goal as well of 'softer' sciences. Is psychology somehow less 'authentic', somehow a 'lesser science', if it fails to state laws holding between quantitative properties? Is a science which is confined to ascertaining orderings – e.g. being able to determine that Person *A*'s rage is greater than Person *B*'s rage, without being able to measure *how much* one person's rage exceeds than of another – any less a *science*? Is the hallmark of a genuine science its ability to produce quantitative laws, i.e. laws stating relationships between quantitative properties, or is that merely a fortuitous feature of a few select sciences, e.g. physics, chemistry, and (perhaps) economics?

It is an innocent-sounding philosopher's distinction at first glance: that between those comparative properties which do not permit further quantification and those which do. And yet, on this seemingly subtle distinction rests one of the longest-lasting and intensely personal debates in the philosophy of modern science. Scientists, particularly those in some of the social sciences, are put on the defensive by their present inability to posit properties having the quantitative features of those of physics. While physicists may invoke mass, energy, heat, etc., all of which are quantifiable, social scientists, it seems, often have to make do with 'softer' properties: intelligence, anger, hostility, covertness, caring, etc., all of which may be (roughly) ordered, but none of which seems to be nonarbitrarily quantifiable. What is at stake is a very fundamental view, call it metaphysical if you will, of the ultimate nature of physical reality. Certain particularly tough-nosed physicists are likely to conceive of the world as ultimately constituted of things bearing quantitative properties; other researchers believe that no such account – restricted solely to such properties – could ever do justice to the richness and diversity of reality. The debate cuts right to the quick of scientists' view of the world and of the validity of their professional pursuits. For in this arcane distinction lurks a challenge to the very basis of the practice in which scientists daily engage.

9.2.4 *Intensive versus extensive properties; eliminable and ineliminable concepts*

Properties of properties of properties of ... – there seems to be no limit to our ingenuity to classify, to subclassify, to subsubclassify, and so on. And thus it should come as no surprise that the very category of quantitative property itself should be further subdividable, i.e. that certain quantifiable properties should themselves have properties which other quantifiable properties lack.

One of the most interesting, and at the same time peculiar, set of properties to appear in the philosopher's inventory is that of intensive and extensive properties. Take a thin aluminum rod. It will have various quantitative properties including, for example, the properties of having a mass of 6 kg and having a density of 2.7 g/cm³. Now break the rod into two equal parts. The mass of each part will be (exactly) half the mass of the original unbroken rod; but the density of each half will be (precisely) the same as the density of the original. How very strange: the mass subdivided with the rod; its density did not. Properties which, like mass, diminish upon objects' being broken down into smaller parts are said to be 'extensive'; those which, like density, do not, are said to be 'intensive'. (These two terms, incidentally, have nothing whatsoever to do with the distinction between "extension" and "intension" which is common in modern semantics.)

The metaphysical significance of this latest distinction is an outgrowth of the immediately preceding one. We have just seen how some physicists believe that the ultimately significant properties of the world are quantitative ones. But some physicists will want to go even further, and want to refine this latter thesis. It is not just quantitative properties which are ultimately 'real' but, more particularly, it is extensive quantitative properties which form the foundation upon which we may hope to erect our understanding of the universe.

You can see why one might have this prejudice toward extensive properties, if one, that is, is going to have a prejudice at all toward the primacy of quantitative properties. Taking density as our example, we can see that the concept of *density* is – in an absolutely clear-cut way – totally eliminable, expendable, in any scientific theory. Any theory which invokes the concept of *density* could, just as well, invoke the concept of *mass per unit volume*. But does the expendability of the *concept* of density imply that the *property* density is 'unreal' or, as some writers put it, just a convenient 'mathematical fiction'. Is the *term* "density" just a convenient shorthand for "mass per unit volume", and should we want to argue that there really is no such *property* as density which is referred to by this term?

It is illuminating to look into the history of the evolution of the interplay of these various concepts. In Newton's *Principia* (1687), for example, we find that the order of definitions is precisely the reverse of today's norms. For Newton, *density* was the primitive concept, and he defined *mass* in terms of density. The opening sentence of the book reads: "The quantity of matter [i.e. mass] is the measure of the same, arising from its density and bulk [i.e. volume] conjointly" ([144], 1). On the modern account, we say that density is equal to mass 'divided by' volume. But given that relationship, it is also certainly true to say of a body – as Newton did – that its mass is equal to its density 'times' its volume. For Newton, density, not mass, was the fundamental, or at least more familiar, concept.[10] It was a well-known fact, for example, that iron floats on mercury, and that gold sinks in mercury. Substances could be arranged in order of ascending density: iron, mercury, gold. This property, determined by what floats on what, and what sinks in what, seemed to be fundamental, intrinsic, and did not depend for its determination on measuring either the mass or the volume of the substances involved. Later, it was recognized that one could assign not just orderings to the densities of substances, but specific numerical values, by using the measure of a substance's mass divided by a measure of its volume. This both introduced a new 'handle' on the concept and allowed persons to measure densities for cases where the float/sink method was inapplicable, e.g. in the case of gold and platinum.

What we find is that one can do physics, both better and more easily, if one takes as one's fundamental concepts *mass* and *volume*, rather than *density* and *volume*. (A parallel account can be constructed for the logic of the concept of *speed*.[11]) Even so, this still leaves open the question whether the *property* of density is 'real' or 'unreal'.

---

10. See, also, Cajori's notes to the *Principia* ([144], 638-9).

11. "Speed" is eliminable in favor of "distance covered divided by elapsed time" (e.g. kilometers per hour). But children have the concept of *speed* without having the latter concept of *distance covered per unit of time*. (Remember, too, that mariners use a concept of speed, *knots*, which makes no reference either to distance or to time. It is not "knots/hour", but "knots" *tout court*.) Children have the former naive concept of *speed* insofar as they know such things as that Alice can run faster than Betty (i.e. has greater speed than Betty), and that Betty, in turn, can run faster than Carol. But these same children may be several years away in their intellectual development from having the more sophisticated concept of *distance covered per unit time*. For one thing, the latter concept involves the mathematical operation of division, and that concept – if it comes at all – comes much later in a child's comprehension.

It should be clear that there can be no simple truth or falsity in any forthcoming answer. Someone who argues for the 'unreality' of the property of density (or of speed) is, tacitly, advancing the metaphysical thesis that our decisions about what is real and what is not should be decided by the test of what is taken to be fundamental and ineliminable in physics (and perhaps in other sciences as well). Physics (and science in general) on this account gives us an access to what is ultimately 'real'.

But one is by no means forced to adopt that particular metaphysical thesis. And indeed, it is more than just a little resistible. Certainly one can, with coherence and conviction, argue that the foregoing metaphysical theory is overly parsimonious. One can argue that the fundamental concepts of science probably do match fundamental features of the world without having to subscribe to the stronger thesis that the *only* features there are in the world are those which play important and central roles in science. One can, that is, accept the revelations of science without subscribing to the claim that nothing else is real.

There is a more direct objection as well. It is not at all clear that there is any particular way of recognizing fundamental as opposed to definable properties. That is, there may not be any particular property that properties themselves have which identifies them as being ineliminable or not. I have already argued (in chapter 5) that there well may not be any one way of doing science; indeed I think it overwhelmingly likely that there is not. What may be fundamental, ineliminable, in one scheme of science may be definable and eliminable in another. We have already seen how, in certain reconstructions of Newtonian physics (footnote 8, p. 85), the very concept of mass itself dropped out.

There is an important conclusion to draw from this debate about the reality or unreality of those properties which correspond to eliminable concepts. We are often tempted to regard questions about what is real as if all of them were empirical questions to be settled – if not always in practice, then at least in principle – by scientists pursuing the experimental method. But it should be clear that science is, by itself, impotent to answer even as simple a question as whether *density* (or *speed*) is a 'real' property or merely a 'fiction'. How much more impotent science must be, then, to answer the significantly more difficult question whether there is such a property as *intelligence* (or *evil* or *free will*). The answers to such questions simply cannot be had by scientific means. The answers to such questions reside in proposing, debating, and choosing among alternative metaphysical theories.

. We are tugged in two different directions. It seems strange to deny that density is a real property, and yet we fully appreciate the arguments and motivations of someone who promotes that thesis. But the ensuing tension we might feel evidences the fact that we standardly operate with a variety of criteria for invoking the very concept of *reality* itself. In the case of intensive properties, those criteria can be made to conflict with one another. And what is ultimately at stake is not a truth about whether intensive properties are 'real' or not: there could not possibly *be* an answer to such a question given the tensions inherent in our very concept of what it is to be 'real'. Rather what is involved in our trying to decide whether intensive properties are real is an effort to try to decide which of our various criteria of reality we want to give primacy to. The answer to this latter question cannot be one of mere random choice. We will choose, both in light of our pre-philosophical intuitions and in light of what future mileage we hope to get out of the revised concept.

9.2.5 Emergent versus nonemergent properties

Philosophers' fascination with properties seems endless. In the 1920s, a number of philosophers – including, among others, C. Lloyd Morgan ([138]), J.C. Smuts[12] ([196]), and S. Pepper ([150]) – picking up from some provocative, but undeveloped, notions in Mill's theory of causation ([135], book III, chap. VI) proposed a theory of emergent properties. The principal figure among this group was C.D. Broad.

> ... most of the chemical and physical properties of water have no known connexion, either quantitative or qualitative, with those of Oxygen and Hydrogen. Here we have a clear instance of a case where, so far as we can tell, the properties of a whole composed of two constituents could not have been predicted from a knowledge of the properties of these constituents taken separately, or from this combined with a knowledge of the properties of other wholes which contain these constituents.

---

12. Jan Christiaan Smuts (1870-1950) had an astounding career. Not only was he a philosopher, albeit a minor one, he was also a player on the world's political stage. From 1919 to 1924, and from 1939 to 1948, he served as prime minister of South Africa.

... It is clear that in *no* case could the behaviour of a whole composed of certain constituents be predicted *merely* from a knowledge of the properties of these constituents, taken separately, and of their proportions and arrangements in the particular complex under consideration.

... Take any ordinary statement, such as we find in chemistry books; e.g., "Nitrogen and Hydrogen combine when an electric charge is passed through a mixture of the two. The resulting compound contains three atoms of Hydrogen to one of Nitrogen; it is a gas readily soluble in water, and possessed of a pungent characteristic smell." If the mechanistic theory be true ... [a mathematical] archangel could deduce from his knowledge of the microscopic structure of atoms all these facts but the last. He would know exactly what the microscopic structure of ammonia must be; but he would be totally unable to predict that a substance with this structure must smell as ammonia does when it gets into the human nose. The utmost that he could predict on this subject would be that certain changes would take place in the mucous membrane, the olfactory nerves and so on. But he could not possibly know that these changes would be accompanied by the appearance [i.e. occurrence] of a smell in general or of the peculiar smell of ammonia in particular, unless someone told him so or he had smelled it for himself. ([35], 63 and 71)

Broad is actually advancing here two theses, a positive one and a negative. On the positive side, he argues that certain properties of 'wholes' are deducible (he uses the term "predictable" as a synonym) from a knowledge of the properties of their parts. For example, he suggests that a knowledge of the properties of hydrogen and nitrogen would allow us to deduce that atoms of these elements will combine in the ratio of three to one. On the negative side, he argues that this feature just remarked for the combining ratios does not hold universally. He suggests, for example, that the existence of the distinctive smell of ammonia *could not* be deduced from a knowledge of the properties of hydrogen and nitrogen.

There really is a very gripping metaphysical thesis at play here. For Broad is operating with the intuitive notion that somehow certain physical properties of things are 'contained within' the properties of their parts; but that other properties are, in some sense, unexpected or novel. These latter properties are said to be "emergent". In some metaphorical sense, they seem to be a step above on the ladder of reality.

Is the theory viable? As Broad stated it, the theory contains a striking logical fallacy. Ernest Nagel has adroitly exposed the error ([139], 366-97). Nagel argues that there is no absolute or ahistorical sense of "emergent". Whether a property is emergent or not, i.e. whether the existence of some property may be deduced from some body of knowledge, depends entirely on the information contained in that body of knowledge.[13] But there is nothing, nor could there be, which counts definitively as knowledge of hydrogen and nitrogen. It is up to us to decide just what we choose to include and to exclude in any such body of knowledge. If certain information is included, we will be able to deduce certain facts about ammonia; if not, then not. The only sense in which a property can justifiably be said to be emergent is within a historical setting. At some stage in the development of scientific knowledge no proposition describing the smell of ammonia may be deducible from then-current scientific knowledge; but with the growth of knowledge, we may add to our storehouse of information so that such a proposition does become deducible. Emergence, then, in Nagel's reconstruction, is no metaphysical property at all, merely a historical footnote to the progress of science. What may be emergent today may well be nonemergent tomorrow.

Is Nagel's dismissal of Broad's intuitions too swift, too damning? Might it be that Broad expressed himself carelessly, but was, nonetheless, onto something of fundamental importance? Did he really glimpse an important metaphysical distinction or was he merely the victim of a logical confusion? In short, are there emergent properties?

Let's return for a moment to Broad's example. The motivating intuition in all of this was his tacit belief that there is something *fundamentally different* between ammonia's ability to, for example, dissolve in water and its ability to cause in us a certain kind of reaction. The former seemed somehow 'physical', or at least it was a disposition to

---

13. Logicians will know that the principle has been stated casually. A more precise formulation – intended for technically trained readers – is: "(1) Whether a statement containing a given predicate is deducible or not depends on the information logically contained in the premises. (2) A predicate can occur *nonvacuously* in the conclusion of a deductively valid inference which has a self-consistent premise-set only if that predicate occurs explicitly in at least one of the premises."

bring about a physical state, while the latter was somehow 'more mental', or at least was a disposition to bring about a mental state. Is this a 'real distinction' worthy of preservation, and indeed encapsulation, in the distinction between physical and nonphysical, between nonemergent and emergent? Again, it must be clear that the question is not a scientific one. It concerns not one's scientific theorizing, or one's laboratory practice, but a metaphysical view as to what ultimately one is looking at and trying to make sense of.

The situation is this: If you are convinced that there is some important, metaphysical distinction between 'the physical' on the one hand and 'the mental' on the other, you may well find yourself attracted to the theory of emergence and may try to so restrict the class of physical properties as to allow for the occurrence of emergent properties. The trouble with this procedure, however, is that it skirts the very edge of arbitrariness. It is exceedingly difficult to draw a nonarbitrary dividing line between the physical and the mental. If your metaphysical instincts lie on the other side, you may well want to allow virtually any property to count as 'physical', in which case there will not be emergent properties. The point is that the answer to the question "Are there emergent properties?" has no ready answer. It depends on the metaphysical views one has of the world and on one's abilities to preserve those views in theories which are logically sound.

The metaphysical instincts of the Emergentists of the 1920s seem clear enough. But none of them was ever able to capture those instincts in a theory which satisfies the rigorous strictures of logic. Whether their goal can ever be realized, or indeed is even worth realizing, is a chapter of philosophy not yet written.

9.2.6 *Qualities versus relations*

In his novel *The Red and the Black*, Stendhal offers the following description of Julien Sorel:

> His cheeks were flushed, his eyes downcast. He was a slim youth of eighteen or nineteen, weak in appearance, with irregular but delicate features and an aquiline nose. His large eyes, which, in moments of calm, suggested a reflective, fiery spirit were animated at this instant with an expression of the most ferocious hatred. Hair of a dark chestnut, growing very low, gave him a narrow brow, and in moments of anger a wicked air. Among the innumerable varieties of the human coun-

tenance, there is perhaps none that is more strikingly characteristic. A slim and shapely figure betokened suppleness rather than strength. In his childhood, his extremely pensive air and marked pallor had given his father the idea that he would not live ... ([28], 28-9).

The only thing remarkable about this passage is its familiar formula: it is one of a piece with countless other descriptive passages all of us have read. In particular, it is far more remarkable for what it does not say, what it chooses to leave out, than what it does say.

There is in principle no end of descriptive detail one can produce. But there are *conventions*. Although it may be true (I do not know whether it is or not) that my son Efrem sits in front of his friend Todd in English class at their school, I would not normally think to include this information if asked to describe Efrem. No more so did Stendhal include in his description of Julien such possible data as that Julien was – at the moment of being described – standing 22 meters from the one oak tree on the property or that Julien was twice as old as the priest's nephew in Paris. We simply do not usually consider such 'peculiar' properties as *sitting in front of*, or *standing 22 meters from*, or *being twice as old as* as being proper, or intrinsic, properties of things. In describing things, we usually omit to mention such properties.

These latter sorts of properties – *sitting in front of, standing 22 meters from*, or *being twice as old as* – are *relations*, that is, they are properties which hold between *two* or more things. *Being red* is a property of individual items; *being more intensively red than* is a property which holds between two items. Properties which may be predicated* (to use the technical term) of single items – e.g. *being red, being square, having a mass of 6.2 kg*, even *being flammable* – are said to be 'qualities' (alternatively, 'attributes'). (Note, in this technical sense, "quality" does not mean being valuable or of superior manufacture, etc. A 'quality' is simply a property which a single thing may bear.) *Being to the left of, being heavier than, being twice as old as*, etc., are not qualities of things, but relations among things.

One common way philosophers sometimes try to draw the distinction between qualities and relations is to take recourse to some facts about the terms we typically use for these properties. To form a grammatical sentence using the phrase "... is rectangular", we need to provide the name of but one thing, e.g. "Boston Symphony Hall is rectangular." To form a grammatical sentence using the phrase "...

is higher than ...", we need to supply two names, e.g. "Mt Rainier is higher than Mt Hood." In addition to two-place relations ("... is higher than ..."), there are three-place relations ("... gives ... to ..."), and four-place relations ("... combined with ... tastes a lot like ... combined with ..."). Indeed relations may, and do, obtain between any number of things whatsoever.

According to this latter, linguistic, reconstruction of the distinction between qualities and relations, there is nothing remarkable whatsoever about their difference. Qualities appear as nothing other than one-place relations.[14] They are merely the first in a series of stepwise increase. But if there is nothing remarkable about qualities when viewed from the standpoint of logic or mathematics, do they nonetheless have some special status metaphysically? The four-place relation we just cited as an example, "... when combined with ... tastes a lot like ... combined with ...", will undoubtedly strike many persons as being somehow bogus. While they may be perfectly prepared to acknowledge the reality of such qualities as *being red* or *having a mass of 6.2 kg*, these persons will regard this latter, four-place, relation as being artificial. Is this mere prejudice, or are there good reasons for regarding relations as 'artificial'? Two different facts about our metaphysical views may help to explain the naturally felt antipathy some persons have toward relations.

First is the strongly held intuition that things can change their relations without losing their identity. A delicate crystal vase, for example, in being moved from a high shelf to a tabletop remains the 'same vase': the change in its spatial relations (from having been two meters above the floor to now being only one meter above the floor) has not affected its identity. But let that same vase drop from the shelf to the tabletop so that it shatters, so that it loses its property of wholeness or cohesiveness, then it ceases to be the 'same thing'. What had been a vase is no longer; the vase has gone out of existence to have been replaced by a collection of glass shards. Or, again, a person may move across town: the change in her spatial relations to other things does not (generally) affect her identity. She is still the same person. But let her lose her memory, or let her undergo a radical change in

---

14. Below, unless it is explicitly qualified as "one-place" (or "monadic"), the term "relation" will be used to designate the class of dyadic (two-place), triadic (three-place), etc., relations. We will continue to use the term "quality" for "one-place relation".

personality, and the resulting individual is not the 'same' person. Such conceptions are very deeply seated in our world-views. In asking about the identity and 'nature' of things, we almost invariably inquire after their qualities. Qualities (or at least some important subset of qualities), not relations, are generally taken to constitute a thing's 'essence'. And thus Stendhal describes Julien as: *being flushed, having downcast eyes, appearing weak, having irregular features, having delicate features, having animated eyes, possessing a fiery spirit, having chestnut hair*, etc. Relations, in contrast, are regarded as extrinsic, as mere accidents or incidentals. "My son's being good-natured is a 'real' property of him; his happening, at the moment, to be standing two feet from my desk is just an accidental feature, it has nothing to do with who or what he *is*", many persons might be inclined to argue.

This first reason why persons might feel uneasy about ceding full reality to relations, refusing to deem them real properties of things, lies pretty close to the surface as it were. But there is a second, much deeper, reason which additionally informs the thinking of some persons and makes them antagonistic toward granting the reality of relations. In ancient philosophy, Aristotle had advanced a logic which treated certain kinds of propositions: singular propositions (e.g. "Alexander the Great was a soldier") whose subjects are individual things (persons, places, times, etc.); and general propositions, whose subjects are classes of things. General propositions are further subdividable into universal propositions (e.g. "All men are mortal") and particular* (e.g. "Some men are blue-eyed"). But what is common to all these kinds of propositions is that they single out *one* subject (e.g. Alexander the Great; the class of men) and then proceed to predicate of the subject a quality (attribute). Such propositions are standardly known as 'subject/predicate' propositions. But are these the only types of propositions? Does every proposition predicate a quality of a subject?

For over two thousand years, until the early part of the current century, most philosophers believed so. Few, if any, were inclined or bold enough to propose that logic should and needed to be expanded to encompass relational propositions as well. Their resistance came about through the belief that relational propositions could – in principle – be replaced by, or be 'reduced to', subject/predicate propositions. This belief was in turn prompted by the belief that relations themselves, e.g. *being west of* or *being taller than*, were eliminable in favor of qualities. How might this be argued?

There are two different ways one might think it possible to eliminate relations.

Consider what we might take to be a paradigmatic instance of a relational proposition, e.g. the proposition expressed by the sentence "John is west of Toronto." In modern logic, this proposition would be taken to refer to three 'things': the two individual items, John and Toronto, and the relation, *being west of*. But there is a way to parse the English sentence, a way that is commonly taught in high-school grammar classes, a way that reflects its origins in the theory that all sentences are of subject/predicate form. According to that grammatical theory, the subject of the sentence (or proposition) is "John" and the predicate is "is west of Toronto". On this classical account, there are just two things being referred to in the sentence: the one individual thing, viz. John, and one quality (attribute), viz. the quality of *being west of Toronto*. Such 'properties' as *being west of Toronto* are sometimes, understandably, called 'relational properties'.

Which is it? Is *being west of Toronto* a quality (a relational property) of John, or is *being west of* a relation holding between John and Toronto? Two considerations favor plumping for the latter – the relational – account.

Suppose a person says, "My father and mother are divorced." How would we construe this if we were to adopt the theory that makes relations simple qualities? What shall the subject of this sentence be taken to be? Shall we construe it this way: "My father is (i.e. has the quality of being) divorced-from-my-mother"; or in this: "My mother is (i.e. has the quality of being) divorced-from-my-father"? Either choice seems wholly arbitrary. It is far less arbitrary to regard both father and mother 'equally' as subjects, standing to one another in the relationship of *being divorced from one another*. The point is that if one argues that all relational propositions are 'convertible into' subject/predicate propositions, then one can often, if not always, choose the subject only arbitrarily. Is the sentence "John is west of Toronto" any more 'about' John than it is 'about' Toronto? Is the sentence "Ronald and Nancy are married (to each other)" any more 'about' Ronald than it is 'about' Nancy?

The second consideration suggesting that we might prefer to construe such sentences as "John is west of Toronto" as relational rather than as being subject/predicate has to do with the peculiarity of the relational-property of *being west of Toronto*. Compare the (single-place) quality *being west of Toronto* with the (two-place) relation of *being west of.* The quality, but not the relation, in a sense invokes or refers to an individual*, viz. Toronto. One might, on metaphysical grounds, regard 'qualities' which refer to individuals as being no 'real' qualities at all: one might, that is, want to advance a theory which makes individuals, on the one hand, distinct kinds of entities from qualities, on the other. If so, then the hybrid expression "is west of Toronto", inasmuch as it refers to an individual (the city of Toronto), would be deemed not to refer to any quality at all.

Perhaps, though, there may be another way to eliminate relations, one which would, again, offer qualities in their place, but which would not take recourse to 'hybrid-qualities' (relational properties) such as *being west of Toronto*. Can this be done? This brings us to an examination of a more radical approach some philosophers have taken in their attempts to argue that relations are in principle eliminable in favor of qualities.

Here we might take as our example the relational proposition that object O_1 has twice the mass of object O_2. How might one argue that such a proposition can be replaced by a proposition containing only one-place predicates, i.e. terms referring to qualities? In this way: remember that every material thing has a mass. When one asserts, then, that object O_1 has twice the mass of object O_2, one could argue that what was being asserted was true only insofar as O_1 had some particular mass (an attribute) [e.g. 40 g] and O_2 had some particular mass [e.g. 20 g]. The relational claim – that O_1 has twice the mass of O_2 – could be regarded, then, as reducible to *two* nonrelational, subject/predicate claims about the masses of O_1 and of O_2 respectively. Or again, consider the relational proposition that Lincoln was similar to Washington. The natural reaction in someone's being told this might well be to ask, "In what respects were they similar?" And the answer may be, "They were both Presidents", or "They were both excellent public speakers", or "They were both elected to second terms", etc. In these latter cases, attributes – *being President, being elected to a second term*, etc. – are predicated of each person individually. The relational proposition "Lincoln was similar to Washington" is replaceable by the two nonrelational propositions "Lincoln was a President" and "Washington was a President." With examples such as these at hand, some philosophers have argued that attributes (qualities) are to be regarded as ineliminable and 'real', while relations are to be regarded as eliminable and 'unreal'.

There are, however, at least two problems with the theory that relations are in principle eliminable in favor of qualities. First is the difficulty that relational propositions and their supposed nonrelational replacements in general do not *mean* the same thing (or more exactly, they are not logically equivalent). Consider, again, the claim that O_1 has twice the mass of O_2. Suppose, as above, that this relational claim is true just because O_1 has a mass of 40 g and O_2 a mass of 20 g. The latter conditions will 'make' the relational claim true. But are the latter conditions implied by the former, relational, claim? Clearly not. Someone can assert that O_1 has twice the mass of O_2 without having any idea what the mass is of either object: only that the mass of the former is double that of the latter. The former, relational, proposition can be true without either of the latter, nonrelational, propositions being true. There are, in fact, an infinite number of pairs of nonrelational propositions which could 'make' the relational proposition true.

The second difficulty comes about through the challenge that some relations do not seem, even in principle, to be eliminable in favor of qualities. Consider a possible world consisting of three physical objects, *A*, *B*, and *C*, spatially arranged so that *B* is *between* the objects *A* and *C*.[15] What *quality* does any of these objects possess which accounts for the truth that *B* is between *A* and *C*? We might try to say that *A* lies to the left of *B* and that *B* lies to the left of *C*. But saying this will not have eliminated relations: it will simply have invoked a different relation, viz. the relation of *lying to the left of*. Or, to take another example, suppose that line L_1 *lies parallel to* line L_2. What qualities might we imagine each line to possess 'all on its own' which might account for its being parallel to the other? Nothing whatsoever suggests itself as a plausible candidate.

What, finally, are we to make of all this? When all is said and done, are relations 'real' or are they not? There have never been any knockdown arguments on either side: neither party to the dispute has ever

---

15. We often, naively, suppose that the relation of *betweenness* is unproblematic. But it is not. If I am right in what I earlier argued (see section 8.6), viz. that visual space need not correlate with tactile space, then there is the possibility that an object which is *seen* to be between another two might not be *felt* to be between those two. Indeed I suspect that the successful use of the concept of *betweenness* usually rests on our presupposing a certain context: we assume that we are talking about spatial distribution; or visual; or tactile; or mass; or temperature; or ... But we need not trouble ourselves here over this complication. For the purposes of the present example, we can simply stipulate that we are talking about three objects in *visual* space.

shown that the other's arguments are self-inconsistent. And, of course, it is in the very nature of the debate that no empirical evidence could possibly settle the question. Nonetheless, the view which would make relations every bit as 'real' as qualities has clearly in the twentieth century almost entirely vanquished the theory that qualities alone are real and that relations are unreal. The change in attitude has come about principally through the remarkable successes and power of modern logic, which has abandoned the straitjacket of subject/predicate sentences for relational ones. Subject/predicate sentences have become in this modern account merely a special case – that of one-place relations – of relational sentences. The ground has shifted, not because the old theory was ever demonstrably shown to be false or mistaken, but because the new theory is so much more congenial and so much more powerful. To the extent that one believes that aesthetic features – such as beauty and elegance – and simplicity are indicative of truth, then, to that extent, one can believe that the modern theory is true. But no one should believe that the truth of the theory which makes relations as 'real' as qualities has been demonstrated. It has not. Its acceptance comes about, necessarily, through softer, metaphysical considerations.

But even with all this said, a problem remains. We have talked uncritically, at some length, in the first instance of qualities as being 'real', and later of relations, as well, as being 'real'. But what, exactly, might this mean? What are philosophers saying when they say that qualities are real and that relations are real?

9.3 Realism and its rivals; abstract and concrete entities

The concept of *property* encompasses both the concept of *quality* (or *attribute*) and the concept of *relation*. As understood here, a thing's properties may include its *being red* (a quality), but also its standing in the two-place relation of *being north of* some second thing, as well as its standing in the three-place relation of *being between* two other things, etc.

It is important to emphasize that properties – qualities and relations – are neither physical things themselves, nor *parts* of things. A piece of chalk, white though it is, is not literally whiteness itself. Neither is the chalk's whiteness a *physical part* of the chalk. Physical *parts* of material objects are themselves (smaller) physical parts and may in their turn be physically separated from the larger thing of which they are parts. One might for example remove chips of chalk from a larger piece of chalk. The chips are (or were) *parts* of the original chunk. But the property of whiteness is no part of that chunk. The whiteness cannot be removed so that we could then say: "Here on the left is the whiteness which used to be in the chalk, and here on the right is what remains of the chalk, that is, the chalk with its whiteness removed." Or, to take a second example, imagine the impossibility of trying to remove the *weight* of the chalk: "Here on the left is the weight of the chalk; and here on the right is what remains of the chalk with just its weight and nothing more taken from it." Relations, too, are not parts of things. John may be taller than Bill; but the relation of *being taller than* is neither part of John nor part of Bill. In short, properties – qualities and relations – are not parts of things. But if properties are not parts, what, then, might they be?

The one feature of properties which is universally acknowledged is that properties are *general*. Although only one thing in the world may happen to exhibit, for example, some specific shade of blue, there is nothing in principle preventing any number of other things from also exhibiting that specific shade of blue. And similarly for any other property: zero, or one, or two … or countless numbers of things may be square; zero, or one, or two … or countless numbers of pairs may stand in the relation of *being friendly with*; etc. This distinction between, on the one hand, particulars* – individual things, such as persons, places, times, or material objects – and, on the other, their qualities and relations is acknowledged to be perhaps *the most fundamental* distinction in our conceptual scheme.

But what account are we to give of the relationship between particulars and their properties? Plato struggled mightily with this problem throughout his lifelong philosophical writings. Every theory he advanced he was soon to realize was beset with difficulties. And his own experience was to presage virtually every successor's. The problem has turned out to be the most enduring of all philosophical puzzles. Today, more than two thousand years later, no theory has won anything like universal acceptance; indeed there is probably nothing that can even be called the 'received' account.

These are the data Plato believed had to be accounted for in a theory of properties: (1) two or more existing things can share the same property; (2) properties (e.g. the property of being square) are not *parts* of things; and (3) properties can exist without anything instancing that property (e.g. squareness would exist even if nothing in the world happened to be square). The last of these three claims is the most problematic and is the one most often challenged. Whether or not one subscribes to this last claim will determine whether one opts, like Plato, for a so-called Realist theory of properties or for a non-Realist theory.

Why might one think that each property exists even if nothing happens to bear that property? Why, for example, might one believe that squareness exists in a world where nothing whatsoever is square?

Consider the sentence: "Everything is such that it is not square" (or more idiomatically, "Nothing is square"). Although this sentence happens to express a false proposition, we can perfectly well conceive that what is being claimed *could have been true*. It is not necessary that the universe contain square things; it just happens to be a contingent truth that it does. Suppose, for the sake of argument, that there never were any square things in the universe at any time, past, present, or future. The proposition under examination – that everything is such that it is not square – would then be true.[16] But how could it be true? For on the face of it, it would seem to be referring to two quite different concepts, that of *every (existing) thing* and that of the property *squareness*. The concept of *squareness* must refer to *something or other*. But, by hypothesis, it cannot be referring to the property of any actually existing thing. Therefore, in some sense, squareness would have to 'exist' even if nothing whatsoever at any place or any time in the universe happened to be square.

Although the foregoing argument is not Plato's, but a more modern version of the reasoning leading to his conclusions, Plato argued that the properties of things must exist 'independently' of those things. But what might this mean? If the properties of things exist independently of those things, what are we to make of the nature of this 'existence'?

---

16. Having never experienced anything which was square, perhaps persons may never come to formulate and entertain either the proposition that things might be square or the proposition that nothing is square. But what propositions persons formulate and subsequently come either to believe or to disbelieve is irrelevant to whether those propositions are true or false. There are innumerable propositions which we never formulate, still less do we have opinions about their truth or falsity. And there probably are countless numbers of propositions which we are incapable of considering, if for no other reason than that their constituent concepts lie outside the conceptual capacities of human beings (see pp. 84-5 above). The point is that a proposition such as that nothing is square does not depend on human beings' beliefs; even more strongly, it does not depend even on there being human beings or any conscious creatures.

Physical objects – things which are actually square, blue, etc. – exist in both space and time. If their properties are hypothesized to exist, but neither as parts of objects nor as physical objects themselves, then – it would seem reasonable to maintain – they must exist *outside of* space and time.

On purely combinatorial grounds, there are four possibilities: (1) something exists both in space and in time; (2) something exists in time, but not in space; (3) something exists in space, but not in time; and (4) something exists neither in space nor in time. Physical objects, including human beings, exist in space and time. They are said to be 'spatiotemporal' objects or existents. Are there any 'things' in any of the other three categories? Does anything exist *outside* of space and/or of time?

I am not quite sure, but perhaps some religions have posited a god who exists in time, but not in space. But I must confess ignorance on this score. In any event, some philosophers have argued that minds satisfy this second category, i.e. they have advanced the theory that minds exist only in time but not in space. G.E. Moore counterargued, however, that from the difficulty of attributing some particular length, width, and depth to minds, it does not follow that minds are not *in* space:[17] "... our acts of consciousness ... occur *in the same places* in which our bodies are. ... When ... I travelled up to Waterloo by train, I believe that my mind and my acts of consciousness travelled with me. When the train and my body were at Putney, I was thinking and seeing at Putney. When the train and my body reached Clapham Junction, I was thinking and seeing at Clapham Junction. ... My acts of consciousness take place in my body; and yours take place in yours: and our minds (generally, at least) go with us, wherever our bodies go" ([137], 19-20).

Is there anything which might plausibly be regarded as falling into the third category, i.e. of things in space but not in time? Offhand, I cannot think of a single example where a philosopher has proposed such a thing. I know of no alleged examples of things which are supposedly spatial but are not temporal. Of course one can neglect to mention a spatial object's temporal extent. One could talk about the geographical features of Paris without ever mentioning at what time they happened to exist. But failing to mention their time of existence

---

17. Moore seems to be echoing here a similar argument in Locke. See [124], book II, chap. XXIII, §§18-20.

does not make them nontemporal objects. The Champs Elysées has temporal existence even if one happens to neglect it in describing that boulevard.

The fourth category, that of objects which are neither spatial nor temporal, is the focus of the most intense controversy in this scheme. For it is here that followers of Plato, "Realists" as they have come to be known, will assign properties. Objects which are neither spatial nor temporal, which lie 'outside' of both space and time, are known as 'abstract objects'. Objects which lie within space and time, e.g. this page you are reading, your body, the planet Earth, the Sun, or the Milky Way, are known as 'concrete' objects. Concrete objects have spatiotemporal positions.[18]

There is a certain irony in the name "Realism". Philosophers who argue for Realism, i.e. the theory that properties 'really' exist outside of space and time, seem to be bucking ordinary notions of what is 'real'. In the ordinary way of invoking the concept of reality, one would be inclined to identify reality with spatiotemporal existents, i.e. with concrete objects. But by a curious twist of history, the name "Realism" has been attached to the theory that abstract objects are 'real'. (Sometimes vocabulary, other than that adopted here, is used to label abstract objects. Sometimes in place of "abstract", the term "subsistent" is used. And some philosophers prefer to used the verbs "subsist" or "have being" in place of "exist" in the case of abstract

---

18. Sometimes we tend to view 'the entire universe' as the *class* of all the things it contains; othertimes as a kind of super-object, a gigantic *scattered object* of the sort we discussed earlier on p. 195. But can this latter mega-object, the entire universe, itself have a place? a time? If we try to persist with the relational theories of space and of time advanced in the preceding chapter, and if we were to try to say *where* or *when* the entire universe exists, wouldn't we be illicitly supposing that there was something *else* – outside of the universe – which stood in some spatial or temporal relation to it? I think we need not be too troubled over this difficulty. Once again we can use the techniques of section 8.8. Just as we can say where the Mississippi River is located in space by specifying where its spatial parts are (it is at Memphis, Vicksburg, Natchez, Baton Rouge, New Orleans, etc.), we can say where the entire universe is: it is simply where any of its spatial parts are. Similarly, it exists in time whenever any of its temporal parts exist. Thus the entire universe can be regarded as a spatiotemporal object and there is no need to posit anything in space and time outside of the universe.

entities in order to contrast their 'manner of existence' from that of objects which are in space and time.)

Having posited that properties are outside of space and time, i.e. are abstract entities, a Realist is posed a formidable problem. Plato quickly realized this. At various times, he proposed a variety of alternative explanations. At one point he thought that these abstract entities (squareness, justice, etc.) – "forms" he called them (their more modern name is "universals"*) – were perfect particulars of which the concrete existents, the spatiotemporal objects, were somehow imperfect 'copies'. But he recognized that no such account could be made to work. If blueness itself were a particular, the sort of thing which might be copied, then it itself would have to have the property of blueness, and one would merely have deferred the problem, not have solved it; one would in fact thus have an infinite regress.

If particulars are not copies of universals, perhaps they 'participate' or somehow 'share in' the universal. But this notion is mere metaphor. We understand how two children might share a toy: by both handling it at the same time or by taking turns. Or, again, persons might participate in a stock offering or own a share in a company: they have a legal right to certain assets or profits. But there is only so much of the company to go around. Sharing cannot go on indefinitely; eventually the asset runs out, or at the very least, each 'sharer' gets a steadily diminished portion. But universals do not 'run out': any number of things can be blue without in the slightest detracting from the blueness of other things.

All attempts to explicate the relation obtaining between universals and particulars (i.e. their instances) in terms of other, more familiar relations have proved equally insupportable. We can give a name to the relation obtaining between a particular and its properties, i.e. we will say that the particular 'instances' or 'exemplifies' certain universals, but we seem unable to explicate the relationship any further. It seems, so far at least, after two thousand years of philosophers' trying, to have eluded explication. It seems, so far, to be wholly *sui generis**.

Some persons find the theory of universals exceedingly attractive. They take delight in positing another 'world', a world of abstract objects outside of space and time. To have found the need for such a posit appears to persons of this temperament to be one of the great triumphs of metaphysics. But, equally, there are persons of the contrary temperament who regard the positing of a world of abstract entities as the greatest blot possible in metaphysics and try, with enormous effort, to construct theories which have no need to posit such strange entities. These latter, anti-Realist, theorists typically take one of three approaches. They will try to construct either a Conceptualist theory, a Nominalist theory, or a theory positing the existence of what have come to be called 'tropes'.

Conceptualists attempt to argue that there are no abstract entities, that certain items in our minds – our *conceptions*[19] of squareness, extension, etc. – are all we need posit in order to explain such facts as that two or more objects may share the same property. But making the analysis depend on the existence of conscious creatures has one immediate consequence which is wholly unacceptable to most contemporary philosophers: it makes it impossible for things to bear properties in worlds in which there are no minds. Few philosophers are disposed to make the existence of the world depend on the existence of *us*. The favored modern belief strongly seems to be that a world could exist devoid of consciousness. There may be conscious creatures in this world, but there did not *have to be*. It would still have been a world, even if we had never existed.

The preferred anti-Realist approaches today are through Nominalism and through the Theory of tropes.

Nominalists argue that the only things that exist, that are 'real', are individuals. There are no entities existing (subsisting) independently of individuals, i.e. nothing exists outside of space and time. Squareness, for example, might be explicated by invoking either the class of square things or – in some accounts – the complex individual (or scattered object[20]) which just is all the square things in the universe.

---

19. *Conceptions* are not to be confused with *concepts*. What *sorts* of things *concepts* are is a question which has prompted a great diversity of replies. Above (p. 97) I gave only a minimal characterization of *concept*, one which was (deliberately) silent on the question concerning what sorts of things concepts are. But *conceptions* allow for a slightly fuller characterization. Whatever final account we might want to give of *concepts* and *conceptions* – their ontological status and their relations one to another – we can say at the outset (pre-analytically) that *conceptions* are *in the mind*. For there to be a *conception* of, let us say, blueness, there must be a mind (or consciousness) which 'has' or 'entertains' that conception. Conceptions are 'mental entities'; concepts may, or may not, be in the mind. (Many, perhaps most, current accounts lean toward treating *concepts* as non-mental entities.)

20. See p. 195 and footnote 18, p. 265 above. We will return, again, to this notion of a 'complex individual' in chapter 11, p. 334.

Three problems beset Nominalism. If properties are to be explicated in terms of classes of similar individuals, then it would seem that Nominalism has dispensed with one sort of abstract entity, viz. universals, only to persist with another, viz. classes. For, in most standard accounts, classes are themselves abstract entities. But even allowing for classes, another problem arises. If redness, for example, is to be explicated by invoking the class of all red things, then the members of this class are members in virtue of their *being similar to another* (in respect of their color). But then the relation of *similarity* (or *resemblance*) would seem to be an irreducible property, i.e. one not capable of being explicated solely in terms of some class of things. And finally there is the aforementioned problem of unsatisfied (or unactualized) properties. According to Nominalism, if there were, for example, no actual squares, then squareness would be identified with the null (i.e. empty) class. But similarly, if there were no actual circles, then circularity, too, would be identified with the null class. Thus, in a world where there were neither squares nor circles, both squareness and circularity would be identified with the same, viz. the empty, class. Nominalists believe that none of these objections is fatal and that each can be met in a well-crafted theory. But, in the meantime, another anti-Realist theory has been attracting attention.

I began this section by saying that the properties of material things are not *parts* of things, in the sense that they are not themselves material things. But if properties are not *parts*, then – according to this third anti-Realist theory – they are very much more like parts than they have earlier been regarded. Donald Williams, who is generally credited for resurrecting this theory in the 1960s (elements of the theory were current in the 1920s and 1930s), argued that the properties of specific individuals, e.g. the redness and sphericity of some particular lollipop (not redness and sphericity 'in general'), are – if not exactly parts, then at least – 'components' ([214]). (Williams sometimes called these components "subtle", "thin", "diffuse", or "fine" parts. See, for example, [214], 76.) In any event, he labeled individual properties further, dropping explicit reference to their being either 'parts' or 'components', by introducing the technical term "tropes".[21]

---

21. Williams appropriated the word, but not the meaning, from George Santayana ([184]). His justification for assigning a new meaning was somewhat imperious: "I shall divert the word, which is almost useless in either his [Santayana's] or its dictionary sense" ([214], 78). Williams also used the expres-

> I propose now that entities like our fine parts [i.e. tropes] ... are the primary constituents of this or any possible world ... They not only are actual but are the only actualities, in just this sense, that whereas entities of all other categories are literally composed of them, they are not in general composed of any other sort of entity. (78)

> That things consist of tropes does not imply either that they were made by putting tropes together or that they can be dismantled by taking tropes apart. (98)

There are, then, in this scheme no universals of the sort posited by Realists, i.e. there is no universal redness instanced in this lollipop and in that lollipop. There is rather the particular redness of this lollipop and the particular redness of that lollipop. But certain problems are seemingly solved only to leave others unsolved, and perhaps even in a worse state.

Once again relations seem to pose a formidable challenge. There is a powerful attraction in the theory of tropes when the examples (Williams's own) are of such qualities as redness, sphericity, and aridity. But the theory seems less attractive when one turns to relations, such properties as ...*-is-to-the-left-of-*... and ...*-is-between-...-and-*.... The particular redness of a specific lollipop can plausibly be argued to be coextensive* with the lollipop itself, i.e. it can plausibly be argued that redness of a particular lollipop is – like the lollipop itself – an individual (more exactly, a trope) having spatiotemporal properties. But what about that lollipop's being on the table? Is *being on* a trope which is a 'component' (a 'thin part' in Williams's terminology) of the pair of objects, the lollipop and the table? Neither Williams originally (1966) nor Keith Campbell, who promoted the theory in the 1970s ([41]), addressed how, exactly, relations were supposed to be accommodated within the theory of tropes. It is only more recently that Campbell

---

sion "abstract particulars" as a synonym for "tropes" adding, however, that this "good old phraseology has a paradoxical ring" (78). Since Williams used "abstract" in a way quite different from that adopted in this book, I will scrupulously avoid adopting the expression "abstract particular".

"Theory of tropes" should not be abbreviated as "tropism". "Tropism" is a term too well entrenched in biology, where it has a distinct technical use, to be profitably co-opted for use in philosophy.

has tried to adapt the theory to this vexing problem (see e.g. [42]). His current approach recapitulates some of the techniques we have explored earlier (in section 9.2.6) by which philosophers have tried to eliminate relations in favor of (monadic) qualities.

There is another problem as well: Plato's problem of the One and the Many. In a theory of tropes, how is it possible for two or more concrete particulars to 'share the same property in common', e.g. for two or more individuals (my apple, your tomato, and her scarf) all to be red? At the first level of analysis the answer is clear: each of them has as a component, i.e. has as a trope, its own individual redness. But what makes each of these tropes the 'same' trope? Plato's original problem – asked of physical things themselves – returns with an even greater sting as a problem about tropes. What makes two tropes similar? The trouble now is, however, that we cannot say that they, the particular tropes, share some trope in common. We have just seen that Williams has insisted that tropes "are not in general composed of any other sort of entity". In a way, the very problem that the positing of tropes was supposed to forestall has itself reappeared to infect that theory itself. One proposal which has been made is that the similarity of two (or more) tropes, e.g. the similarity of this red trope to that one, is an 'irreducible brute fact'. But such an explanation – to philosophers who have not themselves adopted the theory – seems more of a resolute avoidance of the difficulty than a satisfactory solution. Like the Nominalists with their earlier theory, those philosophers who lately posit tropes as a way to avoid Realism believe that the problems within their theory are not insuperable.

Although I generally prefer negative theories – those which posit as few unempirical concepts*[22] as possible – my own leanings in this particular case are toward Realism.[23] My attraction to the theory is

----

22. For definition of "unempirical concept" in Glossary, see under "empirical".

23. I was surprised to find in Steven Goldman's combined review of my book *The Concept of Physical Law* ([201]) and of David Armstrong's *What Is a Law of Nature?* ([13]) that he has characterized me as being a Nominalist: "Swarz [sic] argues a nominalist position in which particular events, in virtue of being all there is to reality, are both logically and ontologically prior to universals" ([79], 97). Goldman has obviously read something into my book that is not there at all. Nowhere in that book do I even raise the matter of Realism versus Nominalism. And while I certainly did argue that par-

bolstered by one further consideration: I can see no way to account for the existence of certain items, e.g. pieces of music, plays, and novels, other than by conceiving of them as abstract entities. Here I am considerably influenced by the arguments of C.E.M. Joad (1891-1953). Joad argued ([105], 267-70) that the play *Hamlet*, for example, could not reasonably be identified with any particular in the world: neither with an idea in Shakespeare's mind,[24] nor with any manuscript he wrote, nor with any printed edition of the text, nor with any particular production, nor with any audio or video recording of any particular production. For *Hamlet* could exist even if any one or several of these were not to exist. While Joad, himself, rightly expressed some diffidence about his own arguments, I think that they add considerable impetus to a theory which would posit abstract entities.

Although I am a Realist, I am a reluctant Realist. For, to be frank, there is something exceedingly peculiar about positing entities with exist (subsist) outside of space and time. I, personally, would prefer a theory which could dispense with such mysterious entities. But I find the problems inherent in the various anti-Realist theories even more

---

ticular events are logically prior to physical laws, I never argued, nor do I believe, that physical events are logically prior to universals. If anything, I believe precisely the opposite. I suspect that Goldman's mistaken characterization of my position arises out of my having staked out a position contrary to Armstrong's. Armstrong believes that there are ontically necessary relations obtaining between universals; I do not believe that there are. But this does not mean that I deny that there are universals. I deny only that there exist ontically necessary relationships between them. I regard myself as much a Realist about universals as Armstrong. While both of us are Realists, he is a Necessitarian and I am a Regularist.

24. The expression "idea in someone's mind" is ambiguous. Sometimes when we use this expression, we refer to some particular idea on some particular occasion, in effect, to some *act* of thought which is (at least) some temporal particular. Othertimes in using this expression we refer to an idea which other persons may share. If so, then we are talking of a universal. Note that if we mean by "an idea in Shakespeare's mind" some particular act of thought, then insofar as Shakespeare is now dead, that act is now as nonexistent as any of his pains or his visual sensations of the English countryside. If, however, by "idea in his mind" we mean something which could be shared by other persons, which could exist as well in other persons' minds, then we are talking of a universal, and that would not be to deny Joad's argument, but to concur with it.

troubling. Realism is simply the better, in my estimation, of the available theories. But, like many other Realists, I do not much care for Realism. Recently one of my colleagues professed his repudiation of Realism by saying that he found the positing of abstract entities "unintelligible". I share his displeasure. But I find myself unable to adopt his own anti-Realist position because I cannot in turn believe that the anti-Realist theories provide any better answer or that they can be developed without themselves having to posit at least some abstract entities.

The debate between the Realists and the anti-Realists, we may be sure, will continue for some time. And we may equally be sure that passions will flare.

Some years ago I was present at a conference where Bas van Fraassen spoke about the problems in positing, or abstaining from positing, abstract entities – in particular, sets – in mathematics. He began his talk (which he subsequently published) with the following two paragraphs:

> Once upon a time there were two possible worlds, Oz^{25} and Id. These worlds were very much alike and, indeed, very much like our world. Specifically, their inhabitants developed exactly the mathematics and mathematical logic we have today. The main differences were two: (a) in Oz, sets really existed, and in Id no abstract entities existed, but (b) in Id, mathematicians and philosophers were almost universally Platonist, while in Oz they refused, almost to a man, to believe that there existed any abstract entities.
>
> They all lived happily ever after. ([207], 39)

In his final paragraph, he added:

> I am not arguing that there are no sets. First, it is philosophically as uninteresting whether there are sets as whether there are unicorns. As a philosopher I am only interested in whether our world is intelligible if we assume that there are no sets, and whether it remains equally intelligible if we do not. Personally, I delight in the postulation of occult entities to explain everyday phenomena, I just don't delight in taking it seriously. As a phi-

---

25. Doubtless further homage to L. Frank Baum. See p. 207 above.

losopher, however, I look forward to the day when we shall be able to say, "Yes, Virginia, there is a null set," and go on to explain, as the *New York Sun* did of Santa Claus, that of course there isn't one, but still there really is, living in the hearts and minds of men – exactly what a conceptualist by temperament would hope. ([207], 50)

Some of van Fraassen's listeners were amused by his fable. But at least one, Reinhardt Grossmann, a dear teacher of mine from graduate school, was not. Indeed, Grossmann was outraged. Several times he was heard to protest, "How can he believe it makes no difference? There is all the difference between abstract entities really existing and their not."

As I said, the debate continues.

It is now time to apply the concepts explored in these last two sections to the problem introduced at the outset of this chapter, viz. whether qualitative identity – the sharing of all properties in common – confers numerical identity.

CHAPTER TEN

Individuation

In the previous chapter we previewed the topic of this current chapter: How are we to account for the possibility of there being numerically distinct things which are qualitatively identical? If two or more things are qualitatively identical, i.e. share their properties in common, what then accounts for their multiplicity? To be able to pursue such a question has required us to devote virtually all of chapter 9 to an examination of the concept of *sharing properties in common*.

10.1 Physical objects

One of the facts of our experience, perhaps the most familiar, is that the world contains an enormous number of physical objects. It may, as well, contain many other kinds of things, e.g. minds, souls, numbers, universals, and forces. But we will confine our attention in the earlier parts of this chapter principally to physical objects.

Ordinarily we do not much wonder about the commonplace. It is the unusual, the out-of-routine, the unfamiliar, which stands out and demands our attention. One may wonder how it is possible, if indeed it is, that extrasensory perception might occur, or that certain human beings can walk on burning coals, or that the influenza virus of 1918-19 which killed 20 million persons disappeared as abruptly as it had initially appeared. But few persons would be similarly tempted to wonder about something as familiar and commonplace as the existence of material objects. And yet, when one does think about material objects, the more one thinks about them, the more mysterious they seem.

First of all there is the most basic question of all: Why is there something, rather than nothing? Many persons are tempted to give a theological answer: God has created the world. But that answer only raises another: Why did God create the world? There is no satisfactory answer forthcoming from rational theology. Various religions may offer answers; but religious answers are, more often than not, glaringly deficient when judged on the grounds of rational theology and are usually terribly unconvincing to persons who do not share the same religious orientation.

Some modern thinkers, adopting what they have called "the anthropic principle", have turned the question and its answer round about, arguing that unless there were a world, complete with material objects, we could not even ask the question "Why does anything exist?" While the claim is undeniably true, many critics object that it does not provide a satisfactory answer to the question.[1] It is analogous to someone's answering the question "Why does Joan love classical music?" by replying that if Joan's mother had not become pregnant then Joan would not have been born and hence would not have loved classical music. Although Joan's mother becoming pregnant was a necessary condition for Joan's being born and hence a necessary condition for Joan's liking classical music, neither of these events (or states) – Joan's mother becoming pregnant and Joan's liking classical music – critics will insist, explains the other. Similarly, if the world did not exist, none of us could ask why it does; but neither of these events (states) – the world's existing and our asking why it does – critics will insist, explains the other.[2]

Although I have read what a great variety of writers have had to say on this subject, I have never found an answer which has had (for me) a

---

1. The anthropic principle has received considerable attention in the last decade, both in academic circles (see, e.g., [22] for a sustained defense, and [62] for a criticism – the latter contains a good bibliography) and in the popular media (see, e.g., [74]). But it is not a new principle by any means. Its promoters advance it explicitly as a resurrecting of the teleology of ancient and medieval science (again see [22]). It is a specialized version of the very sort of principle which Bacon, as we have earlier seen (p. 58), was intent to dispel from physics nearly four hundred years ago. As I explained, the arguments for and against adopting such principles cannot be decided by experimental science. These are metaphysical principles which require us to examine the very core of our conception of what a satisfactory model of explanation may be. I, like Bacon, regard such principles, whether in their old-fashioned guise or in their latest raiment, as inappropriate within physics and cosmology. But, clearly, other writers do not share this view.

2. Even more recently (1984), Nicholas Rescher has taken a new departure and has pursued a boldly speculative proposal: that certain very basic physical laws (laws of Nature) – "protolaws" he calls them – necessitate the exist-

significant degree of plausibility. I have become steadily more convinced that the question is ill-conceived. It is as ill-conceived as, for
example, one way of posing the question "Where is the universe?"
One can, as I suggested earlier (footnote 18, p. 265), answer the latter
question by saying (fairly uninformatively): "It is where any of its
spatial parts are." But one cannot, of course, rationally demand an
answer which specifies where the universe is in relation to something
outside of the universe. Similarly, one can explain why some specific
event occurs in the history of the universe by citing antecedent events
(and – depending on one's theories of historical explanation – possibly historical laws, generalizations, or truisms as well). But one can-

---

ence of material objects; and that the truth of these protolaws, themselves,
come about through their maximizing certain 'cosmic values' ([170]). There
are two forbidding hurdles lying in the path of this solution.

The first problem lies in the exceptional role assigned to the protolaws. In
virtually all contemporary accounts, physical laws state the relationships
between existent or possible entities; but they do not 'require' or 'necessitate'
the existence of those entities. That is, physical laws are regarded as being
logically conditional, not categorical, i.e. as *not* implying the existence of
their subjects. For example, the law which states that an isolated planet and a
star will revolve around a common focus in elliptical orbits is, in fact, never
realized. There are no fully isolated planetary systems anywhere in the universe. Physical laws state (conditionally) "such and such would happen
if ..."; they do not state (categorically) "such and such actually exists and
behaves thus ..." So we see that Rescher's hypothesized protolaws would be
considerably different from 'ordinary' physical laws. To explain the *existence*
of material objects, they would have to be an ontologically different kind of
thing than familiar physical laws. We would have, as it were, two 'tiers' of
physical laws.

The second difficulty arises from Rescher's suggestion that the protolaws
maximize certain 'cosmic values' ('cosmic' in that these values have nothing
to do with human concerns, i.e. are not ethical, aesthetic, etc.). We are not,
however, given an example of any of these cosmic values, and hence are in
no position to judge whether they can explain protolaws. But we can
anticipate certain severe problems. Insofar as these cosmic values are further
characterized as being self-justificatory, it is highly improbable that they
could serve as the explanatory basis of protolaws which include, Rescher
suggests, quantum mechanics, general relativity, and the like. It is difficult, if
not impossible, to imagine self-justifying cosmic values with the kind of
specificity needed to explain why quantum mechanics rather than a logically
possible, but incompatible, alternative should be true.

not extrapolate indefinitely and think that one can ask meaningfully why the universe as a whole exists. Just as there is nothing outside of the universe against which the spatial position of the entire universe may be gauged, there are no events outside of the universe whose occurrence can be rationally posited as explaining the existence of the universe.

This conclusion may seem overly pessimistic. Many of us hate to think that our understanding must be limited. But the world provides no guarantee of its being fully comprehensible. Given how we standardly explain events and states, it seems to me that we are positively precluded from being able to formulate an intelligible answer to the question "Why is there anything, rather than nothing?" The only possible reply must be: "We cannot answer such a question. It can have no answer."[3]

I take it as a datum that the universe exists and that it has material objects in it. To be sure, some philosophers – in the two thousand years of written philosophy – have challenged even this assumption. I have no particular desire here to recount their arguments. As I have said (p. 240), I do not think that there can be any conclusive refutation of their theories. But I do believe that the contrary posit, that there are material objects, is rationally supportable. In any event, I am sufficiently comfortable with it that I am perfectly happy to accept it as a working hypothesis if for no other reason than to get on to what I do want to examine. (If this latter claim strikes you as evidencing an excessive tentativeness, let me state explicitly that I firmly believe that there *are* material objects. It is just that I am not interested here in making a diversion into a discussion of what, for most persons, requires no justification whatsoever.)

There are material objects – this is the starting point for this chapter. I do not ask *why* there are material objects. But I do want to ask

---

3. Robert Nozick strongly rejects this pessimistic verdict. But he cautions that very odd theories will have to be generated. Characterizing his own theories (1981), he writes: "The question cuts so deep, however, that any approach that stands a chance of yielding an answer will look extremely weird. Someone who proposes a non-strange answer shows he didn't understand this question. Since the question is not to be rejected, though, we must be prepared to accept strangeness or apparent craziness in a theory which answers it" ([146], 116).

how it is *possible* that there are material objects. The two questions
are very different.

Physical objects, material things, in spite of their familiarity turn
out to be conceptually puzzling. What accounts for the numerical distinctness of material objects? We might discover, in due course, that
this question, too, just like the ones I dismissed a moment ago, may be
unanswerable; it may be ill-conceived in ways unapparent at the outset. But whether this is so remains to be seen. We must make an
attempt to answer it. In that attempt we must be prepared for one possibility: discovering that our initial question was ill-conceived and the
enterprise we have embarked upon must eventuate in frustration. But
we cannot decide this in advance. 'Nothing ventured, nothing gained'
is true; unfortunately, its positive counterpart 'Something ventured,
something gained' may be false. Without making the attempt, we will
gain nothing. However, in making the attempt, we are not assured of
any success. We are not even entitled to the belief that success is possible, still less that it is probable.

10.2   Identity-at-a-time versus identity-through-time

It has become customary to break the question of the numerical identity of physical objects into two stages. We begin (in this chapter) with
the question of the numerical identity of objects at some given
moment of time. This might be called 'snapshot' identity. For
example, we might ask, "Is the book I am now looking at the selfsame
book you are now looking at?" This is 'momentary' or 'instantaneous' identity. That is, this is identity which disregards the fact, if it
is a fact, that the 'things' being identified may also happen to endure
through time. The instantaneous aspect of the identification is perhaps
better expressed in a formal statement. The question we will be intent
to pursue may be formulated this way:

> Under what conditions may O_1-at-T_1 be regarded as being
> numerically identical with O_2-at-T_1?

Identity-at-a-time is often spoken of as 'synchronic identity' and
equally as 'individuation'. It is easy to see why the concept of individuation is invoked in this context: to specify the conditions under
which O_1 and O_2 are numerically identical (or distinct) is just to
specify the conditions under which O_1 is (or is not) to be regarded as
being the same *individual* as O_2. To specify conditions of numerical
identity just is to specify the conditions of individuation.

Having once addressed the question how numerical identity, or individuation, is to be accounted for at some specific moment of time, one can then go on to ask how identity-through-time might be explained. The latter question presupposes an answer to the former. Objects must be individuated – i.e. we must be able to pick out individual objects – before we can hope to be able to trace their evolution through time. Thus we will separate the two problems, tackling individuation (or synchronic identity) in this chapter and identity-through-time (or diachronic identity) in the next.

10.3   Positive and negative theories of individuation

Attempts at solving the problem of individuation divide into two distinct classes: those which argue that what individuates objects is their properties; and those which argue that properties alone can never individuate objects, and hence which find it necessary to posit something 'beyond' or 'behind' an object's properties, a special 'individuator', viz. its 'substance'. Theories which attempt to solve the individuation problem by invoking *nothing more* than a thing's properties are spoken of as 'negative' theories. Negative theories are also sometimes colorfully called "bundle theories" since they argue that there is nothing more to a thing than its being (metaphorically) a 'bundle' of properties. Theories which try to solve the individuation problem by positing that there is *more* (e.g. substance) to a thing than just its properties are said to be 'positive' theories.

Negative theorists will, like Leibniz, take as their point of departure the principle of the identity of indiscernibles (see p. 232 above), arguing that numerical identity can be accounted for strictly in terms of the properties which things instance. In the previous chapter we introduced symbols for numerical identity and for qualitative identity. The principle of the identity of indiscernibles may be stated in a specialized version for identity-at-a-time:

$$(O_1\text{-at-}T_1 \varpropto O_2\text{-at-}T_1) \rightarrow (O_1\text{-at-}T_1 = O_2\text{-at-}T_1)$$

This principle states that O_1 is numerically identical to O_2 at some particular moment of time if, at that moment of time, O_1 and O_2 share all their properties in common. The philosophical task confronting the negative, or bundle, theorists then becomes one of examining under what conditions this principle might turn out to be true.

Questions of numerical identity are interchangeable with questions of numerical difference. For, if we can state under what conditions O_1

and O_2 are numerically identical, then we have also stated, implicitly, under what conditions O_1 and O_2 are numerically distinct. Simply: O_1 and O_2 will be numerically distinct when the conditions for their being numerically identical do not obtain. Thus we may interchange the two questions at will. This explains why we often find theorists, both those promoting a negative theory and those promoting a positive theory, focusing their attention on examples of numerical difference as readily as on numerical identity. From a psychological point of view, it may be somewhat easier to focus on numerical difference than on numerical identity. But both approaches are equally valid.

10.4   The metaphysical and epistemological dimensions of the problem of individuation

There are two quite distinct, although closely allied, problems of individuation.

On the one side, there is the metaphysical problem. What must we assume about physical things *themselves* in order to account for their numerical distinctness? If possible, we want this answer not to invoke any special perceptual or cognitive abilities of conscious creatures since we can readily imagine possible worlds in which there are distinct physical objects and yet which do not contain any conscious creatures. We should no more want to make the numerical distinctness of physical objects depend on some feature or capacity of conscious, perceiving, knowing creatures than we should want, for example, to make the charge on an electron, or the mass of a proton, or the speed of light depend on some fact about *us*.

On the other side, there is the epistemological problem. We human beings *can* and regularly *do* individuate objects, i.e. we are able to distinguish them one from another, and we can even *count* objects (in stipulated regions of space and intervals of time).[4] How are we able to do this? What is there about physical objects and about us which allows us to individuate them? Do we human beings have 'access' to whatever it is which – metaphysically speaking – individuates material objects, or – somehow – do we individuate objects in some other way? But if so, how?

It is a regrettable fact about English that we use the same word

---

4. Our being able to *count* objects is often taken as equivalent to our being able to *individuate* objects. See, for example, [217].

"individuation" both for the metaphysical basis of numerical difference and for our human ability to discern the multiplicity of things. We could, somewhat artificially, deliberately avoid the verb "individuate" in the latter case and take recourse instead to something like "tell things apart". But the trouble with that maneuver is that it is only a temporary solution. Other writers standardly use "individuation" in both senses, the metaphysical and the epistemological. We will follow suit. But we must be aware that although we use a single word, there are two different concepts at play. What we would like is a solution to both problems of individuation, the metaphysical version and the epistemological version.

10.5 Positive theories: Substratum as individuator

Certain terms in philosophy – "form", "principle", "substance", etc. – have been in vogue for millennia, first in Greek and Latin and, later, in English translation, and have acquired a bewildering number of different meanings. "Substance", for example, occurs frequently in the writings of Aristotle and is used there in no fewer than six different senses (see e.g. [147]). In this chapter and in each of the next two, we will invoke respectively three different concepts of substance. In this chapter, we will examine whether substance need be posited to explain individuation (identity-at-a-time); in the next chapter, whether substance need be posited to explain identity-through-time; and in the last chapter, whether substance need be posited in order to explain personal identity.

Of the many concepts of substance, the principal one for attention in this chapter is that which is sometimes called "the substratum". Although the concept is certainly not original with Locke, it was his version – or at least a version conventionally attributed to him – which came to figure prominently in later discussions and is the one which modern philosophers most often have in mind when they talk of "substratum". Locke offered this explanation as to why he thought it necessary to posit substance:

> ... when we talk or think of any particular sort of corporeal [material] substances[5] ... though the *idea* we have ... of them

---

5. Locke, in this first instance, is not using "substance" in his own technical sense, but in the colloquial or ordinary sense, in which one might talk, for

be but the complication or collection of those several simple *ideas* of sensible qualities, which we ... find united in the thing ...; yet, because we cannot conceive how they should subsist alone, nor one in another, we suppose them existing in and supported by some common subject; *which support we denote by the name substance*, though it be certain we have no clear or distinct *idea* of that *thing* we suppose a support. ([124], book II, chap. XXIII, §4)

... not imagining how these simple *ideas* can subsist by themselves, we accustom ourselves to suppose some *substratum* wherein they do subsist, and from which they do result, which therefore we call *substance*. (§1)

... substance is supposed always *something* besides the extension, figure, solidity, motion ... or other observable *ideas*, though we know not what it is. (§3)

This argument for the introduction of substance is a so-called argument to the best solution: it argues for the existence of something on the basis that that something must be posited as the best (if not the only possible) solution of some puzzle. Substance, it is clear, because it is itself propertyless, could not possibly be known either by sense or by scientific experiment. Its existence is established, not by empirical means, but – it is alleged – by rational means.

As he originally introduces, and justifies, the concept of *substance*, Locke does so for a particular purpose. The problem he is addressing in book II, chap. XXIII is that of trying to explain how the several properties of an individual thing occur at one place and do not seem separable from one another. The properties of gold, "yellowness, great weight, ductility, fusibility, and solubility in *aqua regia*,[6] &c., [are] all united together in an unknown *substratum*" ([124], §37). This first role for the concept of *substance* has, in more modern times, come to be referred to as 'substance-as-ontological-glue'. Substance, in this

example, of gold as being a kind of substance or of water as being a kind of substance. His own examples are of horse and of stone. Roughly, this first, ordinary, sense might be thought something akin to a natural kind of thing.

6. A mixture of nitric and hydrochloric acids

first sense, is regarded as that 'stuff' which 'binds together' a thing's properties and gives it its characteristic unity.

Four chapters later (XXVII), however, Locke addresses a quite different set of problems, viz. those of individuation (although only very briefly) and identity-through-time (at rather greater length). Again he invokes the concept of *substance* in trying to solve the problems he is examining. But Locke seems – like so many other philosophers who have taken recourse to the concept of substance – to overlook the fact that he is assigning a role to substance additional to its earlier one. For there is no logical connection whatever between the concepts of *substance-as-ontological-glue* and of *substance-as-individuator*. That a thing's substance 'binds together its properties' does not imply that that substance also accounts for the thing's numerical distinction from other things. Indeed, even if one were disposed to be sympathetic to the notion of substance, one could still ask: "Is the ontological glue which holds together a thing's properties the same substance or distinct from that substance which accounts for that thing's numerical uniqueness?" To have solved the former problem is not only not to have solved the latter problem, it is not even to have addressed it.

We must, then, distinguish between substance-as-ontological-glue and substance-as-individuator. It is only the latter which is of present concern.

Subsequent philosophers, most especially George Berkeley, found Locke's concept of *substance* unacceptable. Contemporary philosophers (e.g. J.L. Mackie [128], chap. 3) are somewhat dubious about Berkeley's objections, suggesting that perhaps Berkeley and many other philosophers have misinterpreted Locke, that Locke was merely reporting commonly held views and indeed may have been skeptical about their cogency himself. These are questions of historical scholarship best left for another sort of book. Here we need merely ask whether a concept of *substratum* along the lines historically attributed to Locke will solve the problem of individuation. In a trivial sense it will. For so long as substance is described as being something "I know not what", then one can simply assign to it by fiat whatever is needed to solve the individuation problem. Substance, on this account, becomes the individuator by stipulative* definition. Two qualitatively identical things will be numerically distinct, on this account, because their respective substances differ. It is of the essential nature of each substance to be numerically distinct from every other substance.

Whether or not they are tilting against a notion of substance which was uniquely Locke's, or whether they are objecting to a notion which is merely representative of a certain type of approach to solving the problem of individuation, a great many philosophers will eschew the concept of substance-as-individuator and will try to solve the individuation problem without resorting to such a notion. The objections to substance-as-individuator are threefold.

First and foremost is the fact that substance seems to be nothing more than an invented notion imbued with just those features needed to solve the problem. From a purely explanatory point of view, the methodology underlying the introduction of the concept of *substance* is ineffective. It is as if one were to try to explain, for example, why opposite poles of magnets attract one another by saying that each pole has within it 'an affinity for its opposite'. A new description has been given of the phenomenon, but nothing more by way of explanation.

The second objection stems from the fact that inasmuch as substance-as-individuator is essentially propertyless, i.e. its assigned role is to lie 'behind' or 'beneath' the properties of a thing, then it is essentially undetectable by sense or by scientific instrument.[7] It is as unempirical a concept as one can possibly define.

And third, and perhaps most significantly, substance-as-individuator solves the metaphysical version of the individuation problem but not the epistemological version. We can and do individuate physical objects. And just as surely we do not perceive their substances. We must, then, be able to individuate physical objects *on some other basis*. If we can explain how we are able to do this, then perhaps we will have no need to posit substance-as-individuator. Whatever it is which allows *us* to individuate things perhaps might serve as well to account for the metaphysical numerical difference of things.

10.6   Negative theories: Qualities and relations as individuator

Leibniz's attempted solution was a classic negative theory: he tried to solve the problem of individuation solely by recourse to the properties of things. His solution, recall (p. 233), was that every thing whatsoever has a set of properties unique to it, i.e. there are, as a matter of

---

7. The model of substance as lying 'beneath' the qualities (the monadic properties) of a thing may have some minimal virtue in evoking certain suggestive images, but it is hard to understand how substance might be supposed to ground the relations in which particulars stand.

fact, no qualitatively identical things in the universe. Although it is logically possible that there should be two or more qualitatively identical things, Leibniz argued that their existence would be incompatible with God's perfection. God sees to it that there are no qualitatively identical things, that any two things, however much apparently alike, do in fact differ in some detail or other, i.e. that *each* thing consists of a *unique* bundle of properties.

Apart from its unacceptable appeal to highly dubious theological principles to solve a metaphysical problem, there are two other flaws in Leibniz's solution. The first is that his solution, even if it were to be accepted as the solution to the metaphysical version of the individuation problem, would not solve the epistemological version. For the undeniable fact is that we are often able to individuate items *at a glance* without taking cognizance of any particular differences in their qualities, let alone – as Leibniz would have it – differences, in some instances, in their microscopic features. The second flaw is that Leibniz conceived of 'qualitative identity' and 'qualitative difference' in terms of monadic *qualities* alone. In dismissing the reality of dyadic (two-place), triadic (three-place), and higher-place relations (see section 9.2.6), Leibniz cut himself off from a possible solution which has attracted a great many twentieth-century negative theorists, viz. that what individuates physical things is not their qualities, but their relations.

But before we turn to examine relations as individuator (sections 10.6.2 and 10.6.3), we must examine some present-day attempts to argue, once again, for monadic qualities as individuator.

10.6.1 Relational properties; haecceity

Various recent philosophers have – like Leibniz – tried to argue that the principle of the identity of indiscernibles is true. But they do so nowadays on the basis that the principle is logically necessary, eschewing any appeal whatever to theological principles about God's perfection, etc.

Thomas Foster, for example, argues that two or more objects *must* differ in some property or other ([73]). His arguments depend on his claim that so-called relational properties (see above p. 258), e.g. *is-older-than-the-Eiffel-Tower* or *is-to-the-left-of-a*, are bona fide monadic qualities applying to single individuals and are not merely disguised relations – e.g. *is-older-than* or *is-to-the-left-of* – holding between ordered pairs*[8] of individuals. (Remember, the terminology is a bit confusing. *Relational properties* are not relations: they are monadic qualities.) His argument may be summarized this way:

> Consider two numerically distinct objects, *a* and *b*, that are separate from one another. Then *a* has the relational property (monadic quality) of *being-separate-from-b*. But if the principle of the identity of indiscernibles were not true, i.e. if it were possible for two distinct things to have *all* properties in common, then *b*, too, would have to have the property of *being-separate-from-b*, i.e. of being separate from itself. But this latter condition is impossible; nothing can be separate from itself. Thus the principle of the identity of indiscernibles is necessarily true and any two numerically distinct things *must* differ in their (monadic) properties. That is, qualitative identity between numerically distinct things is a logical impossibility.

There are several objections to Foster's argument.[9] Chief among them is his treating *n*-place relations as monadic qualities rather than as relations.

Unlike Foster, some other philosophers have argued that it is logically possible for two or more numerically distinct things to share all their properties in common. Max Black, for example, has described a world consisting solely of two numerically distinct, but qualitatively identical, iron spheres ([31]). According to Black, such a world is logically possible; according to Foster, such a world is not.

"It all depends on what is meant by *sharing all properties in common*", we might say. If we allow that *is-separate-from-b* is a genuine quality (monadic property), then, of course, the two iron spheres must differ in their properties, since sphere *a* will have this property, and sphere *b* will not have it, indeed it is impossible that *b* should have this property. On the other hand, if we insist that *is-separate-from* is a *relation* holding between two things, then – clearly – *a* stands in this relation to *b*; and *b*, in its turn, stands in this very same relation to *a*. In an account, then, which resists treating *n*-place relations as relational properties (i.e. as monadic qualities), the two iron spheres – just as

---

8. For definition of "ordered pair" in Glossary, see under "set".

9. Foster, himself, reviews some which I do not discuss. See [73].

Black hypothesizes – can share all qualities in common and can also share all *n*-place relations in common.

The debate turns, then, on whether or not to allow so-called relational properties (e.g. *is-separate-from-b*) to be regarded as qualities (monadic properties). The major thrust of philosophical writing in the twentieth century has been explicitly away from such a notion. From Russell's initial forays into this area, early in the century, onward, the theory has been that such relational properties as *is-separate-from-b* or *is-west-of-Toronto* should be regarded not as qualities instanced in single particulars (e.g. *a* and Edmonton, respectively), but as disguised proxies for two-place relations instanced in ordered pairs of particulars, e.g. in the ordered pairs $\langle a, b \rangle$ and $\langle$Edmonton, Toronto$\rangle$. (We have earlier reviewed [section 9.2.6] the very considerable difficulties, insuperable perhaps, in trying to 'reduce' relations to monadic qualities.)

But even if there were not the pressures of logical considerations against Foster's relational properties, there would remain the objection that such 'peculiar' hybrid properties do not effectively solve the epistemological version of the individuation problem. If two numerically distinct physical objects, a_1 and a_2, differ only in instancing, respectively, such properties as *being-separate-from-a_2* and *being-separate-from-a_1*, it is very hard to see how we might take cognizance of such properties in discriminating between those objects. Suppose you were to take these objects, place them in an opaque box, shake them about in that box, and dump them out onto a tabletop. Clearly I would be able to see that there were two objects. But which is a_1 and which is a_2? Even though I would be able to see there are two objects, I could have no way of knowing whether the one on the left had the property of *being-separate-from-a_1* or had the property of *being-separate-from-a_2*. If the item on the left is a_1, then it has the property of *being-separate-from-a_2*; and if the item on the left is a_2, then it has the property of *being-separate-from-a_1*. But which of these relational properties an item has will depend on its being a_1 or a_2; i.e. its relational properties depend on, and do not determine, its numerical identity.[10]

---

10. This little thought experiment – where the objects might exchange places – must not be confused with the problem of *re*-identifying a_1 at a later time, T_2, with itself at an earlier time, T_1. (This latter problem will be dealt with in chapter 11.) The point here is to challenge the theory that we discriminate between items, e.g. a_1 and a_2, by recognizing that a_1 has the property of

Another approach, along lines similar to Foster's, is to restrict the class of relational properties to one, very special, class of individuation-conferring relational properties. In this latter account, individuation is secured for each individual, $a_1, a_2, ..., a_n$, by that thing's instancing a monadic quality utterly unique to it alone, viz. the property *being-identical-to-a_1*, *being-identical-to-a_2*, ..., or *being-identical-to-a_n*. Such properties are said to be *haecceitist*[11] *properties* or *individual essences* (see e.g. [2], [126], and [122]).

All the objections already leveled against relational properties apply to haecceitist properties inasmuch as haecceitist properties are relational ones. But there is an additional objection to haecceitist properties (or individual essences): they seem to defy the very concept of what a *property* is supposed to be. If we examine our working inventory of 'ordinary' properties and relations – *redness*, *triangularity*, *being to the left of*, etc. – we find that each and every one of these is *general* in the sense that there is a large (potentially infinite) class of things which are eligible candidates for having that property or relation.[12] But haecceitist properties are strikingly different. There is one and only one thing in the entire universe which could possibly instance the 'property' of *being-identical-to-a_1*, namely a_1 itself. Similarly, there is one and only one thing in the entire universe which could possibly instance the 'property' of *being-identical-to-a_2*, namely a_2 itself; etc. Haecceitist properties seem to lack the very feature – generality – which one might well believe is essential to the concept of *property* itself.

Moreover, proposing haecceitist properties as a solution to the individuation problem seems to present a circularity. We want to know

---

being-separate-from-a_2 and that a_2 has the property of *being-separate-from-a_1*. I contend that it is impossible to determine which item has which property prior to having discriminated between them. Put another way, I am arguing that to see that a_1 in fact has the property *being-separate-from-a_2*, one must already have seen that there are two objects. Relational properties do not account for numerical difference; it is, in fact, the other way around.

11. "Haecceity" (pronounced *hex'-ee-i-ty*) is the translation of the Latin "haecceitas" (literally "thisness"), a term coined by the medieval philosopher John Duns Scotus (c. 1266-1308).

12. This is true even of ordinal properties. Any number of mountains *could have been* the twelfth-highest mountain, although at most one actually is. (We will examine ordinal properties in the next subsection, 10.6.2.)

what it is about a_1 which accounts for its numerical difference from a_2. In the haecceitist account we are offered the 'property' *being-identical-to-a_1*. But what kind of property is this? On the face of it, it looks like an invented 'property' having just the requisite features needed for the individuation of a_1.

But even if one were to allow that haecceitist properties provided a solution to the metaphysical version of the problem of individuation, it is unclear that they solve the epistemological problem. Can one literally see such properties? If I am able to tell by looking at two highly similar physical objects (e.g. newly minted pennies pressed from the same dies) that they are numerically distinct, do I do this by recognizing that the first (on the left) has the property of *being-identical-to-a_1* and the second (on the right) has the property of *being-identical-to-a_2*? Again, as in the case of 'ordinary' relational properties, suppose someone switches a_1 and a_2 without my seeing her do so. I can still see that there are two objects although I might well now believe (mistakenly) that the one on the left has the property of *being-identical-to-a_1*. Even though I now have got their haecceitist properties wrong, I have still managed to individuate the objects. How could I have done this, if haecceitist properties account for individuation?

If there are haecceitist properties, then there must be as many of them as there are individuable things in the world. Moreover, to be able to individuate things never before encountered (e.g. the individual flakes of corn in my cereal bowl), I must be able to respond to the stimulus of their haecceitist properties, without of course ever having encountered such properties before in my life. I find such a theory implausible. From a psychological point of view, that is, of being able to learn one's way about in this world on the basis of past experience, one must assume an ability to generalize from acquaintance with a variety of properties: redness, triangularity, etc. But haecceitist properties (remember these are monadic qualities, not *n*-place relations) are never instanced in more than one thing. How could one ever, then, prepare oneself to respond correctly to a haecceitist property not yet encountered? How could I possibly have an ability *now* to individuate flakes of corn tomorrow, if individuation comes down to recognizing the haecceitist property (individual essence) of each individual flake? I cannot see how this would be possible.

My objections to haecceitist properties are not conclusive. To me, proposing that a_1's having the property of *being-identical-to-a_1* is what accounts for the numerical difference of a_1 and a_2 strikes me as not particularly attractive as a solution. It 'feels' too much like simply having invented a variant description of the very thing to be explained and then offering that description as explanation. But can we do any better? We can find out only by trying.

10.6.2 Ordinal properties

The theory that ordinal properties individuate has the considerable attraction that it invokes no esoteric or 'peculiar' properties like relational or haecceitist ones. Ordinal properties are gratifyingly ordinary and familiar. Examples include 'is the tallest man' and 'is the fourth largest freshwater lake' (Quinton's examples, [165], 15) and 'is the first dog to be born at sea' (Strawson's example, [200], 26). Ordinal properties assign their bearers to a unique position in an ordering (first, fourth, etc.). Although ordinal properties – like all non-haecceitist properties – are general in that there is a potential infinity of things which are candidates for instancing the property, they differ from other properties in that no more than one thing in actual fact does instance the property. For example, vast numbers of things are red, and a still larger number are candidates for being red. But of these many things – the red things and the possibly red things – no more than one can be *the reddest thing*; no more than one can be *the fifth reddest thing*; etc. In this latter regard, ordinal properties would seem to offer especial promise of solving the problem of individuation: perhaps each and every thing instances a unique ordinal property, i.e. has an ordinal property which is proprietary to it and it alone.

Ordinal properties are not simple qualities; they are, in effect, 'collapsed' relations. When they are 'spelled out' using the resources of modern logic, they can be seen to invoke relations such as *is taller than* or *is born prior to*. For example, the sentence "Rob Roy was the first dog to be born at sea" can be reconstructed this way: "Rob Roy was a dog; Rob Roy was born at sea; all dogs, other than Rob Roy, that were born at sea were born *later than* Rob Roy." Similar paraphrases, or reconstructions, in terms of relations can readily be given for "second", "third", etc.[13]

---

13. Although ordinal properties are 'collapsed' relations, they are not relational properties. The difference is that relational properties, such as *is west of Toronto*, refer to specific individuals (e.g. Toronto). Ordinal properties do not. In the reconstruction just given of "Rob Roy was the first dog born at sea" there is no reference to any individual other than Rob Roy.

As we pass from "first" to "second", and from "second" to "third", etc.,

As promising as ordinal properties may initially appear as offering a solution to the problem of individuation, it turns out that, in the end, they do not. There are two problems.

The first problem is already familiar. Just as with the theory that numerical difference is to be accounted for by difference in qualities (monadic properties), the theory that numerical difference is to be accounted for by difference in ordinal properties suffers at the hands of the requirement that it solve the epistemological problem of individuation. For we regularly individuate things without, for the most part, being in the slightest aware of their ordinal properties. You can glance at two pencils, fresh out of the box, lying on your desk and tell that there are two of them without knowing, or indeed having any way of finding out, which is the older, the slightly longer, the heavier, etc.

The second problem, too, recalls a difficulty we have already seen. Except for the possible exception of haecceitist properties, there is no convincing logical principle requiring that any two things must differ in one or more qualities. Similarly, there is no logical principle requiring that any two things must differ in one or more ordinal properties. Of course no two things can be 'the tallest man' and no two things can be 'the first dog born at sea'. But there is nothing to prevent there being two or more men, of identical height, being taller than all other men, or there being two or more dogs all being born simultaneously at sea and prior to the birth of all other dogs born at sea. In short, there is no logical guarantee that numerically distinct objects *must* differ, or any factual guarantee that numerically distinct objects *do* differ, in at least one ordinal property, from one another.[14] Even if it is not in fact

---

the complexity of the reconstruction grows exponentially. The reconstruction of "Riff Raff was the second dog born at sea" is: "There was some x such that x was a dog and x was born at sea and x is other than Riff Raff; Riff Raff was a dog, and Riff Raff was born at sea, and Riff Raff was born *later than x*; and for any y, if y is a dog and y is born at sea, and if y is other than x and y is other than Riff Raff, then y is born *later than* Riff Raff."

14. Quinton thinks that there is another problem as well, viz. "we can ... only ascribe ordinal properties to things in theory if they are finite in number" ([165], 16). This is a mistake. Consider an infinite class of objects whose lengths are as follows: 1/2, 2/3, 3/4, 4/5, 5/6, etc. Each item in this class has a unique ordinal position, 1st, 2nd, 3rd, etc. While it is true that there is nothing which is 'the longest member in the class' (i.e. is the last item of the ordering), it is still nonetheless true that every one of the infinite number of items in the class has a unique ordinal property. (To be sure, there are some infinite classes which are 'open at both ends', e.g. { ... 1/5, 1/4, 1/3, 1/2, 2/3,

actual, we can at the very least imagine a possible world (again, for example, Max Black's possible world of two qualitatively identical iron spheres [p. 286]) where every object has exactly the same qualities as every other and no object has an ordinal property unique to it alone. Yet, by hypothesis, in such a world there are two or more objects. Their numerical difference is yet to be explained.[15]

10.6.3 *Spatial and temporal relations*

Although the theory that physical things are individuated by ordinal properties cannot be sustained, our examination of that theory has helped to reveal just what it is that we seek: some specifiable and recognizable property, or bundle of properties, which each thing instances and which – by its very nature – cannot be instanced by more than one thing. *Is* there any specifiable bundle of properties which has this feature?

Many negative theorists argue that a physical thing's position in space and time precisely has this sought-for feature, and, thus, position in space and time is what finally individuates physical things. It is important to understand that it is *conjoint* position in space and in time which is alleged to be the individuator. Position in space alone is insufficient; so too is position in time. For the property of being at

---

3/4, 4/5 ...} which may be ordered by the relation "is larger than", but whose members cannot be assigned ordinal properties. We often describe such classes just in terms of their lacking certain *ordinal* characteristics, saying of them that "they lack a *first* member and lack a *last* member". Thus, it is not the infinitude per se of a class which precludes its members instancing ordinal properties, but its being open-ended at both ends.) This correction of Quinton's error is irrelevant to the two objections made in the text above.

15. There is a third problem as well, perhaps in the end even more serious than the two just mentioned. The essential occurrence of the relation *other than* in every reduction of an ordinal property to 'standard' (non-numerical) relations bears comment. (See the example, p. 290, of the reconstruction of "Rob Roy was the first dog to be born at sea".) What does "other than" mean? The most natural way to interpret this relation is that it is equivalent to "not identical to" or "is numerically distinct from". In that case, then even to invoke an ordinal property is to have presupposed a solution to the individuation problem. That is, ordinality, it would appear, is logically dependent on individuation; we will not be able in a noncircular manner to explicate numerical difference in terms of ordinality.

some specific place, e.g. being at P_1, is a property which any number, indeed a potentially infinite number, of physical things might instance (by being at that place at different times). Over the last ten years or so, there will have been hundreds of different books, one after the other, on my desk (i.e. at P_1). The property of *being at* P_1 is one which many, many physical things have (at one time or another) instanced. Similarly, the property of *being (or existing) at* T_1 is one which many things all instance.[16] At this very moment (i.e. at T_1), vast numbers of physical objects – some close at hand, others at appreciable distances – instance the property of *being at* T_1.

But combine the two properties – *being at a place* and *being at a time* – and the number of bearers collapses. Pick any specific place at any specific time: there is at that place either no things or exactly one; there cannot be two or more things there. Quinton waxes metaphorical on this point, soaring to heights of inspired prose:

> There is no limit to the number of things which can be present at a particular map-reference [position in space], provided they occur there at different times. Equally there is no limit to the number of things that can be in existence at a particular moment of time, provided that they are to be found at different places. But this boundless promiscuity of positions in space and time considered separately is replaced by the most rigorous propriety when they are conjoined. A complete, that is to say spatial *and* temporal, position is either monogamous or virginal, ontologically [metaphysically] speaking. ([165], 17)

Positional properties – i.e. *being at some specific place at some specific time* – have one marked advantage over ordinal properties for purposes of individuation. While there is no guarantee that any given physical object instances any ordinal property whatever (recall the example in the preceding section of the two equally-old dogs born at sea), every physical object, it would seem, *does* occur at a unique position in space and time. While most conjoint positions in space and

---

16. Special relativity theory tells us, contrary to our naive intuitions about physics, that the relation *is simultaneous with* must be treated with extreme care. Two events at different places may turn out to be simultaneous with one another viewed from one vantage point (what physicists call a "reference frame") and not simultaneous when viewed from another.

time are empty (there is – colloquially speaking – more empty space in the universe than occupied space), it is still nonetheless true that, 'viewed the other way round', each and every physical object in the universe occupies a position in space and time unique to it alone.

Position in space and time would seem to solve not only the metaphysical version of the individuation problem but the epistemological version as well. *We* individuate objects by attending to their positions in space and time. There are two black pens currently on my desk. For all intents and purposes they share all their monadic qualities in common. If you were to swap them, i.e. exchange their positions, without telling me or showing me, I would not detect that you had done so. And yet I have no difficulty at all in seeing that there are two of them. How *do* I tell them apart? How do I count them? Not by detecting some subtle differences in their qualities. My sight reveals nothing whatever different in their qualities. Nor do I discern their numerical distinctness by taking cognizance of their 'substances'. In this latter regard, I would not know even how to undertake such a task. Rather, I detect their numerical difference at a glance, simply by seeing that they are, at one particular time, each in a place different from that of the other.

Thus, it would appear that we have finally solved both the metaphysical and the epistemological versions of the problem of the individuation of physical objects. Position in space and time is what individuates. There apparently is no need to postulate a mysterious 'substratum' as individuator.

But philosophers are seldom inclined to 'leave well enough alone'. In philosophy, just as in science, there is no natural stopping point. Having given one explanation or theory, there is then always the inclination and desire to delve deeper yet, to try to understand what might account for the truth of the latest theory. In biology, for example, Gregor Mendel (1822-84) – knowing nothing of the 'mechanisms' of heredity – was able to advance a theory which correctly predicted the statistical transference of features from parent to offspring. But what lay behind these statistical laws? It was to be many years before chromosomes were to be discovered in the nuclei of cells, and further decades still before DNA was to be discovered in the chromosomes.

At one level of analysis, the puzzle of individuation is solved: it is position in space and time which individuates. But this seeming solution to the problem of individuation is not quite the end of the matter. For upon probing, this latest answer, in its turn, is found to harbor some further puzzles themselves in need of examination. Just why is it – we might be inclined to wonder – that position in space and time is, as Quinton rakishly puts it, virginal or monogamous? Why is it that no two physical things are in the same place at the same time?

And there is a second problem as well. If, as was argued in chapter 8, we want to posit only a relative space and not an absolute space, then the position of any physical object is not a monadic quality, but a two- or many-place relation. But if position in space (and equally position in time) is a relation, it would seem to be a relation between *numerically distinct* objects. If so, that would, in turn, suggest that to individuate any one object we would antecedently have had to individuate another. The account of individuation in terms of spatial and temporal position would appear to be in imminent danger of becoming circular or of presupposing an infinite regress.

We turn to these latter two problems in the next two subsections.

10.6.4 Impenetrability

The principle that no two physical things can be at the same place at the same time is often referred to as 'the principle of the impenetrability of material objects'. This principle merits careful examination.

. There are two perfectly straightforward ways in which two numerically distinct things *can be* in the same place at the same time.

First, any physical object is at any one time at all the places where any of its parts are. My bedside radio contains, as one of its several parts, a loudspeaker. That loudspeaker is located at some specific place, P_1. In response to the question "What is located at P_1?" it is perfectly proper to reply in either of two ways: (1) "There is a loudspeaker there"; and (2) "There is a radio there". If we designate a *small* place, small in the sense that it is contained within a part of a larger thing, then there will be two things at one place: the part of the thing, and the thing of which it is a part. Remember (section 8.8), a thing does not have to have all of its spatial parts present at a place for it to be at that place. The Mississippi River exists at Natchez although other spatial parts are hundreds of kilometers distant.

Second, if we choose a place which is *large* enough, then it can easily contain two or more objects. My office at the university is a place. It contains not just two, but several objects: a typewriter, two filing cabinets, a desk, a telephone, etc. In this latter example, several objects all occupy the same place at the same time.

Clearly, in their attempt to solve the problem of individuation, when negative theorists invoke the principle of the impenetrability of material objects, they mean to exclude such cases. It is, however, a tricky business to state the intuitive principle rigorously so that it does not immediately fall victim to counterexamples. It is easy to see why. As a first attempt, one might try to state the principle more precisely by formulating it this way: "A place which contains the part of some object O_1 cannot simultaneously contain a part of some other object O_2." But this first try is immediately refuted by the fact that you can place your telephone in the drawer of your desk. There would then be in one place two different things: your desk and your telephone. This latest difficulty arises from the fact that many material objects contain vacuities within their boundaries (e.g. an empty drawer in your desk), and it is perfectly feasible to place other objects within these vacuities.

Persons who have promoted the principle doubtless have had in mind a certain limited number of examples. These examples likely include such commonplace facts as these: Pots do not sink into stove-tops; the metal surface of the burner 'excludes' the pot. One's fingers do not penetrate the keys of a typewriter; although they may depress those keys, human fingers do not enter into the 'internal space', i.e. the interior, of the keytops. One might drive a nail into a wooden beam. But the steel of the nail does not merge into, i.e. form a composite with, the wood fibers; instead the nail 'pushes aside' the wood of the beam and replaces the contents of that region of space, which had been of wood, with steel.

The problem with trying to capture these latter examples in a defensible principle is that not all material things behave in this way. Stovetops and typewriter keys may, but galaxies do not. Although a galaxy may contain thousands of millions of stars, the distances between individual stars are so enormous that it is possible for one galaxy to pass through another and for both to emerge from the collision, not unscathed, but at least identifiable as galaxies ([192], 345-7). But are galaxies material objects? They certainly satisfy most, if not all, of the conditions we pre-analytically ascribe to material objects: their parts are material; they have a certain physical 'cohesiveness' in that they move about in space preserving their general size and shape; they are held together by physical forces; etc. And yet galaxies *are* able to pass through one another.

Someone might protest: "the difference is that galaxies are mostly empty space; bona fide (i.e. 'real') physical objects are far more dense (compact); there are no great 'open spaces', as it were, in stovetops, our fingers, or steel nails." But the trouble with this line of rebuttal is that it is false. The surprising truth is that, viewed at the atomic level, our flesh, our stovetops, our steel nails *are* mostly empty space. Compared to the pressures prevailing in the interior of white dwarfs (collapsed stars), those affecting physical objects in or near the vicinity of the Earth's surface are relatively slight. The material of white dwarfs is the same basic sort of stuff of which stovetops and fingers are composed, viz. electrons, protons, neutrons, etc. But because of the difference in pressure, the density of the interiors of white dwarfs[17] is a millionfold that of water. And thus, while the average density of the physical objects which are common in our own local environment is, in fact, vastly greater than the average density of a galaxy, it remains very much less than the average density of certain stellar interiors. In short, the fact that stovetops 'exclude' the pots placed upon them is a more-or-less 'local' feature of some familiar, ordinary, room-temperature objects. It is not a feature which holds of all material objects, e.g. it does not hold of galaxies.

Over the years, writers have expressed a great many differing attitudes about the logical (i.e. modal) and the epistemological status of 'the' principle of impenetrability. Newton (1687) had thought that we learn the principle by experience: "That all bodies are impenetrable, we gather not from reason, but from sensation. The bodies which we handle we find impenetrable, and thence conclude impenetrability to be a universal property of all bodies whatsoever" ([144], vol. II, 399). Locke (1690) concurred, and expanded Newton's claim, arguing that not only is the idea that all objects are impenetrable learned from experience but, further, the very concept of *impenetrability* itself 'arises' from experience.

> The idea of *solidity* we receive by our touch; and it arises from the resistance which we find in body to the entrance of any other body into the place it possesses, till it has left it. There is no *idea* which we receive more constantly from sensation than *solidity*. Whether we move or rest, in what posture soever we are, we always feel something under us that supports us[18] and hinders our further sinking downwards; and the bodies which

---

17. 10^6 g/cm^3 ([192], 126)

18. This claim – that we always feel something under us that supports us – is overstated. Most of the time we are not consciously aware of the support of

we daily handle make us perceive that, whilst they remain between them, they do, by an insurmountable force, hinder the approach of the parts of our hands that press them. ... If anyone think it better to call it [i.e. solidity] *impenetrability*, he has my consent. ... And though our senses take no notice of it, but in masses of matter, of a bulk sufficient to cause a sensation in us: yet the mind, having once got this *idea* from such grosser sensible bodies, traces it further and considers it, as well as figure, in the minutest particle of matter that can exist, and finds it inseparably inherent in body, wherever or however modified. ([124], book II, chap. IV, §1)

These passages both argue that the principle of impenetrability is learned by experience (i.e. a posteriori) and strongly suggest, but do not state explicitly, that their authors regard the principle as a scientific truth and not as a necessary (or logical) truth.

Certain contemporary philosophers take a quite different point of view. Quinton, for one, takes the principle to be a necessary truth. (Here he is using the expression "metaphysical truth" much as I use the expression "necessary truth"*.)

If we are confronted by two distinct things between which we can find no strictly qualitative difference of length or weight or colour we can always distinguish them by reference to their respective positions. What proves this is the familiar but highly important metaphysical truth that no two things can be at the same place at the same time. ... Individuals [i.e. material objects] are, to use an old word, *impenetrable*, which does not mean that they are never soft or porous. ([165], 17)

(In his reference to "soft or porous", Quinton is likely being motivated by a similar sort of distinction discussed by Descartes ([55], vol. II, 225-6).)

Quinton offers no argument for his claim that the principle of the impenetrability of material objects is true. He is content to declare it a

———————

the floor on which we are standing or of the chair on which we are seated. Locke has here confused what we are *capable* of feeling, whenever we like, with what we *do* feel at any time.

'familiar' and 'highly important' necessary truth and to proceed from there.[19] But just as sure as Quinton is of the necessary truth of the principle, other twentieth-century philosophers have been just as sure of its contingency. Friedrich Waismann (1897-1959) offers the following possible-worlds tale:

> Suppose there were two chairs, *A* and *B*, with exactly the same characteristics. The fact that they are in principle distinguishable depends on the property of impenetrability. Suppose now that we lived in a world in which experiences of the following sort were everyday occurrences. When the two chairs are put so that they touch, and pressed together, they gradually merge into one chair; then turn back into two [qualitatively] identical chairs. ([209], 201)

For Waismann, the principle of impenetrability is no necessary truth. He has no difficulty whatever in imagining a possible world in which that principle is false. In his hands the principle is nothing more than a physical law of this particular world.

But can Waismann's possible-worlds tale really be sustained? It is, we note, exceedingly brief. If we were to try to fill in details, what might we find? In particular, although Waismann talks, ostensibly, about 'chairs', can we really regard 'chairs' which merge into one another as 'real' physical objects, or is Waismann playing fast and loose with the concept of *physical object*? Can things behave like Waismann's chairs, i.e. act in violation of the principle of impenetrability, and still be regarded as physical objects?

I think that Waismann was exactly right. But I also think that his possible-worlds tale needs some further elaboration to make it a plausible counterexample to the alleged logical necessity of the principle at stake.

The legions of philosophers who have supposed that impenetrabil-

---

19. He does, however, slightly qualify his claim, allowing for one exception, viz. the first of those we discussed a moment ago: "The only apparent exception to this rule is not an exception in principle. A whole is at every place and time that its parts are. Wholes and parts share positions. But they share only some of their positions. If A has B as a part they are not indistinguishable in position. For although all of B's positions are also A's, not all of A's positions are B's as well" ([165], 17).

ity does, in some way, figure in our concept of what it is for something to be a material object were on the right track. Where many of
them were mistaken, however, was in supposing that *every* material
object must *at all times* be impenetrable. In contrast, I would argue
that a 'thing' can earn the status of material objecthood by instancing
the property of impenetrability from time to time and from circumstance to circumstance.

> Imagine a possible world where select objects are found to be
> able to merge into one another. Two chairs which share all their
> qualities (monadic relations) in common, for example, set upon
> a 'collision' course are found not to rebound from one another,
> but to merge into one place and subsequently to separate. The
> spectacle admittedly would be highly surprising to a native of
> this universe. Any of us, on the first occasion of seeing such an
> event, would probably be inclined to reckon it a hologram or a
> conjuring trick. But as we become more familiar with the phys-
> ics of that world, we recognize that this is no hologram, no con-
> juring trick. These chairs which are able to merge into one
> another are genuine physical objects. Even though they are
> *inter*penetrable with one another, they are not interpenetrable
> with other things. They are tangible, publicly observable, and as
> permanent as any other fixtures in the environment, e.g. tables,
> trees, and lampposts. We can, if we like, sit on these chairs,
> move them about, paint them, weigh them, burn them, etc. In
> short, they satisfy a great many other properties typical of
> material objects. The only caution is that we would have to
> keep these chairs from touching one another, for when they do,
> they temporally 'collapse into one another'.

We must not generalize too extensively on this latter possible-
worlds tale and posit a world in which every material object was interpenetrable with every other, for then we would lose entirely our grasp
of what it is for something to be a material object. A chair which was
interpenetrable with everything else could not be sat upon, or painted,
or cut into pieces, etc. It would not be a *physical* object at all. While
we can allow interpenetrability for some physical objects under some
circumstances, we cannot allow it for all under any circumstances.

In our being able to tell this latter possible-worlds tale, the principle
of impenetrability is revealed to be no necessary truth at all, but only a
contingency, i.e. it is a proposition which is true in some possible

worlds, but not in all. This does not mean that the principle cannot be invoked in an attempt to solve the problem of individuation. What it does mean, however, is that the *justification* for using that principle must rest in experience, not in a priori reason. If typical physical objects in this world are individuable because they are impenetrable to one another, then that is a physical law of this particular world, it is no necessary truth.

What is emerging in our researches is the realization that our ability to individuate physical things, indeed numerical difference itself in physical things, is attributable to certain contingent facts about this particular world. We have found a solution to the individuation problem, but it is by no means one suited for any possible world whatever. Had this world been much different from the way it is, our ordinary means of individuating, indeed our very concept of individuation, would have to be different.

Just for a moment, let us explore how our techniques of individuating physical objects would have to differ in yet another world, where objects are more penetrable than they are in this world. We will pick up, and continue, our last possible-worlds tale.

> Suppose we are able to construct a machine which turns out objects which look like single chairs. But we discover that these are actually Waismannesque chairs: whenever these (seemingly single) chairs are left in bright hot sunlight for an hour, they suddenly separate into two qualitatively identical chairs (i.e. into two chairs sharing all qualities in common). The original chair undergoes something like biological mitosis (cell division) except that the resulting products each have the same mass as the original. (In the world being described, mass is an intensive property [see section 9.2.4], not an extensive property.) The original chair, we are happy to report, cannot separate when someone is sitting on it because that person's body would shield the chair from the sunlight. Chairs, as they come off the assembly line, are called "coupletons"; after they undergo splitting, they are called "singletons". Singletons cannot be further 'split'.
>
> In merely *looking* at a chair, no one is able to tell whether it is a coupleton or a singleton. To ascertain whether it is a coupleton or a singleton, one must either know that it is fresh off the assembly line or subject it to test, by placing it in bright hot sunlight, to observe what becomes of it.

In such a world, the problem of individuation cannot be treat-ed more-or-less independently, as it is in *this* world, from the problem of identity-through-time. How many chairs are in a room at any one time depends not only on how many seem-ingly distinct chairs there are but essentially on how many of those apparently single chairs are in fact coupletons and how many are in fact singletons. But to answer that question depends on determining facts about the chairs' history or future. In that world, no philosopher has ever suggested that the problem of individuation could be handled separately, indeed antecedently to, the problem of identity-through-time. Where *we* see two problems, they see only one.[20]

In searching for a solution to the problem of individuation, we dis-cover, once again, how our concepts are tailored to the contingencies of the world in which we find ourselves. There is no guarantee that the physical objects of a world, more particularly the ready-at-hand most familiar objects of our experience, would exhibit the degree of impen-etrability that we find in this world. We can describe other possible worlds in which objects are more penetrable, and still other worlds in which objects are less (e.g. in which galaxies are torn apart when they collide). We simply find ourselves ensconced in a world where familiar physical objects are so constituted that the principle of impen-etrability can be used fairly successfully in our creating a workable concept of individuation. But the principle is no necessary truth, and it probably cannot be stated very precisely. It is a *vague* principle, adopted and adapted for our everyday needs.

---

20. One can, in fact, describe a series of possible worlds where solutions to the problem of individuation become progressively more remote from the solution in this world. We can, for example, describe possible worlds in which some objects undergo mitosis but without there being anything in their history or among their manifest properties (see section 9.2.2) to account for which will and which will not. In this latter world, whether a chair is a coupleton or a singleton is a matter solely of a disposition. But some chairs will have been burned without their ever having been exposed to sunlight. Given the occurrence of such circumstances, where some physical objects are never subjected to test, individuation could be explicated only counterfac-tually, i.e. it will have to contain a component of this sort: "x is a coupleton if it were to be subjected to test and were to undergo mitosis."

10.6.5 Does individuation presuppose absolute space?

Far more troubling than the vagueness and the contingency of the principle of the impenetrability of material objects is the precise role played by spatial and temporal relations in the negative theorist's solution of the problem of individuation.

If one adopts a theory of relational space and relational time, then a physical object's having a determinate spatial and temporal position involves its standing in spatial and temporal relations to *other* things in the universe. We locate physical objects in space by specifying their whereabouts *in spatial relation to* other things. My scissors are on the desk blotter which, in turn, is on my desk. The city of Burnaby is immediately east of Vancouver. And we locate physical objects in time by specifying their whereabouts *in temporal relation to* other things. The library at Simon Fraser University was built before the Administration Building, and it, in turn, was built before the engineering laboratories. Even when we set up coordinate systems, by which we might say that something is located at 116°32′W and 42°N, or that something exists on 18 June 1823, we are tacitly depending on those coordinate systems having been fixed by reference to specific places (Greenwich and the two poles) and to the conventionally assigned date of the birth of Jesus.

But if fixing the position of some physical object in space and time involves a reference to *other* physical things, then the negative theorist's proposed solution to the problem of individuation would seem to involve either an infinite regress or circularity. To be able to individuate one thing, it would seem that we would have had to have individuated another.

One might think that this current difficulty constitutes good reason for positing an absolute space and an absolute time. But, on reflection, we can see that an absolute space and an absolute time will not solve the problem either. The trouble with an absolute space and an absolute time is that they are each *amorphous*, i.e. each point of space is indistinguishable *to us* from any other point of space, each point of time is indistinguishable *to us* from any other point of time. Thus, even if one were to adopt a theory of absolute space and time, one would still have to take recourse to relations to determine an object's position. Newton, who did posit an absolute space and time, saw this difficulty clearly: "... because the parts of space cannot be seen, or distinguished from one another by our senses, therefore in their stead we use sensible measures of them. For from the positions and distances of things from any body considered as immovable [i.e. taken as the fixed point of our coordinate system], we define all places; and then with respect to such places, we estimate [judge] all motions, considering bodies as transferred from some of those places into others. And so, instead of absolute places and motions, we use relative ones ..." ([144], vol. I, 8). No theory of absolute space and time can solve the epistemological version of the individuation problem, but a theory of relative space and time seems to solve the epistemological version of the individuation problem at the unacceptable cost of an infinite regress or of circularity. Is there any way out of this bind?

Quinton thinks there is. He argues that, for each observer, there is *one* position which is, in a sense, epistemologically 'privileged' or 'primary', viz. that person's 'here-and-now': "The position where I am at the present moment is, then, the absolute point of origin of all my positional characterisations of things. It is the one position I do not have to pick out by its relation to something else and by their relation to which in the end everything else is individuated" ([165], 20). Even if you were to wake out of a deep coma, not knowing what year it was, or where on the face of the Earth you were, you would presumably still be able to individuate local objects, e.g. the furniture of your room, by reference to your own 'there-and-then'.

And yet, I think that in two different ways Quinton's solution, invoking each individual observer's own 'here-and-now', is unsatisfactory.

What Quinton has done is to underscore the fact that of all the possible points which one might choose as one's starting point, or so-called fixed point, on which to construct a phenomenological (perceptual) coordinate system, there is one point which is not arbitrary but which virtually forces itself upon us, viz. the point from which we 'view the world'. For visual space, this 'point' is our eyes. We 'look out on' the world from sockets on the front of our heads. But while this is true, it – in its own way – raises problems as serious as those it was meant to solve.

Quinton has 'reduced' the general epistemological version of the problem of individuation to that of individuating other things with respect to one's own body. But this is no ultimate solution. It is tantamount to my saying, "I can solve the individuation problem if you will allow me to begin with individuating some one thing, and then I can individuate others with respect to it." The question remains: "How are you to get the process started?" It does not matter whether the fixed point is one's own body, the Tower of Pisa, or lines of longitude and latitude. The problem remains basically the same: how can any of this be done without an infinite regress or circularity?

At some point in each of our own personal histories, we had to individuate our own body. None of us is born into this world knowing that he/she has a unique body. The connection between our bodies and our perceptions and kinesthetic sensations is something we had to *learn*, by trial and error, during the first few years of our lives. We had to *learn* the difference between consciousness and externality; we had to *learn* where our bodies 'leave off' and other things begin. Having done that, we were then in a position to rely on the correlation between certain kinds of sensory data and the external objects which cause that data as our guide in individuating, at a glance, external physical things. But that we are *now*, as adults, able to do this must not conceal from us the fact that we had to spend a considerable time sorting this all out as youngsters. What we do now habitually, we once did only by trial and error. We may now, as adults, use our bodies, and their unique positions in space and time, as the locus of our individual perceptual coordinate schemes, but this is not innate, it is learned. And what still needs explaining is what we must suppose true of the world so as to warrant our creating such a conceptual scheme.

You perhaps may detect that I am pushing the epistemological version of the individuation problem back toward the metaphysical version. That we are *able* to discriminate physical objects needs explaining. But it needs explaining, I would suggest, in a way which depends not only on facts about us, but equally on facts about physical objects which account for their being individuable *logically prior* to our discriminating between them. And this brings me to the major criticism I have of Quinton's solution of the epistemological version of the problem of individuation: it abandons the metaphysical problem.

No ultimately satisfactory solution of the problem of individuation can make individuation depend solely on abilities of human beings and overlook whatever it is about physical objects themselves which accounts for their numerical difference. If *we*, human beings, are able to discriminate among physical objects, they must have been *discriminable* before we exercise our abilities. We want an account of individuation which explains the numerical distinctness of physical objects not only in worlds in which there are conscious perceivers but in worlds devoid of consciousness altogether. Numerical distinctness of physical objects is not just a feature of worlds in which there are conscious creatures, but of lifeless worlds as well.

In short, Quinton's account of how *we* individuate objects leaves unexplained what it is about objects themselves which permits us to discriminate among them.

The dilemma is this. The metaphysical version of the individuation problem would seem to require positing an absolute space, a space 'in' which each and every physical thing would have a unique position distinct from that of every other thing and independent of the knowledge or perceptual abilities of any conscious creature. But an absolute space cannot solve the epistemological version of the individuation problem. We human beings cannot discern any difference between the points of an absolute space. We would seem, then, to have to take recourse to a relative space. But a relative space just *is* the set of spatial relations instanced by numerically distinct objects. That is, a relative space is logically dependent on our discriminating physical objects: the logical and psychological order is that objects are primary, and that space is derivative, i.e. space is 'constructed out of' the relations obtaining among physical objects which are antecedently individuated.

There are only two ways out of this dilemma. The first is the way adopted by Newton. He embraced *both* theories of space (see above, pp. 303-4). He posited an absolute space in which God, but none of us, would be able to know the absolute position of each thing. And he posited a relative space which we human beings use to individuate and to gauge the motion of physical objects.

Such a 'Newtonian' solution is to be resisted. In positing an absolute space, we invite the inevitable incoherence which we explored at some length in Buber's befuddlement. Having struggled, both in physics and in philosophy, for three hundred years to shed the incoherent theory of an absolute space, we should hardly want to reintroduce that theory in a desperate attempt to solve the metaphysical version of the individuation problem. And in positing a theory of relational space to solve the epistemological problem, we precipitate a vitiating circularity. In short, were we to adopt both the absolute and the relative theories of space, the one as a supposed solution to the metaphysical problem and the other as a supposed solution to the epistemological problem, we would create a composite theory incorporating the worst features of *both* of the originals. Moreover, the resulting theory would have more than just internal defects. Any such blended solution offends aesthetic sensibilities. It is untidy and profligate. It

violates the methodological principle[21] not to multiply entities beyond
need. It would grate against our desire for comprehensiveness in our
theories. It would be unacceptably piecemeal.

I think there is another way, one which solves both the metaphysical and the epistemological versions of the individuation problem and
which does not require the positing of an absolute space or saddle us
with the circularity of a relative space.

10.6.6 The solution: A more radical negative theory

The problem of the individuation of physical objects will forever
remain insolvable so long as negative theorists persist in trying to
explain numerical distinctness in term of space and of properties and
relations instanced at positions in space. This is the post-Leibnizian
picture with which negative theorists have been working for generations. But it is a mistake. To procced along these lines is to have
failed to appreciate the profound difference between a theory of relative space and a theory of absolute space. The typical negative approach to trying to solve the problem of individuation has been, in
effect, an unwitting illicit amalgam of the two incompatible theories.
These attempts have uncritically borrowed from the theory of absolute
space the notion that the points of space, or perhaps I should say the
places within a space, were distinct from one another independent of
the objects 'in' that space. But this hybrid theory cannot be made to
work. If one is going to adopt a theory of relative space one must be
prepared for a more wholesale conceptual reorientation.

In a theory of relative space, space is itself, both in a logical and in
a psychological sense, 'constructed out of' the spatial relations among
numerically distinct physical objects. Objects are not 'in' space – that
is the old, absolute theory. In the theory of relative space, what exists
are physical objects at varying distances from one another and moving
about with respect to one another; space is then 'constructed' out of
these objects. What is logically primitive, and the conceptual foundation upon which the rest of the theory is constructed, is the existence
of numerically distinct physical objects. It is little wonder, then, that it
becomes impossible to explain the numerical distinctness of physical
objects in terms of space: the conceptual order is being inverted. One
can never explicate the primitive concepts of a theory in terms of that

---

21. Known as 'Ockham's razor'

theory's derived concepts: the explication becomes circular. And this is precisely the situation we find in many theorists' attempts to solve the problem of individuation. Through a historical accident, our having earlier posited a theory of absolute space and having not completely thrown off its conceptual shackles, many theorists persist in approaching certain problems as if they were still working with the earlier theory. They try to explain individuation by invoking properties of space, failing to recognize that a theory of relative space *presupposes* the very existence of numerically distinct physical objects. An incisive discarding of the remnants of the theory of absolute space is what is needed.

We must give up trying to explicate numerical distinctness in terms of space. It is not space which is our 'starting point' and the numerical distinctness of physical objects which needs to be explicated. It is the concept of *physical object* which lies 'at the bottom', as it were, and it is space (relative space, that is) which is 'constructed' – both metaphysically and epistemologically – on that foundation. In a world where there are no physical objects, there is no physical space. To fail to understand that proposition, and thus to fail to understand that the concept of *physical object* is more primitive than that of *space*, is to turn the conceptual order on its head and to saddle oneself with necessarily insolvable problems.[22]

Edwin Allaire, a quarter of a century ago, argued similarly that no appeal to spatial relations could provide an ultimately satisfactory solution to the problem of individuation: "Relations – I'll stick with spatial ones – *presuppose* numerical difference; they do not account for it" ([7], 254). But Allaire was not content to make the numerical difference of physical objects an unanalyzable concept, as I have done. Instead, he posited what he and some others (e.g. Gustav Bergmann) called "bare particulars" to account for the numerical distinction: "Bare particulars are ... the entities *in* things accounting for the numerical difference *of* things" ([7], 253). While bare particulars may, at first, seem like nothing other than Locke's substratum given a new name, Allaire explicitly denied that they were, and argued that, unlike the problematic substratum, bare particulars are supposed

---

22. Although it is notoriously difficult to design experiments to reveal clearly the conceptual framework children devise, there does seem to be anecdotal evidence that children form the concept of *physical object* much before, indeed perhaps years earlier than, an abstract concept of *physical space*.

to be accessible to experience. In a paper written two years earlier ([6]), Allaire had argued that we are 'acquainted' with bare particulars, meaning by "acquainted" what Russell had meant when he introduced a technical definition for that term in 1912: "We shall say that we have *acquaintance* with anything of which we are directly aware, without the intermediary of any process of inference of any knowledge of truths" ([178], 46).

It is clear Allaire and I agree that we are directly acquainted with the numerical difference of physical objects. We human beings can literally *see* that there are numerically distinct objects.[23] But I decline to take Allaire's last step: positing 'bare particulars' to account for that numerical difference. I do not believe that there is any 'entity' (Allaire's own term) under or behind or accompanying or 'in' the physical object itself which accounts for that physical object's numerical difference from other physical objects. Still less do I believe that we are acquainted with bare particulars or that they are 'presented' to us like the properties of things, while not, of course, being properties themselves (see [7], 256). Such a theory of perception is empirically untestable and philosophically suspect. A bare particular, like a substratum, is nothing but an *invented* entity, posited by fiat as a solution to the problem. But just as in the case of substance, the posit amounts to idle wheel-spinning. Allaire was correct in arguing that spatial relations presuppose numerical difference of objects. But I resist, as creating a mere illusion of further analyzing the concept of numerical difference, his positing of bare particulars. At some point, analysis must end. I suggest that Allaire has gone one step, an unnecessary step, beyond that stopping point.

How, in the end, do we solve the problem of individuation? We solve the problem by recognizing that the concept of *physical object* is a primitive notion in our conceptual scheme and that the numerical distinctness of physical objects cannot be explicated in terms of anything (e.g. relative space) which is derivative in that scheme. This solution, which argues that the original question was in some sense improper, is bound to dissatisfy some readers. (Recall our discussion of the 'Barber paradox', p. 152 above.) On the face of it, the question

---

23. I am not making the stronger claim, however, that we literally see *how many* physical objects are within our field of view. There may be ten objects in my field of view, and I may be aware of all of them without being aware that there are ten.

"What accounts for the numerical distinctness of physical objects?" looks as if it ought to have a straightforward answer. Grammatically it is like the question "What accounts for the green color of grass?" But, upon examination of the problem, it can be seen that the concept of *physical object* plays a very special role in our conceptual scheme, one so basic that it does not allow for further analysis, at least not in terms of the categories *space* or *position in space* which require, themselves, to be explicated in terms of it.

In short, what it all comes down to is a radical, and I think necessary, conceptual about-face. It is not *space* which is the primitive concept in terms of which *physical object* is to be explicated; it is the concept of *physical object* which is primitive and in terms of which *space* is to be explicated. In the fifteenth edition (1952) of *Relativity*, Einstein said this in his preface, previewing a newly added appendix: "... space-time is not necessarily something to which one can ascribe a separate existence, independently of the actual objects of physical reality. Physical objects are not *in space*, but these objects are *spatially extended*" ([64], vi). And in that appendix itself, he writes: "It appears to me, therefore, that the formation of the concept of material object must precede our concepts of time and space" ([64], appendix v, 141). What is here true for physics is true as well for metaphysics. And once we have understood the order of priority, there is no special problem of individuation. At the very least, it is not a problem 'over and above' that of explicating *physical object* itself. We do not have a concept of *physical object* of which it is then proper to ask what accounts for the numerical distinctness of physical objects. The concept of *numerical distinctness* lies at the bedrock of our conceptual scheme; there is nothing more basic than it in terms of which it might be explicated. Numerical difference is not to be accounted for in terms of a 'presented' entity (a bare particular), of a 'know not what' (a substratum), or of any specially favored properties (e.g. spatial relations). To have the concept of *physical object* is already to have the concept of *numerical difference*. And the latter concept is not further analyzable.

In finding that a particular concept is not further analyzable, we have learned something of enormous importance about our conceptual scheme. In learning that the problem of individuation cannot be solved by appeal to substance, to bare particulars, to qualities, or to relations, we have learned that we had mistakenly got the order of logical precedence wrong in our thinking about these notions. We had imagined physical objects strewn about in space and their numerical difference accounted for in terms of their different positions in that space. Our studies reveal, however, that such a view is ultimately untenable. Our starting point must be that of numerically distinct physical objects lying at varying distances from one another and moving about relative to one another. From such a view we can construct a workable concept of space. But such a view is grounded upon the primitiveness of the notion of physical object and numerical distinctness. We cannot – on pain of circularity – try to explain those notions by invoking properties of space.

We may think that we have abandoned the theory of absolute space, have fully switched over to the theory of relative space, and have seen clearly the implications of the latter theory. But in cold fact, many of us have not fully done so. Some philosophers believe that the problem of individuation can be solved by invoking spatial relations, but in so doing they overlook the fact that spatial relations *presuppose*, and do not ground, the numerical difference of physical objects. Simply put, there are no places logically or epistemically independent of, or prior to, the existence of numerically distinct physical objects. The order of dependence is from physical things to places; not the other way around.

10.7 Nonphysical objects[24]

Identity is a two-place (dyadic) relation. In that regard, it is like *is taller than* and *is envious of*. But unlike all other two-place relations, identity is unique in that it can hold only between one thing and itself; it cannot – like *is the same height as* or *is the same age as* – ever hold between two numerically distinct things. One might think, then, that it would be particularly easy to establish in practice when the relation of identity holds. But it turns out that on occasion it is exceedingly difficult to do so. This is so because we often have several logically independent ways of individuating one and the same thing. We may individuate some 'thing' in one way and may individuate some 'thing' in another way, and we might not quite be sure whether in doing so we

---

24. I have explored the issues of this section previously in "Can the Theory of the Contingent Identity between Sensation-States and Brain-States Be Made Empirical?" in *Canadian Journal of Philosophy* 3, no. 3 (Mar. 1974), 405-17. I thank the editor of that journal for permission to reprint selected passages below. Most of this section is, however, newly written for this book.

have individuated two numerically distinct things or have individuated one thing twice.

For example, I sometimes talk about 'my red car' and I sometimes talk about 'my Oldsmobile'. Each of these descriptions individuates[25] exactly one thing in the universe: I have only one red car, and I have only one Oldsmobile. But if you were to overhear me using both expressions you might have no way of knowing whether my red car is (one and the same with) the Oldsmobile, or whether I have (at least) two cars, one red but not an Oldsmobile, and the other an Oldsmobile but not red. If, however, you were to have access to my cars and were to examine my red one, you would quickly discover that it is an Oldsmobile; or, if you were to examine my Oldsmobile, you would quickly discover that it is red. You would be able, as an empirical matter of relative ease, to establish the identity of my red car with my Oldsmobile.

With an example such as this in mind, one might get the mistaken idea that identity can always be readily established by direct observation. We need only, one might mistakenly believe, simply examine the referent of the one individuating description and examine the referent of the other individuating description and the identity (or not, as the case may be) of the 'things' referred to would be altogether obvious. But the example of my red car and of my Oldsmobile is not, in the end, a fair representation of the general methodology involved in identifying *A* with *B*. For there are large classes of 'things' whose identity poses methodological and metaphysical puzzles which are not solvable by simple observation or direct empirical examination. To identify one of these things with 'another' we will have to grapple with metaphysical issues which transcend mere observation.

In the case of the synchronic identity of physical objects, the focus of the problem is usually on trying to create a viable account of their numerical difference in the face of qualitative identity. But in the case of nonphysical objects, the focus is usually on the other side of the same coin, on the problem of trying to account for numerical identity in the absence of perceived qualitative identity.

We have already seen one example of this latter problem when I discussed, in chapter 8 (pp. 181-3), the case of identifying the causes of our visual sensations with those of our tactile sensations. Each of

---

25. Or, more exactly, is a uniquely referring expression which may be used to individuate

these kinds of sensations, the visual and the tactile, exists in a sensory 'space', i.e. comprises its own self-contained modality* (as it is some-times described), and the problem becomes one of trying to 'identify across sensory modalities'. As I argued, there is no necessity that the data of various sensory modalities correlate highly with one another; it is a brute contingency of this world that they do correlate as highly as they do. Capitalizing on this correlation, as children we learned to synthesize a unitary sensory space out of these distinct kinds of data, so that now, as adults, we hardly if ever give a moment's thought to the profound differences between visual and tactile space. Apart from shape,[26] the features of things which we discern visually – e.g. their hues, their distances, their transparency or opacity – do not overlap with the features we discern tactually – e.g. their texture, their degree of pliability, their viscosity, their weight. And yet, in spite of the nearly complete difference in the two sets of data furnished by our eyes and by our hands, we posit the *identity* of the sources of the one with the sources of the other, saying that the thing seen is one and the same with, i.e. is numerically identical to, the thing felt. This iden-tification is not a matter of observation (like identifying my red car with my Oldsmobile), but involves making a posit which carries us well beyond anything 'given' in perception or demonstrable by empir-ical means. The identity of the visual with the tactile is a posit which helps 'to make sense' of the sensory data, but is not itself anything perceived, nor, for that matter, is it anything perceivable.

If we fail to recognize that identification is possible, even when the descriptions of the 'things' to be identified are profoundly unalike, we may fall into the error some philosophers have made in arguing that it is impossible *in principle* scientifically to identify mental states with brain states.

For several generations, a certain element of popular metaphysics was in advance of that of professional philosophers. For the past hun-dred years at least, many persons who would not regard themselves as philosophers had adopted a particular view about the nature of human

---

26. Although both sight and touch seem to furnish the 'same' data pertaining to shape, we know that identifying visual shape with tactile shape is some-thing that we had to learn to do; that ability is no more innate or logically mandated than is our ability to identify colors and temperatures (in those few cases where they do correlate, e.g. where an object is heated to incandes-cence). (See p. 181, esp. footnote 20.)

consciousness which was at distinct odds with what many skilled philosophers were then arguing. This popular view held that consciousness was, in some sense, to be identified with the (higher) workings of
a central nervous system. Many philosophers, however, actively
resisted this popular theory, not because they were reactionary by
nature, but because they thought that the theory was logically flawed.
They pointed out that mental states and brain states ostensibly have
different properties. For example, brain activity consumes a certain
amount of electrical power and gives it off as heat, and is – like any
other physical activity – subject to the physical laws of thermodynamics. But mental states do not seem to have these features at all.
Then, too, a mental state, such as your seeing a red apple or hearing a
loud noise, does not seem to be paralleled by a corresponding feature
in your brain. There are presumably no apple-shaped red patches in
your brain, nor, presumably, are there any loud noises there either.
Invoking the principle of the indiscernibility of identicals,[27] many philosophers were then prone to argue that it was not just false, but –
more strongly – that it was *impossible*, that mental states could be
brain states. But the entire debate was reversed at the end of the 1950s
with the virtually simultaneous publication by three different philosophers – U.T. Place ([153]) in 1956, H. Feigl ([70][28]) in 1958, and
J.J.C. Smart ([193]) in 1959 – of what has come to be known as the
Identity theory of mental states and brain states. These philosophers
argued that the standard, historically long-lived objections to the identifying of mental states with brain states were not valid.

Their rejection of the standard philosophical arguments against
identifying mental states with brain states turned on two flaws they
claimed to find in those arguments. The first was that even if a description of a mental state did not, in any obvious sense, demand a reference to properties appropriate to physical objects, that in and of

------

27. The principle of the indiscernibility of identicals states, recall, that whatever are numerically identical are qualitatively identical. A logically equivalent statement of this same principle reads: "Whatever are not qualitatively
identical are not numerically identical." It is the latter version which is being
invoked in the present context. If we wanted a name for this alternative formulation, we could call it the principle of "the nonidentity of discernibles".

28. The reprint (1967) of Feigl's original monograph contains a supplementary bibliography. Between the original and the supplement, the compilation
comprises 565 items published on the mind-body problem.

itself did not mean that mental states were not states of physical things: the description may be incomplete, and incompleteness is no indicator of incompatibility. That we do not typically describe mental states using terminology drawn from neurophysiology, physics, and chemistry does not prove that those states cannot be so described. The second flaw these philosophers claimed to find in the standard argument dealt with the objection that when a person sees, for example, a red apple, there is no apple-shaped red patch in his brain. The way around this supposed difficulty was to counterargue that it was not the 'contents' or the 'objects' of consciousness which were to be found in the central nervous system, but the *state* or *activity* of consciousness. What was being identified was not a red patch in one's visual field with a publicly observable red patch in one's brain – by all accounts the latter patch does not exist – but it was the *activity* (or state) of seeing red which was being identified with some *activity* (or state) in the central nervous system.

In the ensuing thirty years, the Identity theory has gone through a variety of refinements as philosophers have struggled to improve it and to make it more specific.[29] The precise details are best left to other books. Here my sole concern is with certain arguments which allege that the Identity theory – in any version whatsoever – can never aspire to the status of being a scientific theory.

Brain states are not physical objects, but are *states* of physical objects. Mental states, too, are not physical objects, but are states of something: of physical objects, if the Identity theory is true, or of something else (of minds or of persons), if the Identity theory is not true.

Is it possible to identify one property, P', with a property P''? Is it possible to identify one state, S', with a state S''? Two sorts of objections have been leveled against the proposal that the Identity theory might be testable by laboratory experiment. One of these is a general

---

29. The original proponents of the Identity theory claimed that the identity was *contingent*. Some subsequent theorists, also sympathetic to the Identity theory, have argued that if the relation is identity, then it cannot be contingent, but must instead be *necessary*. (See, for example, Kripke, [116].) This issue need not be pursued here. In this section, I am not concerned with the modal status of the Identity theory (i.e. whether it is contingent or necessarily true), but with the metaphysical presuppositions we bring to bear in determining the theory's epistemological status.

objection pertaining to the very possibility of establishing empirically the identity of any properties whatever. The other has to do with some alleged special peculiarities of the identification of mental states with brain states.

On the first score, some philosophers have argued that property-(and state-)identification is possible only when there is an equivalence in meaning between the expression used to refer to the one property (or state) and the expression used to refer to the other. For example, one might argue that the properties *azure* and *cerulean* are identical because the term "azure" means the same as the term "cerulean". But since "*a* is having a throbbing pain in his hand" and "*a*'s brain is in state *x*" do not *mean* the same thing (however "*x*" may be interpreted), it may be argued that the experience of having a pain can never be identified with any brain state whatever.

But against this theory is the hard evidence provided, within the history of science, of actual examples where property-identification has been successfully carried through. Scientists have, on occasion, identified one property, P′, with 'another', P″, without there being any meaning-equivalence between the terms used to refer to each. Scientists have, for example, identified electric current with the flow of electrons in a conductor; diabetes with elevated glucose levels in the bloodstream; radioactivity with the emission of subatomic particles; and visible light with electromagnetic radiation of wavelength 4000 to 7000 angstroms. In each case, at the time when the identification was made, there was no meaning-equivalence between the terms used. "Electric current" did not originally mean "flow of electrons". "Diabetes" did not originally mean "elevated glucose level". Indeed, diabetes was recognized as a distinct illness long before modern chemistry distinguished glucose from other sugars. It was an *empirical* discovery that diabetes is elevated glucose levels; it was no linguistic or semantic discovery.

We can see, then, that it is sometimes possible to identify properties with one another, even if the expressions we use to refer to them do not mean the same thing (or, more specifically, even though the expressions we use to refer to these properties are logically independent of one another). This latter is a important result, for without it, it would be impossible from the outset to subject the Identity theory to empirical test.

But having found that, on occasion, it is possible to identify some properties with one another even though the expressions referring to those properties are not equivalent, certainly does not by itself guarantee that we will be able to contrive an empirical test of the hypothesis that mental states are brain states. Indeed, at least one philosopher, Peter Herbst, argues that it is impossible in principle, because of the peculiar nature of mental states and of brain states themselves, ever to demonstrate empirically their identity with one another.

> Let us then investigate a proposition that there is a particular mental entity which is ... identical with a particular brain state. In order to be able to test it, we must know which mental entity is supposed to be identical with what brain state. Therefore we need at least two clear and independent identifying references to serve as the basis of our proposition of identity. They must each be sufficient to individuate an entity, or else we cannot say what is identical with what, and they must be independent of each other, or else the identity proposition expressed in terms of them becomes tautologous. ([93], 57-8)

But having pointed out what he takes to be a logical requirement for putting the theory to empirical test, viz. having independent ways of individuating brain states and mental states, Herbst proceeds to express the gravest pessimism about our ever being able to carry out the task in practice.

> ... it will not do to individuate experiences of having-a-sensation by their alleged neurophysiological properties. For exactly the same properties would also have to individuate the brain state, and therefore the two identifying references would fail of logical independence. Thus, for purposes of testing the empirical identity thesis [Identity theory], the ascription of neurophysiological properties to experiences is not only question-begging but useless.
>
> By what shall we individuate them? It is no use trying to individuate them by their spatio-temporal position alone, because, for one thing, we are not in a position to assign spatial positions to them unless the identity thesis is true, and it cannot be shown to be true unless sensation-experiences can be individuated.
>
> ... individuation by neurophysiological properties is question-beggingly useless; individuation by spatial position likewise, and individuation by temporal position not useless but insufficient. ([93], 58-9)

The model Herbst is working with lies just beneath the surface. He is assuming that, in order to be able to demonstrate in a scientific experiment the identity of A with B, we must have some unique description of A, i.e. a way of individuating (singling out) A and we must have some *other* way, a logically independent way, of picking out B. For, as he points out, if the two descriptions are not logically independent of one another, if, that is, either one logically entails the other, then the identification of A with B is not a matter of scientific experiment at all but is simply a matter of logic (in Herbst's terminology, the identity proposition is 'tautological', i.e. true as a matter of the meanings of the terms involved). Applying these general requirements specifically to the Identity theory would imply that for that theory to be testable by empirical means we would have to have a way of individuating mental states and a way of individuating brain states which do not – as a matter of logic – entail that the one is the selfsame thing as the other. Then, having picked out, or isolated, the 'two' states, we must be able to demonstrate that the states (or properties) so individuated are really one and the same state (or property).

But he argues that we will, in principle, be unable to individuate mental states and brain states in a manner suitable for experimentally identifying the one with the other. This is so, he argues because (1) if we were to individuate mental states by their physical properties, i.e. by the neurophysiological features we use to individuate brain states, then we will have prejudged the very theory we are trying to prove; similarly, (2) if we were to individuate brain states by mentalistic properties (e.g. by their being painful, or clever, or incoherent), then, again, we will have prejudged the very theory we are trying to prove. But what about individuating brain states and mental states each by their spatiotemporal properties? Might we not be able to identify one with the other if we can show that they are both in the same place at the same time? Herbst argues (3) that we cannot assign precise spatial and temporal positions to mental states in advance of having accepted the Identity theory. Suppose you are now (having the experience of) recalling what you ate for breakfast today. Where, precisely, is this current memory experience? It is insufficient to offer a vague answer of the sort "somewhere in my head", since the identification at which we are ultimately aiming is with some very specific state located in particular nerves and lobes of the brain. In general, if we are depending on spatial positions as the basis for making an identification, it is unsound to identify A which is located 'in the vicinity of P_1' with B which is located 'exactly at P_1'. Herbst thus argues that an answer to the question about the location of experiences can be given with the requisite degree of specificity only if one has *already* accepted the Identity theory. But if one accepts the Identity theory, then one's testing procedure has become viciously circular, presupposing as a premise the very thing to be established as a conclusion.

We seem, then, to be faced with what looks to be an intractable dilemma: unless one assumes that the Identity theory is true, one cannot precisely assign spatiotemporal positions to experiences; but unless one can assign spatiotemporal positions to experiences, one cannot *test* the Identity theory. If this argument is accepted, it would appear, then, that the theory that there is an identity between mental states and brain states is in principle untestable.

Is there any way out of Herbst's stark dilemma? I think there is, but it requires that we back up and reject the naive methodology which Herbst has presupposed. His idea of the methodology involved in property-identification is the analog of the example we described of identifying one physical object with 'another': recall the case of your identifying my red car with my Oldsmobile. He seems to believe that to identify one property with another we must isolate instances of each, and then in examining them, we must be able to 'discover' their identity (in much the same way, for example, that we might 'discover' that two objects have the same length). But when we turn once again to the pages of the history of science, looking now to learn how scientists actually go about making property-identifications, we discover that their methodology is nothing remotely like what Herbst has envisaged.

In the later half of the nineteenth century, James Clerk Maxwell and Ludwig Boltzmann, in their celebrated dynamical (kinetic) theory of gases, were able to identify the temperature of a gas with the [total translational] kinetic energy of the molecules of that gas.[30] The term "temperature" certainly did not *mean* (at that time at least) "total kinetic energy". The identification plainly was not a matter of discerning any meaning-equivalence between the *terms* used. But neither did the identification take place in the manner presupposed by Herbst's model. These brilliant theoreticians did not proceed by first experimentally individuating the temperature of a gas and experimentally individuating the [translational] kinetic energy of its molecules, and

---

30. More exactly, with the mass of the gas multiplied by the root-mean-square speed of its constituent molecules

then discovering at a second stage – by some sort of unexplained observation – that these two properties of the gas instance the relation of *identity*. The identification of the temperature of a gas with the kinetic energy of its molecules came about, rather, on the basis of a certain highly controversial *theory* about the nature of gases, and on a great number of assumptions about the behavior of gas molecules, e.g. about their relative sizes, their numbers, their interactions, and the nature of their activity on striking the walls of a container. The subsequent empirical confirmation of their bold hypothesis of identity rested upon the predictions their theory made of observable macroscopic phenomena such as rates of diffusion, measures of specific heats, and viscosity. The empirical confirmation of the identity relation has never – not even now, more than one hundred years later – rested on an independent measure of the kinetic energy of the molecules. And yet the identification is taken to be so well established as to be no longer a matter of debate.

There are, as well, many other counterexamples to Herbst's flawed methodology.

One of the great mysteries in classical Newtonian physics was the unexplained proportionality between so-called inertial mass and gravitational mass. Physical objects attract one another with a force proportional to the product of their 'masses'. Physical objects also are accelerated by forces in proportion to their 'masses'. These are two – seemingly – quite distinct properties, and physicists distinguished *two* concepts of mass: a physical object's *gravitational mass*, and a physical object's *inertial mass*. Newton, himself, noted that these two 'masses' are apparently proportional to one another, but offered no explanation for it (see [144], book I, defs. I-III; book III, prop. VI). In the nineteenth century, the Hungarian physicist Lóránd von Eötvös[31] constructed an apparatus to measure how closely gravitational mass correlated to inertial mass. His torsion balance (c. 1890) was accurate to one part in 100 million (i.e. 10^{-8}). Within the limits possible with his device, he found no discrepancy whatever between the two measurements ([68]). Later measurements, in this century (1971), have extended the accuracy to one part in a million million (i.e. 10^{-12}) ([195], 534). But clearly no such measurements, however refined, are capable of showing anything more than a correlation. It is impossible

_____

31. Pronounced *ût'-vûsh*

for measurement, even if perfect, to demonstrate the identity of the properties being measured.

For more than 225 years, experimental physicists had been able to individuate the inertial mass and the gravitational mass of objects in logically independent ways and with increasing precision. In so doing they had satisfied the first and, on the face of it, the only problematic part of Herbst's methodology. Were Herbst's methodology sound, it would seem, then, that physicists ought to have been able, in a relatively effortless manner, to go on to determine whether they were observing one property or two. But having individuated inertial mass and gravitational mass, from as early as 1687 through to 1916, physicists were up against a brick wall. There was no observation possible, or any direct test conceivable, which could answer for them whether they were observing one property of physical matter or two distinct, but highly correlated, properties. The question defied answer by any appeal to direct observation. The eventual identification of inertial mass with gravitational mass, when it was finally made by Einstein early in this century, did not occur as a result of his making finer measurements or by observing some telltale feature overlooked by other physicists.

Einstein's posit that inertial mass was not just highly correlated with gravitational mass, but was, in fact, one and the same property, proceeded by his identifying the so-called gravitational field as being itself an inertial field. (See [63] and [64], esp. chaps xix and xx.) *Fields* are not observable entities. They are what are often called 'theoretical' or 'hypothetical' entities. This is not to say that they are unreal or fictitious, although some philosophers and physicists have been wont to so regard them. To say that an entity is 'theoretical' is to say that it cannot be observed 'directly'; that its existence is posited and confirmed by its explanatory role in a scientific theory. Gravitational fields are posited to explain the mutual attraction of physical bodies (just as electric fields are posited to explain the attraction and repulsion of charged bodies) (see [64], 144-8). Inertial fields are posited to explain the acceleration of bodies subjected to forces. By identifying gravitational fields with inertial fields, it followed as an immediate consequence that the gravitational mass of a body would be the selfsame as its inertial mass.

The identification of gravitational mass with inertial mass did not, then, come about in the sort of naive manner imagined by Herbst. One did not individuate inertial mass, individuate gravitational mass, and then 'experimentally discover' or 'directly observe' that the relation of identity held between the two properties. The identification came about because at a higher theoretical level, far removed from the observational base, Einstein posited the identity of gravitational fields with inertial fields.

Why does making such a posit count as doing empirical science? Because *predictions* which can be derived from the theory in which such a posit occurs are testable. In identifying gravitational fields with inertial fields, Einstein's theory – unlike Newton's – entailed that the axis of the orbit of the planet Mercury would gradually rotate (precess) ([63], 163-4), that the light emitted from a massive star would experience a so-called red-shift, and that light rays would bend in a gravitational field. These dramatic, and unexpected, predictions fit observed astronomical data better than did Newton's theory. And thus Einstein's theory won confirmation at the expense of Newton's theory, and Einstein's posit of the identity of gravitational fields with inertial fields was taken to be *indirectly* confirmed.

The empirical route to the confirmation of identity – of temperature with total kinetic energy, of gravitational mass with inertial mass – is no simple or direct matter. It is certainly not a matter to be settled by 'direct observation'. Identity is often established, not by direct observation, but indirectly, through layer upon layer of theory and of assumption.

Such historical examples shed light on the possibility of confirming the Identity theory because they tell us that if an identification of mental states with brain states ever should be made empirically, it will not come about by individuating instances of states of the one sort, by individuating instances of the other, and then by discovering that there is a relation of identity between them. The identification, if it ever is made, will be far more roundabout and far more protracted. And it will involve not only observation and experiment, but also vast amounts of theory.

The identification of mental states and brain states is, at present, a working hypothesis. It provides the motivation for a far-reaching research program, but its fine details are decades or more away from being stated. It will take generations to spell out precisely which brain states are supposed to be identical with which mental states. There will never be any particular laboratory findings, there will never be a crucial experiment, to which future historians will be able to point and say, "That experiment finally tipped the scales and showed once and for all that mental states are brains states". The transition, if it occurs, can only come about through a gradual and steady accumulation of vast storehouses of data along with theorizing of ever greater sophistication and refinement.

Sophisticated scientific theories seldom, if ever, appear suddenly, fully articulated. The Identity theory of mental states with brain states, if it is to prove successful, will doubtless follow the historical course we have earlier seen of the kinetic theory of heat: a succession of scientists will adopt it as a working hypothesis, and these generations of researchers will steadily improve the theory, filling in details, expanding its compass, piece by piece, over a course of time. In the case of heat theory, the transition to the kinetic theory took two hundred years.

Much of the future impetus for the Identity theory will come as much from research in Artificial Intelligence as it has, historically, derived from neurophysiology and experimental psychology. As engineers and theoreticians working together create electronic (and perhaps chemical and atomic) devices to emulate the cognitive processes of human beings, there will be a steadily increasing incentive to regard our own actual mental states as being nothing other than brain states. Present-day computers are not conscious; they do not think. But are computers capable *in principle* of consciousness? Of course it all depends on what one means by 'a computer' and what one means by 'consciousness'. If by 'a computer' one means an electronic device operating in a linear manner (one step after another), i.e. as a so-called Von Neumann device ([4], 32-3), then there seems to be accumulating evidence, both experimental and theoretical, that such a computer will never be able to mimic the conscious and cognitive processes of an adult human being. But if we mean by 'a computer' nothing more than 'a manufactured device containing no organic materials', then it is very much an open question whether such a device could replicate the mental processes of human beings. To date, there do not seem to be any compelling reasons to believe that it is impossible in principle. We are beginning to be able to build computers which, in a rudimentary way, imitate some of the cognitive processes of human beings: in pattern recognition; in sensorimotor skills; in ability to play chess; in language translation; etc.

If, over the next several decades (centuries perhaps), computers can be built which imitate still better the abilities of human beings – e.g. our ability to understand a spoken language, our ability to communicate, our ability to reason, our ability to recognize features of our environment, our ability to learn, our ability to generalize – there will be less and less reason to refrain from attributing consciousness to them.[32] And once we have begun to attribute consciousness to our computers, we will very likely find that we regard our own mental processes as being nothing other than the processes of our own built-in computers, i.e. of our brains and their associated peripheral nervous systems. The Identity theory will have come to be accepted with the kind of natural inevitability at present enjoyed by the theory that the temperature of a gas is the [total translational] kinetic energy of that gas and by the theory that inertial mass is gravitational mass.

There is a loose end in this scenario, however. To isolate it, we will back up one last time, virtually to the conceptual roots, at it were, of the debate about the Identity theory. "Why", it is profitable to ask, "in spite of the fact that so many philosophers and scientists remain undecided about the truth of the Identity theory, have so many others uncritically accepted it?" Why do so many nonphilosophers and non-scientists even now believe the Identity theory to be true? What evidence promotes that belief?

The evidence cited is well-known. Many persons believe that the Identity theory is true because they are familiar with laboratory findings that certain electrical stimulations evoke vivid memories; that other electrical stimulations cause or assuage pain; that certain chemicals introduced in the bloodstream will cause vivid hallucinations, euphoria, panic, sleep, etc. In short, most of us already know that a great deal of what goes on in our consciousness, perhaps all of it, is profoundly intimately related to what is happening in our brains. And

---

32. See Turing's "Computing Machinery and Intelligence" ([206]) and Scriven's "The Compleat Robot: A Prolegomena to Androidology" ([187]). Turing's suggestion that we should want to attribute consciousness to a machine which could 'imitate' a human being in a question-and-answer game (the 'imitation game') has been subjected to severe criticism, probably the most well-known being that by John Searle in his "Minds, Brains, and Programs" ([188]). Searle's critique, in its turn, provoked a firestorm of counterargument (see, e.g., Hofstadter's reply, along with a reprint of Searle's original paper, in [99], 373-82). To a certain degree, Searle's criticisms are becoming moot, insofar as they were directed principally against a particular model – the so-called computational model – of Artificial Intelligence instantiated in a Von Neumann machine. But both of these targets are gradually giving way to newer techniques and bolder architectures which one may, reasonably, regard as approaching more and more the structure and functioning of the human brain.

thus many persons have assumed that our mental states just simply *are* brain states.

But of course the latter conclusion is not strictly warranted by the empirical data which are cited in its support. Descartes, too, believed that most if not all of what goes on in our consciousness is intimately related to what goes on in our brains, but he, unlike many persons today, did not believe that mental states were brain states. Indeed, he believed that it was impossible that they could be. He was, as we have said (pp. 93ff.), a dualist, believing that there was causal interaction between the mental states and brain states, but that they could not be identified one with another.

The very possibility of maintaining dualism, as did Descartes, in the face of an exceptionless correlation between mental states and brain states tells us that something more must be added to the account of the methodology of identity. Given that one can always, in principle, be a dualist about any alleged identification – one could, for example, be a dualist about temperature and kinetic energy, about inertial and gravitational mass, etc. – we must explain why identity is sometimes the preferable hypothesis. In short, the hypothesis of identity always competes against the hypothesis of 'mere correlation'. Any two quantitative properties (or states) which are identified must be correlated. Why should we ever want to pass beyond positing mere correlation to posit a stronger relationship, viz. identity? What empirical evidence could we ever have for warranting a hypothesis of identity over and above one of mere correlation?

Suppose someone were to be a dualist, not with regard to mental states and brain states, but with regard to inertial mass and gravitational mass, arguing that all that has ever been experimentally demonstrated (e.g. in Eötvös's experiment and its successors) is a remarkable correlation between the two properties and that there has never been, nor could there be, an experimental demonstration that showed anything more, i.e. that it is impossible to demonstrate that there is an actual identity between the two. How could such a challenge be met?

It is at this point that two powerful metaphysical principles involved in the identification of properties with one another must come into play. In the end, the choice of identity over mere correlation is made in part on the basis of the desire for ontological or metaphysical economy. We want not to multiply entities beyond necessity. Mere correlation posits two ontologically distinct entities; identity posits but one, and is thus preferable. But the latter choice is also mandated by our desire that our theories be explanatorily powerful. In positing 'mere correlation', an intractable problem remains: "Why are the two states correlated? What is the nature of the connection between the two?" Descartes, himself, was crucially aware of this latter difficulty and struggled to offer a cogent answer, but neither he, nor any other dualist, ever could satisfactorily fill that gaping hole in the theory. In a theory which posits identity, in contrast, there is nothing further to be explained. If mental states *are* brain states, then there is nothing to explain in their being correlated. Correlation follows immediately, as a logical matter, from identification.

By transcending the empirical data of correlation, in particular by positing an identity, we satisfy at one stroke two intensely powerful metaphysical desiderata: we effect an economy in our ontology and we avoid the need for further explanation carrying, as it might, the requirement of positing still further kinds of entities and hidden interactions. In short, when it comes down to positing an identity or a 'mere correlation', if there is not good reason to desist from making the identification, identity – not 'mere correlation' – is the preferred hypothesis. The naive model, which portrays correlation as being demonstrable and identity as being a relation which takes 'something more', over and above 'mere correlation', to warrant its being posited, has turned the metaphysical requirements upside down. Identity is the preferred hypothesis; 'mere correlation' a decided second-best, to be invoked only when there are grounds to believe that identity does not obtain.

A scientific version of the Identity theory of brain states and mental states has not yet been well enough confirmed to warrant its acceptance to the degree, for example, that we accept certain identifications made in kinetic theory and in general relativity. The Identity theory is at present a remarkably fruitful research program. But it stands to a fully articulated theory much as Bacon's theory, "Heat is Motion", stood to the theory of Maxwell and Boltzmann (two centuries later) which explained specifically temperature, pressure, viscosity, entropy, free energy, etc., in terms of the physical properties of the microstructure of a gas. (Incidentally, Maxwell's and Boltzmann's theory was hardly the last word. Kinetic theory has continued to evolve, through the Dirac and Einstein-Bose repairs, and will continue to evolve for the foreseeable future.)

The Identity theory is in principle empirically testable. Testability is, however, a matter of degree. The Identity theory, which is today only minimally testable, may well grow steadily more testable as it becomes, slowly, over many decades, better articulated. Testability never resides in a single, one-shot, laboratory experiment. It is a much more global affair, encompassing observation, creative imagination, theory construction, constant revision, and a metaphysical model of what constitutes ontological economy and explanatory power. The testing of the Identity theory will involve hundreds of researchers painstakingly assembling countless tens of thousands of pieces of data into a comprehensive whole. It will no more be tested by a single experiment, or a few, than was Newtonian mechanics or kinetic theory. And like these latter theories, it will have a penumbra of metaphysical assumptions, assumptions which are as vital to the theory as any of the most directly testable predictions of that theory.

CHAPTER ELEVEN

Identity-through-time

Different philosophers have used a variety of expressions to refer to the concept of *identity-through-time*. Some writers refer to it as "diachronic identity"; some as "genidentity"; some as "re-identification"; and still others, without qualification, as "identity". The latter term is potentially confusing because it is sometimes also used to refer to the concept of *individuation*. In this chapter, "identity" is used only to refer to the concept of *identity-through-time*, never to *individuation*.

11.1 Is the problem of identity solely an epistemological one?

In his landmark book *A Treatise of Human Nature* David Hume (1711-76) devoted the single longest (by far) section to the topic "Of scepticism with regard to the senses" ([101], book I, part IV, section II). Ostensibly this was a discussion of the grounds for believing in a material external world (of 'objects' or 'bodies' in Hume's terminology) which is the cause of our sensations ('perceptions' as Hume called them). He was, that is, focusing on the inherent difficulties which we mentioned earlier (p. 237) in Locke's theory. Hume adopted a skeptical position. He found that the arguments which would posit objects as the causes of our perceptions were – for him, according to his standards – inconclusive, and hence, he argued, belief in such objects was not rationally well-founded.[1] (I have suggested earlier that currently such conclusions as Hume's are less attractive simply be-

---

1. Hume did not, however, argue the stronger position, viz. that one rationally ought not to believe in the existence of external objects. He claimed that even if such a belief were not well-founded, we remain nonetheless committed to it: "We may well ask, *What causes induce us to believe in the existence of body?* but 'tis vain to ask, *Whether there be body or not?* That is a point, which we must take for granted in all our reasonings" ([101], 187).

cause we have altered our understanding of what may reasonably be regarded as standards of rational belief.)

But there is another strain running throughout that section of the *Treatise* which warrants our attention here. Time and again in that section, Hume raises the issue of discontinuous perception. He asks about the existence of objects "even when they are not perceiv'd" ([101], 188), of mountains, houses, and trees "when I lose sight of them by shutting my eyes or turning my head" (194), and of the fire burning in his hearth "when I return to my chamber after an hour's absence" (195). It is easy, in reading these passages, to come away with a totally mistaken notion as to just what the problem of the identity-through-time of material objects is supposed to be. I have known students who, having read these passages, have come to believe that the problem of identity-through-time arises solely through the occurrence of interrupted observation. They have believed – mistakenly – that identity is problematic only when we wish to identify something perceived at some time or other with something perceived at another time and when we have not observed the earlier thing as it continuously 'evolved' into the latter. They have believed that there is no problem of identity if one continuously observes a scene.

To subscribe to this belief is to fail to comprehend the depth of the problem. The problem of identity does *not* come about through interrupted perception. To be sure, the case of interrupted perception complicates ascriptions of identity considerably. But the problem of identity exists even in cases of continuous (uninterrupted) perception. More specifically, the problem of identity-through-time is not a perceptual problem, but a conceptual one. This may be understood by recognizing that even under circumstances of continuous perception, problems of identity arise. There are two such problems.

First, suppose no change whatever occurs in one's perceptions over some particular time interval. Let's say, for example, that someone is keeping careful watch on a valued painting. Over a period of continuous observation, five minutes we'll say, no change whatever is perceived to have occurred. Must we conclude that the painting which exists at the end of this interval is the selfsame (numerically identical) painting as that observed at the beginning? We would, naturally, be inclined to say that it is. But really, there are a host of metaphysical assumptions informing our answer. In the Middle Ages, some philosophers believed that physical objects owed their existence to their being 'created'. They also believed that no material object could 'create' another of the same kind, particularly if that other existed at a later time. For a material object to exist a minute from now it would have to be created; but no object existing *now* had within it the capacity to 'create' a similar kind of material object existing at a different (later) time. Thus it was argued that God, and God alone, could create the future object. What may look, on the face of it, to be one material object enduring through time was taken – in this medieval account – to be an infinite succession of material objects, each lasting for only an instant, each created by God in such a manner as to give the appearance (illusion really) of one object enduring through time.[2] In such an account, it was impossible to observe a material object over a period of time: there were no such things. Instead what one actually observed were an infinity of successive instantaneous objects. Today this theory of successive creations is no longer seriously credited, but it serves to remind us that it is not a simple 'fact' that we see objects enduring through time. Various medieval philosophers thought otherwise. The point is that the very description "*O* was perceived throughout the period T_1 to T_2" presupposes a certain metaphysical theory about the nature of material objects and their existence through time. The merits of that theory are something to be examined, not simply assumed.

The second reason why there is a problem of identity, even under conditions of continuous observation, has to do with precisely the opposite possible results of continuous observation. Suppose now, in contrast, that the 'object' was seen to change in some way: perhaps it grew larger, then smaller; perhaps it changed color, or temperature; perhaps it disappeared from sight (maybe even 'went out of existence') and some time later a qualitatively identical thing appeared.

---

2. Thomas Aquinas (1225-74) writes: "... all creatures [i.e. created things] need God to keep them in existence. For the *esse* [being] of all creaturely beings so depends upon God that they could not continue to exist even for a moment, but would fall away into nothingness unless they were sustained in existence by his power ..." ([8], 1a. 104, I, p. 39).

This idea of sustained creation endured into the early modern period of philosophy. Descartes writes (1641): "... it is quite clear to anyone who attentively considers the nature of time that the same power and action are needed to preserve anything at each moment of its duration as would be required to create that thing anew if it were not yet in existence. Hence the distinction between preservation and creation is only a conceptual one, and this is one of the things that are evident by the natural light [of reason]" ([55], "Third Meditation" in *Meditations on First Philosophy*, 33).

What shall we say? Has identity been preserved? Has it been lost? It is clear that the mere fact of observation provides no answer whatsoever to this question. The problem of identity in this latter case has to do with what we want to make of what it is that has been continuously observed. The observing was uninterrupted, but the problem of identity is every bit as severe as in the case of interrupted observation. In short, we need *theories* to settle questions of identity, not just observations. The problem is principally a metaphysical one, not an epistemological or observational one.

11.2 Is identity incompatible with change?

There is a great temptation to regard any change whatever, however slight, as destroying a material thing's identity. For example, if there were to be a scratch, however minute [no pun], on my wristwatch today which was not on my wristwatch of yesterday, there would be an inclination – on the part of some persons – to argue that today's wristwatch could not, strictly speaking, be identified as being the watch which existed yesterday. I have had many students who have argued precisely this thesis. But it is certainly not a modern thesis. It is, we learn, one which has apparently commended itself naturally to many persons since antiquity ([189]). Two hundred and fifty years ago, Hume commented upon it in his *Treatise*:

> ... suppose any mass of matter, of which the parts are contiguous and connected, to be plac'd before us; 'tis plain we must attribute a perfect identity to this mass, provided all the parts continue uninterruptedly and invariably the same, whatever motion or change of place we may observe either in the whole or in any of the parts. But supposing some very *small* or *inconsiderable* part to be added to the mass, or subtracted from it; 'tho this absolutely destroys the identity of the whole, strictly speaking; yet as we seldom think so accurately, we scruple not to pronounce a mass of matter the same, where we find so trivial an alteration. ([101], book I, part IV, sect. VI, 255-6)

Hume has here considered only a change of parts, but he equally well could have been talking of a change in properties. He is making two points: one, that however small a change, 'strictly speaking' that change destroys the identity of the object; and two, that when these changes are in fact small (inconsiderable or trivial), we do not – in our ordinary conception of identity – regard these changes as destroying identity. He then goes on to illustrate with several examples how our ordinary notion of identity is invoked through all sorts of changes: the replacement of parts in a ship, the growth of an oak tree, the change in weight of a human being, etc.

It would appear, then, that there are two concepts of *identity*: a 'strict' one and a 'looser' common, ordinary, or everyday one.

Perhaps there are, or have been, some philosophers who have adopted this 'strict' sense of identity. Perhaps it was something like this that Heraclitus (6th-5th cent. BC) had in mind when he declared that it is impossible to step into the same river twice. But even if there are a few examples of persons adopting the 'strict' notion and thereby coming to believe that almost nothing endures through time, this 'strict' notion is emphatically not the notion virtually all of us operate with nearly all of the time when *we* think about identity.

The 'strict' notion is a fairly *useless* notion. Even if, for some misguided reason, one were to adopt it as the 'correct' explication of the concept of *identity*, it is clear that one would have, almost immediately, to supplement it with another notion, for all intents and purposes the 'ordinary' notion, in order to get on in this world. Virtually everything you own, virtually everything you touch, virtually everything you see changes in subtle (or gross) ways from minute to minute, hour to hour, and day to day. If any alteration whatsoever were to count as destroying that thing's identity, then you could practically never lay claim to owning anything, to touching anything twice, or to seeing anything twice. You could never, for example, have a right to complain of your neighbor's having broken your lawn mower since your lawn mower would not have endured through time in any event: had it been in your own possession, it would have rusted ever so slightly, and that rusting would have destroyed its identity anyway. And so on.

It is easy to state conditions for 'strict' identity-through-time: an object preserves a 'strict' identity if it does not change its monadic properties and has no change in parts. But having stated these conditions for 'strict' identity we are now left with the considerably more difficult job of stating the conditions for 'ordinary' identity, the concept we need and use daily to get on in this world where objects undergo constant change, where some of these changes are reckoned not to destroy a thing's identity, and other changes do destroy a thing's identity. (From this point on, we will drop the qualifications "strict" and "ordinary". Hereinafter, "identity" will be understood to refer to 'ordinary' identity.)

11.3 Qualitative identity and identity-through-time

The problem may be stated formally: under what conditions is O_1-at-T_1 to be regarded as numerically identical to O_2-at-T_2? (I stipulate that "T_2" always signifies a time *later than* "T_1".)

Immediately we must state a profound difference between identity-at-a-time and identity-through-time. In the former case, identity-at-a-time (synchronic identity), it was essential that the objects, O_1 and O_2, being identified shared all properties in common at T_1. But in the case of identity-through-time, where (some) change in properties is given as permitted and indeed something to be accommodated within our theory, we cannot demand that O_1-at-T_1 have all and only the properties of O_2-at-T_2. Numerical identity-through-time does not require that the properties of O_1 remain the same as it evolves through time to become O_2. The situation is a bit more complicated. It may be stated this way:

(P1) $(O_1$-at-$T_1 = O_2$-at-$T_2) \rightarrow (O_1$-at-$T_1 \approx O_2$-at-T_1 & O_1-at-$T_2 \approx O_2$-at-$T_2)$

But we do not have:

(P2) $(O_1$-at-$T_1 = O_2$-at-$T_2) \rightarrow (O_1$-at-$T_1 \approx O_2$-at-$T_2)$

The first of these principles, (P1), states that if an object O_1 at an earlier time T_1 is identical with (i.e. is the selfsame object as) O_2 at some later time T_2, then whatever properties O_1 had at T_1, O_2 – in being the selfsame object as O_1 – also had the very same properties[3] *at that earlier time*. But the second of these principles, (P2), states, falsely, that if O_1-at-T_1 is identical to some object O_2-at-T_2, i.e. will become over time the latter object, then its properties at the earlier time were the very same as they will be at the later time. To repeat, this second principle is false; an object need not retain all its properties unchanged in order to remain the 'same thing'.

11.4 Parts and properties revisited

One theory which suggests itself to many persons is that what iden-

---

3. Throughout the rest of this chapter, "properties" will be understood as "monadic properties" and "qualitative identity" will be understood as "sharing all monadic properties in common".

tifies O_2 at T_2 with O_1 at T_1 is that all, or nearly all, of the *parts* of O_2 should be parts that had been those of O_1, i.e. that what identifies physical objects is the identity of their parts. Certain sorts of physical objects – e.g. a person's library, or wardrobe (understood as being the clothes a person owns, not the closet in which they are stored), or an heirloom set of dishes – in general the sorts of things which are known as 'assemblages' ([165], 65-6), do seem to be identified by their parts.[4]

But most physical objects are not assemblages and are not identified by their parts. For most physical objects, the gradual replacement of their parts with fairly similar parts – just like a gradual and relatively minor change in their properties – is compatible with their 'remaining the same thing'. The red car garaged in my carport is the car I bought eight years ago even though in the interim it has had the bulb in the left taillight replaced at least a dozen times,[5] has worn out two sets of tires, has had its brakes and exhaust system replaced, etc. And yet, for all that, it remains the same car, and would remain so even if the replacements had been more extensive, e.g. if the engine had been replaced, all four fenders, both bumpers, the seats, the axle, the igni-

---

4. Some authors prefer the term "clusters", "ensembles", or "mereological sums". I, myself, earlier used the term "scattered objects" (p. 195). See also footnote 18, p. 265, and p. 267.

If one replaces each of the books of my library with a totally different book – e.g. my copy of Copi's *Symbolic Logic* with a copy of Flaubert's *Madame Bovary*, etc. – then the resulting assemblage cannot be regarded as being identical with my original library. But some, relatively few, assemblages can withstand replacement of all their parts and still remain the 'same' assemblage. For example, the United States' Navy might, one by one, replace each of the ships in the Seventh Fleet, and the resulting assemblage of ships could, reasonably, or at least arguably, be regarded as being one and the same as the original Seventh Fleet. And we do sometimes talk this way: "The Philadelphia Orchestra under Muti maintains the lustrous string sheen it had three generations ago under Stokowski." Here, the suggestion is that it is the same orchestra even if, as is probably true, there has been a total change in personnel in the intervening sixty-year period. Although it is useful to bear such examples in mind, one must not regard them as definitive or as uncontroversial, however.

5. Why the left rear bulb, but not the right one, keeps burning out, regardless of the manufacture of the replacement bulb, has defied explanation by anyone whom I have consulted. Alas.

tion system, the fuel system, the cooling system, etc. There is no part, or any number of parts, whose continued presence is essential to the car's remaining the same car. (Whether *every* part can be replaced in a thing, and still have the resulting thing remain the same as the original, is a question we postpone until subsection 11.6.3 below.)

But the objection to making the parts of things their identifiers does not rest wholly, or even principally, on the fact that most things are not identified by their parts. The difficulty is more fundamental.

The theory that the parts of a thing are its identifier – even for the case of assemblages – cannot be the primary account of identity-through-time but must remain derivative, or parasitic, upon a more basic theory. For the *parts* of physical objects (recall the discussion on p. 261) are themselves physical objects. To identify a thing by the identity of its parts requires that those parts be themselves identifiable. If parts were identifiable by *their* parts, and so on, we would have an infinite regress. Eventually, identification by parts must come to an end and we must take recourse to some other, more basic, identifier.

11.5   Positive theories: Substance as identifier

Physical objects endure: some for relatively short times, e.g. ice sculptures; others for much longer times, e.g. mountains and planets. But whether they endure briefly or for long, most physical objects undergo change during their existence. They grow and then decay (or are eaten) if they are alive; they tarnish, have parts replaced, and are painted, bent, folded, or spindled, etc., if they are inanimate. Sometimes the changes things undergo are so drastic as to warrant our saying that one thing has ceased to exist and another has come into being, as for example when we sell the family silver serving pieces and allow them to be converted into a photographic emulsion. The (atoms of) silver may endure through such a radical transformation; but the teapot and sugar bowl are gone out of existence, and a new physical object, a photographic transparency, subsequently comes into existence. The material (silver) – or to use an old-fashioned word, the "stuff" – has endured, but the original physical objects whose material it was have not.

During its 'lifetime' (the period of its existence), the silver teapot underwent a number of changes. It tarnished constantly and was cleaned monthly. In each of those polishings, it lost a thin layer of silver. Over time, the teapot became successively more scratched. At one point, its spout sprang a leak and had to be resoldered. And five years before it was sold, it had been engraved with its owner's insurance number to aid in recovery if it were stolen. And yet, throughout this series of successive and numerous changes, one could reckon it the 'same' teapot. The teapot endured.

There is in any such account something that strikes many persons as paradoxical, if not outrightly inconsistent. The very thing which is alleged to have remained the same, i.e. to have endured, is also alleged to have changed. To resolve the conceptual tension, some persons have constructed positive theories which would attribute to enduring physical objects two 'aspects': a deep, or hidden, unchanging permanent 'substance', and an outward, variable set of properties. In such theories, the 'substance' of a physical object is what endures, i.e. persists unchanged through time; what changes are the properties grounded in that substance.

Just as substance has been proposed as the individuator (see section 10.3, p. 279, and section 10.5, p. 281), substance has been sometimes proposed as the *identifier*, i.e. as that 'thing' which confers identity on an enduring object.

The many roles often assigned to substance are logically distinct. Even if one were to promote a concept of substance as the solution to the problem of individuation, one would have to argue further for a (perhaps) different concept of substance, or at least for an expanded role for substance, to assert that a thing's substance was what conferred its identity-through-time. Substance, understood as being the 'individuator', need not, it is clear, endure through time. Thus positive theorists might be inclined to supplement their initial account, arguing that not only is it the nature of substance to 'take up space' (i.e. to be extended in space), it is also the nature of substance to 'take up time' (i.e. to be extended in time).

But whatever objections there were to positing substance as individuator are paralleled, and indeed even multiplied, in positing substance as identifier. The most obvious problem recalls an earlier objection leveled against substance as individuator: positing substance as identifier does nothing whatsoever to solve the epistemological problem of the re-identification of physical objects. We often have no difficulty whatsoever in re-identifying many familiar objects. I recognize immediately the wristwatch sitting on my desk as being the very same wristwatch I placed on the desk an hour ago. And yet I make the re-identification without being in the slightest aware of the enduring substance of the watch. Indeed, I could not possibly *be* aware of that substance, if by 'substance' one means 'that constituent of the watch which endures unchanged through all incidental changes the watch undergoes'. Certainly no such 'unchanging thing' is given to me perceptually when I examine the watch.

But there is another problem as well, having to do not with the epistemological side of the problem, but with the metaphysical. I must confess to not understanding fully what the substance of a physical thing is supposed to be. But whatever it is, it would seem to be something which is spatially coextensive with the object, i.e. is at all places where the object is. But if so, what happens when a physical part of the object is removed from it? Suppose you own a piano and remove one string. Presumably the substance of the piano has been marginally diminished. But suppose you now replace that string with one qualitatively identical to the one removed. The piano with the new string is still the same *piano* as the one before the swap. (Remember, the goal is to explicate our workaday notion of identity, not a 'strict', artificial notion.) But is the substance of the piano as it exists after the swap the very same substance as that of the piano prior to the exchange of strings? If it is, then it would seem that the substance of the new string has become part of the substance of the piano. This smacks of mysticism. But if we do not claim that the substance of the piano has at first decreased and then increased and indeed latterly been restored, then – according to the theory of substance as individuator – the identity of the piano has been lost: this latest piano cannot be identified, because their substances differ, with the earlier piano. In short, the very concept of substance itself precipitates the very problem it was invoked to solve. For now we should have to have a theory as to how much change a substance might undergo to be deemed to have remained the 'same' substance.

In foisting the solution of the problem of identity off onto substance, the metaphysical problem has become aggravated, and the epistemological problem has become insolvable. Clearly, a negative theory is to be vastly preferred.

11.6 Negative theories: Identity without enduring substance

Negative theorists will dispense with such unempirical entities as substance. They will attempt to explicate identity-through-time by means of certain *relations* obtaining between entities existing at successive moments of time. Recall (from section 8.7, pp. 186ff.) the argument that physical objects ought to be conceived as being extended not only in space but in time as well. The task of the negative theorist then becomes one of trying to explain how identity is preserved as things change over time.

11.6.1 Space-time paths

The fundamental concept in the negative theorists' arsenal in their attack on the problem of identity is that of a *space-time path*. Consider a physical object at rest with respect to its surroundings and undergoing no changes in properties or parts. That is, it is simply 'growing older', and nothing more. Its path through both space and time, its so-called space-time path, is a 'straight line': it is, so to speak, moving straight along the 'time-axis' (see figure 11.1.A, p. 339). But now suppose this object were to rotate about some fixed point. A coin placed on the edge of a rotating disk will do as a example. The coin starts out at a certain place, P_1, at a certain time, T_1, moves away from that place so that at T_2 it is at P_2, and eventually returns to its original place, P_1, but at a still later time, T_3. It then moves away again, and still later returns yet again, and continues to alternate in this manner a great number of times (figure 11.1.B). If, however, we trace the path of the coin on the edge of the rotating disk, not through time alone, where it follows a straight line, and not through space alone, where it follows a circular path, but through space and time together, we discover that it follows a corkscrew (or helical) path (figure 11.1.C). And if someone were to trace your own path, as you move about in space over the course of a day, we would discover that your path through space-time was neither a straight line, nor a smooth corkscrew, but a jagged zigzag of connected segments of unequal lengths and a variety of directions.

We can abstract from the notion of the actual space-time paths of actual objects to a generalized notion of a space-time path itself, independent of whether or not anything happens to follow that particular path. Just as there are an infinite number of paths through space connecting any two spatial points,[6] there are an infinite number of space-time paths connecting any two positions in both space and time. There are, for example, in principle an infinite number of paths through

---

6. The points need not be distinct. There are an infinite number of different spatial paths connecting any point with itself. For example, if you were to set out upon a walk, there are in principle an infinite number of different spatial paths you could follow to return you to your initial point of departure.

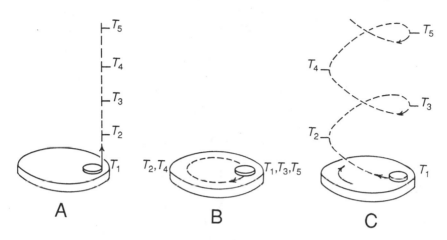

Figure 11.1

space and time which an object might follow to 'get itself' from the center of London on 11 July 1888 to the dark side of the moon on 18 June 2056.

There are a (nondenumerable) infinity of space-time paths. And just as most points of space are devoid of physical objects (see pp. 293-4), most space-time paths are not followed.[7] For a path to be occupied means that some physical object, having at least some finite duration in time, follows that path. But of course finding that a space-time path is occupied (or followed) does not mean that some one physical object has endured along that path. A path will be said to be occupied whether one object has followed that path, or whether a succession of different objects has followed that path. For example, a single object, a pumpkin, might follow some space-time path. But it is possible for two or more numerically distinct objects to occupy successive parts of one path. A pumpkin, for example, might miraculously be replaced by a horse-drawn coach. Thus, to explicate the concept of identity-through-time, we will need the concept of an occupied space-time

---

7. Indeed the actual number of occupied, or followed, space-time paths in the universe is not even a finite fraction of the nondenumerably infinite number of potential paths.

path, but we will need considerably more as well. We will need additional distinctions so as to be able to account for the difference between one thing persisting over time and a succession of things replacing one another over time.

For a negative theorist, then, a theorist who eschews substance as identifier, the task becomes one of specifying what sorts of features one must look for in an occupied space-time path to warrant our saying that that path constitutes the history of a single object rather than the history of a succession of different objects. In short, we must look to see what confers unity on one occupied space-time path and diversity on some other.

One might begin by thinking that to explicate the notion of a physical object evolving through time and preserving its identity, we need require only that for each point along some space-time path there must be a bundle of properties which is qualitatively identical to the bundle of properties found at every other point along that path. Stating this rather more formally, we might put it this way:

CRITERION 1: O_2 at (P_2, T_2) is (numerically) identical to O_1 at (P_1, T_1) if and only if there exists some space-time path connecting (P_2, T_2) with (P_1, T_1) such that for every point, P_i and T_i, along this path (including P_2 and T_2) there exists an object, O_i, which is qualitatively identical to O_1.

This first criterion is, obviously, too strong: it precludes change. Our ordinary notion of identity-through-time does *not* require that the later stage of an object be qualitatively identical to its earlier stages. We must find some way to weaken this initial formulation.

Before we try, however, there is an important point to be made about the very nature of this particular manner of proceeding which the negative theorist has adopted. Notice how radically the approach of the negative theorist differs from that of the positive theorist. The positive theorist looks for something permanent 'in' the very objects themselves to account for identity-through-time. The negative theorist instead looks not 'within' objects to account for their enduring through time, but looks along a space-time path for certain kinds of features, for a succession of 'stages' as it were, bearing certain sorts of relationships to one another. And yet this is not to have replaced the concept of a single object with the concept of an infinite series of instantaneous objects. Although we have written of "O_i existing at P_i and T_i", where "i" is understood to range over all the infinity of real numbers between those assigned to the starting and end points [i.e. lying between (P_1, T_1) and (P_2, T_2)], we need not be thought to be describing an infinitude of numerically distinct objects. Recall that it is an implicit understanding, in our use of variables, that different variables may refer to one and the same thing. Although the *symbol* "$O_{0.24721}$" may be distinct from "$O_{0.3119872}$", it remains an open question whether the two objects *referred to* by these symbols are numerically identical or distinct. They will be numerically identical – according to the negative theory – if they stand in certain important relations to one another; otherwise they will be numerically distinct. One of the necessary relations is that these objects occur along the same occupied space-time path. But considerably more is needed besides. What that 'something more' might be, we turn to next.

11.6.2 Identity-preserving relations

Since qualitative identity is too strong a relationship to insist upon in our attempt to explicate *identity-through-time*, we might try a weaker relationship, that of *qualitative similarity*:

O_1 and O_2 will be said to be 'qualitatively similar' if and only if

either O_1 and O_2 are qualitatively identical,

or O_1 and O_2 differ only very slightly in their respective (monadic) properties,

or   virtually all of the parts of O_1 are numerically identical with parts of O_2 (and conversely).[8]

With the concept of *qualitative similarity* in hand, we might try to substitute it for *qualitative identity* in our first criterion. Intuitively, the revised account would be to the effect that at each stage (P_i, T_i) along a space-time path connecting the earlier object, O_1, with the later object, O_2, there is an object, O_i, which is *qualitatively similar* to its immediate predecessor (and successor). But this intuitive notion immediately encounters a certain mathematical difficulty.

Although some physicists have occasionally speculated otherwise (see e.g. [211], section 4.5), to the best of our knowledge, time is infinitely divisible; it is, in the terminology of mathematics, continu-

---

8. Remember, identification by parts is dependent upon identification by properties. If O_2 is identified with O_1 in virtue of their parts being identified, then those parts, in turn, must at some point be identified by appeal to their differing not at all, or only slightly, *in their properties* from earlier parts.

ous. This means that for any moment (or instant) of time that one may choose, there is no such thing as the 'immediately preceding' moment or the 'immediately following' moment, since between any two moments there are an infinity of other moments. *Immediate predecessor* and *immediate successor* are concepts applicable only to discrete orderings, not to continuous ones. In cases where it is improper to speak of immediate predecessor and immediate successor, mathematicians take recourse to the concept of *neighborhood*. Roughly (very roughly), we may conceive of the 'neighborhood' of a point as being other points (along the space-time path) which are 'close to that point'.[9] Thus, using the concept of *neighborhood*, we might try the following account of identity-through-time:

> CRITERION 2: O_2 at (P_2, T_2) is (numerically) identical with O_1 at (P_1, T_1) if and only if there exists some space-time path connecting (P_2, T_2) with (P_1, T_1) such that for every point, (P_i, T_i), along this path (including P_2 and T_2) there exists an object, O_i, which is qualitatively similar to every object in the neighborhood of (P_i, T_i).

Unfortunately, this latest repair does not quite work. Where the earlier version – in terms of qualitative identity – was too strong, this later version is too weak.

The trouble is that as we trace the successive objects occupying the path from (P_1, T_1) to (P_2, T_2), we may find that although stages close together in time may be only slightly qualitatively different, these differences may accumulate over long time intervals so as to constitute

---

9. Smith and Albrecht provide the following rigorous definition of "neighborhood": "Let M be any set. We say that d is a *distance function* or *metric* with respect to M if and only if for every two elements p and q of M there is associated a real number $d(p, q)$, called the distance from p to q, satisfying the following properties:
1. $d(p, q) \geq 0$
2. $d(p, q) = 0$ if and only if $p = q$
3. $d(p, q) = d(q, p)$
4. $d(p, q) + d(q, r) \geq d(p, r)$ for all p, q, and r in M.
Let (M, d) be any metric set. Let p be a fixed point in M, and let ε be any positive real number. We define a *neighborhood* $N(p, \varepsilon)$ of p, with radius ε as follows: $N(p, \varepsilon) = \{q \mid q \in M$ and $d(p, q) < \varepsilon\}$" ([194], 58 and 60).
    For our purposes above, we choose a value of ε which is small relative to the 'distance' between (P_1, T_1) and (P_2, T_2), i.e. $\varepsilon \ll d((P_1, T_1), (P_2, T_2))$.

wholesale changes between the endpoints. For example, a paper-punch may gradually, over time, be converted into a writing pen. Although 'nearby' stages of the evolving object may be considered to be stages of thc 'same' thing, the last point cannot be deemed to be numerically identical with the first.[10] Qualitative identity is too strong a relation to require for identity-through-time; qualitative similarity, by itself, is too weak. We shall have to add a further restriction to qualitative similarity.

The counterexample just cited suggests what sort of further restriction is called for. We should want to require not only qualitative similarity, but that at each stage along the path, the object O_i should be the *same type* of object as those in its neighborhood. It is not enough just to demand that the objects at the endpoints, O_1 and O_2, be of the same type, for that condition would be satisfied by a paper-punch being transformed into a writing pen, the pen into a bracelet, the bracelet into a scalpel, and the scalpel into a paper-punch. Although the material (or stuff) of the original paper-punch would have been preserved through all these many changes, it seems incorrect to claim that the later paper-punch is *the very same punch* as initiated the series of transformations. For a later punch to be identified with an earlier punch, it seems entirely reasonable – and consistent with our ordinary notion of identity – to require that the two be joined by a series of intermediate stages all of which are themselves paper-punches. Through a series of successive approximations, we arrive at our third, and final, attempt at formulating a criterion of identity-through-time:

> CRITERION 3: O_2 at (P_2, T_2) is (numerically) identical with O_1 at (P_1, T_1) if and only if there exists some space-time path connecting (P_2, T_2) with (P_1, T_1) such that for every point, (P_i, T_i), along this path (including P_2 and T_2) there exists an object, O_i, which is qualitatively similar to each of the objects in the neighborhood of (P_i, T_i) and which is the same type of thing [tree, wristwatch, piano, leg, etc.] as O_1.

For convenience, we will hereinafter call this last criterion "the strengthened criterion of spatiotemporal continuity". It is understood to require qualitative similarity as well as identity of kind (i.e. of type or of sort).

---

10. In technical vocabulary, the relation of 'qualitative similarity' is said to be nontransitive.

344   *Beyond Experience*

There is an important consequence implicit in our adopting the strengthened criterion of spatiotemporal continuity. On such an explication, there simply does not exist a *general* account of identity-through-time for a 'thing' which is unqualified as to kind. We can, that is, give an account of the conditions under which a car, or a hammer, or a book is to be regarded as preserving its identity-through-time, but we will not be able to give an account – because none is possible – of the conditions under which a 'thing', in general, i.e. of unspecified type, is to be regarded as preserving its identity-through-time.[11]

Let us now examine this strengthened criterion of spatiotemporal continuity by applying it to two case studies.

11.6.3 Case study: The ship of Theseus

In legend, Theseus killed the Minotaur; in historical fact, he did not of course: the Minotaur is mythical. Whether Theseus himself is cut from the fabric of sheer myth or was a genuine historical character is quite another matter. Modern scholarship has not been able to settle this question ([210]), although it has identified the historical elements in the legend as occurring in the Bronze Age. Thus when Plutarch (c. 46-120 AD) wrote a biography of Theseus, it would have been at least a thousand years later, ample time for the story to have been considerably altered and embellished.

––––––––––––––––

11. Marjorie Price dissents from this latter claim, arguing that she can adduce examples where we would want to say that some 'thing' had persisted through time, but where we would be unable to classify that 'thing' further. Her principal example is this: "To determine the effects of the Martian atmosphere on higher animals, NASA sends Rover [a terrier] to Mars. After a successful landing and take-off, Rover returns to Earth, where he is continuously observed for six months. Film cameras record every moment of his existence. During this time, Rover undergoes a gradual change, so that by the end of the isolation period he is an amorphous mass of cells. Even the chromosomal constitution of his cells has changed: its nature is not identifiable as the sort to be found in members of any known organism ... No one can deny that the entity in the isolation unit at the end of the interval in question, call it 'Clover,' is Rover. ... Yet we cannot justifiably classify Clover as a dog. For the only biologically significant property Clover shares with any dog that ever lived is the property of being composed of cells" ([160], 203).

Price argues in this possible-worlds tale (1) that identity has been preserved (i.e. Clover is Rover); (2) that Rover was a dog, Clover is not; and

Theseus's father was Aegeus, king of Athens. When Theseus was about to set sail from Athens to seek and to try to slay the fearsome Minotaur, he promised his father that on his ship's return, if he had been successful, the black sails would be replaced with white ones stowed on board. But on returning to Athens, Theseus forgot his promise and, although he had slain the Minotaur, did not change the sails. His father, sighting the ship and seeing the black sails, believed his son had perished at the hands of the Minotaur and in his grief hurled himself from a cliff to his death. Theseus, thus, ascended the throne.

But at this point in his chronicle, Plutarch pauses for a brief moment. He postpones his recounting of Theseus's subsequent exploits just long enough to tell us something quite curious about the fateful black-sailed ship: "The ship on which Theseus sailed with the youths

---

(3) that in this identification all that is preserved is thinghood, i.e. that there is no *sort* of thing which Rover was (e.g. a dog or a terrier, etc.) and which Clover is. In short, thinghood itself is preserved, but no specific kind of thing.

I am sure that many readers will not share Price's own strong intuitions and convictions about the case she has constructed. I certainly do not. When she writes, "No one can deny that the entity in the isolation unit at the end of the interval in question ... is Rover", I will protest. For my own reaction is that this entity – whatever it is – is *not* Rover: Rover has at some point in the six-month interval ceased to exist and has been replaced (sorrowfully) by this amorphous mass. Moreover, I think that a reluctance to subscribe to Price's intuitions can be explained. Were one to allow such an example, then it would seem that *any change* whatsoever, just so long as material 'stuff' endures, would qualify as a preservation of 'identity'. Such a liberalized concept of identity errs in much the same way as the earlier, overly restrictive concept of 'strict' identity (section 11.2), viz. it does violence to our pre-analytic concept which allows for some, but not too drastic, change in a thing for identity to be preserved.

But there is more wrong with Price's arguments than the fact that she has overestimated the degree to which her own intuitions will be shared. There is a more central issue in the debate, and I believe that she is mistaken about it as well. If someone were to argue that the later, amorphous mass, although not a dog or more specifically a terrier, is to be identified, as Price says, with Rover, then that – by itself – is not sufficient to establish that identity-through-time is possible for 'things' which are unqualified as to kind. For Price to argue this latter point, she must show that there is no *sort* of thing which has been preserved through this remarkable transformation. But one could argue that there is. Indeed Price, herself, characterizes this later 'thing'

and returned in safety, the thirty-oared galley, was preserved by the Athenians down to the time of Demetrius Phalereus [c. 310 BC]. They took away the old timbers from time to time, and put new and sound ones in their places, so that the vessel became a standing illustration for philosophers in the mooted question of growth, some declaring that it remained the same, others that it was not the same vessel" ([157], *Theseus*, XXIII.1). Where Plutarch reports that the philosophers' disputes concerned 'growth', we would today understand that it was identity-through-time which was at issue (see [189]).

Anyone who adopts the strengthened criterion of spatiotemporal continuity is in a position to give a determinate, and reasoned, answer

---

as a "mass of *cells*" (my italics). We might want to add that it is living tissue. Although this later mass is not a dog, it does have a spatiotemporal identity with the original *tissues* of Rover. To be sure, we have no *term* (in English) for this sort of thing (and this is no surprise since what Price is presenting is merely a possible-worlds tale and does not describe anything actually existent). But the lack of a descriptive word does not imply that there is no determinate sort of thing being described. There is a (hinted-at) sort of thing in Price's example: Clover is living; Clover is cellular; Clover has a biological unity; Clover (presumably) exchanges gases with its environment; Clover (presumably) requires energy for its survival; etc. What Clover lacks is a biological classification.

If Clover were not a fiction but an actual existent and if biologists were to find their intuitions pulling them in the direction of wanting to say that identity had been preserved in this kind of transformation (and that is an important "if"), then they well might want to fill the gap in taxonomy by inventing a new term for designating the sort of thing which both Rover and Clover are. Price seems to have confused there not being a name for what sort of thing both Rover and Clover might be with their not both being of any particular sort whatever. But it is difficult to conceive of there being two physical objects which did not share something more in common than the bare fact that they are both physical things. That Clover is not a dog does not prove that Clover is not some sort of thing, α, which Rover also was, and that what has been preserved in the transformation is a thing of the sort α. Price has not shown that Rover and Clover are not both α, and indeed, I believe that it is impossible to show it.

I have never seen a plausible case where we would want to say that identity had been preserved and were also prepared to assert that no particular sort of thing had been preserved. There is, and can be, no criterion of 'bare' or 'unqualified' identity-through-time. Identity-through-time is always identity of some determinate sort: of a hammer, of a dog, of a human body, etc.

to the puzzle. The ship, with its replaced timbers, *is* the ship of Theseus. There is an unbroken spatiotemporal path connecting the later, repaired, thirty-oared galley with the original ship. At each point along that path there is a *ship* (or, more exactly, a ship-stage) which is *very like* the ships (ship-stages) which are to be found on neighboring (i.e. close-by) points on that same path. We can trace the evolution of the ship through time as timbers are occasionally replaced. But it remains the same ship. (Its changes may be likened to those of the human body where parts [cells] are constantly being replaced, and yet where identity is preserved.)

Two millennia after the debate reported by Plutarch, when the problem – which has come to be known simply as 'the ship of Theseus' – was recounted by Thomas Hobbes (1588-1679), we find that a new complicating wrinkle has been introduced. (William Molesworth's translation, dating from 1839, is deplorable. I will paraphrase it.)

> If the ship of Theseus were continually repaired by the replacing of all the old planks with new, then – according to the Athenian philosophers – the later ship would be numerically identical with the original. But if some man had kept the old planks as they were taken out and were to assemble a ship of them, then this ship [containing all the original parts of the earlier ship] would, also, without doubt be numerically identical with that original. And so there would be *two* ships, existing at the same time, [in different places,] both of which would be numerically identical with the original. But this latter verdict is absurd. ([97], part II, chap. 11, §7)

What we find in Hobbes's version is the head-on conflict of two *reasonable* theories of identity-through-time. There are good reasons (as I have just rehearsed) for arguing that the ship with the new parts is numerically identical with the original, earlier, ship: it has an unbroken spatiotemporal continuity with that ship. But there are also good reasons for arguing that the ship assembled out of all the discarded parts is numerically identical with the original: its timbers are several hundred years old; it 'looks like' an ancient sea-worn ship; and its parts were present in the original ship. Which one, then, of these latter ships *is* Theseus's ship? (We will assume that at least one of them is.)

It is important not to believe that the resolution of this puzzle depends on some objective truth, some fact which is there to be discovered in the way, for example, one might put to an empirical test the question whether today's ship is larger than some other or whether it is painted blue. Hobbes's puzzle is not at all amenable to empirical resolution. For our purposes, all the relevant empirical data are in hand. The question is: "What are we to make of these data?" Ought we to believe that the ship with the new parts is the original? Or ought we to believe that the ship with the old parts is the original? We must choose between two competing – both prima facie plausible – theories. These theories, since they yield conflicting answers, cannot both be regarded as 'right'. But where theories collide and appeal to empirical data is precluded, how is it possible rationally to choose? The decision must rest on *weighing* the merits and demerits of each theory.

For my own part, I am convinced that it is the ship with the spanking new parts, the seaworthy one, not the one recently assembled out of the original parts, which warrants being regarded as the one which is numerically identical to, i.e. is a temporally later stage of, the ship Theseus sailed. A variety of factors inform my choice.

First of all is the fact that the strengthened criterion of spatiotemporal continuity is *more fundamental* than the criterion of sameness of parts insofar as the latter criterion presupposes the former and not conversely. To identify a thing by its parts requires that the parts, at some point or other, be identified by their being spatiotemporally continuous with earlier parts. Other things being equal, the criterion of spatiotemporal continuity takes precedence over the criterion of identification by parts.

But *are* 'other things' equal in this case? If the discarded parts had not been assembled into a ship, then, doubtless, most persons would be willing to allow that the ship with the replaced parts is identical with the original. But the case is not that simple. The discarded parts have been collected and assembled into a ship, and insofar as they have been, might that ship not be a viable contender for the title of 'ship of Theseus', and indeed, might that ship not have the stronger claim?

My own reply is to liken the ship assembled from the discarded parts to a cousin laying claim to an inheritance when the deceased has left no will. The cousin is the rightful heir if among the surviving relatives he is the closest in kinship. But let a son or a daughter be factored into the equation and that child then has a stronger claim than the cousin.

This is not to say, however, that the claim supported by the criterion of spatiotemporal continuity is absolute or inviolable. Such claims are regularly superseded, for example, in the case of assemblages (p. 334). In technical terminology, the priority of the claim sanctioned by the strengthened criterion of spatiotemporal continuity is 'defeasible', i.e. it can be overridden by other, confounding, factors. Might ships, then, be assemblages? Might they be things which we standardly identify by their parts rather than by spatiotemporal continuity?

We are certainly not normally inclined to believe so. We standardly treat ships much as we do cars, lawn mowers, radios, etc.: we regard them as preserving their identity even as parts are occasionally changed. But still there lurks the specter of the ship assembled from the discarded parts, with its ancient timbers and leaky hull, faintly calling out for acknowledgment as being the rightful heir to the title 'ship of Theseus'.

There can be no verdict in this case which will prove satisfying to every disputant. Persons' intuitions are bound to differ. But there is one further factor which may help to sway some persons toward the claim made on behalf of the repaired ship with its new timbers. Hobbes introduced the wrinkle of having someone collect, and then assemble, the discarded parts. I will introduce a further, final, wrinkle: suppose there were a first mate who lived on board the ship of Theseus and never left it. (He suffers, we may suppose, a debilitating case of terraphobia.)

Matey (as he's called) learns that someone has collected the discarded planks from the ship of Theseus and has assembled them into a ship. Matey is totally uninterested. But then Matey learns that this impertinent scavenger is claiming that the assembled ship *is* the ship of Theseus. Matey is enraged. "That's preposterous", he bellows. "That ship is miles inland. The ship of Theseus has never left the water since the day it was launched. I, myself, have never been off this ship since that day. Since I've never left the ship of Theseus, and since I am here on board *this* ship, not the one in dry dock, that ship cannot possibly be the ship of Theseus."

Who is correct? Were the dispute to end in court, and were I to be on the jury, I would vote for the ship under Matey's feet and not the one assembled inland of the original timbers. Although Theseus himself may never have trod the actual planks of the repaired ship, he did tread its decks, he slept in the captain's stateroom (although never on the present mattress [straw?]), and he took his meals in the galley, although of course not on the wood of the present table. My verdict: the repaired ship *is* the ship of Theseus even though its *parts* may not have been present in that earlier ship. The ship assembled from the discarded parts of the original is a curiosity, but it is not the historical ship of Theseus. Although its parts are ancient, its history *as a ship* goes back only a few months: it cannot, then, be the ship of Theseus.

Someone might protest, invoking the example of London Bridge. The latter, we know, was disassembled and its parts were carefully numbered, catalogued, and shipped to Arizona. There the parts were reassembled into a bridge standing in the desert at Lake Havasu City. Is this latter structure London Bridge? Certainly. But if so, then how is this case different from collecting the parts discarded from the ship of Theseus and assembling a ship out of those parts? If the structure in Arizona is London Bridge, why is not the recently assembled ship to be regarded as being the ship of Theseus?

Again, the analogy with the case of the inheritance of property is apt: the cousin will inherit just so long as a son or daughter does not lay claim. Identity of parts will prevail as the identifier just so long as nothing lays claim to being the spatiotemporal successor of the original. If the ship of Theseus had been disassembled and its parts labeled and catalogued, moved inland, and there reassembled into a ship, then that ship would be the ship of Theseus. But that is not what happened. The original ship was never disassembled. The original ship stayed afloat. The all-important difference is that between *replacement* and *disassembly*. In cases of replacement, the criterion of spatiotemporal continuity is paramount. In cases of disassembly and subsequent reassembly, we fall back upon identification by parts.

It may seem to you bizarre to explicate the concept of identity-through-time by taking recourse to analogies pertaining to inheritance and the like. You may tend to think of identity as a metaphysical notion totally removed from the conventions of a legal system and of human practices. You may, for example, conceive of the relation of *identity-through-time* as being more like the relation of *being heavier than* than like the relation of *being before x in line to succeed to the Crown*. One may, that is, believe that the criteria for identity-through-time should be something wholly objective, free from any taint of conventionality.

The *core* of the concept of identity-through-time is, in fact, fairly free of conventional trappings. The strengthened criterion of spatiotemporal continuity invokes such concepts as *space-time path* and *neighborhood* (in its mathematical sense, not demographic). But even in the core concept, a bit of convention may be seen to be creeping in: *qualitative similarity* is not a precise notion. There is an unavoidable element of conventionality in our determining what are to count as being similar, but not exactly alike, in their properties; or what is to count as comprising 'most' of the parts of a thing.

But the strengthened criterion of spatiotemporal continuity comprises merely a *necessary* condition (and a defeasible one at that) for identity-through-time. In actual cases it must be supplemented with a variety of other conditions. Another example will help to illuminate the nature of these further conditions.

11.6.4 Case study: Mitosis

Hobbes's version of the problem of the ship of Theseus provides an example where two different criteria of identity-through-time – the strengthened criterion of spatiotemporal continuity and the criterion of identity of parts – yield conflicting results. The prospect of mitosis (fission), however, provides an example where the fundamental criterion of identity itself – viz. the strengthened criterion of spatiotemporal continuity – might be thought on occasion to yield conflicting, or at least profoundly problematic, results.

Every space-time path has an infinite number of possible (or potential) branch points. In this (the actual) world, physical objects as they follow a space-time path, at arriving at each branch point, pursue one branch to the exclusion of the other possible ones. (Just as a person arriving at a fork in a road may follow one fork but not both.) Of course this fact that physical objects do not split (like the 'coupleton' chairs described earlier [see pp. 301ff.]) is just a contingent fact about this world; it is no necessary truth, which means of course that there are possible worlds where objects do split, i.e. sometimes do follow *both* branches at a junction point along a space-time path.

Amoebae might be thought to constitute a counterexample to the normal behavior of inanimate objects. I remember my biology teacher in high school explaining that amoebae reproduce asexually, by splitting (i.e. by mitosis). He then went on to add the astounding claim that every amoeba alive today "thus was alive twenty million years ago". In other words, my high-school biology teacher subscribed to the theory that when an amoeba splits, each offspring is identifiable with the original, single, amoeba which existed prior to the split.

There is a considerable conceptual difficulty inherent in this notion.[12] Suppose the original amoeba and its two offspring were to be

---

12. We will ignore the fact that each offspring at first has only half the mass

given names: "*a*", "*b*", and "*c*" respectively. If *b* were to be identified with *a* and if *c* were to be identified with *a*, then *b* and *c* would, although in different places, paradoxically be the selfsame thing. (We are here invoking the principle which bears the name 'the Euclidean Axiom', viz. that if *y* is identical to *x* and if *z* is identical to *x*, then *y* and *z* are identical to one another; or, as it is sometimes expressed, 'any two things identical to a third are identical to one another'.) Such a case is radically different from the case, e.g., of the Mississippi River's being in two places at one time, or of a time traveler's being in two different places at the same time. In the case of the Mississippi River, as we have seen, what is involved is two different *spatial parts* of the river existing in different places at one time. In the case of a time traveler what is involved is two different *temporal stages* of one and the same person existing at different places at the same time (i.e. the space-time path curves back upon itself). But the case of the amoebae, *b* and *c*, is different. The two exist simultaneously at different places; they are each 'complete' amoebae (i.e. they are not spatial *parts* of a larger organism or of a scattered object); and neither one is a later temporal stage of the other come back in time.

How might we handle such a case? Although there is nothing compelling us to treat it this way, we standardly regard the case of mitosis as the annihilation of the 'parent' organism and the 'creation' (or 'birth') of two offspring. Contrary to the claim of my biology instructor, we do not treat the offspring as identical with the parent. Amoebae alive today were not alive twenty million years ago: their ancestors, of several million generations previously, were alive then; but no amoeba living today was alive then. What this amounts to is modifying the strengthened criterion of spatiotemporal continuity: we will invoke that criterion only for space-time paths where there is no actual branching. An actual branch-point will be taken to mark the end of the existence of one thing, and the creation in its place of two successors. But neither successor will have a claim to being identical with the single 'ancestor' prior to the branching.

But if this is the standard manner of handling such cases, *must* we handle them this way? What if not only amoebae, but tables, chairs, human bodies, etc., were to undergo mitosis? And what if the physical laws of the world were different, so that, for example, objects emerg-

---

and half the volume of the parent. While true, this is not particularly relevant for the points below.

ing from such a splitting were not half the mass and half the volume of their 'parents' but were qualitatively identical to their parents? How might we handle cases of desks, or chairs, etc. suddenly being replaced by pairs of desks, chairs, etc.? *Could* there be a concept of *identity-through-time* in such a world?

It would be foolhardy to venture an answer with much insistence. We can have only very tentative grounds on which to predict how we might choose to conceptualize cases which depart so radically from the ordinary. What is important in broaching such cases is not so much anticipating their resolutions, but becoming aware of the extensive penumbra of conditions obtaining in our ordinary use of the concept of identity-through-time.

The criterion we have latterly adduced (p. 343) – viz. that identity-through-time requires (i) qualitative similarity along a space-time path and (ii) identity of kind – is well suited for the peculiarities of this particular world. But it is not a criterion which would be satisfactory for any possible set of circumstances whatever. It is, rather, tailor-made by us for this world, a world in which mitosis is nonexistent (or at least a relative rarity) for ordinary physical objects.

The problem posed by the prospect of widespread mitosis is not just metaphysical or epistemological. It dovetails importantly with an extensive network of concepts drawn from as far afield as ethics, the law, and economics. For the concept of identity interplays in intimate fashion with questions of ownership and of responsibility and liability. How is ownership to be ascertained? responsibility for damage? If a person owns a boat which spontaneously splits into two boats, would he have a right to claim ownership of both? We can imagine a possible world where the very suggestion would be regarded as outrageous; where it would be 'obvious' that he was morally obliged to choose one and the other would become public property. And what of the person who had damaged the original boat, and failed to repair it before it split into two qualitatively identical (damaged) boats? Would he be responsible for repairing the pair of later boats? We cannot predict how we might handle such an eventuality. Much might depend on how frequently objects split, whether their splitting was foreseeable or not, etc.[13]

---

13. The possible-worlds case of fusion (merging) is in various ways more problematic even than the case of fission (splitting). What if qualitatively similar objects, when brought within a diameter's distance of one another,

11.6.5 Ineliminable vagueness in the criterion of identity

There are further residual problems with the strengthened criterion of spatiotemporal continuity.

Suppose a Volkswagen were to be refashioned, piece by piece, at the Peugeot plant so as to evolve into a Peugeot; and suppose that that Peugeot were then to be refashioned at the Volkswagen plant back into a Volkswagen. There is a space-time path connecting the latter car with the original such that at every stage along the path there is a car. But is the car at the end of this process, even though a Volkswagen, to be regarded as being numerically identical to (i.e. one and the same as) the original Volkswagen? Again I am sure that opinions will differ.

Some persons might see in this latter sequence of events certain analogies with the case of, let us say, a house being painted. The later house is identical with the earlier house, even though the earlier one might have been a white house and the later one a brown house. One might try, in light of such an analogy, to argue that the later vehicle is the selfsame *car* as the original, but is not the same *Volkswagen*, since at every point along the path connecting the two there was a car, but there was not a Volkswagen. But this answer, we may be confident, will not commend itself to everyone. We can imagine someone arguing, "Being a Volkswagen is not like being white. If a white house is painted brown, and then repainted white again, the later white house is identical with the earlier white house. But if a car is transformed from a Volkswagen into a Peugeot and back into a Volkswagen, it is not to be regarded as the same Volkswagen."

Frankly, I do not believe that there is any way a priori to settle this latter debate. I think prephilosophical intuitions are bound to vary from person to person. Some will regard the last car in the series as identical to the first; others will, just as determinedly, regard it as different. If we had a precise, agreed-upon, theory of identity-through-time, we could appeal to that theory to settle the matter. But the trouble is that it is the very theory itself which is at issue. Our prephilosophical intuitions are sufficiently unclear, and differ enough from

---

suddenly collapsed into one object which could not be made to split into the two originals? How, then, should we want to adjust our concepts of ownership, of liability (for damage), etc.? I will leave the pursuit of such questions as an exercise for your amusement.

one person to another, as to make it problematic just how we might want to refine our theory further.

Philosophical theories are not spun out of thin air. They are devised, first, with an eye to fitting some paradigm cases. If they can be contrived so as to overcome that first hurdle, then – but only then – might they be appealed to in our attempt to settle some borderline disputes. But in the current case, the dispute itself lies not so much at the borderline as it does at the center. We discover, very early on, in trying to formulate an account of identity-through-time, that persons have strongly, if not irreconcilably, different intuitions about identity. Its seems unlikely that we could possibly devise a single theory which accommodated such a diversity.

It should be pointed out explicitly, however, that the problem we see in the case of the Volkswagen-Peugeot-Volkswagen does not arise from the fact that we have attempted to offer a negative theory. This latter problem would have arisen for a positive theory as well. A positive theorist, confronted with the spectacle of a Volkswagen being transformed into a Peugeot, and the Peugeot in its turn being transformed into a Volkswagen, would be no better off in answering the question whether the latest car is identical with the earliest one. According to a positive theory, the latest car would be identical with the earliest one if and only if the substance of the latest were one and the same with the substance of the earliest. But what is the criterion of sameness of substance through the sorts of changes we have just described? The problem is displaced, but not solved. The problem is a *prephilosophical* one, infecting any theory whatever that one might try to construct for identity-through-time, irrespective of whether that theory is a positive or a negative theory.

If our prephilosophical intuitions are – as I believe – so vague and so variable from person to person as to make selecting a precise theory of identity-through-time arbitrary, then what, if anything, have we accomplished in adducing and promoting the strengthened criterion of spatiotemporal continuity? My own opinion is that this latter criterion – vague as it is – is just about the best we can hope to achieve. This last account offers us the common conceptual core of our concept of *identity-through-time*. But beyond this point, there is, and can be, no further common (i.e. shared) account.

What constitutes identity-through-time for a valued heirloom wristwatch may be strikingly different from that for a wristwatch carrying no sentimental value. What makes the heirloom watch the watch it is, in your regard, is the fact that your father personally engraved a message on the back of the watch on the occasion of your twenty-first birthday. Were the back of the watchcase to be destroyed, or replaced, indeed even replaced by a qualitatively identical part complete with a copy of the original engraving, the resulting watch might, as far as you were concerned, simply no longer be worthy of being regarded as the same watch. What is essential, for you, in identifying the watch may be the fact that your father himself engraved the back. Replace that back and what results is a watch, but not the heirloom you treasure. In contrast, your other watch, the one carrying no sentimental value, can have its parts replaced ad infinitum and it would still remain 'the same watch'.

Should we allow such variable, such seemingly extrinsic, factors as sentimental value to play a role in determining a thing's identity-through-time? "Isn't the watch really the same (or different)", one might be inclined to argue, "quite independent of anyone's *attitude* toward the watch? Surely identity-through-time is a determinate notion, not subject to the vicissitudes of anything as variable and unpredictable as persons' attitudes. Virtually everyone else would regard the current watch, with its new back, as being identical with the earlier watch. Surely one person's idiosyncratic predilections cannot carry any weight in determining whether identity has been preserved. Identity is an *objective* matter, to be settled by objective general criteria, not by one person's sentiment or peculiar requirements."

It is a common human failing to be overly ready to dismiss perfunctorily philosophical intuitions and expectations which differ markedly from one's own. It would be easy, and I know that many persons are tempted and some succumb to that temptation, to argue that such properties as sentimental value have no 'proper' or 'legitimate' role to play in a philosophical account of identity. Many persons bring to philosophy the firmly held belief that philosophical analyses should abjure the subjective and should aim for objectivity and determinateness.

But that such attitudes may inform, and indeed explain, the manner of someone's doing philosophy does not, of course, *justify* doing philosophy in that way. One must beware not to mistake one's own convictions as to what a proper philosophical theory ought to look like for a justification for rejecting another's approach.

Identity-through-time is a *practical* concept, tailored by generations of persons to reflect the contingencies of this world, our particular practices of law, our institutions of inheritance and ownership, and our attributions of responsibility and liability. It is naive to believe that it can be analyzed in a compact formula, or that there are but a determinate handful of conditions which dictate its use. It is, instead, as complex a notion as any of those of ethics or aesthetics.

In saying this of the identity-through-time of material objects, I anticipate the thrust of the next, final, chapter. There I will argue that the concept of *personal* identity is more complex still, and will argue that far from there being any *one* determinate concept of personal identity, there is only a *core* concept to which we then append a diverse array of further conditions.

CHAPTER TWELVE

Persons

I, a stranger and afraid
In a world I never made.
– A.E. Housman ([100], 109)

12.1 The raccoon's tale

In the fall of 1982, my department at Simon Fraser University mounted its fourth annual public-issues conference. The theme for that year was "Challenges to Science" and was widely advertised off-campus. The meetings attracted persons from many backgrounds. On the first day, a buffet lunch was served. Having taken a bit of tuna salad, my wife and I seated ourselves at a table with some strangers. The man on my left struck up a conversation.

"In my previous life, I was a raccoon", he said.

Thinking this a bit of an odd icebreaker, I replied in what I assumed was the same spirit that the remark had been offered.

"I see. Do you feel a compulsion to wash your food in a mountain stream?"

I quickly discovered my mistake, however. The stranger had been in dead earnest. He firmly rejected my suggestion, and then persisted, not aggressively, but determinedly, in his claim.

"I was a raccoon before I was a person."

Perhaps he said "human being" rather than "person". My memory is not as precise as I would like on this particular point. I pressed him a bit.

"How do you know that? What makes you believe that you were a raccoon?"

The stranger was unable to offer any evidence beyond his own unshakable conviction that this was true. In some way, totally unanalyzable, and apparently not causing him any particular concern, he just 'knew' he had been a raccoon. At that, the topic had reached a dead end and we turned to other, more usual, sorts of conversation.

In looking back on what was one of the most unusual exchanges of my life, I have had to ask myself several questions. What could it possibly mean for a person to have been a raccoon? Is such an idea even intelligible? Of course, if we try hard, we can imagine what it would be like to be 'housed' in a raccoon's body: instead of having a nose, one would have a snout; instead of hands, claws; etc. But this was not what that man had been claiming. He had not claimed that he – a person – had been housed in a raccoon's body; he claimed that he had *been* a raccoon. Putting aside the question why he might have thought such a thing, one must wonder what sort of theory of personhood we would have to adopt which would allow us even to imagine such a thing. For a raccoon to 'become' a person, for some 'thing', let us say *x*, to 'become' some later 'thing', let us say *y*, it is essential that something or other be preserved in the transformation: there has to be some 'important' connection between the earlier *x* and the later *y*. But what could this possibly be in the supposed case of a raccoon's becoming a person? According to the man who believed this of himself, it was not the *body* of the one which became the *body* of the other. Was it the mind? By his own admission, he had no memory of having been a raccoon. But how essential is memory for mind? Could the mind of a raccoon now be the mind of a man but without the man having a memory of having been a raccoon? If it was not mind, might it have been something else? Perhaps the *soul* of the raccoon became the soul of the man. But is this intelligible? What are souls? What counts for or against a soul's enduring and changing through time? In short, the claim provokes – and for our purposes serves to introduce – the cluster of problems concerning the analysis of personhood and of the identity through time of persons.

12.2   Persons and human beings

Every person I have ever known has been a human being. By "human being" I do not mean, as this term is sometimes used, "a decent, upright person", but rather I mean a living animal of the species *Homo sapiens*: a flesh-and-blood mammalian creature having a head, a torso, and typically two arms, two legs, etc., standing upright, breathing air, eating a variety of organic produce, etc.

While every person I have met, and expect to meet, is a human being, it is not at all clear that persons *must* be human beings or that all human beings are persons. At least for the moment we want to leave it as an open question whether a person could have a nonhuman body (an animal body[1] or an electromechanical body[2] perhaps). Then, too, anacephalic infants (human beings born with no brain) who may be able to carry on some basic life processes are not conscious and have no prospects of consciousness. They are human beings, in that they have human (albeit defective) bodies, but it is arguable whether such grievously deficient, nonconscious human beings can be reasonably regarded as being *persons*.

One of the most difficult problems some persons have when they first approach these questions is to sort out the difference between the *legal* criteria for personhood and the *conceptual* criteria. The Law is a poor touchstone for deciding conceptual issues. The Law, in some jurisdictions, may rule, for example, that a fetus is a person. But although the Law may so rule, one can always ask, "Does this law comport with what our concept of personhood is? Do we have good philosophical grounds for accepting that law, or should we want to argue that it rests on a conceptual mistake and ought to be changed?" We are not logically, legally, or morally bound to accept the decisions of Law in constructing our own best concept of personhood. Ideally, the order of precedence ought to be the other way round: Law ought to try to capture the best thinking of the society; it ought to follow the best thinkers, not lead them.

Thus, even if 'the Law' (and of course 'the Law' is hardly monolithic, but varies from jurisdiction to jurisdiction, society to society) were to say "anyone is (legally) a person who satisfies the conditions *a*, *b*, and *c*", that would certainly not answer for us the question how we ought best to conceive of personhood. Even if in the eyes of the Law every human being were to be considered a person, that would not tell us whether from a considered philosophical point of view that was a warranted conclusion or not. We may be legally obliged to act in accord with the Law, but we surely do not have to believe or think in accord with the Law.

Then, too, the Law is nearly always reactive. It responds to needs

---

1. We are reminded of Kafka's Gregor Samsa (a gigantic insect), of Lucas's Chewbacca (a Wookiee), and of assorted Ewoks, werewolves, frog princes, etc.

2. Recall such fabulous characters as Pinocchio (more mechanical than electrical) and, of course, See-Threepio (also known as C-3PO) and Robo-Cop.

and disputes as they arise and become issues in the community. The Law seldom anticipates changing beliefs and thus does not plan in advance for them. But metaphysics, and philosophy in general, is different. Metaphysicians are free to speculate, and indeed considerably enjoy speculating, on situations which have not arisen – and indeed may never arise – in their attempts to refine our concepts. For metaphysicians, the Law may be a storehouse of case studies, a repository of much of traditional thought, but it can hardly serve as the arbiter of the cogency of a conceptual reconstruction.

The problems, then, to be addressed are these. Virtually every person is a human being; virtually every human being is a person. But *must* persons be human beings; *must* human beings be persons? Could a person have a nonhuman body? Might a human being be other than a person? In short, what is the *conceptual* connection between *being a person* on the one hand and *being a human being* on the other?

12.3 Why individuation and identity collapse in the case of persons

Anthony Quinton does philosophy in an admirably painstaking and systematic fashion. It is thus somewhat surprising to find, in reading *The Nature of Things* ([165]), that although he seems to be proceeding in a careful step-by-step fashion, examining first the problem of individuation of material objects and next the identity-through-time of material objects, when he comes to the subsequent discussion of persons, he skips over the question of the individuation of persons and proceeds immediately to the question of the identity of persons. Why the apparent omission? On the face of it, there is an entire chapter missing in his book, and yet – so far as I can tell – he offers not a single sentence of explanation as to why he departed from what looks to be the obvious and natural game plan. Might there be some reason why one would not treat the question of persons in a parallel manner to that already established for material objects, that is, by beginning with the question of the individuation of persons and then, in due course, graduating to the question of persons' identity-through-time?

I think there is a reason for *not* treating the question of persons in this two-step manner. And even if Quinton neglected to address the issue at all, I think we might do well to pause over it for a moment.

It is, of course, truistic to say that persons are not 'just' material bodies. Persons may have material (in particular, human) bodies, but they also have properties and moral rights which no mere physical body possesses. Persons can think and can act in ways that no 'mere' physical object, particularly a nonliving object, can remotely replicate. But these remarkable transcendent abilities are not what warrants leapfrogging over the question of personal individuation directly to the question of personal identity. The reason is slightly more concealed.

Material objecthood, i.e. being a material object, can be predicated of an existent thing on the basis of properties it instances, if not exactly all at one moment of time, then over a very short period of time. To count the objects in a room, for example, a procedure which requires that we individuate them, we will have to see which ones occupy space in the sense that they exclude other objects from the same space. We need this latter test to tell, for example, which are mere holographic images and which are 'real' physical (material) objects. But we do not need much of their history to individuate them; theoretically, a millisecond of endurance is adequate.[3] But there is no such equivalent determination possible for individuating persons.

Of course one could count the human bodies present. But while that is a good *practical* means, it is not entirely theoretically satisfactory. Some human bodies, even if alive, hardly are the bodies of persons. Human bodies born without brains, in which there is no consciousness whatsoever, can hardly be regarded as the bodies of *persons*. And again, it is theoretically possible that a person should have other than a human body. In short, at the very least, at the outset of our examining the question of the individuation and identity of persons we do not want to prejudice the issue by assuming that persons *must* be identified with living human beings. Perhaps at the end of our researches we may want to assert such a thesis. But if we do, then such a thesis is something to be argued for, not assumed from the outset. It ought, that is, if it is to be promoted, to be argued for as a conclusion of an argument and not assumed as a premise.

In skipping over the question of the individuation of persons, directly to the question of their identity, we do so because we already have an eye on our eventual conclusions. To be a person is essentially,

---

3. That this is so depends very much on certain physical facts characteristic of this particular world. In a Waismannesque world, recall (p. 301), it would be necessary to know something of the remote history, viz. the details of its manufacture, of a seeming single chair to know whether it was in fact one chair or a pair.

among other things, to be the sort of thing which does (or, in the case of newborns, will) have memories. But to have memories requires that the person be extended in time. There logically cannot be short-lived persons (e.g. having a duration of a millisecond) in the way, for example, there can be short-lived physical objects, e.g. muons whose lifetime is of the order of two-millionths of a second. It is of the essence of being a person that one have a history of experiences.

12.4 Is there a self?

In *A Treatise of Human Nature*, David Hume begins his discussion of personal identity with what, at first, seems to be nothing more than a casual, innocuous, recounting of a common belief among philosophers about our direct acquaintance with our selves.[4] (Although Hume restricts his discussion to the beliefs of fellow philosophers, he might just as well have spoken of vast numbers of persons educated and living in Western culture.) "There are some philosophers, who imagine we are every moment intimately conscious of what we call our SELF; that we feel its existence and its continuance in existence; and are certain, beyond the evidence of a demonstration, both of its perfect identity and simplicity" ([101], book I, part IV, section VI, 251). But Hume does not broach this topic of self to lend his assent to the commonly held view; he raises this issue of self in order to probe it and, eventually, to reject the common conception. In one of the most celebrated passages in all of philosophy, he shortly continues:

> For my part, when I enter most intimately into what I call *myself*, I always stumble on some particular perception or other, of heat or cold, light or shade, love or hatred, pain or pleasure. I never catch *myself* at any time without a perception, and never can observe any thing but the perception. When my perceptions are remov'd for any time, as by sound sleep; so long am I insensible of *myself*, and may truly be said not to exist. And were all my perceptions remov'd by death, and cou'd I neither think, nor feel, nor see, nor love, nor hate after the dissolution of my body, I shou'd be entirely annihilated, nor

---

4. This way of putting the point is not Hume's, but a modern reconstruction using terminology, viz. the term "acquaintance", which has been borrowed from Russell. See p. 309 above.

> do I conceive what is farther requisite to make me a perfect non-entity. If any one upon serious and unprejudic'd reflexion, thinks he has a different notion of *himself*, I must confess I can no longer reason with him. All I can allow him is, that he may well be in the right as well as I, and that we are essentially different in this particular. He may, perhaps, perceive something simple and continu'd, which he calls *himself*; tho' I am certain there is no such principle [elemental thing] in me. ([101], 252)

If this passage is read superficially, it gives the appearance of being self-refuting, for Hume writes "*I* enter ...", "*I* call ...", "*I* conceive ...", etc. Do not his very own words betray the impossibility of his maintaining what he claims, viz. that he cannot find *himself*? Is not saying, as Hume does, "I am insensible of *myself*", as self-refuting as saying, "I do not exist"?

Once again (recall our earlier discussion, p. 171), we find a philosopher denying that something exists which is thought to be familiar to great numbers of other persons. And again, just as in other cases, we find in this instance that the philosopher is denying one thing only to assert another.

Hume is not, of course, denying that he exists. He is perfectly comfortable speaking of himself and using the personal pronoun "I" of himself. What he is denying is that 'self' is anything 'given' in perception. And what he is offering on the positive side is the thesis that self is "a bundle or collection of different perceptions, which succeed each other with inconceivable rapidity, and are in a perpetual flux and movement" ([101], 252). In short, Hume's theory is that self is nothing more or less than 'a bundle of perceptions', or – to use a more modern vocabulary, and one not restricted solely to perceptions – self is a 'stream of consciousness'.[5] Sometimes this theory is also called the 'no-ownership' theory, since it argues that there is no self which owns or possesses the succession of items in that stream of consciousness: the items follow one another, as Hume says, "with inconceivable rapidity", but they are not 'in' or 'of' a self.[6]

---

5. More exactly, he maintains that self is a punctuated, or interrupted, stream, since we all have periods of dreamless sleep.

6. Some persons have argued that Hume's experiment is naive in that absolutely constant things are, by their very nature, imperceivable and that what Hume was trying to perceive is something which would amount to a

Some philosophers have agreed with Hume. Richard Taylor, for one, goes even further than Hume ventured.

> One imagines that he is deeply, perpetually, unavoidably aware of something he calls "I" or "me." The philosopher then baptizes this thing his *self* or perhaps his *mind*, and the theologian calls it his *soul*. It is, in any case, something that is at the very heart of things, the very center of reality, that about which the heavens and firmament revolve. But should you not feel embarrassment to talk in such a way, or even to play with such thoughts? As soon as you begin to try saying anything whatever about this inner self, this central reality, you find that you can say nothing at all. It seems to elude all description. All you can do, apparently, is refer to it; you can never say what is referred to, except by multiplying synonyms — as if the piling of names upon names would somehow guarantee the reality of the thing named! But as soon as even the least description is attempted, you find that what is described is indistinguishable from absolute nothingness. ([204], 122)

Taylor knows full well the common conception of self which he is bucking. And he is as eloquent in presenting the view he wishes to refute as he has been in denying it. Taylor gives expression to the commonly held, opposing, view this way:

> There seem to be two realities – myself and all the rest. By "all the rest" is meant the whole of creation except me. ... This rest, this everything else, all that is outside, other, is perpetually

---

constant element in perception. The objection continues by arguing that perception operates, essentially, by taking cognizance of *differences*. An undifferentiated, constant element of perception, coextensive* in time with one's entire existence, would be an impossibility since it would lack a contrast.

Such an objection relies on certain empirical claims about perception, claims which are exceedingly difficult to test. We know that we become desensitized to long-lasting stimuli: for example, we grow inured to a constant aroma, being unable to smell it at all after a long exposure. But still, such data fall short of proving that it is impossible to detect a truly constant element in perception. The claim is more metaphysical than empirical and, even at that, not particularly self-commending or self-evident. I mention this debate, but side with neither party to it.

changing, never two moments the same. But at the heart of it all, at that point which is the metaphysical center of my reality, is that self, that which is not something "else" – and it does *not* change, or at least does not become something *else*. It remains one and the same, throughout all the changes it undergoes, preserving its identity through an ever elapsing and growing time. Except for this – that it does finally suffer that calamitous change, which is its own extinction! And that is a pretty awesome thought, a dreadful thought, a cosmic insult. ([204], 122)

Taylor argues (not at all well or convincingly, in my opinion) against this latter view of *self*. And he concludes:

We wanted something [i.e. a self] to present as an ultimate reality, to contrast with everything else, and we found total, perfect nothingness! It isn't there. Imagination creates it. Intellect distinguishes it. Metaphysics builds intellectual fortresses upon it. Religion guarantees its salvation – always, of course, on certain terms – and promises to push back the nothingness that approaches it. And all the while, it is itself the most perfect specimen of nothingness! One does indeed feel like a child discovered making a face at himself in the mirror. One wants somehow to cover up what was going on, embarrassed at his own ridiculousness. ([204], 123)

Taylor's counsel, then, for those afflicted with the Dread of Death: The self cannot die, for there is no self.

Hume's and Taylor's extreme ideas about self are heady, perhaps alarming, and for some persons, even frightening.[7] But they are also important, if for no other reason than to cause us to shake off our complacent, comfortable misconception that there is any *universal* idea of selfhood. For theirs is but one of a bewildering array of quite different notions of what *self* might be.

Visit any well-stocked library and look at the number of books catalogued under the subject heading "self". (And look, too, at the number dealing with "death".) The figures are staggering, and writers from an

---

7. They are also threatening if read by someone reared in a religious tradition where *self* (or soul) is a central concept and where children have been taught not to question church dogma.

enormous number of fields all contribute to the froth: philosophers, to be sure; but also psychologists (of every imaginable stripe, Freudian, Jungian, Existentialist, Experimentalist, Behaviorist, etc.); sociologists; anthropologists; educators; criminologists; novelists; essayists; historians; etc.[8] There is, in fact, a veritable industry given over to generating an endless supply of articles, novels, and learned books on the topic of *self*. Our collective curiosity on this topic (like that on sex and diet) seems limitless.

We will confine our attention to the major philosophical theories of personal identity.

12.5   The principal contemporary theories of personhood

For a person a-at-T_1 to be identified with a person b-at-T_2, there must be some thing, or set of features, which unifies the two, which accounts for their being two stages of one and the same person. The principal theories are these:

- The unifying principle is soul (self, or mind).
- The unifying principle is physical body (usually, if not invariably, a human body).
- The unifying principle is similarity between successive bundles of sensations.
- The unifying principle is personality and memory.
- The unifying principle is an amalgam of various of the preceding.

Although I have never taken a poll, my own educated guess, arising from my having been brought up and exposed to much the same sort of culture as everyone around me, is that the theory that it is soul (or self) which accounts for a person's identity is the most widely held one of the lot. It has, however, steadily, and perhaps at a quickening pace in the last century, been losing some of its original religious trappings. Many persons who are not religious still cling to a concept of soul not terribly unlike that historically promoted by Christianity. Many non-Christians retain the belief that the soul is, in some fashion, not a physical thing, but a supernatural sort of entity. Where their

---

8. I will ignore all the execrable "self-help" books written by an army of poseurs and dilettantes whose scientific credentials are often vanishingly close to nil.

notion departs from traditional religious views is in their abandoning the further belief that souls endure beyond bodily death. They have come to adopt a 'secular' concept of soul. Soul is posited to be what makes one person different from another, while at the same time souls are believed, somehow, to be dependent for their existence upon the existence of a living human body. All in all, soul appears as a mysterious 'I know not what' which plays the theoretical role of providing the basis for personal identity. Soul, while not physical, is what is conceived of as being what is essential in a person. The positing of soul as a solution to the problem of personal identity is a positive theory analogous to the positing of substance as a solution to the problems of individuating and re-identifying physical objects. And like the theories of material substance, it encounters similar sorts of metaphysical and epistemological difficulties.

Some persons, we all know well, have an unshakable conviction that souls exist. They are as sure of the existence of souls as they are of tables and chairs. Other persons are less sure; and some persons, of course, are convinced that souls do not exist. Souls (if they exist) are not publicly perceivable things. We cannot prove or demonstrate the existence of souls by holding them up for public display, or by pointing to one, or even by directing persons to introspect and thereby to discover their own souls. Hume, as we saw a moment ago, tried the exercise and reported abject failure. So did Taylor. This is not to say that everyone who tries the exercise must fail. Hume knew that some persons might try the experiment and come to believe that they had succeeded in finding their souls. But Hume's, Taylor's, and many other persons' reported failures do tell us that searching for one's soul by introspection is not a test which yields anything like universal agreement. And it is not unreasonable to hypothesize that persons who do report success in administering the test to themselves are persons who were antecedently disposed strongly to believe that they had souls. From a methodological point of view, successful reports of the experiment must be regarded as tentative at best and, perhaps, suspect as well.

But my purpose here is not so much to argue against the existence of souls as it is to point out that their existence is problematic. And that their existence is problematic is all that is needed to render souls inappropriate platforms on which to erect solutions to the problem of personal identity.

There are, to be sure, some exceedingly troubling cases in which we might be terribly unclear whether personal identity has been preserved or not. (We shall turn to some of these cases presently.) But in both ordinary and troublesome cases, we never actually proceed by trying to detect the person's *soul* and asking ourselves whether it is, or is not, identical with some earlier (or later) soul. The fact is that, whatever might be our final opinion about the existence of souls, we never actually invoke the concept of soul in our day-to-day re-identification of other persons or even, for that matter, of ourselves. You may catch a glimpse of someone on the street who looks like a long-lost friend. "Could that be Jim?" you ask yourself. In an impulsive mood, you shout, "Jim!" He turns, stares blankly for several embarrassing seconds, and then flashes a familiar grin of recognition. Identification has been made. And neither you nor Jim has examined the other's soul.

If one adopts the theory that sameness of soul confers personal identity, then one can make sense of the claim of the man who believed that he had in a former life been a raccoon. He had been a raccoon if the soul he now has formerly had been the soul of a raccoon.[9] But while we may, by adopting this theory of soul, be able to attribute a *meaning* to his claim, we will not have succeeded in making that claim *rational*. To make such a claim rational, we would have to have some account of how it is possible to *know* such a thing or to have good evidence for it. And inasmuch as the very existence of soul seems so problematic, the belief that there could be objectively valid criteria for re-identifying souls seems utterly forlorn. The price of adopting a theory of souls as personal re-identifier is the abandoning of rational grounds for making identifications.

From an epistemological point of view, souls are idle: they play no role in our day-to-day identification of other persons. From a metaphysical point of view, positing souls as the principle of personal identity is, as was the case with material substance, regressive. It simply displaces the problem of identity, but leaves it otherwise unresolved. By arguing that person *a* is identical with person *b* if and only if the soul of *a* is identical to the soul of *b*, we have merely deferred the question, but not answered it. For now we must ask whether the soul of *a* is identical to the soul of *b*. And whatever way

---

9. This is of course also to assume that raccoons' souls are not so different from persons' souls that the one could not become the other. I shall not pursue this baroque question whether raccoons' souls, horses' souls, turtles' souls, etc. are interchangeable or not. As you might suspect, I regard the exercise as ludicrous.

we might go about answering this latter question, we might well have pursued directly, that is, without having interposed the superfluous intermediary concept of *soul* in our attempt to answer the original question. In short, introducing the concept of *soul* does no useful work in helping us solve our real problems: it merely retards the progress toward a solution.

Positing soul is, thus, not going to be of much help in solving either the epistemological or the metaphysical problems of personal identity. We must seek another identifier of persons.

The theory that it is the human body which is the identifier is considerably more promising: it is economical in the sense that it assimilates the problem of personal identity to that of the identity-through-time of a particular material object, viz. a person's own body, and it invokes no hidden or exotic substances. Moreover, it is, after all, clearly the criterion we daily use in identifying other persons. How did you recognize Jim, and he, you? By noticing certain familiar physical features in the appearance that one presents to the rest of the world. (Human beings have an uncanny ability to recognize extremely subtly different features of physiognomies.)

But John Locke, recall (section 6.4 above, pp. 108ff.), argued strenuously against using the practical criterion of bodily identity as the theoretical criterion of personal identity. Although the body may be used as a surrogate criterion, it was not to be regarded as ultimately satisfactory: "… should the soul of a prince, carrying with it the consciousness of the prince's past life, enter and inform the body of a cobbler as soon as deserted by his own soul, everyone sees he would be the same person with the prince, accountable only for the prince's actions" ([124], book II, chap. XXVII, §15). The talk here of the transference of soul from the prince's body to the cobbler's is incidental; the essential aspect is not the transference of soul – Locke is very emphatic on this point, reiterating it several times – but the element of the transference of *consciousness*. It is the transference of consciousness, alone, which makes for the transfer of the prince to the cobbler's body. The identity of persons is grounded in consciousness, not soul. Indeed, Locke argues at some length that a person could successively have different bodies, that a person could take turns sharing a body with another, that a person could have different souls and might even now have the soul of some former person, but that none of this would affect that person's identity. For a person's identity is not a matter either of body or of soul, but strictly of consciousness.

For Locke, the element of consciousness which played the crucial role in personal identity was memory. To the extent that a person has the memories of an earlier person, to that extent he/she may be identified with that earlier person. In one of his not infrequent heroically convoluted sentences, Locke writes:

> Had I the same consciousness that I saw the ark and *Noah's* flood as that I saw an overflowing of the *Thames* last winter, or as that I write now, I could no more doubt that I write this now, that saw the *Thames* overflowed last winter, and that viewed the flood at the general deluge, was the same *self*, place that *self* in what substance you please, than I that write this am the same *myself* now whilst I write (whether I consist of all the same substance, material or immaterial, or no) that I was yesterday. ([124], book II, chap. XXVII, §16)

More simply: "If I had memories of seeing Noah's Ark and the worldwide flood as well as memories of the Thames overflowing last winter which were as compelling as the perceptions I am now having of writing this passage, then I could not doubt that *I* did indeed see the Ark and Noah's flood and that *I* saw the Thames overflow last winter."

Joseph Butler (1692-1752), writing more than thirty years after Locke's death, challenged Locke's theory by arguing that Locke had got the order of logical priority reversed, that it was personal identity which accounts for memory, and not the other way around:

> But though consciousness of what is past does thus ascertain our personal identity to ourselves, yet to say, that it makes personal identity, or is necessary to our being the same persons, is to say, that a person has not existed a single moment, nor done one action, but what he can remember; indeed none but what he reflects upon. And should one really think it self-evident, that consciousness of personal identity presupposes, and therefore cannot constitute, personal identity; any more than knowledge, in any other case, can constitute truth, which it presupposes. ([39], 298)

Memory, for Butler, is *evidence* for personal identity, but does not itself constitute personal identity. For memory to be evidence of personal identity, personal identity must itself exist *independently* of the evidence for it. He continues, giving voice to an intuition which is antithetical to Locke's own:

> ... though present consciousness of what we at present do and feel is necessary to our being the persons we now are; yet present consciousness of past actions or feelings is not necessary to our being the same persons who performed those actions, or had those feelings. ([39], 298)

That Locke and Butler disagree, and that their disagreement stems from totally different prephilosophical beliefs about the centrality of the concept of *memory* to the concept of *person*, is apparent.[10] But is this the end of the matter? Must this debate simply be regarded as a clash of intuitions, and must it be left at that?

In the very last paragraph of his essay, almost as an afterthought, Butler raises an issue which has come to be seen as essential in tackling these problems. For Butler reminds us that memories can be *mistaken*. And although Butler, himself, does not particularly pursue this problem, it really does pose a crucial difficulty for Locke's theory.

According to Locke, personal identity is constituted by memory. But what if one's memory is mistaken? What if someone is convinced that he recalls something, but his report is about an event at which he could not possibly have been present? (This need not be regarded as a pathological condition. All of us have mistaken memories about some things. Sometimes we might believe that a dream was a 'real' memory. And modern empirical research has shown just how much eyewitness accounts of 'one and the same event', even among persons

---

10. Compare Butler with Hume (publishing three years later [1739]): "Who can tell me, for instance, what were his thoughts and actions on the first of *January* 1715, the 11th of *March* 1719, and the 3d of *August* 1733? ... Will he affirm, because he has entirely forgot the incidents of these days, that the present self is not the same person with the self of that time; and by that means overturn all the most establish'd notions of personal identity? In this view, therefore, memory does not so much *produce* as *discover* personal identity. ... 'Twill be incumbent on those, who affirm that memory produces entirely our personal identity, to give reason why we can thus extend our identity beyond our memory" ([101], book I, part IV, sect. VI, 262).

who are trying their level best to be scrupulously honest, can differ markedly.)

Locke's own example is of someone (himself, of all people) possibly recalling having witnessed the biblical Flood. Locke certainly is consistent: he allows that any person who has such memories was present at the Flood.

Most other persons, from Butler onwards, are far less likely to be quite so liberal. Were any of us to meet someone who claimed to have been present at the Flood, most of us, I am sure, would be skeptical in the extreme, probably believing in the first instance that the person making the claim was mentally ill or suffering some sort of delusion. Does this mean that one must, then, adopt Butler's theory, that personal identity is the basis for memory, and reject Locke's, that memory is the basis for personal identity?

That there is a problem in Locke's theory does not, of course, mean that Butler's opposing theory is correct. Butler's would be the preferred theory only if these two theories were the only ones possible. But they are not. And indeed, what I want to suggest is that what is needed is not the wholesale rejection of Locke's theory, but a repair.

I am convinced, like Locke, that memory does play a central role in personal identity. But the role cannot be as simple and direct as Locke imagined. For Locke's insights can be invoked only for correct memory (or veridical memory, as it is sometimes called), and not for mistaken (or falsidical) memory.

But what is the test of veridical memory? We have already explored this question (in section 8.10, pp. 220ff.). There I argued that one way to test memories is to compare one's own 'seeming' memories with those of other persons. If they agree, then one has good prima facie evidence of the correctness of one's own memories. But what if others' memories do not bear out one's own, or what if other persons were not witnesses to the event you believe you recall, or what if – even more extremely – your memory is of an event predating the birth of anyone alive today? How then shall it be tested? As I argued earlier: by consulting the testimony provided by physical facts. Ultimately the reliability of memory, and our ability to sort out veridical from falsidical memories, at some point must rely on the evidence of the physical world.

If this were a world where persons never had bodies, where they were just thinking things, then one might want to argue that insofar as there would be no way to distinguish veridical from falsidical memories, there would not be such a distinction, and that having a memory, any memory however wild or bizarre, would then be a memory of one's own personal history. But such a world is vastly different from this world.

In the last few decades, there has been a marked shift in much writing about personal identity. Whereas in centuries past philosophers were disposed to ground personal identity in souls, in substance, and other empirically problematical entities, many recent philosophers are disposed to seat personal identity, as did Locke, in memory and, many would add, personality. But they do not rest there. There is more to the concept of personal identity. Not just any memory, or seeming memory, will do. It must be authentic, or veridical, memory. And for memory to be veridical, we normally require that the body (of the person whose memory it is) was present at the remembered event. In short, although the body is not the identifier itself, it plays a crucial role in determining the authenticity of the identifier, viz. memory and personality.

Persons are essentially identified by their personalities and by their authentic (veridical) memories. But for memories to be authentic, the person must be embodied, i.e. the test of cogency of memories depends on causal links in the physical world. (This is not, of course, to argue that memories are not themselves physical entities. They may be. As we saw in chapter 10, memories perhaps are states of our central nervous systems. But the theory of personal identity being proposed here does not require any particular decision in that latter case. All that is required is that memories – whatever their ontological fate, whether regarded as themselves physical states or not – be *testable* by the evidence furnished by physical states.)

Interestingly, another consideration, from quite another direction, also favors the theory that persons must be embodied. Recall our earlier discussion (p. 131) of Plato's allegory of the cave. There I argued that were persons not to be embodied, they could not tell 'themselves' apart from 'other persons', there could be no concept of *personal identity*.

What is emerging is a theory of personal identity which to a certain degree mirrors that of physical object identity. What confers identity is not the endurance of a mental or spiritual substance, but a succession of 'person-stages' unified, or integrated, by certain sorts of relationships they bear to one another.

Hume had grasped a fragment of this modern account. He, too, conceived of personal identity as a series, a succession, of stages. When he looked for the 'organizing principle' he singled out a pair of relations which together he supposed conferred the identity: resemblance and causation. But these relations will not do. The role of causation is overstated. Some items in the stream of consciousness *may* causally bring about their successors, but an equal if not greater number of these episodes are induced by external stimuli. And resemblance fares little better.

> For what is the memory but a faculty, by which we raise up images of past perceptions? And as an image necessarily resembles its object, must not the frequent placing of these resembling perceptions in the chain of thought, convey the imagination more easily from one link to another, and make the whole seem like the continuance of one object? In this particular, then, the memory not only discovers the identity, but also contributes to its production, by producing the relation of resemblance among the perceptions. ([101], book I, part IV, sect. VI, 260-1)

In commenting on this passage, Quinton offers this counterexample: "Suppose two men, A and B, take turns looking through a keyhole at moments 1 and 2. Then experiences A1 and B2 will probably be more alike than A1 and A2 or B1 and B2" ([165], 320). Quinton seems to be suggesting that Hume had argued that the relation of similarity was supposed to obtain between a person's *successive* perceptions. But that is not what Hume claimed (at least it is not what I take him to be writing in the passage above). Rather Hume claimed that in the stream of consciousness there will recur similar episodes (not necessarily successive to one another), and it is these recurring and similar episodes which contribute to the appearance of a unity.

The precise interpretation is a quibble, however. For it is clear that resemblance among the episodes in the stream of consciousness, whether those episodes are neighboring ones or remote from one another, will not unify the series. The point is that the series will be unified if the episodes are those of one person, and it will not be unified if the episodes – however much alike, regardless whether immediate neighbors or remote in time from one another – are those of different persons. You and I might at virtually the same time have qualitatively identical perceptions of a scene, and yet your perception is yours and mine is mine. And nothing intrinsic to our perceptions –

certainly not any relation of similarity (or dissimilarity) obtaining between the two – accounts for the one's being mine, and the other's being yours.

Any viable theory of personal identity is going to have to accommodate a remarkable variety of data.

- Introspection does not seem to reveal any organizing 'principle' (e.g. soul).
- Different persons, a and b, may have experiences, e_a and e_b, which are more alike one another than those experiences are like other experiences of a and of b respectively.
- Personality and veridical memory seem to play a crucial role in determining a person's identity.
- That a memory is veridical can be objectively established only if a person is (or at least has been) embodied.
- If persons are not embodied, then there is no objective test for distinguishing between self, hallucinatory 'other persons', and genuine other persons. Without a body, the distinction between 'self' and 'other' collapses.
- We virtually always use, as our practical criterion of personal identity (particularly that of other persons), the bodily criterion.
- It is perfectly intelligible to describe two persons swapping bodies. Few of us have any difficulty imagining ourselves having (being housed in?) a different body. The body, then, is not the ultimate, or sole, criterion of personal identity.
- Memories are constantly being lost. Some of what I did remember yesterday, and some of what I could have remembered yesterday, I cannot recall today. Some memories are very long-lasting; but others fall away. Memories may be likened to the physical parts of an object which are from time to time discarded and replaced by others. But whereas physical parts are often replaced by qualitatively identical parts, the greater part of our store of memories often changes markedly over a period of years.
- Both memories and personality traits are *dispositional*. Each of us is capable of recalling vastly greater numbers of events than any of us actually recalls at any one moment. Each of us acts and reacts to situations in idiosyncratic (personal) ways, but only one, or very few, of these will be exhibited at any one time. That is, the bulk of one's own memories and personality lies dormant, metaphorically speaking, ready to be activated,

but generally is not manifest. The only respectable theories we have of the nature of (instanced) dispositions are theories which would make of them (instanced) properties of some persisting, or enduring, thing. In the case of memories and personality, this would mean that memories and personality must be seated in 'something' which endures. If souls are not to be invoked for this latter role, then the most plausible alternative candidate is an enduring physical body. And of physical bodies, the human central nervous system is, by far, the most attractive and likely candidate to fill the role.

The term "personality" bears intimate etymological ties to "person-hood". That it does attests to some of the metaphysics built into our language. But for the moment, I do not wish to invoke this question-begging aspect of "personality". I want to use the term "personality" in a more neutral way, without presupposing that personality is conceptually tied to the concept of personhood. Let us, then, for a while, suspend our recognition of the verbal link, and let us conceive of persons' personalities as the characteristic ways they react to situations. Obviously, one's character (one's moral and ethical dispositions) is part of one's personality, but "character" and "personality" are not synonyms. It may be part of your personality to like piano sonority, but we would not be much inclined to regard that liking as part of your character. In any event, for a moment, let's use "personality" as an abbreviation for "characteristic behavior".

Imagine a world where the personalities (as just defined) and the memories of persons could be swapped between bodies. Assume, too, that such swapping occurred universally, quite naturally, i.e. as an operation of Nature itself, to all persons, every day, worldwide at local noon.

What sort of social practices would a society have to institute to cope with such a phenomenon? Suppose a woman left her house at 8:00 AM. At noon her personality and memories are suddenly switched to another body. (We'll assume that body switching is always from male to male and female to female, youngster to youngster, and senior to senior.) At 4:00 PM she sets out for home. Which house should she return to: the house she recalls leaving that morning, or the house from which her body departed that morning? (Since she has no memory of the house from which her body would have departed, we would have to assume that were the latter alternative to be the adopted one, human bodies would have to be tattooed with their home addresses.)

I think *most* of us would be strongly inclined to opt for the first alternative, arguing that personhood is carried by personality and by memories, not by body. Were we to adopt this suggestion, then in the world just described, the practical criterion of identifying persons by their bodies would be fairly useless (it would never work over a time interval of twenty-four hours). Instead we would probably set up some manner of greeting one another whereby we would exchange names or other information which would uniquely identify ourselves to one another.

Of course, there is no *necessity* – either physical or logical – to adopt the practice just described. A society theoretically could adopt the second practice, i.e. of identifying persons by their bodies, not by their personalities and memories. In such a society, when husband and wife greeted one another each evening, the bodies returning home would be those pictured in the photograph on the mantle, but the interests, memories, and personality of each person would be entirely unfamiliar to the other. Such a practice might work. (And some among you might even be intrigued by the prospects, believing that it would relieve the humdrum in ordinary life and make the principal causes of marital breakdown disappear at a stroke.) But the fact is that the concept of personhood which would be implicit in this latter practice is not the concept we use. In this world, in our circumstances, we conceive of personhood as seated, not in body, but in personality and memory.

How can we tie this all together? I suggest in this way. Our concept of *person* is built on the requirement that identity of persons is secured through (genuine) memory and personality. (We will explore each of these requirements further in the subsequent two case studies.) But personality and genuine memory *presuppose* embodiment. Persons must be embodied in order to individuate them and in order to distinguish genuine memory from hallucination and delusion. But this is not to say that a person must have exactly one body throughout his/her lifetime. The requirement of embodiment is satisfiable by a person's having a succession of bodies. What is essential is memory and personality, but that memory and personality must be embodied.

This criterion conceals several imprecisions. From day to day we might recall the greater part of what we could recall the previous day. Today's memories are fairly similar to those of yesterday. But this similarity of memories, from day to day, does not hold for days much further separated. When relatives tell me of things I did when a toddler, I have no memory at all of having done them. I can, today, recall nothing whatsoever of my fourth birthday. There is certainly a spatio-temporal continuity between that youngster's body and my own: I still bear the physical scars of some of his mishaps. But am I to be regarded as the *same person* as that four-year-old of yesteryear? I am sure intuitions will diverge significantly on how to answer this latter question. And even among persons who will want to insist that the adult is the 'same person' as the former child, there may well be a debate as to whether their grounds for saying this depend on their making the identification on the basis of the spatiotemporal continuity of the human body or whether they depend on there having been a day-to-day (but not year-to-year) similarity of memories and personality.

There will inevitably be a strong temptation to assimilate this present conundrum to that examined earlier, viz. Hobbes's version of the problem of the ship of Theseus (pp. 347ff.). In that earlier instance, there were two competing criteria of identity: the spatiotemporal one and the compositional one (i.e. the criterion of re-identification by material parts). I argued that the former is primary, but in situations where it is inapplicable, then it is appropriate to fall back upon the latter criterion. Were we to apply that sort of reasoning to the present case, we might argue that inasmuch as the adult cannot remember having been the child (i.e. where the criterion of continuity of memory and of personality is not satisfied), one may fall back upon the strictly physical criterion of the spatiotemporal continuity of the human body.

But the analogy is not nearly so simple. There are profound implications in identifying persons. Locke warned of the danger in our falling back upon the bodily criterion of personal identity. For instance, he considered it an abomination to punish a person for misdeeds of which he had no memory:

> ... if it is possible for the same man [i.e. human being] to have distinct incommunicable consciousness at different times, it is past doubt the same man would at different times make different persons; which, we see, is the sense of mankind in the solemnest declaration of their opinions, human laws not punishing the *mad man* for the *sober man's* [i.e. the normal man's] actions, nor the *sober man* for what the *mad man* did ... .
> ([124], book II, chap. XXVII, §20, 287-8)

There is something deeply troubling in the prospect of punishing a person for a crime of which he has utterly no memory.[11] The spectacle of a person suffering a heavy fine, or sitting in a jail cell, for having done something which he cannot recall at all strikes many of us as a miscarriage of justice. There can be no contrition by a person who has no memory of having committed an offense; there can be no personal guilt.

Thus, the decision to use the bodily criterion of personal identity as a fallback option must not be undertaken lightly. It is not a mere convenience. Adopting the bodily criterion of personal identity in cases

---

11. There are exceptions. Locke, himself, allowed for the case of punishing a person who committed an offense while intoxicated. But Locke was troubled over the rationale, or justification, for this practice. He believed that punishment was permissible because we "cannot distinguish certainly what is real, what counterfeit [in cases of drunkenness or sleepwalking]; and so the ignorance in drunkenness or sleep is not admitted as a plea" ([124], book II, chap. XXVII, §22). This is certainly a wretched justification for our legal practice. (I will ignore the case of the sleepwalker and concentrate solely on the case of the offense committed while intoxicated.) Locke argues that since there is no way to prove that a person who claims ignorance of his drunken actions is telling the truth, it is permissible to punish him. This seems to have turned the principle of 'innocent until proved guilty' on its head, placing the burden of having to prove himself innocent on the accused instead of placing the burden of having to prove the accused guilty on the prosecution. Locke defends this violation of the principle on the grounds that on "the Great Day" (i.e. Judgment Day), it will all be put right. (But see section 12.8 in this chapter.)

There is, however, a far more reasonable justification – stemming from Aristotle ([11], book III, 1113b29-1114a3) – for punishing a person for his offenses while drunk even if he cannot now recall committing those offenses. When persons *choose* to drink alcohol, they do so in full knowledge that they might commit an offense and might lose the memory of having done so. The subsequent loss of memory is not something which just randomly happens to befall the drinker; quite the contrary, he chose to do something (drink alcohol) which he knew might very well blot out memory. It is this aspect of the affair – knowingly taking a drug which might precipitate one's committing an offense and which also might blot out one's memory – which justifies our subsequently holding the person responsible for his misdeed. If we did not have such a practice, then if there were a memory-erasing drug, anyone could absolve himself of guilt by taking that drug after having committed a crime and wiping clean his memory of the offense. I think few of us would be inclined to regard his after-the-fact self-induced loss of memory as warranting the dropping of proceedings against him.

where the criterion of continuity of memory and personality is inapplicable has profound *legal* implications.[12]

In any event, it is not my purpose to pursue the nuances of legal reasoning. I am prepared to leave the debate at this point, to return to an exploration of some of the other implications of adopting the sort of analysis which has been evolving here. In the course of the ensuing case studies, I will try to expose something more of the vagueness of the concept of identity and will suggest that the idea that there is, or can be, some precise notion as to the complete set of essential ingredients in the concept of personal identity is impossible to realize.

12.6   Case study: Tim's plaint

One of my closest friends in graduate school was a history buff. Tim (not his real name) felt himself a misfit in the twentieth century. He loathed the pace of life, the congestion, and especially the suffering and devastation wrought by modern warfare. Often, in perfect seriousness, he would lament to me that he had been born in the wrong century. Tim sincerely wished that he had been born in and had lived his entire life in the seventeenth century, whose life-style he regarded as being far better suited to his own particular temperament, needs, and attitudes.[13]

On those occasions, twenty-five years ago, when Tim would begin to express such unrealizable desires, I was fully prepared to enter with him into his fantasy and to 'play' by his rules. At that time my usual response was to remind him of all the benefits which living in the twentieth century bestowed and of all the advantages persons living in the seventeenth century did without. I reminded him that he had been

---

12. It is interesting that we probably would feel rather more sanguine about adopting the bodily criterion where the consequence would be the bestowing of a good rather than the exacting of a punishment. Those of us who might protest the punishing of a man who had no memory of having committed an offense might be far less moved to complain in the case of an adult's inheriting a legacy even though he has lost his memory of having earlier been the child whom the legator had originally designated as being the recipient.

13. Tim wanted to have been born earlier, not to have never been born at all. Bernard Williams reports that there is an 'old Jewish reply' to the latter request, i.e. to have never been born. It is: "How many are so lucky? Not one in ten thousand" ([212], 232).

seriously ill a few years earlier and that modern pharmaceuticals had saved his life. Persons in the seventeenth century who had such illnesses never recovered. And I reminded him, too, that persons living in the seventeenth century knew nothing of the music of Beethoven, Schubert, Brahms, Dvorak, Verdi, Puccini, Prokofiev, Weill, Gershwin, and Brel. Persons living in the seventeenth century were ignorant of the writings of Hemingway, Tolstoy, Dostoevsky, and Dickens. They would never have heard the voices of Caruso, Gigli, Galli-Curci, Robeson, Bjoerling, Milanov, Piaf, Jolson, and Lenya. They would never have heard performances by Heifetz, Horowitz, and Gould. They would never have seen the films of Bergmann, of Welles, and of Hitchcock. They would never have savored the wit of William Gilbert, Ogden Nash, and Lewis Carroll. They would never have seen the sculptures and paintings of Rodin, Picasso, and Miro. And the list went on and on.

That was twenty-five years ago. As you can see, my argument focused on selling the triumphs of our own century, and it involved a recitation of a variety of highlights of the last one hundred years or so. In the intervening quarter-century, however, I have often reflected on Tim's plaint, and I have come to have a totally different perspective.

Earlier (in section 8.11) I argued that the concept of accelerated backward time travel is perfectly logically coherent. We can, with perfect consistency, describe an adult who travels backward in time, let us say from the twentieth century to the seventeenth, and there lives several years, perhaps even the rest of his life. But traveling backward in time from the twentieth to the seventeenth century was not what Tim had wanted. Tim wanted to have been born in the seventeenth century and to have lived his entire life in the seventeenth century, having the experiences and the knowledge of a seventeenth-century man. He wanted to have had the memories of having grown up in the seventeenth century and to have had no knowledge whatever concerning what the future would hold for the eighteenth, nineteenth, and twentieth centuries. In short, he wanted *to have been*, not a time traveler to, but an inhabitant of, the seventeenth century. (The fact that he would now not be alive, and indeed would have been dead for more than 250 years, did not trouble him in the least.)

Tim and I had not thought through his daydream in a careful, critical manner. We assumed that Tim was making sense, that what he wanted, although bizarre and physically impossible, was nevertheless logically possible. But his expressed desire was, even though the two of us may have thought otherwise, subtly incoherent on virtually any viable account of what it is to be a person. (And that it was stands as a object lesson in the possibility of engaging in incoherent discourse. Some self-contradictory desires are very unobvious: their incoherence emerges only upon thoughtful and deliberate probing.) And thus today, were someone to express a similar desire, I would challenge it on altogether different grounds: not on the practical or aesthetic grounds that in living in the seventeenth century one would have to forgo so much that is valuable in the twentieth century, but on the logical grounds that no one alive today could possibly have lived in the seventeenth century. For Tim, or any other twentieth-century person, to want to have lived in the seventeenth century is of the same order of desire as wanting there to be a five-sided square or a colorless red apple. Such things, because their descriptions are self-contradictory, logically cannot possibly occur.

One way to focus on the incoherence is to try to imagine what it would be like, not for some anonymous other person to have lived his/her entire life in the seventeenth century, but for you yourself to have done so.[14]

Suppose a twentieth-century historian were to find both a portrait and a detailed diary of some seventeenth-century person. The painting is remarkable. It is of virtually photographic quality and it displays a person who, in outward appearance, is your physical double. And the diary is equally remarkable. It reveals a person who, knowing nothing what you know of the twentieth century, reacts to the events and persons of the seventeenth century in much the way that you react to similar persons and events in the twentieth.

Could this earlier person have been *you*? Suppose the current-you (i.e. the you alive today) had never been born. Would this earlier person, this seventeenth century look-alike and act-alike (to coin a word), have been *you*? Is it enough for a person to look like you and to act like you to really *be* (or to have *been*) you?

If you are not quite sure how you want to answer this question, try

---

14. I have often heard Professor Jonathan Bennett urge the 'first-person' test for various theories of personal identity. He cautions, for example, that one can imagine what it might be like for another person to undergo 'splitting' (mitosis), but one cannot, Bennett has argued, be so sanguine when it comes to imagining it of oneself. "Imagine your body undergoing mitosis during sleep. On which side of the bed would *you* wake up?" Bennett argues that *you* cannot imagine *yourself* waking up on *both* sides.

switching the centuries. Suppose, instead, that you were to be told by a seer, who has a perfect track record in all her short-term predictions, that sometime in the far future there will be a person who will look like you and who will act like you, but who will have no memories of you, or even for that matter any secondhand knowledge of your having lived earlier. Suppose you are inclined to believe the seer.[15] That still leaves open the question what you are to infer from her prediction. Would you regard this future person as *you*? Would you now feel that somehow you will escape earthly death to be reborn (resurrected, reincarnated, or what you will) in the future? Can you identify yourself with this future person, believing that that person is a future stage of *you*?[16] I think most of us will resist the suggestion that such a future person could 'really' be oneself.

If you do not share this intuition, then perhaps you might ask yourself how you would react to the news that someone who looks and acts just like you lives some four thousand miles away, right now, at this very moment. Suppose you were to meet that person. Would you be meeting a look-alike; or would you be meeting *yourself*? I think most of us, even if we were hesitant about the former cases – of the earlier and the later look-alikes – would be more reluctant still to acknowledge this contemporary person as being *oneself*. Our concept of *self* simply does not allow that we should learn that we exist not only here and now (e.g. in 1991 in British Columbia), but – surprise! – also at some distant place, e.g. in Moscow or in Paris. I may have a look-alike in Paris, he may even act remarkably like me, but whatever else is true of him, it surely is not that he is *me*.[17]

In saying this, I am of course appealing to your own sense of identity, and am assuming that, for most of us, our reactions and intuitions

---

15. If the spectacle of a seer is too much for your skeptical imagination, you might alter the example to that of a time traveler who has met this future person and brings back to you firsthand knowledge of your future look-alike.

16. If you are comfortable with the notion that time travel is coherent, then ask yourself what if this future person were to enter a time machine and were to travel back in time to the here-and-now and were to confront you face to face? Would you be shaking hands with yourself?

17. Recall Dickens's *A Tale of Two Cities*. The case is more problematic, however, if the two persons share similar thoughts. Lorne Michaels (one of the producers of the television show "Saturday Night Live") jokingly told the story that he had "become obsessed with the notion that somewhere in the

would be pretty much the same for the circumstances described. This is not to say that if your philosophical intuitions are radically different from mine then they are, somehow, wrong. The point of the exercise is not to judge a particular concept of personal identity right or wrong, but to try to bring into focus what one's concept of personal identity is. If your concept of personal identity is enough like mine to cause you to withhold identifying yourself with some former, later, or distant person just on the basis of similarity of features and of personality, then you, like me, will find Tim's request incoherent.[18]

For some person to *be* Tim (or to be *you*), it is not sufficient that that person share Tim's (or your) physical appearance and personality. Clearly something more is needed. (If not, then you could – even at this very moment – theoretically, if not in actual fact, exist at several widely separated places, e.g. London, Paris, or Moscow, having entirely different sets of experiences.) But I think most of us will be prepared to reply to the suggestion that we might be in several different bodies in several different places all at the same time by rejecting the suggestion, not as false, but as incoherent, i.e. as logically impossible. The suggestion is inconsistent with our concept of what it is to be a *person*.

12.7   What more might there be to the concept of *personal identity*?[19]

Tim's imagining that he could have lived in the seventeenth century overlooks certain ingredients which are essential to personal identity. That there might have been someone who looked and acted like Tim was certainly insufficient for that person to have *been* Tim. Something, perhaps a considerable amount, more is required for personal identity. I have earlier suggested that the 'something more' which is

---

world there was a person having the exact same thought he was at exactly the same moment. He decided to call that person, but the line was busy" ([95], 36, footnote). Would even this establish the identity of the two persons?

18. See (i) Thomas Nagel, "Death" ([141], 67) and (ii) Derek Parfit, "How Our Identity in Fact Depends on When We Were Conceived" ([149], §119, 351-6).

19. My thoughts about the topic of this section are in a state of flux and hence the discussion below is at best tentative. Thus, this particular section should be read with more than the usual degree of forbearance.

required includes veridical memory. Without veridical memory, there cannot be personal identity.

But are these two 'dimensions' all there is to personal identity? Does sharing veridical memories with, and having much the same personality as, an earlier person suffice to make the later person identical with the earlier? Many writers have assumed that veridical memory and shared personality comprise a set of sufficient conditions for identity of persons. But some writers are not satisfied with even these two fairly rigorous requirements; they believe that yet more, or something quite different, is required for personal identity.

Saul Kripke, for example, has argued that being born of the parents one actually has is a necessary condition for being the person one is. You could not possibly be identified with anyone having parents different from your own. Using Elizabeth II as his example, he writes:

> How could a person originating from different parents, from a totally different sperm and egg, be *this very woman*? One can imagine, *given* this woman, that various things in her life could have changed [i.e. been different]: that she should have become a pauper; that her royal blood should have been unknown, and so on. One is given, let's say, a previous history of the world up to a certain time, and from that time it diverges considerably from the actual course. This seems to be possible. And so it's possible that even though she were born of these parents she never became queen. Even though she were born of these parents, like Mark Twain's character [footnote: in *The Prince and the Pauper*] she was switched off [exchanged] with another girl. But what is harder to imagine is her being born of different parents. It seems to me that anything coming from a different origin would not be this object. ([116], 113)

For Kripke, Tim's plaint – whatever else might have been incoherent about it – would have been impossible because it imagined that someone having different parents from Tim's could, nonetheless, have been Tim. For Kripke, no one born in the seventeenth century could possibly have been Tim, since no one born in the seventeenth century was the child of Tim's parents.

In a recent article in *Psychology Today*, Russell Belk, reporting on some recent experimental studies, writes:

> What we possess is, in a very real way, part of ourselves. Our

thoughts and our bodies are normally the most central part of our self-concept. But next in importance are what we do – our occupations and skills – and what we have – our unique set of possessions. ... We generally include four types of possessions in our personal sense of self: body and body parts, objects, places and time periods, persons and pets. ... We found that academics were especially likely to cite books as favorite possessions, perhaps because they represent the knowledge on which their work is based. For other people, sporting goods represent what they can or could do ... Many studies have shown that the loss of possessions that follows natural disasters or that occurs when elderly people are put in institutions is often traumatic. What people feel in these circumstances is, quite literally, a loss of self. ([25], 51-2)

In Belk's view, for some persons the loss of material possessions (including external bodily parts) will constitute a radical discontinuity in *self*.

John Perry, in his estimable *A Dialogue on Personal Identity and Immortality* ([151]), presents to us the dying Gretchen Weirob. Her body has been fatally injured and will soon die. On her deathbed, she has been offered the choice of having her intact brain transplanted into the healthy body of a brain-dead patient. She refuses on the grounds that she cannot identify herself now with the future person who will have her brain but not her (present) body; that is, she has no *anticipation* of being that later person. Here Perry jolts our intuitions. Although he does not pursue the question explicitly, there is in the dialogue at least the suggestion that there is a certain *symmetry* between *anticipation* and *memory* in determining personal identity.

Virtually all discussions of personal identity involve cases of *re*-identification, i.e. of identifying later person(-stages) with earlier ones. But why this particular prejudice or bias? Why are there not equal numbers of discussions of *pre*-identification, i.e. of identifying earlier person(-stages) with later ones? Should the anticipating of being a future person – as sometimes occurs in discussions of eschatology* – be factored into the equation of personal identity on a equal footing with memories of having been a past person?

As we collect these many suggestions – Kripke's, Belk's, Perry's, and others' – as to further (or different) necessary conditions for personal identity – having the parents one does, owning the things one does, having an anticipation of being some future person – difficult

and disturbing questions arise about the very practice itself of metaphysics.

There is always a desire in doing philosophy to construct economical theories, ones which seek the minimum set of conditions which are
individually necessary and jointly (i.e. altogether) sufficient for the
correct application of a concept. In analyzing the concept of *personal
identity* it is natural to want an analysis which is as neat and tidy and
free from loose ends as is possible. And thus there is a strong temptation to find grounds on which to reject most suggestions forthcoming
as to further necessary conditions for personal identity. We want to be
able to say: "These conditions, *x*, *y*, and *z*, are necessary; any further
conditions are superfluous or redundant."

Thus, a while ago, when I and several of my colleagues were discussing Weirob's claim that she would not be identical with a future
person who had her memories and personality but not her body, some
of my colleagues argued that Weirob was simply mistaken: that when
the surgery (brain-transplant) had been completed, and the patient
woke out of anesthesia, that patient would recall having been Weirob
and would insist that identity had been preserved. In short, these colleagues were prepared to tell the dying Weirob that she was *mistaken*,
that she would survive if she would but consent to the surgery. In
other words, some of my colleagues were prepared to place their own
theory of personal identity above that of Weirob.

Is there some 'objective' theory of personal identity whose essen-
tials might be grasped and the adoption of which would warrant our
telling someone that he or she was wrong in conceiving of himself or
herself in some particular way?

Not too many years ago, I myself argued in just the way my colleagues argued last year. I, too, believed that Weirob was simply mistaken: that hers was an *incorrect* view of personal identity, and that
she had made a mistake not unlike believing that squares must be red
or that material objects must be soluble in water. Her error, I thought,
consisted in believing that some feature (anticipation, in this case) was
necessary to the concept of *personal identity* when in fact it was not.

I no longer am so ready to insist on that particular view of the philosophical enterprise. Were someone to suggest that all squares must
be red, I would be quick to object, arguing that that person had got the
concept of *square* wrong. And the reason I would be comfortable
arguing in that way would be because I do believe that the concept of
square is fairly universally shared, that most of us do have virtually
the identical concept of *squareness*. And in other cases, I might object

to someone's analysis – an analysis of *probability*, for example – on the basis that it was inferior to others or that it did not work particularly well, e.g. was confused or clumsy or applicable to too few circumstances. That is, in some cases I am prepared to argue that certain analyses of a given concept are better than, or preferable to, certain others.

But the concept of *personal identity* seems to me to be different. Indeed it now seems to me something of a mistake to talk or write about 'the' concept of identity. The more I read what other persons have written, and the more I talk with my students about their own concepts of personal identity, the greater looms the diversity between the many variants of the concept.

The concept of identity which is used in Law is probably a fairly minimal concept in that it invokes a minimal set of necessary conditions. (The Law could not function with a highly variable concept of personhood, no more than it could function with a highly variable concept of *property* or *responsibility*.) But this same concept may not be particularly useful, for example, in psychiatry, where a patient whose memory is intact may feel himself totally detached from earlier actions.

I think philosophers err if they believe that they can construct some one viable theory of personal identity. That particular goal is as illusory as trying to construct some one theory of, for example, what constitutes quality in music or beauty in art. The trouble is that if we look broadly across our culture, and particularly if we step outside it, we find immense differences in the prephilosophical intuitions persons have about personal identity.[20] The occupational danger for philosophers lies in our too often creating philosophy for other philosophers, indeed not even for all other philosophers, but only for philosophers who belong to the same 'school'. The hazards of inbreeding and of tunnel vision are ever-present.

I remain convinced that memory and personality are the essential

---

20. A great many articles and books published by psychiatrists and psychologists treating the concept of *self* arise out of their clinical experience with patients who have 'immature', 'defective', or even 'pathological' concepts of *self*. One must beware, however, not to draw from these writings the idea that the diversity of concepts of *self* arises out of arrested growth or psychological disorder. When we talk with persons whose concept of *self* is in no way dysfunctional, we find an equally prodigious range of difference.

core of the concept of personal identity. But I am no longer so sure that other factors might not also play an important role, and I am not confident that there are not, in fact, a great number of diverse, yet viable, concepts of personal identity, some of which are not merely different from one another, but even incompatible. In short, I am making a plea for tolerance in the matter of explicating the concept of identity. I think it hopeless, and indeed inappropriate, to argue that there is, or could be, one best concept of personal identity. Our concepts of personal identity are too varied to allow a single reconstruction.

With this said, I turn to our closing case study. If personal identity is not carried by a changeless soul, if personal identity requires continuity of memory and preservation of personality, and if personality, in turn, includes such things as intense desires and mental capacities, then there are some profound consequences in the changing of persons' desires and mental capacities.

12.8   Case study: Can there be justice after death?[21]

There are, I think, two principal egoistic motives which prompt us to desire an afterlife: a desire to maintain what is valued in our lives – including perhaps, but hardly limited to, the sensual, the intellectual, and the aesthetic – and a desire to achieve what we wanted but did not have in life – including perhaps, but hardly limited to, material goods, honor, power, creative talents, and physical abilities.

But for many persons, the desire that there be an afterlife is in part motivated by reasons which transcend individual, personal considerations. This world, we all know – and are constantly reminded throughout the day on the electronic news media and in the newspapers – is unfair. Indeed the world is grossly unfair. A catalogue of its injustices ranges widely from physical handicaps, sickness, and grief to starvation, slavery, flood, avalanche, wanton acts of terrorism, and so on so as to overwhelm the imagination.

Doubtless many of us find the notion of an afterlife appealing, not just because it holds out the promise of thwarting eternal personal Nothingness, but equally – and probably for some of us, even more strongly – because it offers the prospect of finally putting right the injustice in this world. It is in the afterlife, we have been so often

---

21. This section is a revised version of an essay which originally appeared in [104].

propagandized by religion, that virtue will be rewarded and evil punished. Our sense of morality craves this, whether or not it is in fact actual or even, for that matter, possible.

Usual philosophical discussions of justice concern the problems of realizing greater justice in this world. Such discussions typically rely heavily on specifying, and trying to work within, a variety of constraints: ignorance, scarcity of goods, legal systems, and – although often overlooked – physical possibility itself. Indeed so pervasive is the constraint of physical possibility, it hardly even is acknowledged. It is simply an unarticulated presupposition.

But what happens if one seeks to maximize justice in a world (e.g. the afterlife) which is not subject to these usual kinds of constraints? In an afterlife (heaven or hell or some other place), could the Dispenser of Justice (whether an individual or several minds working together) achieve perfect justice? What if, by simply willing it, the Dispenser of Justice could bring into existence any number and variety of goods? What if, that is, there were not scarcity but infinite plenitude? What if physical possibility were to become coextensive* with logical possibility, i.e. the only constraint on the actual (afterlife actual, that is, not this-world actual) were the requirement that no self-inconsistency were to be realized? What if every veil of ignorance were to be lifted?[22] What if, that is, we should all know – if not everything – at least whatever we wanted to know? What if, in particular, every person's every deed were known? What if every person's every desire, doubt, hope, longing, envy, animosity, lust, love, were also known?

Could an omniscient, omnipotent Dispenser of Justice bring about perfect justice under these circumstances? Many religious believers, for millennia, have thought so. I find it difficult to share such optimism. Even in the afterlife, perfect justice – I am afraid – is unrealizable. My pessimism stems from several considerations.

---

22. Although I will not pursue the matter here, I must mention that an afterlife in which this world's physical laws do not hold true will present severe problems for epistemology. All human knowledge of contingent universal propositions presupposes a background of physical laws. Without there being a relatively fixed set of knowable physical laws, human empirical knowledge would seem to be significantly curtailed. In an afterlife where physical possibility expands to nearly the compass of logical possibility, a substantial part of human knowledge would have to flow from (what are in this world) unknown a priori sources, and not from a posteriori ones.

The principal difficulty, as I see it, is that persons sometimes have intensely painful desires which may be satisfied in but one single way. This is particularly awkward when the desire is not for a kind of material possession or a physical skill or a bodily appearance (a desire which the Dispenser of Justice could easily indulge), but for the company, love, or companionship of – not just some person or other, but – some particular person. How could the problem of, let us say, unrequited love be solved by the Dispenser of Justice in the afterlife? For it often happens that one person will form strong emotional bonds – of caring, of longing, of needing – to some particular other person, where the latter person loathes and actively avoids the former.

There seems to be no fully satisfactory, i.e. uncompromised, solution to this problem, although there are a number of apparent solutions. We might begin, for example, by arguing that justice does not demand the elimination of every possible pain. Justice, we might try to argue, demands only eliminating persons' pains when to do so does not infringe on the rights of other persons.

Are we then to ignore the pain of the person whose love is unrequited? Not much of a heaven, we might be inclined to protest, in which there is still so much pain. An innocent person whose love is unrequited might be suffering the pains of hell. How come this is permitted in heaven? What can be done to alleviate the undeserved suffering of this person?

The immediate temptation, since we are talking of heaven, where everything short of the logically impossible is possible, is to argue that the Dispenser of Justice could simply will away the sufferer's pain. If desire is causing intense pain to its owner, and if that desire cannot be satisfied because to do so would conflict with the rights of others, then it would seem that the next best alternative would be for that desire to be expunged, i.e. nullified, by an act of the Dispenser of Justice.

But the trouble with such solutions, and so many others which would have existence in the afterlife sanitized, sterilized, perfumed, rendered conflict-free, etc., is that they sometimes do violence to the very concept of personal identity. Consider the case of the parent whose entire reason for being is directed toward caring for and loving his/her daughter. But suppose the child reacts by asserting her autonomy. Above all else she wants to be free of, and distant from, her parent. Suppose, too, that these differences are irreconcilable. We might suppose that the parent's love in this case is overbearing; perhaps it is even irrational.

In a world unconstrained by physical laws, the Dispenser of Justice could remove the parent's pain by eradicating the desire which engendered it. But would this be justice? We can imagine the prospect of having the painful longing removed being put to the parent before the Dispenser of Justice acted. And we can imagine the parent protesting: "To blot out this particular desire would be to destroy me. What makes me ME is my love and longing – however much grief it causes me – for my child. If I cannot have the love of my child reciprocated and you were to rob me of this pain, you will have annihilated me. This living body might remain, but whatever survives such a drastic alternation will not be ME."

Some persons do have such desires, desires which are intensely painful and yet which justice – because of the conflicting rights of others – cannot satisfy. But justice cannot always then fall back to a 'next best' solution, viz. eliminating the pain by nullifying those desires. For justice, surely, also demands the preservation of personal identity. And these latter two demands – the elimination of the pain of innocent persons and the preservation of personal identity – will sometimes be impossible to satisfy together. There are certain unsatisfiable desires, some of them intensely painful, whose elimination would be tantamount to extinguishing the person who had them.

There is a second sort of difficulty for the belief that justice might be realized in an afterlife. Do virtue and do wrongdoing have just deserts? Is the rehabilitation of the wrongdoer, is his/her contrition, is his/her restitution of wrongly appropriated property all that justice demands? Certainly for many cases the answer must be yes. But something deep inside many of us resists this answer for all cases. Some crimes are so heinous as to make rehabilitation and contrition wholly inadequate. Some crimes are of such magnitude as to make any thought of restitution insulting to the offended. Nothing humanly doable in this world could be fit justice for the crimes of, let us say, a Mengele, and he was – sad to say – not the worst.

For some crimes nothing short of punishment of the offender will satisfy the longing for justice the offended-against demand. But – and here's the rub – punishment often cannot be meted out to the guilty without causing pain to the innocent. I am not talking of the pain of persons opposed to punishment – although their pain may be real and deep – but of the more immediate pain of the wives, husbands, mothers, fathers, daughters, sons, friends, and lovers of the punished. Persons do not become guilty themselves and warrant punishment for loving a wrongdoer. And yet their pain may well be, very likely will be, intense when he is suffering his punishment.

Here, rationality takes a back seat to emotions. While knowledge that the child is in fact guilty and is being punished justly and deservedly may quell a parent's outrage and stifle his objections, that knowledge may do little to numb his anguish. Indeed, it may even make it worse by denying the parent the vent of a righteous fury.

Were the Dispenser of Justice to will away the grief and pain of the innocent person for his/her loved one's punishment, the grieving person would have been rendered less than human. Consider the case of a serial child molester and murderer. A very great deal of our horror, revulsion, and demand for his punishment is grounded in our empathy with the pain caused his victims' surviving families. That is, part of our outrage flows from our certain knowledge of the grief families will feel at the injury and death of one of their members. And yet when we demand punishment of the wrongdoer, his own – innocent – family will suffer because of his pain. What choices are then open to the Dispenser of Justice? Eschew punishing the guilty? render their innocent families insensible of the punishment? render their innocent families uncaring? The consequences of each of these alternatives seem to be forswearing justice, adopting subterfuge, and inducing callousness, respectively. None of these strikes me as compatible with perfect justice.

But this is hardly the end of the problem. There is yet a third difficulty. If there is an afterlife, what age are we each to be in that afterlife? Few, if any, nonagenarians would want to endure an eternity 'housed' in the body they had at the time of their death. No, justice would seem to require getting back your body when it was at its fittest and healthiest: a twenty-five-year-old body for most persons (that is, if the Metropolitan Life Insurance Company is to be believed in these matters). But what of the mentally and physically handicapped? What of the legions of children who died in childhood and never had an adult body? What bodies, what age, what capacities are these latter persons to have in the afterlife?

Surely the infant who died in this world at the age of two is not to remain an infant for eternity in the afterlife. Granted there are certain pleasures of childhood, but I think it the rare person who would willingly swap those of adulthood for those of childhood. But if the child who died at the age of two years in this world is not to remain an infant in the afterlife, what sort of person is he to be in that afterlife? Is he to mature in that afterlife, both bodily and mentally, as he would have done had he not died in this world?

One possibility would be to accelerate the two-year-olds immediately to adulthood. But this solution poses fresh problems of injustice. It strikes me as unfair to rob anyone of childhood. Having reached adulthood, I prefer it to childhood; even so, I would not want to have missed childhood.

If children who die in this world are to be given in the afterlife the childhoods they missed, the afterlife is going to have to resemble the planet Earth far more than it resembles traditional images of heaven. Put bluntly, heaven is no place for a human child to grow up. A place of plenitude and where physical possibility is – more or less – coextensive with logical possibility just does not strike me as the fit playground for a young inquiring mind. On the contrary, it strikes me as a place where one cannot have much fun. To be a proper environment for a human child, the afterlife ought to be awfully like this world, complete with swings, trees, frogs (or similar sorts of exotica), schools, cuts and bruises, successes and failures, joy and heartbreak, etc. At the very least, it has to resemble Earth, not so much in appearance, but in physical law. It has to be a place in which much the same sorts of things have to occur as happen typically on Earth, and that means it has – of its very nature – to be a place where there is much unfairness. So while unfairness need not be a permanent feature of heaven, it must be of a part of heaven for at least as long as it takes the last-dead child to reach adulthood.

This still leaves the problem of the mentally handicapped. Are they in the afterlife to be made rational and intelligent? After all, it was unfair that they were not more rational and intelligent in the first instance. But how can rationality and intelligence be conferred on a severely mentally handicapped person without thereby destroying that person's identity? Marked increases in rationality and intelligence are certain to alter a person's personality radically: the desires, the expectations, the abilities, the typical reactions, the human relationships, etc. that the original person had are bound to change significantly. But these kinds of changes are just the sorts of ones which we regard as altering personal identity. A person who speaks fourteen languages, who runs a mile in 3:51 minutes, who discourses on the subtleties of Quine's philosophy, and who choreographs ballets to the music of Villa Lobos cannot in any but the most Quixotic sense be identified with an earlier person whose body he may have inherited, but who was deaf, dumb, halt, and incapable of understanding language.

My nagging fear is that the injustice which befalls some of us – particularly those so unfortunate as to be born profoundly mentally and physically handicapped – cannot be undone or recompensed.[23] The 'not' operative here is the 'not' of 'not logically possible', not 'not humanly possible'. To undo a severe mental handicap is not to give someone something he lacked, but is to annihilate the one person and to substitute in his place another. Personal identity logically cannot be preserved over a change of this kind and this magnitude. The promise is often made by clerics that the injustices and suffering of this world will be 'put right' in the afterlife. But the promise is at best a falsehood or at worst a lie. There is no logically possible way to 'put right' the injustice of a person's being born profoundly mentally handicapped.

In the end, I have a gnawing suspicion that the very existence of an afterlife is a myth. If it is not, then it is hard to see how it could even begin to live up to its billing. If there is an afterlife, it can hardly be the sort of place where justice is finally realized. The trouble is that justice logically cannot finally be realized. Not even a perfect Dispenser of Justice can bestow perfect justice on less than perfect beings, i.e. on the likes of you and me, our friends and loved ones, those we care about, and those we abominate. I find I am driven to agree with Boito's Iago:

> Man's Fortune's fool even from his earliest breath.
> The germ of life is fashioned
> To feed the worm of death.
> Yea, after all this folly all must die.
> And then? And then there's nothing,
> And heav'n an ancient lie.[24]

---

23. "… along with Helen Keller, my grandfather [Oklahoma senator Thomas Gore] was one of the most famous handicapped persons in America. We were very close. I was taught to read early so that I could read to him, and I read him the newspapers, the Congressional Record, history. When I was a little boy, a sob sister for a newspaper came to interview my grandfather. She said, 'Senator, there must be so many compensations for your blindness, like a superb memory, sensitive hearing. Could you tell me what they are?' And he said, 'There are *no* compensations.' That phrase has sounded continuously in my head ever since" (Gore Vidal; reported in [36], 53).

24. Arrigo Boito, libretto for Verdi's *Otello*, act II, scene II, 1886

Glossary

accidental property A property of a thing, *x*, is said to be 'accidental' if *x* could still be *x* and lack that specific property. Properties which are not accidental are said to be 'essential'. For example, the property of having straight sides is an essential property of a thing's being a square. But being painted green would be an accidental property of a square.

algorithm An algorithm is a step-by-step procedure (recipe) for finding the solution in a finite number of steps to a specified kind of problem. For example, the algorithm for finding whether a natural number (expressed in base ten) is divisible without remainder by three is: "(1) Strike out all occurrences of the digits 0, 3, 6, and 9. (2) Add the remaining digits, if any, together. (3) If the sum is greater than 9, repeat steps (1), (2), and (3). (4) If the result is nil, 3, 6, or 9, then the original number is divisible by 3; if the result is anything else, then the original number is not divisible by 3."

a posteriori By experience

a priori A proposition (see "proposition") is said to be knowable a priori if it can be known *without experience*. Some persons have mistakenly believed that a priori knowledge is knowledge which is possible *prior* to any experience, e.g. would be knowledge attainable by a newborn infant. This is a misconception. When philosophers say that a proposition can be known without experience, they mean that no particular experience of the world, save perhaps learning a language, is necessary to be able to figure out the truth or falsity of the proposition. Various propositions have been offered as examples of this kind of knowledge, e.g. those of mathematics ("Four squared is sixteen"); of logic ("If P and Q are both true, then P is true"); and of (narrow) conceptual analysis ("If A is older than B, then B is younger than A"). Empiricists believe that there are no factual (see "contingent") propositions which are knowable a priori;

Rationalists, in contrast, believe that there are at least some. (See also the discussion in footnote 8, p. 101.)

begging the question A fallacious manner of arguing in which the very thing that one is attempting to establish is assumed as a premise

belief Philosophers use the term "belief" broadly. Our use includes religious beliefs, but all other beliefs as well: political beliefs, scientific beliefs, etc. In short, we use this term to encompass anything believed, from beliefs about the origin of the universe to ones as mundane as whether the car needs to be washed.

Cartesian Deriving from the philosophy of René Descartes

class See "set".

coextensive 1. Two objects, O' and O'', are coextensive if they occupy precisely the same region of space.
2. Two events, E' and E'', are coextensive if they occupy the same interval of time.
3. Two classes (sets) are said to be coextensive if every member of one is a member of the other and conversely. Thus, for example, the class which is the largest elected legislative assembly on Earth in 1980 is coextensive with the class which consists of the 1980 membership of the United States Senate and the House of Representatives. Note that the class which consists of the United States Senate together with the House of Representatives is, by definition, the United States Congress. But the former class, i.e. the largest elected legislative assembly on Earth, is not – by definition – the Congress; it just happens – as a matter of fact – to comprise the same membership. An alternative way of saying that two classes are coextensive is to say that they are *extensionally equivalent*.

confirmation A hypothesis is said to be confirmed if a new prediction derived from that hypothesis is shown to be true. Confirmation is not, however, verification. To verify a hypothesis is to show it to be true. Confirmation is a weaker relation than verification. To confirm a hypothesis is to offer in support evidence which falls short of establishing the truth of that hypothesis. That is, to confirm a hypothesis is to offer evidence which raises the probability of that hypothesis being true, but which does not prove it to be true. For example, someone might try six different chords on a piano and find them all in tune. Such evidence would confirm the hypothesis that *all* strings on the piano were in tune, but would not verify that hypothesis. It remains possible that some of the untested strings are out of tune.

contingent A proposition *P* is said to be contingent if neither it (i.e. *P*) nor its denial (i.e. not-*P*) is self-contradictory. Contingent propositions thus are ones which, from a logical point of view, could be true *and* could be false (e.g. that the Titanic struck an iceberg), i.e. ones which could have *either* truth-value (see p. 28). Whether a proposition is contingent or not has nothing whatever to do with anyone's *knowing* its truth-value; it is wholly a matter of whether or not both it and its denial are free of self-contradiction. Non-contingent propositions are those which are either self-contradictory themselves (e.g. that someone's brother is an only child) or whose denials are self-contradictory (e.g. [the necessary truth] that all squares have four sides). Some philosophers explicate the distinction between contingency and non-contingency by saying that a contingent proposition is one which is true in some possible world(s) and is false in some (other) possible world(s), while a non-contingent proposition is either true in all possible worlds or is false in all possible worlds.

"Contingent" used in its technical sense, as it is in this book, does not mean, as it often does in ordinary English, "conditional upon", as when, for example, one might say, "Their attending the picnic will be contingent upon the weather." This latter, ordinary, use of "contingent" is simply not used at all in this book.

counterfactual "Counterfactual" means "contrary-to-(actual)-fact". One of the most common devices philosophers use to try to discover persons' dispositions to use a certain term, *x*, is to ask questions of the sort, "What would you say if such-and-such were (counterfactually) to be so-and-so? Would you describe it as being *x*?" For many philosophical purposes, "counterfactually" and "in another (i.e. non-actual) possible world" may be used interchangeably. (See section 6.4, pp. 108ff.)

descriptive definition A descriptive definition is one which reports the standard usage of a term. It may be contrasted with normative and with stipulative definitions. A normative definition is one which attempts to refine a usage, as we see, for example, in some dictionaries warning readers not to use "infer" and "imply" interchangeably. See also "stipulative definition".

empirical 1. "Empirical" is most often used as a modifier of "knowledge". When so used it describes the *mode* by which that knowledge is obtainable. Some authors use the term "empirical" as equivalent to "a posteriori", i.e. as equivalent to "by experience". In this book, however, I adopt the stricter (narrower) meaning prescribed by Immanuel Kant in which "empirical" means not "by experience" but "*only* by experience" (see [34], 149-56). When I write that something, *P*, is knowable empirically, I mean that *P* cannot be known (by human beings) in any way other than by experience. Whatever is humanly knowable, but in a way other than by experience, is knowable a priori. (See definitions of "a priori" and "a posteriori".)

2. Occasionally "empirical" is also used as a modifier of "concept". An empirical concept is one whose referent is observable or detectable through experience. *Weight* is thus an empirical concept; *soul* and *substance* are often regarded as nonempirical concepts.

epistemology One of the principal branches of philosophy, epistemology is the theory of knowledge. Its subject matter includes the role of sense perception in the acquisition of knowledge, the possibility of attaining objective knowledge, the psychological aspects of knowledge, and – on some accounts – the sociological aspects of knowledge. (The adjectival forms are "epistemic" and "epistemological".)

eschatological Pertaining to the end of the world, life after death, etc.

exobiology The term "exobiology" was coined (c. 1960) ([21], 355) by the geneticist, Joshua Lederberg ([69]). It refers to the study of (or, for the present time at least, the search for) life beyond the Earth's atmosphere, in effect on other planets. Whereas the program SETI is the search for *intelligent* extraterrestrial life, the scope of exobiology is wider: it is the search for alien life itself, intelligent or not.

formal "Formal" pertains to structure; its contrast is content. For example, the two sentences "Sally sees Richard" and "New York is larger than Boston", while having different content, share some of the same structure, i.e. are formally alike to a degree, in that both consist of a relational term flanked fore and aft by proper names. In section 8.8, I write about certain formal properties shared by spatial and temporal relations. For example, the spatial relation of *being north of* is, to a certain degree, formally equivalent to the temporal relation of *being earlier than*. Both are so-called 'ordering relations': locations in space (along a line of longitude) may be arranged in order according to the relation *is north of*; similarly, events (subject to certain constraints within special relativity theory) may be ordered according to the relation *is earlier than*. (In logical terms, both these relations bear the formal, or structural, properties of *transitivity*, *asymmetry*, and *irreflexivity*. See, e.g., [34], 339-42.)

half-truth There are only two truth-values (see p. 28): true and false. There is nothing 'intermediate' between truth and falsity. That is, there is no 'third', or 'middle' truth-value. (This latter claim has since ancient times been known as the law of the excluded middle.) Thus no single proposition can be either half-true or half-false. However, a *set* of two or more propositions may contain some members which are true and others which are false. Although any set of propositions which contains even a single false proposition is, taken as a whole, false, it is sometimes convenient to designate sets which contain some false propositions and some true propositions as being a 'half-truth'. A half-truth is thus a 'mixed' set of propositions: some of its members are true, but only some; the others are false.

idealism Idealism is the theory that the only things that exist are minds and their contents, e.g. pains, beliefs, desires, sensations of sounds, afterimages. Although "idealistic" is often used in ordinary speech to describe persons who have 'ideals', i.e. ambitions to better themselves or the world at large, this is not the sense of "idealism" being used in this book. Here, "idealism" is the name of a metaphysical thesis which contrasts, in the first instance, with materialism. (See also "materialism".)

individual (*noun*) In ordinary speech, "individual" usually means a person. But in philosophical terminology, "individual" is given a wider meaning. As often used by philosophers, "individual" means not just persons, but any particular thing whatever: individual noises, cars, violins, pains, memories, molecules, stars, etc. An individual is, then, anything which is located in space and time. Another term which is used virtually interchangeably with "individual" is "particular". (Note: some philosophers will use "individual" in an even broader sense. They use "individual" to refer to anything whatsoever which may be talked about as the subject of discourse.

Thus they will include the number two, the number three, etc. in the class of individuals even though they may be disinclined to believe that such 'entities' are located in space and time. The mere fact that one can attribute properties to numbers, e.g. "The number two is even", suffices – on this latter account – to win for numbers the status of being individuals.)

materialism Materialism is the theory that the only things that exist are material (physical) things: subatomic particles through to human bodies and their brains, and on through to stars, galaxies, and galactic clusters. But beyond these things and their distinctive properties, there are no other sorts of things, e.g. minds or supernatural beings, in the world. This technical sense must be distinguished from the more familiar, ordinary sense in which "materialism" is used to describe the greed of persons who are overly acquisitive of material possessions. (See also "idealism".)

methodology The body of techniques, rules, and procedures adopted for the pursuit of some discipline, e.g. science. Methodological assumptions are sometimes adopted, not so much because they are themselves believed to be *true*, but because their adoption is believed to offer a profitable manner of pursuing truth. For example, some psychologists will adopt behaviorism as a methodological principle, not so much because they believe that all mental acts can in some sense be 'reduced to' overt behavior, but because they believe that studying behavior provides the best – and in some instances, the only – access scientists have to the mental states of other persons.

modality 1. In philosophy, "modality" refers to that family of properties which includes possibility, impossibility, contingency, and necessity. To specify, then, the *modal status* of a proposition is to say something about its possibility, impossibility, contingency, or necessity. One particularly fashionable way to explicate modal concepts in contemporary philosophy is through the idiom of possible worlds. A proposition is said to be (logically) possible, for example, if it is true in at least one possible world; a proposition is said to be (logically) impossible if it is true in no possible worlds; etc. *Modal status* is often contrasted with *epistemic status*, the latter having to do with whether a proposition is knowable or unknowable, known or unknown. (Modal and epistemic status can link in sixteen different combinations. See [34], esp. 156-75.)

2. In psychology, "modality" refers to any of several different kinds of sensory abilities (or senses), e.g. seeing, hearing, smelling. Sight comprises one sensory modality (or mode); hearing, another; smelling, still another; etc.

necessary condition "*x* is a *necessary condition* for *y*" means "if *x* did not exist (/did not occur /was false), then *y* would not exist (/would not occur /would be false)". For example, *being more than twelve years old* is a necessary condition for *being twenty years old*, inasmuch as a thing/person which was *not* more than twelve years old would *not* be twenty years old. Pulling a face card from a deck of cards is a necessary condition for pulling a Queen, but it is not a sufficient condition: the face card pulled may be a Jack. (See also "sufficient condition".) If *x* is a necessary condition for *y*, then *y* – in turn – is a sufficient condition for *x*.

necessary truth A proposition (see below) is a necessary truth if its denial is self-contradictory. Synonyms for "necessary truth" include "logical truth" and "non-contingent truth". Using the possible-worlds idiom, a necessary truth may be explicated as a proposition which is true in all logically possible worlds, i.e. true under any logically possible circumstances. Necessary truths include such propositions as "2 + 2 = 4" and "All red things are colored."

ontology 1. The fundamental categories of what *sorts* or *kinds* of things there are in the universe. At one level of analysis, tables and chairs might be considered to be distinct kinds of things; but for the purposes of ontology, tables and chairs are (usually regarded as being) the same sort of 'thing', namely physical (or spatiotemporal) entities. Other 'fundamental' sorts of things which have been proposed by various philosophers at one time or another have been: sets (or classes), propositions, facts, states of affairs, universals, numbers, causal connections, forces, substances, souls, minds, spiritual beings, ethical values, purposes, etc.
2. The branch of metaphysics concerned with the fundamental categories of things

particular (*noun*) See "individual".

particular (*adj.*) When used as an adjective, "particular" typically modifies "proposition" or "statement". A particular proposition is one of the form "Some *S* is *P*" or "There are *S*s (which are *P*s)." Another name for "particular proposition" is "existential proposition". Particular propositions should not be confused with *singular* propositions. Particular propositions are *general* propositions: they refer, not to specific individuals, but to classes of individuals. However, singular propositions, e.g. "Brian Mulroney is prime minister", do refer to specific individuals. Just to make life complicated: singular propositions refer to specific particulars; particular propositions do not.

phenomenology A description of the formal structure of the objects of awareness, i.e. a description of the appearance of things, disregarding any account of their origin, explanation, causes, etc. (There is, in addition, a philosophical school called 'Phenomenology', founded by Brentano and extended by Husserl. This latter – different – sense of "phenomenology" is not invoked in this book.)

physical impossibility A situation is physically impossible if its description is inconsistent with physical laws (i.e. with the laws of Nature). For example, it is thought that it is a physical law (law of Nature) that no material object can be accelerated past the speed of light (300,000 km/sec). If so, then it is physically impossible for there to be some material object which is accelerated to, let us say, 375,000 km/sec. But note that although this latter situation is said to be *physically* impossible, its description is not logically self-inconsistent, and hence is not *logically* impossible.

posit (*noun*) A hypothesis or assumption

posit (*verb*) To put forward a posit, i.e. to assume a hypothesis

predicate (*verb*) To attribute a quality or relation to

proposition Some philosophers use the term "statement" as a synonym for "proposition". Propositions are the sorts of things which are true or false; they are the sorts of things which may be believed, disbelieved, known, doubted, etc. In English, propositions often are expressed by so-called 'that-phrases', e.g. "She knew *that the train would be late*" and "He theorized *that the solution contained copper sulfate*". (For a discussion of several different theories about the metaphysical nature of propositions, see [34], 65-127, esp. 65-86.)

question-begging See "begging the question".

reciprocal (*math.*) The reciprocal of a number is its multiplicative inverse, i.e. the number which when multiplied by the original number yields 1 as the product. Thus, the reciprocal of 3/4 is 4/3, and of −2 is −1/2.

retrodiction Retrodicting is the analog of forecasting an event, but directed oppositely in time, i.e. to the past rather than the future. Just as one might forecast, from a knowledge of physical laws along with specific data about the current position and speed of a comet, where it will be ten years from now, one might retrodict where it was ten years ago.

semantics Semantics is the branch of the theory of signs dealing with *meaning*, e.g. with how descriptive terms (or better, their users) *refer* to items and features in the world.

set A set is any class or collection of things. The set (class) may be 'natural', e.g. the set of mammals, or it may be completely arbitrary, e.g. the set consisting of Napoleon, the number two, and Vancouver Island. Sets, on most accounts, are regarded as abstract entities and are not to be identified with their members. E.g. the *set* which consists of my daughter's piano is not itself a piano (nor is it, for that matter, even a physical [material] object). Sets are standardly denoted by braces, e.g. "{Napoleon, 2, Vancouver Island}".

A set A is said to be a ***subset*** of a set B if every member of A is also a member of B. A set A is said to be a *proper* subset of a set B if A is a subset of B, but not conversely. E.g. the set of women is a proper subset of the set of human beings. Although the terms "subset" and "proper subset" are not, strictly speaking, equivalent, many authors write the former for the latter.

A set A is said to be a ***superset*** of a set B if every member of B is also a member of A. A set A is said to be a *proper* superset of a set B if A is a superset of B, but not conversely. E.g. the set of human beings is a proper superset of the set of women. Again, as with "proper subset", many authors omit "proper" when writing of proper supersets.

An ***ordered*** set (denoted by angle brackets) is one in which both its membership and the *order* of the members determine the set. The (non-ordered) set A, $\{2, 5, 8\}$, is identical to the set B, $\{5, 8, 2\}$: A and B have the same membership. But this set also gives rise to six nonidentical ordered sets: $\langle 2, 5, 8 \rangle$, $\langle 2, 8, 5 \rangle$, $\langle 5, 2, 8 \rangle$, $\langle 5, 8, 2 \rangle$, $\langle 8, 2, 5 \rangle$, and $\langle 8, 5, 2 \rangle$.

An ***ordered pair*** is an ordered set having two members.

stipulative definition A stipulative definition is one which lays down a specific, usually specialized and technical, usage for a term. Examples may be found in the definition of "contingent" above and "world" below. See also "descriptive definition".

sufficient condition "*x* is a *sufficient condition* for *y*" means "if *x* exists (/occurs /is true), then *y* exists (/occurs /is true)". For example, *being twenty years old* is a sufficient condition for *being more than twelve years old*, inasmuch as any thing/person which *is* twenty years old is thereby guaranteed to be a thing which *is* more than twelve years old. Pulling a Queen from a deck of playing cards is a sufficient condition for pulling a face card, but it is not a necessary condition: one could pull a face card which was not a Queen, i.e. a King or a Jack. (See also "necessary condition".) If *x* is a sufficient condition for *y*, then *y* – in turn – is a necessary condition for *x*.

sui generis In a class by itself

topology Geometry has two branches: metrical geometry and topology. Metrical geometry concerns measurement and size – such matters as, for example, proportionality; relative sizes of angles; lengths of peripheries; angles formed by the intersection of diagonals; projections of three-dimensional objects onto two-dimensional surfaces; and perspective. Topology, in contrast, is concerned with those aspects of geometry which are independent of the sizes of the figures, indeed which would still obtain even if the figure were to be 'stretched' or 'distorted' (short of 'tearing' it) – such matters as, for example, the existence of paths connecting two or more regions; the equivalence of knots; and the number of colors required (in principle) to color any arbitrary map so that no two adjacent regions have the same color. From a metrical point of view, a sphere, an oval, and an ellipse are all different figures; from a topological point of view, they are identical. Similarly, from a topological point of view, these three figures share the same topological dimensions: they are two-dimensional whatever their sizes or however they are stretched.

underdetermined A hypothesis or theory is said to be underdetermined by the evidence which supports it if that evidence does not logically guarantee the truth of that hypothesis or theory. If some evidence underdetermines a hypothesis, then that same evidence also underdetermines (some) competing theories. Thus, for example, using the (necessarily inconclusive) evidence produced by the Warren Commission, many writers have proposed several different theories of John F. Kennedy's assassination: e.g. that Oswald acted alone, that Oswald was not the assassin, that there was a second shooter, that organized crime planned the operation, and that foreign nationals planned the operation.

universal (*adj.*) The adjectival form of "universal" means "for all of the universe, i.e. throughout all of space and time." "Universal" is not limited just to the planet Earth. (See "world".) "Universal" does not mean "necessary". Something can be universally true without being necessarily true, e.g. that the speed of light is greater than 290,000 km/sec.

universal (*noun*) According to the theory of Realism, the *properties* of particulars (see above) are posited to be (abstract) entities 'subsisting' outside of space and time. Such entities are usually called "universals". In this theory, the class of universals includes greenness, triangularity, solubility, hardness, etc. As well, especially in the twentieth century, it has become usual for Realism to include among universals the *relations* obtaining between particulars, e.g. *being to the left of* or *being older than*. Needless to say, the ontological status of universals, i.e. the 'nature' of their existence, has been a subject of intense controversy in metaphysics since Plato first introduced the topic. For more on universals, see chapter 9, esp. sect. 9.3.

world Throughout this book, when I use the term "world", I mean the entire universe, both what is known of it and what is unknown; I also include all of the world's history, its present, and its future in this all-encompassing term. I never use "world" to mean (just) the planet Earth, or – for that matter – any other planet.

Further reading

Chapter One – Presenting philosophy

The Two Cultures and *A Second Look*, by Charles P. Snow. Cambridge University Press, Cambridge, 1963.

> One of the most acclaimed and, equally, one of the most reviled books in recent decades. Snow argues for the greater appreciation between scientists and 'literary intellectuals' of one another's accomplishments and modes of thought.

Two Cultures? by F.R. Leavis and Michael Yudkin. Pantheon Books, New York, 1963.

> Two of the best known, most virulent attacks on Snow's *Two Cultures*. It is both sad and discouraging to read Yudkin's outrageous proclamation: "To read Dickens, or to hear Mozart, or to see a Titian can be in itself a rewarding activity; but to find out what is meant by acceleration is to gain a piece of factual information which in itself has no value" (p. 54). Inadvertently, Yudkin has provided the strongest possible illustration of precisely the ignorance and frame of mind which Snow was lamenting.

Chapter Two – The metaphysical impulse

Metaphysics (3rd ed.), by Richard Taylor. Prentice-Hall, Englewood Cliffs, NJ, 1983.

> An introduction to metaphysics. Easy reading.

When Bad Things Happen to Good People, by Harold S. Kushner. Avon, New York, 1983.

> A discussion of the existence of natural evil. Although not a 'philosophy' book, it sets out the *problem* better than most philosophical texts. A recent, popular best-seller.

What Does It All Mean? – A Very Short Introduction to Philosophy, by Thomas Nagel. Oxford University Press, New York, 1987.

Covers a number of topics not pursued in this book, e.g. 'How do we know anything?', 'other minds', 'free will', 'right and wrong', and 'justice'. Easy reading (101 pp.).

Mathematics: The Loss of Certainty, by Morris Kline. Oxford University Press, New York, 1980.

A first-rate history of mathematics which argues that modern mathematics has lost its roots in practical problems.

Chapter Three – Theories: What they are and what they are not

Conjectures and Refutations, by Karl Popper. Basic Books, New York, 1962.

An important work, by a major philosopher. The book becomes progressively more difficult. Newcomers to philosophy will want to read selectively in this volume.

Science and Subjectivity, by Israel Scheffler. Bobbs-Merrill, Indianapolis, 1967.

An attempt to rebut the views of Kuhn, Feyerabend, etc., that there is neither objectivity nor truth in scientific theories.

The Structure of Scientific Revolutions (2nd ed.), by Thomas Kuhn. University of Chicago Press, Chicago, 1970.

A modern-day classic. Highly controversial attack, by a historian, on the traditional view that science is objective.

Against Method, by Paul Feyerabend. Verso, London, 1982.

In the same vein as Kuhn, but written by a philosopher.

The Blind Watchmaker: Why the Evidence of Evolution Reveals a Universe without Design, by Richard Dawkins. W.W. Norton, New York, 1987.

A defense of Darwinism against Creationism. The Appendix contains an order form for a Macintosh software program by which to 'breed' biomorphs on one's home computer. A portent of future philosophy instruction?

Chapter Four – Underdeterminism (I)

The Metaphysical Foundations of Modern Science (2nd ed.), by E.A. Burtt. Routledge & Kegan Paul, London, 1932.

"How curious, after all, is the way in which we moderns think about our world! And it is all so novel, too. The cosmology underlying our mental processes is but three centuries old – a mere infant in the history of thought – and yet we cling to it with the same embarrassed zeal with which a young father fondles his new-born baby." (chapter 1)

Dilemmas, by Gilbert Ryle. Cambridge University Press, London, 1954.

Several case studies of clashes between competing philosophical theories.

The Strife of Systems: An Essay on the Grounds and Implications of Philosophical Diversity, by Nicholas Rescher. University of Pittsburgh Press, Pittsburgh, 1985.

Rescher looks at the problem of the superabundance of philosophical theories through the opposite side of the lens used in this book in chapter 4. Where I had argued that factual data *underdetermine* our philosophical theories, Rescher argues that our philosophical theories *overdetermine* their empirical base, in particular that our philosophical theories originate in self-inconsistent sets of beliefs (what Rescher calls "apories" or "aporetic clusters"). These two approaches are complementary.

Chapter Five – Underdeterminism (II)

Plurality of Worlds: The Origins of the Extraterrestrial Life Debate from Democritus to Kant, by Steven J. Dick. Cambridge University Press, Cambridge, 1982.

Not to be confused with David Lewis's similarly named *On the Plurality of Worlds* ([122]). Dick's book traces from antiquity to the eighteenth century the debate about extraterrestrial life.

The Extraterrestrial Life Debate, 1750-1900: The Idea of a Plurality of Worlds from Kant to Lowell, by Michael J. Crowe. Cambridge University Press, Cambridge, 1986.

Between this book and the immediately preceding one the entire history of the debate up to the present century is covered.

Extraterrestrials: Science and Alien Intelligence, ed. Edward Regis, Jr. Cambridge University Press, Cambridge, 1985.

Appearances to the contrary (see preceding two items), Cambridge University Press does not have exclusive rights to this topic. This particular volume is an anthology of fourteen contemporary papers, most of which are written by philosophers. The article by Rescher contains a good bibliography and cites a more complete one.

The Search for Life in the Universe, by Donald Goldsmith and Tobias Owen. Benjamin/Cummings, Menlo Park, Calif., 1980.

A good introduction to modern astronomy and exobiology. Probably easier reading than the three foregoing volumes.

Chapters Six and Seven – Putting concepts under stress, (I) and (II)

Thought Probes (2nd ed.), ed. Fred D. Miller, Jr, and Nicholas D. Smith. Prentice-Hall, Englewood Cliffs, NJ, 1989.

An introduction to philosophy through the vehicle of science fiction. Each topic is illustrated by a short science-fiction story and then followed by a discussion by a philosopher.

Chapter Eight – Space and time

The Planiverse: Computer Contact with a Two-Dimensional World, by Alexander Keewatin Dewdney. McClelland and Stewart, Toronto, 1984.

In the tradition of Abbott's *Flatland* ([1]). Updated in an ingenious fashion for a generation familiar with computers.

The Ambidextrous Universe (2nd ed.), by Martin Gardner. Charles Scribner's Sons, New York, 1979.

The best introduction to problems of symmetry, etc.

Relativity and Its Roots, by Banesh Hoffmann. Scientific American Books, New York, 1983.

There are, gratifyingly, many good books written for the nonscientist on this important topic. Hoffmann's is among the very best.

Zeno's Paradoxes, by Wesley Salmon. Bobbs-Merrill, Indianapolis, 1970.

The best introduction, known to me, to these classical problems. Unfortunately, this volume is currently out-of-print. With luck, your library may have, or may be able to borrow, a copy.

Chapter Nine – Properties

Universals and Particulars: Readings in Ontology, ed. Michael J. Loux. Doubleday & Co., New York, 1970.

An excellent collection. Of intermediate difficulty.

ADVANCED READINGS

Resemblance and Identity: An Examination of the Problem of Universals, by Panayot Butchvarov. Indiana University Press, Bloomington, Ind., 1966.

The term "identity" in the title refers not to an examination of identity per se, but to one of several different theories of the ontology of properties, viz. that instances of a property "constitute an identical quality which is present in distinct individual things at the same time" (p. 7).

Chapters Ten and Eleven – Individuation and Identity-through-time

Mind, Man, Machine: A Dialogue, by Paul T. Sagal. Hackett, Indianapolis, 1982.

A short, eminently readable introduction to the question whether a machine could be conscious.

Thinking Machines: The Search for Artificial Intelligence, by Igor Aleksander and Piers Burnett. Oxford University Press, Oxford, 1987.

A superb introduction to the present state of research in Artificial Intelligence, including both 'top-down' and 'bottom-up' approaches and contemporary controversies in the field. Do not miss this book.

Are Computers Alive? – Evolution and New Life Forms, by Geoff Simons. Birkhäuser, Boston, 1983.

Simons's thesis is that "computers and robots, appropriately configured, can be properly regarded as emerging life forms" (p. ix).

What Computers Can't Do: The Limits of Artificial Intelligence (rev. ed.), by Hubert L. Dreyfus. Harper & Row, New York, 1979.

Dreyfus is one of the major critics of the claims made by researchers in Artificial Intelligence.

Mind Design: Philosophy, Psychology, Artificial Intelligence, ed. John Haugeland. MIT Press, Cambridge, Mass., 1982.

Intermediate to advanced material.

ADVANCED READINGS

Individuality – An Essay on the Foundations of Metaphysics, by Jorge J.E. Gracia. State University of New York Press, Albany, 1988.

Understanding Identity Statements, by Thomas V. Morris. Aberdeen University Press, 1984.

Identity and Individuation, ed. Milton K. Munitz. New York University Press, New York, 1971.

Chapter Twelve – Persons

A Dialogue on Personal Identity and Immortality, by John Perry. Hackett, Indianapolis, 1978.

The best available introduction for the general reader to the problem of personal identity. In just a handful of pages, Perry introduces, and makes live, the major problems addressed by current philosophers on this topic.

Language, Metaphysics and Death, ed. John Donnelly. Fordham University Press, New York, 1978.

An anthology of seventeen philosophical papers on death and dying. The editor provides a Bibliographical Essay. Unfortunately, the book lacks an index. Highly recommended.

The Mind's I: Fantasies and Reflections on Self and Soul, ed. Douglas R. Hofstadter and Daniel C. Dennett. Bantam Books, New York, 1982.

A deservedly well-known collection of articles. Makes for fascinating reading. Highly recommended.

Personal Identity, by Sydney Shoemaker and Richard Swinburne. Basil Blackwell, Oxford, 1984.

A debate waged in the medium of print. Swinburne argues that personal identity can be accounted for only in terms of soul; Shoemaker argues for personal identity in terms of psychological continuity.

The Identities of Persons, ed. Amélie Oksenberg Rorty. University of California Press, Berkeley, 1976.

An anthology of papers by several of the best-known writers on this topic in recent years. Intermediate to advanced.

Body, Mind, and Death, ed. Anthony Flew. Macmillan, New York, 1964.

A selection of major historical writings on mind, body, and consciousness, from c. 400 BC to 1960.

References

Dates in square brackets, e.g. "[1893]", indicate the year of original publication. Later dates signify the editions used by this author.

[1] Abbott, Edwin Abbott, *Flatland: A Romance of Many Dimensions* [1884 (published under the pseudonym "A Square"); 2nd, rev., ed. 1884 (published under author's own name)]. 6th ed., rev., with intro. by Banesh Hoffmann, Dover, New York, 1952.

[2] Adams, Robert Merrihew, "Primitive Thisness and Primitive Identity", in *Journal of Philosophy* 76, no. 1 (Jan. 1979), 5-26.

[3] Adler, Irving, *A New Look at Geometry*, John Day Company, New York, 1966.

[4] Aleksander, Igor, and Piers Burnett, *Thinking Machines: The Search for Artificial Intelligence*, Oxford University Press, Oxford, 1987.

[5] Alexander, H.G., ed., *The Leibniz-Clarke Correspondence*, Philosophical Library, New York, 1956.

[6] Allaire, Edwin B., "Bare Particulars", in *Philosophical Studies* 14, nos. 1-2 (Jan.-Feb. 1963). Repr. in [125], 235-44. Page references are to reprint.

[7] —— "Another Look at Bare Particulars", in *Philosophical Studies* 16, nos. 1-2 (Jan.-Feb. 1965). Repr. in [125], 250-7. Page references are to reprint.

[8] Aquinas, Thomas, *Summa Theologiae*, trans. T.C. O'Brien, vol. 14 ("Divine Government"), Blackfriars, London, 1975.

[9] Arbib, Michael, "The Likelihood of the Evolution of Communicating Intelligences on Other Planets", in [158], 59-78.

[10] Aristotle, *De Anima (On the Soul)*, trans. J.A. Smith, in *The Works of Aristotle*, ed. W.D. Ross, vol. 3, Oxford University Press, Oxford, 1963.

[11] —— *Ethica Nicomachea (Nicomachean Ethics)*, trans. W.D. Ross, in *The Works of Aristotle*, ed. W.D. Ross, vol. 9, Oxford University Press, Oxford, 1963.

[12] —— *De Partibus Animalium (On the Parts of Animals)*, trans. William Ogle, in *The Works of Aristotle*, ed. J.A. Smith and W.D. Ross, vol. 5, Oxford University Press, Oxford, 1958.

[13] Armstrong, David M., *What Is a Law of Nature?* Cambridge University Press, Cambridge, 1983.

[14] Atrens, Dale Michael, and Ian Stewart Curthoys, *The Neurosciences and Behavior*, 2nd ed., Academic Press, Sydney, Australia, 1982.

[15] Augustine, Saint, *Confessions*, trans. R.S. Pine-Coffin, Penguin Books, Harmondsworth, Eng., 1984.

[16] Ayer, Alfred Jules, *Language, Truth and Logic* [1936]. Repr. with new intro., Dover, New York, 1946.

[17] —— ed., *Logical Positivism*, Free Press, New York, 1959.

[18] —— *The Problem of Knowledge* [1956], Penguin, Middlesex, Eng., 1971.

[19] Bacon, Francis, *Advancement of Learning* [1605], Colonial Press, New York, 1899.

[20] —— *The New Organon* [1620], ed. Fulton H. Anderson, Liberal Arts Press, New York, 1960.

[21] Barnhart, Robert K., ed., *The Barnhart Dictionary of Etymology*, H.W. Wilson Company, Bronx, New York, 1988.

[22] Barrow, John D., and Frank J. Tipler, *The Anthropic Cosmological Principle*, Clarendon Press, Oxford, 1986.

[23] Bates, Ralph S., *Scientific Societies in the United States* [1945], 3rd ed., MIT Press, Cambridge, Mass., 1965.

[24] *The Behavioral Sciences at Harvard*, Report of a Faculty Committee, June 1964.

[25] Belk, Russell W., "My Possessions, Myself", in *Psychology Today* 22, nos. 7/8 (July/Aug. 1988), 51-2.

[26] Bennett, Jonathan F., "The Difference between Right and Left", in *American Philosophical Quarterly* 7, no. 3 (July 1970), 175-91.

[27] Berkeley, George, *Principles, Dialogues*, and *Philosophical Correspondence* (three books bound as one), Bobbs-Merrill Co., Indianapolis, 1965.

[28] Beyle, Marie-Henri (de Stendhal), *The Red and the Black* [1830], trans. C.K. Scott Moncrieff, Modern Library, New York, 1953.

[29] Bieri, Robert, "Huminoids [sic] on Other Planets?" in *American Scientist* 52, no. 4 (Dec. 1964), 452-8.

[30] Black, Joseph, *Lectures on the Elements of Chemistry*, rev. and prepared for publication by John Robison, vol. 1, Longman and Rees, London, and William Creech, Edinburgh, 1803.

[31] Black, Max, "The Identity of Indiscernibles", in *Mind* 61 (1952), 152-64. Repr. in *Problems of Analysis*, Cornell University Press, Ithaca, NY, 1954, pp. 80-92.

[32] Bower, T.G.R., *The Perceptual World of the Child*, Harvard University Press, Cambridge, Mass., 1977.

[33] Bradley, F.H., *Appearance and Reality: A Metaphysical Essay* [1893], Clarendon Press, Oxford, 1962.

[34] Bradley, Raymond D., and Norman Swartz, *Possible Worlds*, Hackett, Indianapolis, 1979.

[35] Broad, Charlie Dunbar, *The Mind and Its Place in Nature*, Routledge and Kegan Paul, London, 1925. Repr. by Littlefield, Adams, Paterson, NJ, 1960.

[36] Brower, Montgomery, and Logan Bentley, "In Memory of His Grandfather", *People Weekly* 30, no. 11 (12 Sept. 1988), 53-4.

[37] Buber, Martin, *Between Man and Man* [1947], trans. Ronald Gregor Smith, Beacon Press, Boston, 1959.

[38] Buck, Paul, ed., *Social Sciences at Harvard 1860-1920*, Harvard University Press, Cambridge, Mass., 1965.

[39] Butler, Joseph, "Of Personal Identity", Dissertation 1, in *The Analogy of Religion* [1736], vol. 1 of *The Works of Joseph Butler*, preface by Samuel Halifax, Henry Wainbourne, London, 1843, pp. 287-303.

[40] Butterfield, Herbert, *The Origins of Modern Science* [1949], Macmillan, New York, 1960.

[41] Campbell, Keith, *Metaphysics: An Introduction*, Dickenson, Encino, Calif., 1976.

[42] —— *Abstract Particulars*, Basil Blackwell, Oxford, 1990.

[43] Campbell, Norman Robert, *Foundations of Science* (originally pub. under title *Physics: The Elements* [1919]), repr. by Dover, New York, 1957.

[44] Carnap, Rudolf, "Überwindung der Metaphysik durch logische Analyse der Sprache", in *Erkenntnis* 2 (1932). Translated as "The Elimination of Metaphysics through Logical Analysis of Language" by Arthur Pap, in [17]. Page references are to English translation.

[45] —— *Logical Foundations of Probability* [1950; 2nd ed. 1962], University of Chicago Press, Chicago, 1962.

[46] Carroll, Lewis (pseudonym for Charles Lutwidge Dodgson), *Alice's Adventures in Wonderland* and *Through the Looking Glass* [1865 and 1871], New American Library, New York, 1960.

[47] Cassirer, Ernst, *Substance and Function* and *Einstein's Theory of Relativity* [1910 and 1921], trans. William Curtis Swabey and Marie Collins Swabey, Dover, New York, 1953.

[48] Clarke, Arthur C., *2001: A Space Odyssey*, based on the screenplay by Stanley Kubrick and Arthur C. Clarke, New American Library, Toronto, Ont., 1968.

[49] Cohen, I. Bernard, "Isaac Newton", in *Scientific American* 193, no. 6 (Dec. 1955), 73-80.

[50] Coleridge, Samuel Taylor, *Anima Poetae*, selections comp. and ed. Ernest Hartley Coleridge from S.T. Coleridge's unpublished notebooks, William Heinemann, London, 1895.

[51] Collingwood, R.G., "The Historical Imagination", in *The Idea of History* [1947], Oxford University Press, New York, 1964, pp. 231-49.

[52] Darrow, Clarence, "What To Do about Crime", an unpublished address before Nebraska State Bar Association, Lincoln, Nebr. (28 Dec. 1926) in the Darrow Papers (box 1, folder 14), Joseph Regenstein Library of the University of Chicago.

[53] —— *The Story of My Life* [1932], Charles Scribner's Sons, New York, 1960.

[54] De George, Richard T., *Classical and Contemporary Metaphysics: A Source Book*, Holt, Rinehart and Winston, New York, 1962.

[55] Descartes, René, *The Philosophical Writings of Descartes*, trans. John Cottingham, Robert Stoothoff, and Dugald Murdoch, vols. 1 and 2, Cambridge University Press, Cambridge, 1985.

[56] Dewdney, Alexander Keewatin, *The Planiverse: Computer Contact with a Two-Dimensional World*, McClelland and Stewart, Toronto, 1984.

[57] Doctorow, E.L., *Ragtime*, Random House, New York, 1974.

[58] Donnelly, John, ed., *Language, Metaphysics and Death*, Fordham University Press, New York, 1978.

[59] Drake, Frank D., "Listening for Our Cosmic Cousins", in *Science Year 1980*, World Book-Childcraft International, Chicago, 1979, pp. 56-71.

[60] Duhem, Pierre Maurice Marie, *La théorie physique: Son objet, sa structure* [1906; 2nd ed. with new appendix, 1914]. Trans. as *The Aim and Structure of Physical Theory* by Philip P. Wiener, Princeton University Press, Princeton, 1954. Repr. by Atheneum, New York, 1962.

[61] Dunbar, Kevin, and David Klahr, "Developmental Differences in Scientific Discovery Processes", in [111], 109-43.

[62] Earman, John, "The SAP Also Rises: A Critical Examination of the Anthropic Principle", in *American Philosophical Quarterly* 24, no. 4 (Oct. 1987), 307-17.

[63] Einstein, Albert, "Die Grundlage der allgemeinen Relativitätstheorie", in *Annalen der Physik* 49 (1916). Trans. W. Perrett and G.B. Jeffery as "The Foundation of the General Theory of Relativity", in *The Principle of Relativity* [1923], Dover, New York, 1952, pp. 111-64.

[64] —— *Relativity, The Special and the General Theory: A Popular Exposition* [1916], 15th ed., trans. Robert W. Lawson, Crown, New York, 1961.

[65] —— "Die Ursache der Mäanderbildung der Flussläufe und des sogenannten Baerschen Gesetzes", in *Naturwissenschaften* 14 (1926), 223-4. Trans. as "The Cause of the Formation of Meanders in the Courses of Rivers and the So-called Baer's Law" by Alan Harris, in *The World as I See It*, Covici-Friede, New York, 1934. English translation repr. in various works, including *Einstein: A Centenary Volume*, ed. A.P. French, Harvard University Press, Cambridge, Mass., 1979, pp. 298-301.

[66] Ellis, Brian, *Basic Concepts of Measurement*, Cambridge University Press, London, 1966.

[67] *The Encyclopedia of Philosophy*, Paul Edwards ed. in chief, Macmillan and Free Press, New York, 1967.

[68] "Eötvös, Lóránd von", in [82], vol. 30, p. 257.

[69] "Exobiology", in *The New Encyclopaedia Britannica*, 15th ed., Micropaedia, vol. 4, 1985.

[70] Feigl, Herbert, "The 'Mental' and the 'Physical'", in vol. II of *Minnesota Studies in the Philosophy of Science: Concepts, Theories, and the Mind-Body Problem*, ed. Herbert Feigl, Michael Scriven, and Grover Maxwell,

University of Minnesota, Minneapolis, 1958. Repr., with postscript and additional bibliography, as monograph *The "Mental" and the "Physical"*, University of Minnesota Press, Minneapolis, 1967.

[71] Feyerabend, Paul, *Against Method* [1975], Verso, London, 1982.

[72] Field, Hartry, *Realism, Mathematics, and Modality*, Basil Blackwell, Oxford, 1989.

[73] Foster, Thomas R., "Symmetrical Universes and the Identity of Indiscernibles", in *Philosophy Research Archives* 8 (1982), 169-83.

[74] Gale, George, "The Anthropic Principle", in *Scientific American* 245, no. 6 (Dec. 1981), 154-71.

[75] Gardner, Martin, *The Ambidextrous Universe* [1964; 2nd rev., updated ed. 1979], Charles Scribner's Sons, New York, 1979.

[76] Gauss, Karl Friedrich, "General Investigations of Curved Surfaces" [1827] and "New General Investigations of Curved Surfaces" [1825]. Both papers bound as one book, *General Investigations of Curved Surfaces*, trans. Adam Hiltebeitel and James Morehead, intro. by Richard Courant, Raven Press, Hewlett, New York, 1965.

[77] Gleitman, Henry, *Basic Psychology*, W.W. Norton, New York, 1983.

[78] Glymour, Clark, *Theory and Evidence*, Princeton University Press, Princeton, NJ, 1980.

[79] Goldman, Steven Louis, untitled review of Armstrong's *What Is a Law of Nature?* and Swartz's *The Concept of Physical Law*, in *History of European Ideas* 8, no. 1 (1987), 97-9.

[80] Goldsmith, Donald, and Tobias Owen, *The Search for Life in the Universe*, Benjamin/Cummings, Menlo Park, Calif., 1980.

[81] Goodman, Nelson, *The Structure of Appearance* [1951]; 2nd ed., Bobbs-Merrill Co., Indianapolis, 1966.

[82] *Great Soviet Encyclopedia*, 3rd ed., Macmillan, New York, 1982. Originally published as *Bol'shaia Sovetskaia Entsiklopediia*, A.M. Prokhorov ed. in chief, Sovetskaia Entsiklopediia Publishing House, Moscow, 1978.

[83] Gregory, Richard Langton, and J.G. Wallace, "Recovery from Early Blindness: A Case Study", Monograph no. 2, Experimental Psychology Society, Cambridge, 1963. Repr. in *Perception: Selected Readings in Science and Phenomenology*, ed. Paul Tibbetts, Quadrangle Books, Chicago, 1969, 359-88.

[84] Grünbaum, Adolf, *Philosophical Problems of Space and Time*, Alfred A. Knopf, New York, 1963.

[85] Gurvitch, Georges, *The Spectrum of Social Time*, translated from *La multiplicité des temps sociaux* by Myrtle Korenbaum and Phillip Bosserman, D. Reidel, Dordrecht, Netherlands, 1964.

[86] Haugeland, John, ed., *Mind Design: Philosophy, Psychology, Artificial Intelligence*, MIT Press, Cambridge, Mass., 1982.

[87] Hawking, Stephen W., *A Brief History of Time: From the Big Bang to Black Holes*, Bantam Books, New York, 1988.

[88] Heidegger, Martin, "Was ist Metaphysik?" [1929; postscript added 1943]. Trans. (with postscript) as "What Is Metaphysics?" by R.F.C. Hull and Alan Crick, in *Existence and Being*, ed. Werner Brock, Vision Press, London, 1956.

[89] Helmholtz, Hermann von, "On the Origin and Significance of Geometrical Axioms" [1870], in *Popular Lectures on Scientific Subjects*, trans. E. Atkinson, vols. 1 and 2, Longmans, Green and Co., London, 1898.

[90] Hempel, Carl G., "The Function of General Laws in History", in *Journal of Philosophy* 39 (1942), 35-48. Repr. in *Aspects of Scientific Explanation*, Free Press, New York, 1965, pp. 231-43.

[91] —— "The Empiricist Criterion of Meaning", in *Revue Internationale de Philosophie* (1950). Repr. in [17], 108-29.

[92] Henry, William, "A Review of some Experiments which have been supposed to Disprove the Materiality of Heat", in *Memoirs and Proceedings – Manchester Literary and Philosophical Society* 5, no. 2 (1802), 603-21.

[93] Herbst, Peter, "A Critique of the Materialist Identity Theory", in *The Identity Theory of Mind*, ed. C.F. Presley, University of Queensland, St Lucia, Queensland, Australia, 1967, pp. 38-64.

[94] Hesslow, Germund, "The Problem of Causal Selection", in [96], 11-32.

[95] Hill, Doug, and Jeff Weingrad, *Saturday Night: A Backstage History of "Saturday Night Live"*, Beech Tree Books (William Morrow), New York, 1986.

[96] Hilton, Denis J., *Contemporary Science and Natural Explanation: Commonsense Conceptions of Causality*, New York University Press, New York, 1988.

[97] Hobbes, Thomas, *De Corpore (Concerning Body)*, trans. William Molesworth, in *Hobbes' Works*, vol. 1, John Bohn, London, 1839.

[98] Hoffman, J. Michael, "Minutes of the Physical Anthropology Section (17 Feb. 1988)", AAFS (American Academy of Forensic Sciences) Business Meeting, Philadelphia, Pa.

[99] Hofstadter, Douglas R., and Daniel C. Dennett, *The Mind's I: Fantasies and Reflections on Self and Soul*, Bantam Books, New York, 1982.

[100] Housman, A.E. (Alfred Edward), untitled poem, no. XII, among "Last Poems", in *A.E. Housman – Collected Poems and Selected Prose*, ed. Christopher Ricks, Penguin, London, 1988, p. 109.

[101] Hume, David, *A Treatise of Human Nature* [1739], ed. L.A. Selby-Bigge, Oxford University Press, London, 1888. Repr. 1960.

[102] *IEEE Standard Dictionary of Electrical and Electronics Terms*, 3rd ed., ed. Frank Jay, Institute of Electrical and Electronics Engineers, Inc., New York, 1984.

[103] James, William, *The Principles of Psychology* [1890], vols. 1 and 2. Repr. by Dover, New York, 1950.

[104] Jennings, Raymond E., ed., *In a Word ... Essays in Honour of Steven Davis*, Simon Fraser University, Burnaby, BC, 1987.

[105] Joad, C.E.M., *Guide to Philosophy* [1936], repr. by Dover, New York, 1957.

[106] Kant, Immanuel, *Critique of Pure Reason* [1781; 2nd ed. 1787], trans. Norman Kemp Smith, St Martin's Press, New York, 1961.

[107] —— *Prolegomena to Any Future Metaphysics That Will Be Able to Come Forward as a Science* [1783]. Trans. (1902) Paul Carus and extensively rev. (1977) by James W. Ellington, in *Philosophy of Material Nature*, Hackett, Indianapolis, 1985.

[108] Kaplan, Abraham, *The Conduct of Inquiry: Methodology for Behavioral Science*, Chandler Publishing Co., San Francisco, 1964.

[109] Kelvin, Lord, (William Thompson), "Electrical Units of Measurement", in *Popular Lectures and Addresses*, Macmillan and Co., London, 1891, pp. 80-143.

[110] King-Farlow, John, "Two Dogmas of Linguistic Empiricism", in *Dialogue: Canadian Philosophical Review* 11, no. 3 (Sept. 1972), 325-36.

[111] Klahr, David, and Kenneth Kotovsky, *Complex Information Processing: The Impact of Herbert A. Simon* (21st Carnegie-Mellon Symposium on Cognition), Lawrence Erlbaum Associates, Hillsdale, NJ, 1989.

[112] Kline, Morris, *Mathematics: The Loss of Certainty*, Oxford University Press, New York, 1980.

[113] Korzybski, Alfred, *Manhood of Humanity* [1921; 2nd ed. 1950], International Non-Aristotelian Library, Lakeville, Conn., 1950.

[114] —— *Science and Sanity* [1933], 4th ed., International Non-Aristotelian Literary Publishing Co., Lakeville, Conn., 1962.

[115] Krebs, Dennis, and Roger Blackman, *Psychology, a First Encounter*, Harcourt Brace Jovanovich, San Diego, 1988.

[116] Kripke, Saul A., *Naming and Necessity* [1970; new preface, 1980], Harvard University, Cambridge, Mass., 1980.

[117] Kuhn, Thomas, *The Structure of Scientific Revolutions* [1962; 2nd ed., enlarged, 1970], in *International Encyclopedia of Unified Science*, vol. 2, no. 2, University of Chicago Press, Chicago, 1970.

[118] Kuklick, Bruce, *The Rise of American Philosophy, Cambridge, Massachusetts, 1860-1930*, Yale University Press, New Haven, Conn., 1977.

[119] Langley, Pat, Herbert A. Simon, Gary L. Bradshaw, and Jan M. Zytkow, *Scientific Discovery: Computational Explorations of the Creative Process*, MIT Press, Cambridge, Mass., 1987.

[120] Leibniz, Gottfried Wilhelm, *Die philosophischen Schriften von Gottfried Wilhelm Leibniz*, ed. C.J. Gerhardt, Berlin, 1875-1890, vol. 2, p. 51. Passage quoted is trans. Bertrand Russell and appears in his *A Critical Exposition of the Philosophy of Leibniz* [1900], George Allen & Unwin, London, 1964, p. 36.

[121] —— "The Principles of Nature and Grace" [1714], in *Philosophical Works of Leibnitz*, ed. George Martin Duncan, New Haven, Conn., 1890, vol. 32, pp. 209-17. Repr. in *From Descartes to Locke*, ed. T.V. Smith and Majorie

Grene, University of Chicago Press, Chicago, 1964, pp. 320-9. Page references are to latter edition.

[122] Lewis, David, *On the Plurality of Worlds*, Basil Blackwell, Oxford, 1986.

[123] Lindsley, David F., and J. Eric Holmes, *Basic Human Neurophysiology*, Elsevier Science Publishing Co., New York, 1984.

[124] Locke, John, *An Essay Concerning Human Understanding* [1690; 5th ed. (posthumous) 1706], ed. John W. Yolton [1961], rev. ed., J.M. Dent & Sons Ltd., London, 1965.

[125] Loux, Michael J., ed., *Universals and Particulars: Readings in Ontology*, Doubleday, Garden City, NY, 1970.

[126] —— ed., *The Possible and the Actual: Readings in the Metaphysics of Modality*, Cornell University Press, Ithaca, NY, 1979.

[127] Lucretius, *The Nature of Things*, trans. Frank O. Copley, W.W. Norton & Co., New York, 1977.

[128] Mackie, John Leslie, *Problems from Locke* [1976], Oxford University Press, Oxford, 1984.

[129] McMullin, Ernan, "Persons in the Universe", in *Zygon* 15, no. 1 (March 1980), 69-89.

[130] McTaggart, John McTaggart Ellis, *The Nature of Existence*, vol. 2 [1927], ed. C.D. Broad, Cambridge University Press, London, 1968.

[131] Mandelbrot, Benoit B., *The Fractal Geometry of Nature* [1977], W.H. Freeman and Co., San Francisco, 1982.

[132] Maxwell, James Clerk, *A Treatise on Electricity and Magnetism*, [1873; 3rd ed., 1891], vols. 1 and 2, Dover, New York, 1954.

[133] Mayr, Ernst, "The Probability of Extraterrestrial Life", in [168], 23-30.

[134] Medawar, Peter, *The Limits of Science*, Oxford University Press, Oxford, 1984.

[135] Mill, John Stuart, *A System of Logic* [1843; 8th ed., 1872], in *Collected Works of John Stuart Mill*, ed. J.M. Robson, vols. 7-8, University of Toronto Press, Toronto, 1973.

[136] Moore, George Edward, "Proof of an External World", in *Proceedings of the British Academy*, 25 (1939). Repr. in G.E. Moore, *Philosophical Papers*, Collier Books, New York, 1962.

[137] —— *Some Main Problems of Philosophy* [1953], Collier Books, New York, 1962.

[138] Morgan, C. Lloyd, *Emergent Evolution* [1923], Williams and Norgate, Ltd., London, 1926.

[139] Nagel, Ernest, *The Structure of Science*, Harcourt, Brace & World, New York, 1961.

[140] Nagel, Thomas, "What Is It Like to Be a Bat?" in *Philosophical Review* 83, no. 4 (Oct. 1974), 435-50.

[141] —— "Death", in [58], 62-8.

[142] Nathan, Peter, *The Nervous System*, 2nd ed., Oxford University Press, Oxford, 1982.

[143] Neurath, Otto, "Protocol Statements", in *Philosophical Papers 1913-1946*, ed. and trans. Robert S. Cohen and Marie Neurath, D. Reidel Publishing Co., Dordrecht, 1983, pp. 91-9.

[144] Newton, Isaac, *Philosophiae Naturalis Principia Mathematica* [1687; 2nd ed. 1713; 3rd ed. 1726], translated as *Mathematical Principles of Natural Philosophy* by Andrew Motte, 1729; rev. and ed. Florian Cajori, 1934. Vols. 1 and 2, University of California Press, Berkeley, 1966.

[145] Nikolsky, G.V., *The Ecology of Fishes*, trans. L. Birkett, T.F.H. Publications, London, 1978.

[146] Nozick, Robert, "Why Is There Something Rather than Nothing?" chap. 2 in *Philosophical Explanations*, Harvard University Press, Cambridge, Mass., 1981, pp. 115-64.

[147] O'Connor, D.J., "Substance and Attribute", in [67], vol. 8, 36-40.

[148] ——— ed., *Modern Materialism: Readings on Mind-Body Identity*, Harcourt, Brace & World, New York, 1969.

[149] Parfit, Derek, *Reasons and Persons*, Oxford University Press, Oxford, 1986.

[150] Pepper, Stephen, "Emergence", in *Journal of Philosophy* 23, no. 9 (29 April 1926), 241-5.

[151] Perry, John, *A Dialogue on Personal Identity and Immortality*, Hackett, Indianapolis, 1978.

[152] Piaget, Jean, *La causalité physique chez l'enfant* [Paris, 1927]. Trans. Marjorie Gabain as *The Child's Conception of Physical Causality*, London, 1930. Repr. by Littlefield, Adams and Co., Paterson, NJ, 1960.

[153] Place, U.T., "Is Consciousness a Brain Process?" in *British Journal of Psychology* 47, part 1 (Feb. 1956), 44-50. Repr. in [148], 21-31.

[154] Planck, Max, *The Philosophy of Physics*, trans. W.H. Johnston, W.W. Norton, New York, 1936. Repr. 1963.

[155] ——— "Wissenschaftliche Selbstbiographie" [1948]. Translated as "A Scientific Autobiography" by Frank Gaynor, in *Scientific Autobiography and Other Papers*, Greenwood Press, New York, 1968.

[156] Plato, *The Republic*, trans. Francis MacDonald Cornford, Oxford University Press, New York, 1958.

[157] Plutarch, "Theseus", in *Lives* (also known as *Parallel Lives* and *Plutarch's Lives*) [1914], trans. Bernadotte Perrin, vol. 1, Harvard University Press, Cambridge, Mass., 1967.

[158] Ponnamperuma, Cyril, and A.G.W. Cameron, ed., *Interstellar Communication: Scientific Perspectives*, Houghton Mifflin, Boston, 1974.

[159] Popper, Karl, *Conjectures and Refutations*, Basic Books, New York, 1962.

[160] Price, Marjorie S., "Identity through Time", in *Journal of Philosophy* 74, no. 4 (April 1977), 201-17.

[161] Prior, Elizabeth, *Dispositions*, Scotts Philosophical Monographs no. 7, Aberdeen University Press, Aberdeen, 1985.

[162] Quine, Willard Van Orman, *From a Logical Point of View* [1953; 2nd, rev. ed. 1961], Harvard University Press, Cambridge, Mass., 1961.

[163] —— "Paradox", in *Scientific American* 206, no. 4 (Apr. 1962), 84-96. Repr. in *The Ways of Paradox*, Random House, New York, 1966, pp. 3-20.

[164] Quinton, Anthony, "Spaces and Times", in *Philosophy* 37, no. 140 (Apr. 1962), 130-47.

[165] —— *The Nature of Things*, Routledge & Kegan Paul, London, 1973.

[166] Raup, David M., "ETI without Intelligence", in [168], 31-42.

[167] Rawls, John, *Theory of Justice*, Harvard University Press, Cambridge, Mass., 1971.

[168] Regis, Edward, Jr, ed., *Extraterrestrials: Science and Alien Intelligence*, Cambridge University Press, Cambridge, 1985.

[169] Rescher, Nicholas, "A Critique of Pure Analysis", chapter VI in *The Primacy of Practice: Essays towards a Pragmatically Kantian Theory of Empirical Knowledge*, Basil Blackwell, Oxford, 1973, pp. 105-23.

[170] —— *The Riddle of Existence: An Essay in Idealistic Metaphysics*, University Press of America, Lanham, Md., 1984.

[171] —— *The Strife of Systems: An Essay on the Grounds and Implications of Philosophical Diversity*, University of Pittsburgh Press, Pittsburgh, Pa., 1985.

[172] —— "Technicalities", in *American Philosophical Quarterly* 25, no. 4 (1988).

[173] Riemann, Georg Friedrich Bernhard, "On the Hypotheses which Lie at the Foundations of Geometry" [1854], trans. Henry S. White, in *A Source Book in Mathematics*, ed. David Eugene Smith, McGraw-Hill, New York, 1929, pp. 411-25.

[174] Roller, Duane, "The Early Development of the Concepts of Temperature and Heat: The Rise and Decline of the Caloric Theory", in *Harvard Case Studies in Experimental Science* [1948], vol. 1, ed. James Bryant Conant and Leonard K. Nash, Harvard University Press, Cambridge, Mass., 1957, pp. 117-214.

[175] Roxburgh, Ian W., "Is Space Curved?" in *The Encyclopedia of Ignorance* [1977], ed. Ronald Duncan and Miranda Weston-Smith, Pergamon Press, Oxford, 1978, pp. 85-9.

[176] Rumford, Count (Benjamin Thompson), "An Inquiry Concerning the Source of Heat which Is Excited by Friction" [1798], in *The Collected Works of Count Rumford*, vol. 1, ed. Sanborn C. Brown, Harvard University Press, Cambridge, Mass., 1968, pp. 3-26.

[177] Russell, Bertrand, "On Denoting", in *Mind*, n.s. 14 (1905), 479-93.

[178] —— *The Problems of Philosophy* [1912], Oxford University Press, New York, 1959.

[179] —— "The Philosophy of Logical Atomism", in *Monist* 28 (Oct. 1918), 495-527; 29 (1919), 32-63, 190-222, 345-80. Repr. in *Logic and Knowledge, Essays 1901-1950*, ed. Robert C. Marsh, George Allen & Unwin, London, 1956. Page reference is to reprint.

[180] —— "Vagueness", in *Australasian Journal of Philosophy* 1 (1923), 84-92.

[181] —— "Mr. Strawson on Referring", in *Mind* 66, no. 263 (July 1957), 385-9.

[182] Ryle, Gilbert, *The Concept of Mind*, Hutchinson, London, 1949.

[183] Sagan, Carl, "An Introduction to the Problem of Interstellar Communication", in [158], 1-24.

[184] Santayana, George, "Tropes", in *The Works of George Santayana*, vol. 14, Charles Scribner's Sons, New York, 1937, pp. 288-304.

[185] Sartre, Jean-Paul, "Existentialism", from the book of that name, trans. Bernard Frechtman, in *Existentialism and Human Emotions*, Philosophical Library, New York, 1957, pp. 9-51.

[186] Sciama, Dennis William, *The Unity of the Universe*, Doubleday & Company, Inc., Garden City, NY, 1961.

[187] Scriven, Michael, "The Compleat Robot: A Prolegomena to Androidology", in *Dimensions of Mind*, ed. Sidney Hook, New York University Press, New York, 1961, pp. 118-42.

[188] Searle, John R., "Minds, Brains, and Programs", in *The Behavioral and Brain Sciences* 3 (1980), 417-24. Repr. in [86], 282-306, and in [99], 353-73. The latter reprint is accompanied by a reply by D.R. Hofstadter, pp. 373-84.

[189] Sedley, David, "The Stoic Criterion of Identity", in *Phronesis* 27, no. 3 (1982), 255-75.

[190] Sheaffer, Robert, "The Decline and Fall of SETI", in *Spaceflight* 24, no. 12 (Dec. 1982), 457-8.

[191] Shoemaker, Sydney, "Time without Change", in *Journal of Philosophy* 66, no. 12 (June 19, 1969), 363-81.

[192] Shu, Frank H., *The Physical Universe: An Introduction to Astronomy*, University Science Books, Mill Valley, Calif., 1982.

[193] Smart, J.J.C., "Sensations and Brain Processes", in *Philosophical Review* 48 (1959), 141-56. Repr. with revisions in [148], 32-47.

[194] Smith, Alton H., and Walter A. Albrecht, Jr, *Fundamental Concepts of Analysis*, Prentice-Hall, Englewood Cliffs, NJ, 1966.

[195] Smorodinskii, Ia.A., "Mass", in [82], vol. 15, 533-4.

[196] Smuts, Jan Christiaan, *Holism and Evolution* [1926]. Repr. with new intro. by Edmund W. Sinnott, Viking Press, New York, 1961.

[197] Stevens, Stanley Smith, "On the Theory of Scales of Measurement", in *Science* 103, no. 2684 (7 June 1946), 677-80.

[198] Storey, Kenneth B., and Janet M. Storey, "Freeze Tolerance in Animals", in *Physiological Reviews* 68, no. 1 (Jan. 1988), 27-84.

[199] Strawson, Peter F., "On Referring", in *Mind* 59, no. 235 (July 1950), 320-44.

[200] —— *Individuals: An Essay in Descriptive Metaphysics* [1959], Methuen, London, 1964.

[201] Swartz, Norman, *The Concept of Physical Law*, Cambridge University Press, New York, 1985.

[202] Swinburne, Richard, *Space and Time*, 2nd ed., Macmillan, London, 1981.

[203] Taylor, Richard, "Spatial and Temporal Analogies and the Concept of Identity", in *Journal of Philosophy* 52, no. 22 (27 Oct. 1955), 599-612. Repr. in *Problems of Space and Time*, ed. J.J.C. Smart, Macmillan, New York, 1968, pp. 381-96.

[204] —— *Metaphysics* [1963], 3rd ed., Prentice-Hall, Englewood Cliffs, NJ, 1983.

[205] Traill, Thomas Stewart, "Heat", in *Encyclopaedia Britannica*, 8th ed., vol. 11, Edinburgh, 1856, pp. 260-76.

[206] Turing, A.M., "Computing Machinery and Intelligence", in *Mind* 59, no. 236 (1950). Repr. in various anthologies, incl. *Minds and Machines*, ed. Alan Ross Anderson, Prentice-Hall, Englewood Cliffs, NJ, 1964, pp. 4-30.

[207] Van Fraassen, Bas C., "Platonism's Pyrrhic Victory", in *The Logical Enterprise*, ed. Alan Ross Anderson, Ruth Barcan Marcus, and R.M. Martin, Yale University Press, New Haven, Conn., 1975, pp. 39-50.

[208] Vercors (pseudonym for Jean Bruller), *You Shall Know Them*, trans. Rita Barisse, Little, Brown and Co., Boston, 1953.

[209] Waismann, Friedrich, *The Principles of Linguistic Philosophy*, ed. Rom Harré, Macmillan, London, 1965.

[210] Ward, Anne G., W.R. Connor, Ruth B. Edwards, and Simon Tidworth, *The Quest for Theseus*, Praeger, New York, 1970.

[211] Whitrow, G.J., *The Natural Philosophy of Time* [1961], 2nd ed., Clarendon Press, Oxford, 1980.

[212] Williams, Bernard, "The Makropulos Case: Reflections on the Tedium of Immortality", in Bernard Williams, *Problems of the Self – Philosophical Papers, 1956-1972*, Cambridge University Press, London, 1973, pp. 82-100. Repr. in [58], 228-42.

[213] Williams, Donald Cary, "The Myth of Passage", in *Journal of Philosophy* 48, no. 15 (19 July 1951), 457-72.

[214] —— "The Elements of Being", in *Principles of Empirical Realism*, Charles C. Thomas, Springfield, Ill., 1966, pp. 74-109.

[215] Wilshire, Bruce, *Metaphysics: An Introduction to Philosophy*, Pegasus, New York, 1969.

[216] Wittgenstein, Ludwig, *Philosophical Investigations* [1953], trans. G.E.M. Anscombe, Macmillan, New York, 1962.

[217] Woods, M.J., "Identity and Individuation", in *Analytical Philosophy*, 2nd ser., ed. R.J. Butler, Basil Blackwell, Oxford, 1965, pp. 120-30.

[218] Wyburn, G.M., R.W. Pickford, and R.J. Hirst, *Human Senses and Perception*, University of Toronto Press, Toronto, 1964.

[219] Young, John Zachary, *Philosophy and the Brain*, Oxford University Press, Oxford, 1987.

[220] Zuckerman, Laurence, "TV News' Fallen Star – The Brief Life and Times of Jessica Savitch", *Time*, 27 June 1988, 63.

Names index

In many cases throughout this book, authors have been referred to by a cross-reference to the References section (pp. 415-26), e.g. Alfred Jules Ayer has been referred to by the numbers [16-18]. For convenience in identifying references within the text where numbers have been used, those numbers have been been included below.

Subject index

72820

D